STRATEGY
IN PRACTICE

ICSA STUDY TEXT

STRATEGY IN PRACTICE

THIRD EDITION

ADRIAN PRYCE AND ROSS THOMPSON

icsa

The Governance
Institute

First published as Strategy in Practice by Keith Mattacks (ICSA Publishing Limited, 2011, 2015)

Published by ICSA Publishing Limited
Saffron House,
6–10 Kirby Street,
London EC1N 8TS

Designed and typeset by Paul Barrett Book Production, Cambridge
Printed by Hobbs the Printers Ltd, Totton, Hampshire

British Cataloguing in Publication Data
A catalogue record for this book is available from the British Library.

ISBN 978 1 86072 710 8

Contents

How to use this study text

ICSA study texts developed to support ICSA's Chartered Secretaries Qualifying Scheme (CSQS) follow a standard format and include a range of navigational, self-testing and illustrative features to help you get the most out of the support materials.

Each text is divided into three main sections:

- introductory material
- the text itself, divided into Parts and Chapters
- additional reference information

The sections below show you how to find your way around the text and make the most of its features.

Introductory material

The introductory section of each text includes a full contents list and the module syllabus which reiterates the module aims, learning outcomes and syllabus content for the module in question.

Where relevant, the introductory section will also include a list of acronyms and abbreviations or a list of legal cases for reference.

The text itself

Each **part** opens with a list of the chapters to follow, an overview of what will be covered and learning outcomes for the part. Part openings also include a case study, which introduces a real-world scenario related to the topics covered in that part. Questions based on this case and designed to test the application of theory into practice appear in the chapters and at part endings (see below).

Every **chapter** opens with a list of the topics covered and an introduction specific to that chapter. Chapters are structured to allow students to break the content down into manageable sections for study. Each chapter ends with a summary of key content to reinforce understanding.

Part opening   Chapter opening

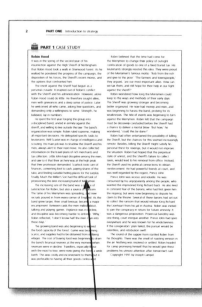

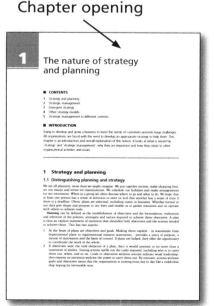

Part case study

Features

The text is enhanced by a range of illustrative and self-testing features to assist understanding and to help you prepare for the examination. Each feature is presented in a standard format, so that you will become familiar with how to use them in your study.

The texts also include tables, figures and checklists and, where relevant, sample documents and forms.

Case Examples

Case examples present short, illustrative case studies which look at how concepts are applied in practice.

Definitions

Key terms are highlighted in bold on first use and defined in the end of book glossary.

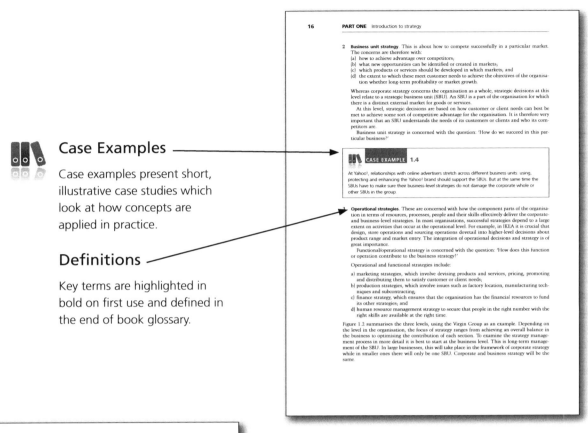

Case Questions

Case questions relate to the case study that opens each part, encouraging you to apply the theory you're learning to a real-world business scenario.

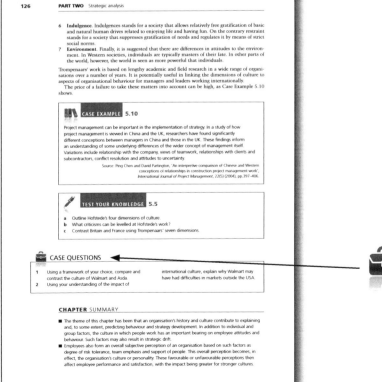

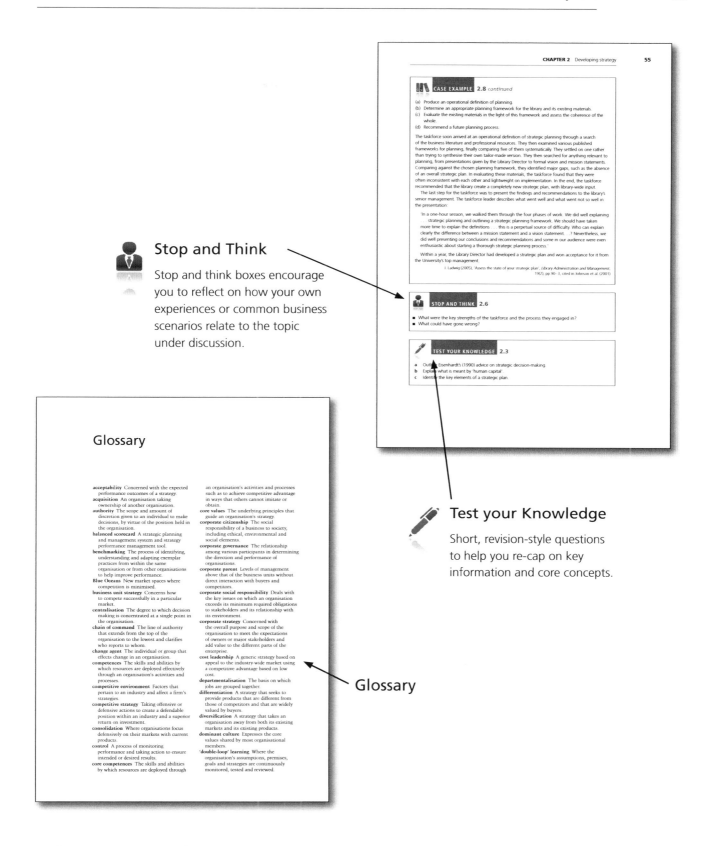

Stop and Think

Stop and think boxes encourage you to reflect on how your own experiences or common business scenarios relate to the topic under discussion.

Glossary

Test your Knowledge

Short, revision-style questions to help you re-cap on key information and core concepts.

Reference material

The text ends with a range of additional guidance and reference material.

Most texts include Appendices which comprise additional reference material specific to that module.

Other reference material includes a glossary of key terms, a directory of further reading and web resources and a comprehensive index.

Strategy in Practice syllabus

Module outline and aims

This module examines the elements, processes and techniques involved in the development and implementation of organisational strategy. As part of the senior management team, Chartered Secretaries have an important role to play in ensuring that strategy fits organisational purpose, is acceptable in terms of risk, and is consistent with good governance as well as with stakeholder requirements and concerns.

The module assesses the critical role played by Chartered Secretaries as part of the senior management team: ensuring the integrity of the policies, systems and processes that deliver the organisation's strategic purpose and objectives. The obligations of directors, officers and senior employees in the strategic planning and delivery of corporate responsibility are also considered. The module will also require you to understand the ethical considerations raised by the development and implementation of strategy, and its impact on reputation.

Learning outcomes

On successful completion of this module, you will be able to:

- Analyse and evaluate an organisation's environment and identify global and local opportunities and threats, taking into account the organisation's internal capabilities and resources and the context in which the organisation operates.
- Advise the governing body on the appropriate policies, systems, processes and risk strategies, within a changing context, to meet stakeholder interests, organisational purpose and safeguard organisational reputation.
- Advise on the roles of directors, officers and senior employees in developing and implementing strategy.
- Advise on the resource management issues that contribute to strategic success.
- Advise the management board on systems and processes needed to deliver strategic objectives and address reputational risk.
- Critically review the nature of organisational ethics in strategy development.

Syllabus content

Introduction

As the pace and volume of change in the environment affecting organisations in the private, public and not-for-profit sectors increases, Chartered Secretaries and other senior administrators must seek to understand what is happening and play their part in determining the organisation's response. All organisations are faced with the challenge of strategic direction, either to grasp new opportunities or to overcome significant problems.

This field of study is potentially vast and it is all too easy to be seduced by the range of frameworks, tools and techniques that abound. They are important, but only in the political and cultural context of the organisation and as a response to the need for practical responses to day-to-day problems with which managers have to grapple. The aim of the syllabus is to focus on those components of corporate strategy most relevant to the practice of a Chartered Secretary.

Syllabus overview

The aim of the Strategy in Practice module is to enable the Chartered Secretary to apply the concepts and principles of strategic management to organisations in order to protect their reputation and promote good governance and accountability to stakeholders.

There are four main areas in the syllabus:

- key strategy concepts
- applied strategic analysis
- strategic purpose
- implementing strategy

To give an insight into the level of understanding and competence required, this section describes in more detail the content of each.

Key strategy concepts – weighting 15%

The nature of strategy and planning is concerned with whether students are able to:

- explain the characteristics of strategic decisions;
- explain what is meant by strategy and strategic management and planning;
- identify levels of strategy and how and why these vary;
- critically review the rational planning model and a range of other models;
- apply a strategic approach to different types of organisation; and
- understand how strategy and planning reflect the values and expectations of stakeholders.

Developing Strategy is concerned with whether students are able to:

- understand the role of the key people involved in the strategy-making process;
- advise on the systems, processes and frameworks underpinning strategy and planning: 'strategising', business cases, strategy projects, and communication; and
- define and understand the interaction of 'risk', 'reputation' and 'sustainability' within the context of organisational strategy.

Applied strategic analysis – weighting 25%

The external environment is concerned with whether students are able to:

- analyse the 'far' environment of organisations using PESTEL and systems maps;
- construct alternative scenarios based on key drivers in the environment;
- assess the attractiveness of industries and sectors and their potential for investment and change; and
- recognise strategic opportunities by identifying market segments, strategic groups and critical success factors.

Strategic capabilities and competences is concerned with whether students are able to:

- distinguish the components of strategic capability including resources, core competences and dynamic capabilities;
- recognise how strategic capabilities provide sustainable competitive advantage;
- assess strategic capability using value chain analysis, benchmarking, and activity mapping; and
- advise on the contribution of organisational knowledge to strategic capability.

Strategy and organisational culture is concerned with whether students are able to:

- analyse how culture influences the strategic position of organisations;
- advise on the implications of strategic drift;
- analyse the influence of an organisation's culture on its strategy using a range of frameworks; and
- understand the relationship between organisational and international cultures.

Strategic purpose – weighting 30%

The governing body's and strategy is concerned with whether students are able to:

- apply the concept of the governance chain to organisations; and
- understand the relationship between stakeholders and governance.

Stakeholder expectations and management is concerned with whether students are able to:

- recognise the importance of determining, challenging and balancing conflict in the risk appetite of differing stakeholders;
- apply the outcomes of stakeholder analysis to manage the influence of different stakeholders and stakeholder groups.

Expressing organisational purpose is concerned with whether students are able to:

- advise on appropriate ways to express the strategic purpose of an organisation: values, vision, strategic intent, mission and objectives.

'Business ethics, social responsibility and good corporate citizenship is concerned with whether students are able to:

- define ethics and take an ethical perspective in strategy development;
- critically review the role of ethics in the organisation;
- understand the different ethical stances taken by organisations;
- advise on ethical decision-making and conflicts of interest amongst stakeholders; and
- advise on the link between sustainability and strategy.

Protecting and enhancing the reputation of the organisation is concerned with whether students are able to:

- understand the nature and sources of reputation;
- advise on ensuring a coherent approach to reputation and risk.

Implementing strategy – weighting 30%

Strategy development is concerned with whether students are able to:

- understand how both emergent and planned strategy development may be found in different organisational contexts;
- understand the elements of strategic leadership that are required in uncertain and complex conditions.

Strategic choice is concerned with whether students are able to:

- critically review the range of methods by which strategy might be pursued: organic development, mergers and acquisition, strategic alliances;
- identify alternative directions for strategy, including market penetration or consolidation, product development, market development and diversification, employing a range of techniques for evaluating strategic options;
- apply portfolio management to create value through corporate level strategy.;
- assess the extent to which strategic business units can provide sustainable competitive advantage; and
- identify sources of competitive advantage in international strategy: Porter's Diamond.

Organising for success is concerned with whether students are able to:

- assess the strengths and limitations of the main structural forms; and
- recognise the role of control processes and relationships, including performance management and evaluation, technical control, and administrative control.

Managing strategic change is concerned with whether students are able to:

- distinguish the nature and significance of strategic change;
- advise on roles in managing change including managers and change agents;
- assess the value of change levers and tactics including political and symbolic processes;
- advise on managing the effects of change on people;
- identify the issues involved in designing and managing strategic change programmes; and
- understand why change may be resisted and how this can be overcome.

Acronyms and abbreviations

AOL	America Online
ATM	automated teller machine
BA	British Airways
BCG	Boston Consulting Group
BP	British Petroleum
BRIC	Brazil, Russia, India and China
BPR	business process engineering
CEO	chief executive officer
CAGE	cultural, administrative, geographic and economic
CSF	critical success factors
CIC	community interest company
CSR	corporate social responsibility
CSV	creating shared value
DRAM	dynamic random access memory
ERP	enterprise resource planning
EU	European Union
GE	General Electric
FDI	foreign direct investment
FRC	Financial Reporting Council
GM	General Motors
HCM	human capital management
HBR	Harvard Business Review
IT	information technology
KPI	key performance indicator
LEAs	local education authorities
M&A	mergers and acquisitions
MoD	Ministry of Defence
NCL	National College for School Leadership
NHS	National Health Service
P&G	Proctor and Gamble
PESTEL	Political, Economic, Social, Technological, Environmental and Legal
PI	performance indicator
quango	quasi-autonomous non-governmental organisation
R&D	research and development
SBU	strategic business unit
SEE	social, economic, environmental
SWOT	strengths, weaknesses, opportunities and threats (sometimes seen as TOWS)
VUCA	volatile, uncertain, complex, ambiguous
VRIN	value, rarity, inimitability, non-substitutability
WTO	World Trade Organization

Acknowledgements

The publishers would like to acknowledge the work of Keith Mattacks who wrote the first and second editions of this book.

The publisher and authors acknowledge the following for the permission to reproduce the figures in this volume:

Figures 1 & 1.5: From *Strategy Safari*, 2nd edition, Mintzberg, Ahlstrand & Lampel, Pearson Education Limited, © Henry Mintzberg, Bruce Ahlstrand and Joseph Lampel 1998, 2009

Figures 2 & 8.4: Republished with permission of John Wiley and Sons Inc, from *What Matters Now: How to Win in a World of Relentless Change, Ferocious Competition, and Unstoppable Innovation*, G. Hamel, 2012; permission conveyed through Copyright Clearance Center, Inc.

Figure 2.2: From Garratt, *The Fish Rots from the Head*, © Profile Books, 2010, reprinted with permission

Figure 2.3: From *Exploring Strategy*, 9th edition, Johnson et al, Pearson Education Limited, © Pearson Education 2002, 2011

Figure 3.3 Reprinted with permission of The Free Press, a Division of Simon and Schuster, Inc., from *Competitive Strategy: Techniques for Analyzing Industries and Competitors* by Michael E. Porter. Copyright © 1980 by The Free Press. All rights reserved

Figure 3.4: From *Exploring Strategy*, 9th edition, Johnson et al, Pearson Education Limited, © Pearson Education 2002, 2011

Figure 3.5: From Dess et al, *Strategic Management*, 7th edition © McGraw Hill, 2014, reproduced with permission of the McGraw-Hill Companies

Table 3.5: From *Exploring Strategy*, 9th edition, Johnson et al, Pearson Education Limited, © Pearson Education 2002, 2011

Figure 4.1: Republished with permission of John Wiley and Sons, from *Contemporary Strategy Analysis*, R. M. Grant, 2013; permission conveyed through Copyright Clearance Center, Inc.

Table 4.1: Republished with permission of SAGE Publications, from Firm Resources and Sustained Competitive Advantage by J. B. Barney, in *Journal of* Management, volume 17, 1991; permission conveyed through Copyright Clearance Center, Inc.

Figure 4.2: From *Exploring Strategy*, 9th edition, Johnson et al, Pearson Education Limited, © Pearson Education 2002, 2011

Figure 4.3: From *Exploring Strategy*, 9th edition, Johnson et al, Pearson Education Limited, © Pearson Education 2002, 2011

Figure 4.5 Reprinted with permission of the Free Press, a Division of Simon & Schuster, Inc., from *Competitive Advantage: Creating and Sustaining Superior Performance* by Michael E. Porter. Copyright © 1985 by Michael E. Porter. All rights reserved

Figure 5.2: From *Exploring Strategy*, 9th edition, Johnson et al, Pearson Education Limited, © Pearson Education 2002, 2011

Figure 5.3: From *Exploring Strategy*, 9th edition, Johnson et al, Pearson Education Limited, © Pearson Education 2002, 2011

Figure 5.5: From Kennedy and Deal, *Corporate Cultures: The Rites and Rituals of Corporate Life*, © Penguin, 1982, reproduced with permission

Figure 5.6: From *Exploring Strategy*, 9th edition, Johnson et al, Pearson Education Limited, © Pearson Education 2002, 2011

Figure 6.1: From Dess et al, *Strategic Management*, 4th edition © McGraw Hill, 2008, reproduced with permission of the McGraw-Hill Companies

Table 6.2: From *Strategic Management*, 7th edition, Richard Lynch, Pearson Education Limited, © Richard Lynch 2015

Table 6.4: From *Exploring Strategy*, 9th edition, Johnson et al, Pearson Education Limited, © Pearson Education 2002, 2011

Table 6.5: From *Exploring Strategy*, 9th edition, Johnson et al, Pearson Education Limited, © Pearson Education 2002, 2011

Table 7.1: From Dess et al, *Strategic Management*, 7th edition © McGraw Hill, 2014, reproduced with permission of the McGraw-Hill Companies

Figure 8.1: Republished with permission of Elsevier Science and Technology Journals, from Strategic Management Style, Archie B. Carroll, in *Business Horizons*, vol 34, issue 4, 1991; permission conveyed through Copyright Clearance Center, Inc.

Figure 8.2: From *Exploring Strategy*, 9th edition, Johnson et al, Pearson Education Limited, © Pearson Education 2002, 2011

Figure 8.3: From ClearlySo, available at www.clearlyso.com/what-is-a-social-enterprise-2/

Figure 9.2: Reprinted with the permission of The Free Press, a Division of Simon and Schuster, Inc., from *Competitive Strategy: Techniques for Analyzing Industries and Competitors* by Michael E. Porter. Copyright © 1980 by The Free Press. All rights reserved.

Figure 9.3: Republished with permission of SAGE Publications, from Blue Ocean Strategy: From Theory to Practice, W. Chan Kim & Renee Mauborgne, in *California Management Review*, vol 47, issue 3, 1958; permission conveyed through Copyright Clearance Center, Inc.

Figure 9.5: From *Exploring Strategy*, 9th edition, Johnson et al, Pearson Education Limited, © Pearson Education 2002, 2011

Figure 9.8: Reprinted with permission of the Free Press, a division of Simon & Schuster, Inc., from *The Competitive Advantage of Nations* by Michael E. Porter, Copyright © 1990 by Michael E. Porter. All rights reserved

Figure 9.9: Republished with permission of SAGE Publications, from Changing patterns of international competition, M. Porter, in *California Management Review*, vol 28, issue 2, 1986; permission conveyed through Copyright Clearance Center, Inc.

Table 10.1: From *Strategic Management: Awareness and Change*, John L. Thompson & Frank Martin, © 2005 Cengage Learning. Reproduced by permission of Cengage Learning EMEA Ltd

Figure 11.2: Republished with permission of South-Western College Publishing, a division of Cengage Learning, from *Strategy Implementation: Structure, Systems, and Process*, 2nd edition, J. R. Galbraith and R. K. Kazanjian, 1986; permission conveyed through Copyright Clearance Center, Inc.

Figure 11.8: From *Organizational Behaviour and Management*, John Martin, © 2001 Cengage Learning. Reproduced by permission of Cengage Learning EMEA Ltd

Figure 12.1: From *Understanding the Theory and Design of Organizations*, International Edition, Daft © 2006 Cengage Learning. Reproduced by permission of Cengage Learning EMEA Ltd

Table 12.3: From *Exploring Strategy*, 9th edition, Johnson et al, Pearson Education Limited, © Pearson Education 2002, 2011

Figure 12.4: From Dess et al, *Strategic Management*, 7th edition © McGraw Hill, 2014, reproduced with permission of the McGraw-Hill Companies

Figure 12.5: From *Using the Balanced Scorecard as a Strategic Management System*, Robert S. Kaplan & David P. Norton, 2007. Reproduced with permission of Harvard Business Publishing

Table 13.1: From *Exploring Strategic Change*, 3rd edition, Balogun and Hope Hailey, Pearson Education Limited, © Pearson Education Limited 2004, 2008

Figure 13.2: From: *Organizational Behaviour and Management*, John Martin, © 2001 Cengage Learning. Reproduced by permission of Cengage Learning EMEA Ltd

Figure 13.3: From *Exploring Strategic Change*, 3rd edition, Balogun and Hope Hailey, Pearson Education Limited, © Pearson Education Limited 2004, 2008

Table 13.3: From *Exploring Strategy*, 9th edition, Johnson et al, Pearson Education Limited, © Pearson Education 2002, 2011

Figure 13.4: From *Organizational Change*, 4th edition, Senior and Swailes, Pearson Education Limited, © Barbara Senior and Stephen Swailes 2010

Figure 13.6: From *The Strategy Process: Concepts, Contexts, Cases*, 5th edition, Mintzberg, Lampel, Quinn & Ghoshal, Pearson Education Limited, © Pearson Education Limited 2013

Every effort has been made to locate and acknowledge sources and holders of copyright material in this study text. In the event that any have been inadvertently overlooked, please contact the publisher.

The publishers would like to acknowledge the work of Keith Mattacks who wrote the first and second editions of this book.

Introduction to strategy

■ **LIST OF CHAPTERS**

Foreword: Strategy in the modern world

■ **OVERVIEW**

In this part, we introduce the study of strategy in practice.

We begin by looking at the nature of strategy and introduce a range of models and approaches available to organisations looking at planning and strategy. We explore what 'strategy' and 'planning' really mean, what 'strategic management' is and why it is important. The second chapter is concerned with the role of the Chartered Secretary in the process of strategic management, and the key systems and frameworks that underpin this. We also look at how the issues of risk, reputation and sustainability interact within the context of organisational strategy.

■ **LEARNING OUTCOMES**

After reading and understanding the contents of Part One, considering the Case Examples and Test Your Knowledge questions, you should be able to:

■   explain the characteristics of strategic decisions;

■   explain what is meant by strategy and strategic management and planning;

■   identify levels of strategy, and how and why these vary;

■   critically review the rational planning model and a range of other models;

■   recognise which elements of the strategy model are likely to be most important in different contexts;

■   understand the role of the key people involved in the strategy making process; and

■   advise on the systems, processes and frameworks underpinning strategy and planning: 'strategising', business cases, strategy projects and communication.

PART 1 CASE STUDY

Robin Hood

It was in the spring of the second year of his insurrection against the High Sheriff of Nottingham that Robin Hood took a walk in Sherwood Forest. As he walked he pondered the progress of the campaign, the disposition of his forces, the Sheriff's recent moves, and the options that confronted him.

The revolt against the Sheriff had begun as a personal crusade. It erupted out of Robin's conflict with the Sheriff and his administration. However, alone Robin Hood could do little. He therefore sought allies, men with grievances and a deep sense of justice. Later he welcomed all who came, asking few questions, and demanding only a willingness to serve. Strength, he believed, lay in numbers.

He spent the first year forging the group into a disciplined band, united in enmity against the sheriff, and willing to live outside the law. The band's organization was simple. Robin ruled supreme, making all important decisions. He delegated specific tasks to lieutenants. Will Scarlet was in charge of intelligence and scouting. His main job was to shadow the Sheriff and his men, always alert to their next move. He also collected information on the travel plans of rich merchants and tax collectors. Little John kept discipline among the men, and saw to it that their archery was at the high peak that their profession demanded. Scarlock took care of finances, converting loot to cash, paying shares of the take, and finding suitable hiding places for the surplus. Finally, Much the Miller's Son had the difficult task of provisioning the ever-increasing band of Merrymen.

The increasing size of the band was a source of satisfaction for Robin, but also a source of concern. The fame of his Merrymen was spreading, and new recruits poured in from every corner of England. As the band grew larger, their small bivouac became a major encampment. Between raids the men milled about, talking and playing games. Vigilance was in decline, and discipline was becoming harder to enforce. 'Why,' Robin reflected, 'I don't know half the men I run into these days.'

The growing band was also beginning to exceed the food capacity of the forest. Game was becoming scarce, and supplies had to be obtained from outlying villages. The cost of buying food was beginning to drain the band's financial reserves at the very moment when revenues were in decline. Travellers, especially those with the most to lose, were now giving the forest a wide berth. This was costly and inconvenient to them, but it was preferable to having all their goods confiscated.

Robin believed that the time had come for the Merrymen to change their policy of outright confiscation of goods to one of a fixed transit tax. His lieutenants strongly resisted this idea. They were proud of the Merrymen's famous motto: 'Rob from the rich and give to the poor.' 'The farmers and townspeople,' they argued, 'are our most important allies. How can we tax them, and still hope for their help in our fight against the sheriff?'

Robin wondered how long the Merrymen could keep to the ways and methods of their early days. The Sheriff was growing stronger and becoming better organized. He now had money and men, and was beginning to harass the band, probing for its weaknesses. The tide of events was beginning to turn against the Merrymen. Robin felt that the campaign must be decisively concluded before the Sheriff had a chance to deliver a mortal blow. 'But how,' he wondered, 'could this be done?'

Robin had often entertained the possibility of killing the Sheriff, but the chances for this seemed increasingly remote. Besides, killing the Sheriff might satisfy his personal thirst for revenge, but it would not improve the situation. Robin had hoped that the perpetual state of unrest, and the Sheriff's failure to collect taxes, would lead to his removal from office. Instead, the Sheriff used his political connections to obtain reinforcement. He had powerful friends at court, and was well regarded by the regent, Prince John.

Prince John was vicious and volatile. He was consumed by his unpopularity among the people, who wanted the imprisoned King Richard back. He also lived in constant fear of the barons, who had first given him the regency, but were now beginning to dispute his claim to the throne. Several of these barons had set out to collect the ransom that would release King Richard the Lionheart from his jail in Austria. Robin was invited to join the conspiracy in return for future amnesty. It was a dangerous proposition. Provincial banditry was one thing, court intrigue another. Prince John had spies everywhere and he was known for his vindictiveness. If the conspirators' plan failed, the pursuit would be relentless, and retribution swift.

The sound of the supper horn startled Robin from his thoughts. There was the smell of roasting venison in the air. Nothing was resolved or settled. Robin headed for camp promising himself that he would give these problems his utmost attention after tomorrow's raid.

Copyright 1991 by Joseph Lampel.

Foreword: Strategy in the modern world

■ **CONTENTS**

1   Definitions and purpose

'Strategy' is a much-used word, one that we use in relation to our everyday lives as well as in a business context. Strategy has many facets and faces. The origin of the word is the Greek term 'strategos', used in military operations and focusing on how to win battles. This aim of 'winning' may be an apt metaphor for business, although, it may not entirely suitable 100% of the time, given the increasing inter-connectedness of business and the growing trend towards strategic collaboration and 'co-opetition'.

Strategy has come a long way since the days of the ancient Greeks, and it is useful to have some understanding of the evolution of strategy as a business and management tool. In this context, and before looking at the history of business strategic thinking, it is appropriate to start with some definitions so that readers can develop their own way of articulating this critical concept for business and its governance.

Here are the definitions of strategy by some business and management authors:

- 'The determination of the long run goals and objectives of an enterprise and the adoption of courses of action and the allocation of resource necessary for carrying out these goals' (Chandler, 1963)
- 'The long term direction of an organisation' (Johnson and Scholes, 2011)
- 'Sound strategy starts with having the right goal.
  'The essence of strategy is knowing what not to do'.
  'Strategy is about setting yourself apart from the competition. It's not a matter of being better at what you do – it's a matter of being different at what you do.' (Michael Porter)
- 'A pattern in a stream of decisions' (Mintzberg, 2007).

The first two definitions emphasise the long-run nature of strategy and the sense of forward direction. Porter focuses on the goal and its differentiation from the competition. Mintzberg suggests less certainty and looking back at what happened, with a kind of post-hoc justification of a series of events – strategy only visible after the event, as it were. None of them mentions the word 'plan' or 'planning', but they do imply action and implementation as well as some future goal or objective.

It is important to stress that strategy is more than a plan. It implies a long-term perspective, and is usually far-reaching in an organisation. As it evolves over time, strategy is dynamic, and indeed interactive in the sense that actions by one organisation will usually generate reactions by others in its sphere of influence or competitive context. There is an element of chess about strategy, with an increasing need to think several steps ahead, given the speed of the modern world and what seems like constant and rapidly accelerating change in the business environment.

How would you define 'strategy' in your own words?

Purpose of strategy

It is clear that strategy has to do with some desired future state, with objectives or goals that can be defined, whether broadly or narrowly. For organisations, this can range from mere survival to target market share or profit levels. It may involve key product, market or pricing decisions, or production and quality issues. Strategy is the hunt for 'competitive advantage' – preferably sustainable competitive advantage, although this is proving increasingly difficult, given the rapid changes in business. Strategy academics now talk in terms of trying to achieve a series of 'transient competitive advantages'.

In hard financial terms, with reference to investors and shareholders, strategy is often focused on a combination of activities that make a return greater than the cost of capital. At the same time, there is a sense of 'winning' a battle in the market place – in simple terms, can an organisation be faster, better or cheaper than the competition in addressing market needs? Note that the target is to be all three at the same time, but in reality, an organisation can only aspire to two out of the three, often within a narrowly defined market segment, given the proliferation of choice now facing buyers in most categories.

Robert Grant (2016) distinguishes between strategy and tactics, although he states that the two must be linked. In his view:

- strategy is the overall analysis and plan for deploying resources to establish a favourable position; and
- tactics are a scheme for a specific initiative that helps achieve this.

Here we see a reference to strategy that implies a commitment of resources to something that is thus not easily reversible. To the extent that implementation of the strategy, and the tactics needed to do this successfully, involve human resources suggests that a good strategist must always consider not only the 'hard' edge of strategy – the return on investment of strategy – but also the 'soft' side – the history and culture of the organisation, the morale and motivation of the staff, and their alignment with the strategy as communicated to them.

So why do companies need strategy, and what are its benefits? Mintzberg et al. (1998) suggest that strategy:

- sets direction – charting a course that creates cohesion (although it may be the wrong direction!);
- focuses effort – promoting coordination and reducing disorder – but it may lead to suffocating 'groupthink';
- defines the organisation – capturing essential meaning and creating a shared identity – but this may lead to a loss of richness and stereotyping or an organisation; and
- provides consistency – reducing ambiguity – but this may also limit creativity.

Furthermore, Mintzberg et al. add that strategy seeks to find a best 'fit' between the organisation and its context or environment. This idea of fit is one we will return to shortly as a core proposition of the strategy process. What should be noted is that these features are quite broadly defined, leaving scope within an overall frame of reference for some flexibility and what Mintzberg refers to as 'emergent' strategy (see Figure 1), the sum of the hundreds and thousands of individual decisions taken day to day by senior, middle and junior management.

This neatly links us back to Mintzberg's terse definition of strategy as 'a pattern in a stream of decisions', and hints at a philosophical difference in viewing strategy among the various strategy schools of thought.

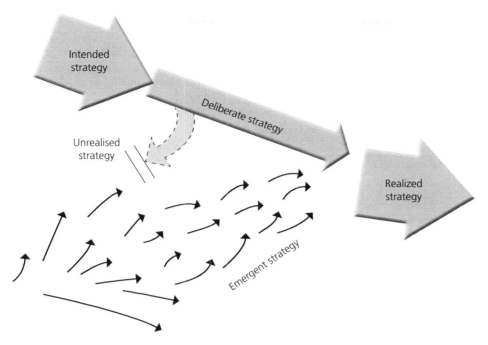

FIGURE 1 Mintzberg's 'emergent' strategy

From *Strategy Safari*, 2nd edition, Mintzberg, Ahlstrand & Lampel, Pearson Education Limited, © Henry Mintzberg, Bruce Ahlstrand and Joseph Lampel 1998, 2009

TEST YOUR KNOWLEDGE

a) What do you think the benefits of strategy are?

b) How does strategy differ from tactics?

2   History and evolution

Strategy and management are intimately linked. As the study of management has evolved over the past 100+ years since business schools were first created, so has strategy. It is the major academic discipline that underpins an MBA, and it is instructive to take a look at that evolution. Mintzberg et al. have identified ten schools of strategy:

1. Design: a process of *conception*
2. Planning: a **formal** process
3. Positioning: an **analytical** process
4. Entrepreneurial: a *visionary* process
5. Cognitive: a *judgemental* process
6. Learning: an **emergent** process
7. Political: a process of *negotiation*
8. Cultural: a *collective* process
9. Environmental: a **reactive** process
10. Configuration: a process of *transformation*

Here we shall concern ourselves with four main schools of thought:

■ **Planning (1950s–60s)**
In many ways, strategic management went back to its roots in terms of applying the sort of planning processes developed during the two world wars, with a new focus on incremental change, which was often related to growth in the overall economy.

■ **Positioning (1980s–90s)**
Strategy owes a great debt to one of the most prolific business strategy academics, Professor Michael Porter, who changed the nature of strategy to consider the relative positioning of an

organisation compared to its competitors. It was no longer enough to grow by the same or more than the economy; it was important to grow by the same or more than your industry or sector grew, and thus analyse your position relative to competitors.

■ **Learning (1990s+)**
  Although it has its origins in the 1960s, this school came more to prominence in the late 1990s/early 2000s as the pace of change grew, and Mintzberg coined the phrase 'emergent strategy' as being loose and adaptive.
■ **Environmental (2000s+)**
  Closely related to the learning school of strategy is the environmental school and a focus on scanning and monitoring the external environment to react to or, better still, anticipate the drivers of change in an industry so as to capture the opportunities or mitigate the threats that may arise.

These schools of thought have evolved as the business environment has changed. Over the years in question, there have been significant shifts of emphasis of strategy, from seeking revenue growth in times of boom to survival and cost control in times of recession and austerity. In that sense, although the hunt for competitive advantage is unchanged, the context in which strategy is crafted varies considerably.

There are other factors and forces that business needs to take into account that are impacting on strategy, covered in this book but introduced here as a fundamental backcloth to any strategy formulation. Where business was once able to pursue the straightforward goal of maximising **shareholder** value, especially for publicly quoted companies which focused on short-term earnings growth, there is now a growing emphasis on **stakeholder** value and the long term.

Business strategists ignore this at their peril, as external forces in society are driving this – with significant political as well as social pressure for business to adapt and respond to major failings in the free market, capitalist economic context that has dominated the global business environment in the past century.

TEST YOUR KNOWLEDGE

a) What are the key four main schools of strategic thinking?
b) What is 'emergent' strategy?

3 Strategy in a VUCA world

Globalisation is a fact of life – we live in an increasingly inter-connected world, well beyond the simplicity of trade between countries, which is not new, to a world of multinational corporations bigger than many countries, operating beyond the jurisdiction of any one nation, with the increasing foreign ownership of productive assets and internationally integrated supply chains. Banking is one of the most globalised sectors. Since 2007 and the financial crisis – indeed since 2001 and 9/11 – we live in what has been described as a VUCA world –: one that is volatile, uncertain, complex and ambiguous. The VUCA acronym resulted from the end of the Cold War and derives from military vocabulary. It has been subsequently applied to the world of strategic management.

The pace of change is getting faster. 'Black swan' events (events that are markedly different from normal situations and are extremely difficult to predict; they are typically random and unexpected) seem to occur more frequently, disruptive technologies arise ever quicker and the internet gives access to vast amounts of information and data overload – often contradictory, and often insufficient for what we need. In this VUCA world, strategy has to cope with a rapidly changing context and moving targets or end goals.

It is with this in mind that we introduce the concept of the 'strategy process', and the first parts of the book are based on this. This is founded on a simple conceptual framework for strategy as a means to determine the following:

■ Where are we now (current state)?
■ Where do we want to get to (future goal)?
■ How do we get there (implementation and plan)?

- Where have we come from (reflection on history, culture and morale)?

The strategy 'process' that answers these questions, which is introduced in Chapter 2, consists of the basic tools and techniques of strategy, essential frameworks to be mastered. Note that strategy is not the same as planning. Planning is part of the strategy process, an important part, but it comes after prior analysis and decision making regarding the strategic objectives. How to get there necessarily involves knowing where you are starting from.

The concepts and frameworks of the strategy process come with some disclaimers:

- They do not give us the right answers, but they may help us to ask the right questions.
- They are necessary but no longer sufficient for good strategy formulation, as they are analytical tools with a bias towards the past and the current, while we increasingly need help to shape our thinking about the future.
- They should be compared with the techniques needed to control a car so as to be able to pass a driving test – after which most of us really learn to drive with the basics of vehicle control becoming second nature. It is similar with the strategy process.

The tools, techniques, frameworks and concepts described in this book should eventually become second nature to the student of strategy. Competitive advantage and thus the added value of the strategy function will come from seeing the future before your competitors – calling for vision and creativity, values and sensitivity, flexibility and agility as well as process and analysis.

In other words, strategy has evolved from a focus on 'hindsight' then 'insight' to 'foresight'. The analytical tools of the strategy process can, however, help organisations to:

- improve the decision-making process;
- identify and understand key issues;
- manage complexity;
- maintain a balance between competing for the present and preparing for the future;
- secure the best fit between our current resources and capabilities and the fast-changing external environment at any one time; and
- identify risks arising from that fast-changing environment.

A VUCA world clearly implies more risk, and in governance terms, risk must be identified, quantified and analysed by the board and senior officers, including the company secretary. One major risk is that any market or competitive advantage can now be quickly eroded, and organisations must accept that Porter's ideal of sustainable competitive advantage is no longer feasible. The best we can hope for, according to Columbia Business School's Professor Rita Gunther McGrath writing in 2013, is 'transient competitive advantage'. She talks in terms of a 'transient advantage economy' and how this impacts upon resource allocation, innovation, leadership and careers.

 STOP AND THINK 2

When thinking about strategy, think like a management consultant. Imagine you have been assigned to your organisation as a new client and have to identify and analyse, with suitable evidence, the key issues from both internal and external factors, challenging the views and assumptions of the management team.

---

4 Strategy and management

As noted above, strategy and management are intimately linked. Managers implement and monitor strategy, through and with the organisation's employees. But what is management? One of the greatest philosophers about management, the late Peter Drucker (1992), wrote that organisations do not exist for their own sake, but to fulfil a specific social purpose and to satisfy a specific need of a society, a community or individuals. Management, in turn, is the organ of the organisation.

Drucker saw strategy in terms of the decisions made today about a future that is inherently uncertain. In his view, management was more of an art than a science, based on a few essential principles:

- Management is about human beings.
- It deals with the integration of people in a common venture.
- Every enterprise requires commitment to common goals and shared values, so management has to set and exemplify those objectives and values.
- Management must also enable the enterprise and each of its members to grow as needs and opportunities change – the importance of innovation.

The task of management is therefore to:

- establish the specific purpose and mission of the organisation – the **what**;
- make work productive and employees effective – traditionally the **how**; and
- manage social impacts and responsibilities – a new component of **how**, growing in importance.

Gary Hamel coined the phrase 'Management 2.0'. He talks about the need for a new management paradigm in the 21st century, given that most of our classic management tools, like the business schools that teach them, were invented in the early 1900s (Hamel, 2011). The challenge of management then was to harness uneducated farm labourers in factory conditions to undertake repetitive manual tasks, as industrialisation and mass production took hold. The focus was on control.

Today, management is still concerned with getting things done through other people, but now employees are more educated and articulate, with far more rights and aspirations, values and creativity. Management today is less about control and more about trust and empowerment, a theme picked up by another leading management thinker, Charles Handy, who also writes about 'new management'. Trust is cheaper, but control is safer – or so we think, certainly in large organisations. However, the rapid pace of change in the external environment means that traditional top-down command and control hierarchies will become like super tankers, slow to change direction. To use another metaphor coined by Harvard's Rosabeth Moss Kanter, how can elephants learn to dance?

The nature of management has changed, as has the nature of strategy. Boards must concern themselves with not only **what** to do, but also **how** to do it. The 'how' is growing in importance and has two dimensions:

1   How best to organise and structure an organisation to implement its strategy is a constant challenge – but now in a fast-changing world with a different profile of employee.
2   How in terms of the style, values and ethics of the organisation, and its alignment with the style, values and ethics of employees in a way that harnesses not only their obedience and diligence, but also their intellect, initiative, creativity and passion. This is reflected in Hamel's pyramid of human capabilities, shown in Figure 2.

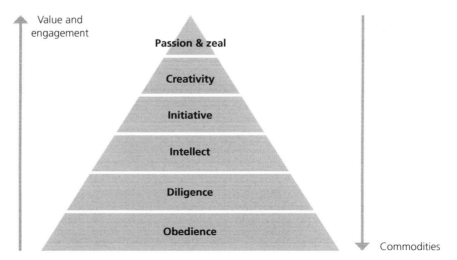

FIGURE 2 Hamel's pyramid of human capabilities

Strategy was never easy. It gets harder all the time. As you read through this book, try to keep in mind the rapidly changing external environment and the demands of society that business serves and the employees drawn from that society, in a way that addresses the essential challenge of business strategy – getting the right things done through other people in the right way.

Organisations that get this right will be successful. If you keep abreast of the somewhat philosophical issues surrounding strategy and management, as well as the technical developments in strategic thinking and its tools and concepts, you will be well placed to serve your organisation and help guide it to success.

 TEST YOUR KNOWLEDGE

a) What are the key elements of strategy in the modern business environment?
b) How are management and strategy linked?

Summary

- The word 'strategy' comes from ancient Greek, with military connotations.
- Definitions of strategy involve long-term goals and how to achieve them, and imply a hunt for competitive advantage, transient though it is likely to be.
- Strategy can be used to set direction, focus effort, define the organisation and provide consistency.
- It must be clearly distinguished from tactics, which are short-term operational matters to help achieve the goals of strategy.
- Strategy has evolved from a focus on planning, through positioning to reaction and innovation – from hindsight via insight to foresight and emergent strategies
- Strategy is dynamic, necessary as organisations operate in a fast-changing and VUCA world – volatile, uncertain, complex and ambiguous.
- A VUCA world clearly involves more risk, which cannot be eliminated but must be managed.
- A good strategist thinks like a management consultant, challenging and testing assumptions about the organisation as the external environment changes.
- Strategy is intimately linked to management, which itself is rapidly evolving with a greater emphasis not only on what organisations do but how they do it, in a way that addresses society's expectation of business and harnesses the values, creativity and even passion of employees.

1 The nature of strategy and planning

CONTENTS

INTRODUCTION

Trying to develop and grow a business to meet the needs of customers presents huge challenges. All organisations are faced with the need to develop an appropriate strategy to help them. This chapter is an introduction and overall explanation of this notion. It looks at what is meant by 'strategy' and 'strategic management', why they are important and how they relate to other organisational activities and issues.

---

1 Strategy and planning

1.1 Distinguishing planning and strategy

We are all planners, more than we might imagine. We put together menus, make shopping lists, set out essays and revise for examinations. We schedule our holidays and make arrangements for our retirement. When in a group we often discuss where to go and what to do. We hope that at least one person has a sense of direction to steer us and that another has a sense of time if there is a deadline. Often, plans are informal, including many in business. Whether formal or not they give shape and purpose to our lives and enable us to gather resources and co-operate with others to achieve ends.

Planning can be defined as the establishment of objectives and the formulation, evaluation and selection of the policies, strategies and tactics required to achieve these objectives. A plan is thus an explicit statement of intention that identifies both objectives and the actions needed to achieve them. This has two aspects:

1 At the heart of plans are *objectives and goals*. Making them explicit – in statements from departmental plans to organisational mission statements – provides a unity of purpose, a means of motivation and the basis of control. If plans are linked, they offer the opportunity to coordinate the work of the whole.
2 If objectives were the only elements of a plan, then it would amount to no more than a statement of wishes. Stating *actions* spells out the tasks required, including who is to carry them out, when, and so on. Goals or objectives without actions indicate weak leadership: they express an intention without the power to carry them out. By contrast, actions without goals and objectives mean that the organisation is moving from day to day like a rudderless ship hoping for favourable seas.

One difficulty is that terms are frequently used interchangeably – terms such as 'goal', 'aim', and so on. For the moment, we shall stick to the one term *objective* as a statement about the future state that the organisation wants to achieve. Good objectives identify both this state and the time when it is to be reached. In brief, an objective we define as a quantified or more precise aim in line with the goal or goals of the organisation.

At its most basic level, **strategy** concerns the long-term direction of an organisation. However, a more complete definition is offered by Johnson et al. (2014). They see strategy as the direction and scope of an organisation over the long term which achieves an advantage for the organisation through the way it configures its resources within a changing environment, to meet the needs of markets and to fulfil stakeholder expectations. In the public sector the term 'policy' is sometimes used instead of 'strategy', though it is slightly broader: expressing the broad purpose of government activity in a particular field, for example, with some desired outcome in mind.

Strategic planning usually consists of step-by-step procedures to develop and coordinate the organisation's strategy. The need for strategic planning arises from the following factors:

- As companies increase in size, the risks of potential losses from the inefficient or ineffective use of resources also increase. Strategic planning helps in managing these risks.
- Strategic planning can give a sense of purpose to people in the company, leading to an improved quality of management, and it can encourage creativity and initiative by tapping the ideas of the management team.
- Companies cannot remain static – they have to cope with changes in their environment. A strategic plan helps to chart possible areas where the company may be involved in the future, as well as offering a framework for dealing with sudden turmoil.
- Strategic plans make explicit the departmental objectives that have always existed. They help to make them more effective and workable.
- A well-prepared plan drawn up after analysing internal and external factors – risks and uncertainties – is in the long-term best interests of the company because better quality decisions will be made (on the whole) and management control can be better exercised.
- Long-, medium- and short-term objectives, plans and controls can be made consistent with one another. It is quite possible, however, that those strategic plans can be made ineffective by budgeting systems with performance measures which have no strategic content.
- Strategic planning might appear to be the very antithesis of entrepreneurship. However, Drucker (1968) has argued that an entrepreneur who builds a long-lasting business has 'a theory of the business' which informs his or her business decisions. In large organisations, the theory of the business has to become public knowledge, as one person cannot take all decisions. As Drucker says, 'business enterprise requires that entrepreneurship be systemised, spelled out as a discipline and organised as work.'

 STOP AND THINK 1.1

When do you engage in planning? Map out the process that you typically use.

1.2 The strategic planning process

Planning is the process of setting out the objectives of an organisation and the means for achieving them. It is sometimes suggested that planning is the primary management function from which all activities follow, but it is not a process independent of other managerial activities. For example, it goes hand in hand with control. The former sets the direction and points the organisation along its route; the latter ensures that the direction is maintained or, if that proves impossible, it warns of the need to choose a new direction. Taken together, planning and control form a cycle with the four elements shown in Figure 1.1.

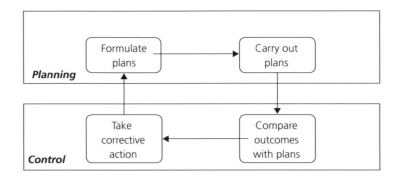

FIGURE 1.1 The planning and control process

While in practice it represents a continuous loop, it is usual to read in a clockwise direction starting from *Formulate plans*. The planning process involves this stage and initiates the next – *Carry out plans*. *Control* includes two elements: comparison and correction. Comparison requires observation of the outcomes of the implementation, or carrying out, stage to discover how closely its results match the plan. The last stage, *Take corrective action*, depends on the mismatches between the plan and its achievement. Changes can be made to the way the plan is being carried out (*Review implementation*). Alternatively, if the gap is such that the plan itself needs review, then it can be adapted (*Review future plans*).

1.3 The characteristics of strategic decisions

What types of decisions are strategic decisions and what distinguishes these from other decisions being taken in the organisation? As we suggested in Section 1.1, 'strategy' and 'strategic decisions', according to Johnson et al. (2014), are concerned with:

1   The long-term direction of an organisation. Strategic decisions are likely to be concerned with, or affect, the long-term direction of an organisation.

 **CASE EXAMPLE** **1.1**

In March 2015, the merger was announced of US food giant Heinz with Kraft Foods Group. The deal was engineered by Heinz's owners, the Brazilian investment firm 3G Capital, and billionaire investor Warren Buffett's Berkshire Hathaway. Current Heinz shareholders will own 51% of the combined company, and Kraft shareholders will own a 49% stake. The merger will create the third-largest food and beverage company in North America and the fifth-largest in the world. It has been approved by both the companies' boards. The move is aimed at reducing costs and improving growth of the two companies, at home as well as enabling Kraft to benefit from Heinz's global reach. The merger has occurred as long-established US food groups like Kraft, which has a heritage stretching back to 1903, have struggled to adapt to new consumer demands for fresher, less-processed foods.

2   **The scope of an organisation's activities**. Strategic decisions are likely to be concerned with the scope of an organisation's activities. Should the organisation concentrate on one area of activity or many? For example, Kraft acquired the UK's Cadbury in a hostile deal in 2010, although this is now owned by Mondelez, the business that was spun off from Kraft in 2012. The issue of scope of activity is fundamental to strategic decisions because it concerns the way in which those responsible for managing the organisation see the organisation's boundaries and what they want the organisation to be like and to be about.

3   **Securing advantage**. Strategic decisions are normally about trying to achieve some advantage for the organisation over the competition or providing higher quality, value-for-money services than other providers in the public or third sector, thus attracting support and funding from government.

4 **Strategic fit with the environment**. Strategy can be seen as the matching of the activities of an organisation to the environment in which it operates. This is known as the search for *strategic fit*, for example, locating in particularly favourable markets or seeking to appeal to particular market segments.

5 **The organisation's resources and competences**. Strategy can also be seen as exploiting the strategic capability of an organisation in terms of its resources and competences to provide competitive advantage or yield new opportunities. IKEA, for example, has built up its logistics expertise, from sourcing products to stock control, over many years and provides a distinct way of operating, greatly valued by customers.

6 **Values and expectations**. The strategy of an organisation is affected not only by environmental forces and resource availability, but also by the values and expectations of those who have power in and around it. In some respects, strategy can be thought of as a reflection of the attitudes and beliefs of those who have most influence on the organisation. For example, whether a company is expansionist or more concerned with consolidation may say much about the values and attitudes of those who influence strategy – the stakeholders of the organisation. These include: shareholders or financial institutions; management and the workforce, buyers and perhaps suppliers; and the local community.

 **CASE EXAMPLE** 1.2

At a company like Google, the senior managers have pursued growth in a number of different directions over the years. They are not the only people interested in strategy. The expectations and values of other managers, employees, suppliers, customers and internet users all have a stake in the future of Google too.

These characteristics mean that strategic decisions are likely to be:

- Complex in nature, especially in organisations with a wide geographical scope, such as multinational firms or those with a wide range of products or services.
- Made in situations of *uncertainty* where it is impossible for managers to be sure. At a company such as Yahoo!, the internet environment is one of constant innovation that is hard to predict.
- Linked to operational decisions. For example, the internationalisation of IKEA required a whole series of decisions at operational level. Management and control structures to deal with the geographical spread of the firm had to change. HR policies and practices had to be reviewed. This link between overall strategy and operational aspects of the organisation has two highly significant implications:
  - If the operational aspects of the organisation are not in line with the strategy, then, no matter how well considered the strategy is, it will not succeed.
  - It is at the operational level that real strategic advantage can be achieved. Companies have succeeded not only because of a good strategic concept, but also because of the detail of how the concept is put into effect.
- Demand an integrated approach to managing the organisation. Managers have to cross functional and operational boundaries to deal with strategic problems and come to agreements with other managers with different interests and priorities.
- Require the management of relationships and networks outside the organisation, for example with suppliers, distributors and customers. Strategic decisions may also involve change in organisations that is difficult both to plan and implement.

Strategic decisions involve change, and so strategic change (see Chapter 13) is a critical component of strategy.

1.4 Mintzberg's Five Ps

Mintzberg (1996) makes it clear that strategy involves more than just following an 'industry recipe', copying a competitor's strategy or carrying on the same as before. He characterises strategic thinking as 'seeing': seeing ahead, behind, below, above and 'for a thinker to deserve the label strategic, he or she must also see it *through*!' (p.83).

Mintzberg suggests that there are five ways in which the term strategy is used:

1 **Strategy as plan**. A strategy is a 'consciously intended course of action'. This reflects the definition of strategy outlined above, and the ideas of Ansoff outlined below in Section 2.2.
2 **Strategy as ploy**. Strategy as a manoeuvre in a competitive game. For example, a firm might add unnecessary plant capacity with the intention not to produce the goods but to discourage a competitor from entering the market. The strategy is not the activity but the deterrence.
3 **Strategy as pattern**. The idea of strategy as a pattern relates to Mintzberg's ideas of emergent strategies that result from unintended decisions assuming a life of their own.
4 **Strategy as position**. A critical aspect of top management's work today involves matching organisational competences (internal resources and skills) with the opportunities and risks created by environmental change in ways that will be effective and efficient. Strategy can therefore be a 'position' in a market, relative to others, from which a return can be gained. Positioning the firm can define or redefine its relationship with the competition and can involve:
    a) carving a niche to avoid competition (by making distinctive products or services, or exploiting a distinct competence);
    b) co-operating with firms in different market niches and with competitors (Microsoft and Apple compete in some markets, but participate in joint ventures in others).
    We can see this developed in the ideas of Ohmae and Porter (see Section 4.5).
5 **Strategy as perspective**. Strategy can construct a unique way of looking at the world, of interpreting information from it and judging its opportunities and choices. As such, it refers to organisation culture.

These five ways of discussing strategy are not mutually exclusive. Arguably they complement each other. In the right circumstances, any of the definitions will be the most apt to describe the approach to strategy taken. Nor is there a necessary hierarchy in which one comes before the other. A perspective can give rise to a plan but the process of planning can result in an alteration of perspective.

 STOP AND THINK 1.2

How is strategy viewed in your organisation or one you know well? Use Mintzberg's framework to help you analyse it.

1.5 Levels of strategy and planning

It is possible to identify three distinct planning levels, although there may be more or fewer in organisations in practice. Typical terms are *strategic, intermediate* and *operational levels*. These are shown in Table 1.1, which also suggests the managers who are responsible and the timescale covered by each plan.

Senior managers display a broader scope in their plans both in terms of areas of the business and the timespan covered. This latter aspect is important. They have different planning horizons. The **planning horizon** is the time that elapses between making and executing a plan. Longer time horizons suggest that strategic planning means greater uncertainty than intermediate or tactical planning. Not only are forecasts likely to be less detailed over a longer period but also there is more time for unexpected events to occur.

TABLE 1.1 Three levels of planning

Planning level	Purpose	Managers	Time horizon
Strategic	Achieving business objectives through making long-term relationships between the organisation and its environment; obtaining key resources.	General managers and heads of functions.	1–10 years or more
Intermediate	Giving direction to, and allocating resources among, sub-units and functions to give each clear objectives and to ensure coordination.	Middle managers working together and also with their departmental teams.	6 months to 2 years
Operational	Accomplishing tasks with available resources to contribute to departmental objectives.	Operating unit managers, supervisors and individual staff.	A few hours to 1 year

The plans at each level have different purposes. In general, senior managers, in giving direction to those at lower hierarchical levels, are expected to absorb some of the uncertainty in the business environment. Intermediate and operational plans can be more specific and concrete because they cover shorter periods and relate (or at least should relate) to the objectives of the next higher level that should already have been clarified. Agreement over objectives in this way reduces uncertainty for managers. At the operations level, roles are assigned to specialist departments such as marketing or purchasing, each with their own strategy.

Strategies therefore exist at a number of levels in an organisation. It is possible to distinguish at least three different levels:

1 **Corporate strategy**. This is concerned with the overall purpose and scope of the organisation to meet the expectations of owners or major stakeholders and add value to the different parts of the enterprise. In the case of IKEA, this took form in the way in which the firm was structured to maintain its independence according to the wishes of its founder. In publicly quoted businesses, corporate-level strategy is heavily influenced by the expectations of shareholders and the stock market. Being clear about corporate strategy forms the basis of other strategic decisions. It may well take form in an explicit or implicit 'mission statement' that reflects such expectations. This is discussed in Chapter 7.

   Corporate strategy is concerned with the question: 'What businesses should we be in?'

CASE EXAMPLE 1.3

BT in talks with Telefónica to buy O2
BT is considering buying back O2, the mobile phone operator it owned until 2001, in a deal that would reverse what has been described as one of the worst strategic errors in UK corporate history. The former telecoms monopoly is so determined to regain a foothold in the mobile phone business it is also in parallel talks to acquire EE, Britain's biggest mobile phone firm, as it explores ways to offer a single package of television, broadband, landline and mobile telephones. The four-way package, which the industry has dubbed 'quad-play', is now viewed as a must-have for success as consumers increasingly prefer to get all their telecoms, television and digital services from one place.

Guardian, 25 November 2014

2 **Business unit strategy**. This is about how to compete successfully in a particular market. The concerns are therefore with:

(a) how to achieve advantage over competitors;

(b) what new opportunities can be identified or created in markets;

(c) which products or services should be developed in which markets; and

(d) the extent to which these meet customer needs to achieve the objectives of the organisation whether long-term profitability or market growth.

Whereas corporate strategy concerns the organisation as a whole, strategic decisions at this level relate to a strategic business unit (SBU). An SBU is a part of the organisation for which there is a distinct external market for goods or services.

At this level, strategic decisions are based on how customer or client needs can best be met to achieve some sort of competitive advantage for the organisation. It is therefore very important that an SBU understands the needs of its customers or clients and who its competitors are.

Business unit strategy is concerned with the question: 'How do we succeed in this particular business?'

 **CASE EXAMPLE** **1.4**

At Yahoo!, relationships with online advertisers stretch across different business units: using, protecting and enhancing the Yahoo! brand should support the SBUs. But at the same time the SBUs have to make sure their business-level strategies do not damage the corporate whole or other SBUs in the group.

3 **Operational strategies**. These are concerned with how the component parts of the organisation in terms of resources, processes, people and their skills effectively deliver the corporate- and business-level strategies. In most organisations, successful strategies depend to a large extent on activities that occur at the operational level. For example, in IKEA it is crucial that design, store operations and sourcing operations dovetail into higher-level decisions about product range and market entry. The integration of operational decisions and strategy is of great importance.

Functional/operational strategy is concerned with the question: 'How does this function or operation contribute to the business strategy?'

Operational and functional strategies include:

a) marketing strategies, which involve devising products and services, pricing, promoting and distributing them to satisfy customer or client needs;

b) production strategies, which involve issues such as factory location, manufacturing techniques and subcontracting;

c) finance strategy, which ensures that the organisation has the financial resources to fund its other strategies; and

d) human resource management strategy to secure that people in the right number with the right skills are available at the right time.

Figure 1.2 summarises the three levels, using the Virgin Group as an example. Depending on the level in the organisation, the focus of strategy ranges from achieving an overall balance in the business to optimising the contribution of each section. To examine the strategy management process in more detail it is best to start at the business level. This is long-term management of the SBU. In large businesses, this will take place in the framework of corporate strategy while in smaller ones there will only be one SBU. Corporate and business strategy will be the same.

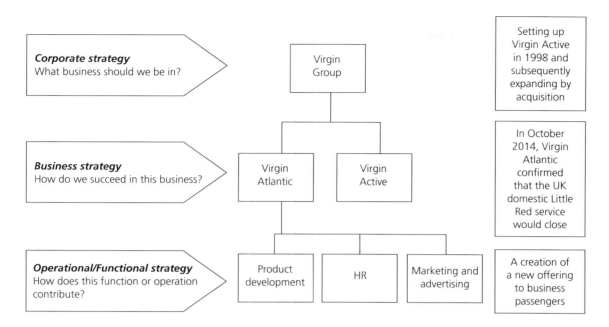

FIGURE 1.2 Levels of strategy at the Virgin Group

There is a hierarchy or cascade of plans and decisions whereby activity at the lower levels is guided and constrained by policy made at higher levels. Figure 1.3 illustrates the process as it might affect marketing; similar cascades would exist in other functional areas.

FIGURE 1.3 The relationship between different levels of strategy and objectives

 **STOP AND THINK** 1.3

Hamlet Ltd sells valves. The finance director recently said: 'We plan to issue more shares to raise money for new plant capacity – we don't want loan finance – which will enable us to compete better in the vital and growing valve markets of Latin America. After all, we've promised the shareholders 5% profit growth this year, and trading is tough.'

Which are the corporate, business and functional strategies in her statement?

The corporate objective is profit growth. The corporate strategy is the decision that this will be achieved by entering new markets rather than producing new products. The business strategy suggests·that those markets include Latin America. The operational or functional strategy involves the decision to invest in new plant (the production function), which is to be financed by shares rather than loans (the finance function).

TEST YOUR KNOWLEDGE 1.1

a Explain what is meant by strategic planning.
b List and briefly describe Mintzberg's Five Ps.
c Define the three levels of strategy.

2   Strategic management

2.1 Introduction

Johnson et al. (2014) argue that strategic management is more than the management of the process of strategic decision making, yet it is also different from the day-to-day decisions that managers have to make. These decisions often concern problems of an operational nature, such as the efficient production of goods or managing a sales force. These are tasks essentially concerned with managing resources *already* deployed in a specific part of the organisation and carried out within the context and guidance of an existing strategy. Although operational management is vital to the effective implementation of strategy, it is not the same as strategic management. Strategic management is concerned with complexity arising out of ambiguous and non-routine situations with organisation-wide rather than operation-specific implications. The issue for organisations is that managers have typically been trained to undertake operational tasks and take operational responsibility. Accountants tend to see problems in financial terms, marketing managers in marketing terms, and so on. The manager who aspires to manage, or influence, strategy must develop a capability to take an overview, to conceive of the whole rather than just the parts of the situation facing an organisation and to handle complexity.

Johnson et al. (op. cit.) stress that strategic management is concerned not only with taking decisions about major issues facing the organisation, but also with ensuring that the strategy is put into effect. Dess, Lumpkin and Eisner (2014) and Barney and Hesterly (2010) suggest that action is involved as well as analysis and choices, and that the ultimate goal of **strategic management** is to secure competitive advantage. It can therefore be defined as the analyses, decisions and actions an organisation undertakes to create and sustain competitive advantage.

Johnson et al. (op. cit) suggest that strategic management has four main elements:

1 **Strategic analysis**. This concerns understanding the strategic position of the organisation. It is the stage of data collection and interpretation, and involves assessing how well the organisation is doing within its changing environment. Questions are asked about the value that the organisation offers to all its stakeholders. There is an appraisal of the resources available and how well they are arranged to provide this value.
2 **Strategic choices**. Involves looking at possible courses of action, evaluating them and choosing between them. The chosen strategy will build on the capabilities or strengths of the organisation in relation to the environment. It will look to develop and exploit relative advantages and sustain them over time.
3 **Strategy implementation**. Both planning how the choice of strategy can be put into effect and managing the changes required, ensuring that it is carried out through the organisation. In large businesses this may mean a hierarchy of strategies – corporate, business and functional – that fit together.
4 **Strategic control**. Since as every aspect of strategy is in a state of flux, managers need to monitor continually the outcomes of their choices and to adapt the policies or the way they are carried out.

An outline of the process is shown in Figure 1.4. The model is not meant to suggest that the process of strategic management must follow a neat and tidy path. In practice, the elements of strategic management are interlinked. One way of evaluating a strategy is to begin to implement it, so strategic choice and strategy implementation may overlap. Since strategic analysis should be a continuing activity, it will overlap with the implementation of strategy.

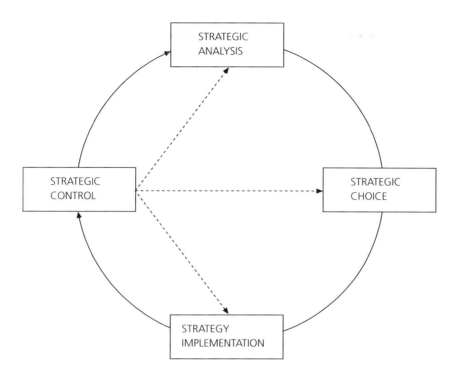

FIGURE 1.4 The strategic management cycle

2.2 The emergence of strategic management

The emergence of strategic management in organisations occurred largely in the second half of the twentieth century. Several schools of thought have emerged, each with its own foundations and arguments. These range from a focus on large-scale corporate planning in the 1950s, through disillusionment with general prescriptions and the failure of complex planning when circumstances change rapidly to new ideas based on chaos and complexity theory. Since the 1950s, strategic management thinking has fragmented into several schools.

Rational planning

Ansoff (1965) argued that businesses are 'purposive': they pursue objectives. He defined an objective as a criterion by which a firm's success or failure is determined. Objectives may be:

- **Economic**. Concerning the most efficient use of available resources in converting inputs to outputs. This is usually measured by return on equity or investment (profit as a proportion of capital invested – ROI). In the longer term, other objectives must be addressed.
- **Concerned with self-renewal**. The development of new products and markets, management development and the acquisition of new plant and equipment.
- **Flexible**. To deal with unforeseen breakthroughs or catastrophes. It is essential that plans provide sufficient flexibility to enable the business to survive.
- **Non-economic**. Including those that respond to the needs of the firm's stakeholders, for example the management's attitude to risk.

It will not be possible to obtain *all* the information affecting these issues since so much depends on events in the future. Strategic decisions are thus taken in conditions of *partial ignorance*. There is, therefore, an ever-present element of risk. Ansoff believes that a strategy is a *linking thread* for the organisation – strategy provides a business with a common thread that enables the management to provide guidance. To be useful, this must strike a balance between being too vague and being too prescriptive. For instance, an oil company might describe itself as being in the 'energy' business but this does not mean it would be appropriate for it to expand into marketing electricity to domestic consumers. The management and technical skills involved may be too different.

Craft

Ohmae (1982), writing about the leaders of Honda, Matsushita, Toyota and other Japanese companies, showed how intuition, creativity and obsession with being the best were more significant than rational skills at data analysis. Since then, Ohmae has stressed the demands that globalisation places on strategists and how they must combine cross-cultural thinking with financial modelling. Handy (1989) also wrote about the links between policy, accomplishment and structure, stressing that planning should be as much based on intuition as analysis.

Failure of big planning

Porter presented a model of competition – **competitive strategy** – in which firms within industries vie for advantage while at the same time keeping out new entrants. Porter (1980) provided both simple explanations of why some firms are successful and some valuable analytical tools. He introduced into strategy the terms *generic strategy* and *competitive advantage* (there is more on Porter's work later in the chapter). Peters and Waterman (1982) also attempted rigorous analysis. A comparison of leading companies looked for the management ingredients that distinguished them from the rest. Critics point out that many of the chosen excellent companies were beginning to disappoint! Mintzberg (1994) continued to stress the failure of 'big planning' in *The Rise and Fall of Strategic Planning*.

Competence

This concerns the growth of interest in the embedded skills of the organisation. The role of the centre in this setting is as parent of the subsidiaries – a coach and leader, creating growth and ambition and skills that can be applied whatever industry or market the organisation is facing. Senge's *The Fifth Discipline* advocates the 'learning organisation', although the achievement of this plausible idea has been disappointing. Hamel and Prahalad (1994) argue that it is not the current mix of products and markets that gives a firm a secure future. Instead, it possesses core competences that it can enhance and apply to an unending stream of future activities. Nike's core competence is not offering high-quality shoes, but design and marketing. Effective management of competences means being able to nurture them and transfer them from one area of activity to another. In other words, core competences create sustainable competitive advantage.

Chaos and complexity

Stacey (1992) is among those who question the assumptions on which the formal planning process has been constructed. He draws on chaos theory to advocate management processes that learn and interact and are able to adapt to the real nature of the environment – instability in a world that is volatile, uncertain, complex and ambiguous (VUCA).

2.3 The rational model

One influential view of strategic management is that strategy can and should be managed through rational planning processes. This follows a sequence of steps involving setting objectives, the analysis of environmental trends and resource capabilities, continuing through the evaluation of different options, and ending with the careful planning of the strategy's implementation. This was outlined in Figure 1.4.

The underlying principle in this rational model is that strategies are the outcome of careful objective analyses and planning. In this way, managers are able to make decisions that establish the future direction of their organisation. Many organisations do have formal planning systems and these contribute usefully to the development of the organisation's strategy. The sequence is logical rather than chronological. We have already identified the main stages and elaborate on these in the following chapters.

However, not all organisations have a formal process. Even when they do, it would be a mistake to assume that the strategies of organisations necessarily come about because of such processes.

The rational model is based on a number of assumptions.

■ **Most strategies are created 'top down'.** Senior managers or strategists 'think great thoughts' and the results are documented in a plan, and developed into greater and greater detail.

- **Corporate strategies**. These (for the organisation as a whole) are developed before strategies for individual business units or functions.
- **A strategy can be broken down into its components**. The depiction of the strategic planning model as a number of stages suggests that it can be broken down into its components. In its extreme form, this suggests that little creative thinking is required, as strategy will be generated automatically out of the external and internal appraisals.
- **Objectivity**. Strategies are determined on their merits through an objective analysis. In other words, it is possible to make objective judgements unclouded by bias.

In Section 2.2, we saw how Ansoff argues in favour of the rational approach to strategic management. Drucker (1968) is another proponent of the rational model, arguing that *conscious* choices need to be made in relation to:

- what the organisation intends to do in the environment and within the opportunities or threats that this offers;
- what degree of risk it faces – all strategies, because they are made in conditions of partial ignorance, involve a risk. Strategic planning cannot completely avoid risk, but it can avoid unnecessary risk;
- the long term, as decisions taken now have implications for the future; and
- resource development, as decisions must be made about organisation structure and issues such as outsourcing and investment.

Drucker suggests that strategic planning is, therefore, something that organisations *should* do and that it involves three tasks:

1 A continuous process of making present risk-taking decisions. This must be done systematically and with greatest possible knowledge of their future effect. This amounts to discovering which new things need to be done, and when.
2 Systematic organisation of the efforts needed to carry out these decisions. The aim of strategic planning is action now, and its realisation *in processes and behaviour*.
3 Measuring the results of these decisions through organised, systematic feedback.

The emphasis on doing things systematically naturally leads to the importance of planning, deciding what things to do, the order in which they are done and when they should be done. Formal strategic planning is a process that can take several months, and might even be the responsibility of a separate department. The work is carried out in stages.

2.4 Limitations of the rational approach

How far does the rational model accord with the strategic management process in your organisation? Why are there variations?

The rational model has been criticised on a number of grounds. The very notion that strategy making can be reduced to planning processes has come under sustained attack from Mintzberg (1994). He made the following criticisms:

- **Practical failure**. Strategic plans often fail. The environment is, or has become, more unstable. The best-laid plans can be invalidated by a new competitor, changes in technology, and so on. Empirical studies have not demonstrated that planning processes necessarily contribute to improved performance. Data about planning processes are, however, hard to gather.
- **Routine**. Strategic planning often occurs in an annual cycle. But a firm 'cannot allow itself to wait every year for the month of February to address its problems'.
- **Reduced initiative**. Formal planning discourages strategic thinking. Once a plan is locked in place, people are unwilling to question it. Obsession with particular performance indicators can reduce a manager's readiness to cope with uncertainty.
- **Internal politics**. The model ignores the 'political' environment of organisations, in other words the conflicting groups that want power.
- **Obsession with control**. Planning can result in an obsession with control that results in a fear of risk and a reluctance to consider truly creative ideas. Planning gives an illusion of control even though the forecast assumptions on which it is based are wrong.

Mintzberg went on to identify some fundamental fallacies in strategic planning.

- **Formalisation**. The assumption is that strategy formation is a job, which like others, can be analysed into its component parts. However, Mintzberg argues that strategic planners have failed to undertake any proper examination of how strategy is made. How can an intuitive judgement be analysed into a logical sequence of steps? 'We have no evidence that any of the strategic planning systems – no matter how elaborate, or how famous – succeeded in capturing (let alone improving on) the messy informal processes by which strategies really do get developed' (1994, p.296).
- **Detachment**. Divorcing planning from doing. Managers manage by remote control, detaching strategy from operations. Consequently, they do not really need any day-to-day knowledge of the product. However, there are strategic messages within the flow of daily operational information that must be detected. Management at the strategic level can be detached only if good information is available. Unfortunately, information that is easily available may give a distorted picture.
- **Formulation precedes implementation**. Defining strengths and weaknesses is very difficult in advance of testing them. 'The detached assessment of strengths and weaknesses may be unreliable, all bound up with aspirations, wishes and hopes.' It is a waste of time without the context of an actual problem. Furthermore, discovering strengths and weaknesses is a learning process. Implementing a strategy is necessary for learning to see if it works. Where learning is needed, where the future is uncertain, strategic thinking cannot be divorced from implementation.
- **Predetermination**. Planning assumes that the environment can be forecast and that its future behaviour can be controlled by a strategy planned in advance and delivered on schedule.

However, it is clear that forecasting cannot cope with discontinuities in events such as war or volcanic ash! In many cases, Mintzberg argues, forecasting functions as a type of comforting magic. Nevertheless, in conditions of stability, forecasting does better, so that extrapolation makes sense as a forecasting technique.

Incidentally, *military analogies* abound in the realms of strategy. The rational model holds that a strategy is a course of action to reach a desired objective. An example often quoted is that of an army. Its objective is to conquer the enemy. The strategy describes how this will be achieved. It may be easy to grasp but is not necessarily relevant to organisations, as:

1 their objectives may be more complex and perhaps more ill defined than an army's;
2 they compete with other organisations for customers (a well-managed army would not be split into two units each independently trying to defeat the enemy);
3 they are less able to command resources than an army;
4 their employees want the organisation (and their jobs) to remain in permanent existence.

 TEST YOUR KNOWLEDGE 1.2

a   What is meant by 'strategic management'?
b   Outline the key stages in the rational model of strategic management?
c   According to Mintzberg, what are the key limitations of the rational model?

---

3   Emergent strategy

3.1 Introduction

As we saw in Section 2, there are other quite different views from the rational model about how strategy can be managed. Managing strategy can be thought of as the process of crafting, where strategic management is seen, not as a single, formal planning process, but in terms of a series of processes. Strategies develop on the basis of managers' experience, their sensitivity to changes in their environment and what they learn from operating in their market. This does not mean that managers are not thinking about the strategic position of their organisation or the choices it faces, but that it may not be taking place in a highly formalised way as it does in planning systems.

Building on this, Mintzberg (1985) developed the concept of an **emergent strategy**. This does not arise out of conscious strategic planning, but results from a number of ad hoc choices, perhaps made lower down the hierarchy. Initially, they may not be recognised as having strategic importance. Emergent strategies develop out of patterns of behaviour, in contrast to planned strategies that are imposed from above. Case example 1.5 makes the point clear.

 **CASE EXAMPLE** **1.5**

Honda is a leading manufacturer of motorcycles. The company is credited with identifying and targeting an untapped market for 50 cc bikes in the US, which enabled it to expand, defeat European competition and severely damage indigenous US motorcycle manufacturers. By 1965, Honda had 63% of the US market.

But this occurred by accident. Upon entering the US market, Honda had wanted to compete with the larger European and US bikes of 250 ccs and over. These bikes had a defined market and were sold through dedicated motorcycle dealerships. Honda's larger machines developed faults as they had not been designed for the hard wear-and-tear imposed by US motorcyclists. Honda had to recall the larger machines and had made little effort to sell its small 50 cc motorbikes. Sports goods shops and ordinary bicycle and department stores had expressed an interest but Honda did not want to confuse its image in its 'target' market of men who bought the larger bikes.

The faults in Honda's larger machines meant that reluctantly, Honda had to sell the small 50 cc bikes just to raise money. They proved very popular with those who would never have bought motorbikes. Eventually the company adopted this new market with enthusiasm. The strategy had emerged, against conscious intentions.

This example suggests the 'common-sense' rational model will not always work.

According to Mintzberg, *intended strategies* are plans. Aspects of those plans that are actually realised are called *deliberate strategies*. *Emergent strategies* are those that develop out of patterns of behaviour that are adopted and have a strategic impact. In practice, no strategy will be wholly deliberate or wholly emergent. A plan may exist only in someone's head but it is still a plan even though it is private. Figure 1.5 illustrates the process. **Realised strategies** are those determined both by analysis and unforeseen developments in the environment, unanticipated resource constraints and/or changes in managerial preferences.

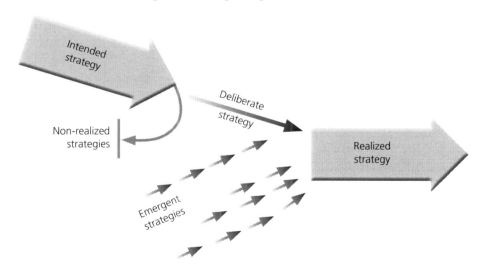

FIGURE 1.5 Emergent strategies

From *Strategy Safari*, 2nd edition, Mintzberg, Ahlstrand & Lampel, Pearson Education Limited, © Henry Mintzberg, Bruce Ahlstrand and Joseph Lampel 1998, 2009

With this in mind, Mintzberg (op. cit.) identified eight styles of strategic management. These are shown in Table 1.2.

TABLE 1.2 Strategic management style (Mintzberg, 1985)

Planned strategies	■ Precise intentions ■ Explicit intentions (documented) ■ Imposed by central leadership ■ Large number of controls ■ Maximises predictability
Entrepreneurial strategies	■ Intended strategy derives from the vision of strong leadership ■ Not always explicit
Ideological strategies	■ Intended strategy is a collective vision of the organisation's members ■ Control is through shared values ■ Involves changing the environment
Umbrella strategies	■ Strategic targets ('ends') are defined and deliberate ■ How they are achieved ('means') is emergent
Process strategies	■ Processes are formal (e.g. hiring) and deliberate ■ Content of strategies (what is done) is emergent
Disconnected strategies	■ Members of sub-units 'do their own thing' loosely coupled to the rest of the organisation ■ Strategies are emergent for the organisation, deliberate for sub-units
Consensus strategies	■ Groups in the organisation converge on common patterns of activity
Imposed strategies	■ Strategy is imposed by the environment (e.g. a strong customer) – which precludes the organisation's own choice

3.2 Crafting emergent strategies

Most of the styles of strategic management identified above contain both deliberate and emergent elements. There will come a point when even an emergent strategy will need some conscious direction, perhaps to change its course. Senior managers, when faced with an emergent strategy, might favour some aspects of it over others. For example, a company might pride itself on the high quality of its products, even though this involves expensive labour costs. If the quality strategy is favoured, management might try to develop work policies that reduce costs.

Mintzberg (1987) uses the phrase 'crafting strategy' to help us understand the idea. Forming a strategy and implementing it are 'fluid processes of learning through which creative strategies evolve'. Mintzberg uses the image of a potter's wheel; the potter gives shape to the clay through a gradual process where feedback is close to the action. In contrast, a sales representative who discovers a new way of providing customer satisfaction may have to convince large numbers of people within the organisation of the idea's merits. The trouble with the long feedback link is that it separates thinking from doing when it comes to strategy. This has the following result:

1 **A purely deliberate strategy prevents learning**. For example, it is hard with deliberate strategies to learn from mistakes, or stumble by accident into strategic growth.
2 **A purely emergent strategy defies control**. It may in fact be a bad strategy, dysfunctional for the organisation's future.

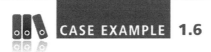 **CASE EXAMPLE** **1.6**

In some organisations, strategic change can be haphazard. Mintzberg mentions the example of the Canadian National Film Board. The Board used to make short documentaries but ended up by chance with a feature film. This forced it to learn the marketing of such films, and so it eventually became much more involved in feature-length productions – strategy arose by accident.

The strategist must be able to recognise patterns and to manage the process by which emergent strategies are created: to find strategies as well as invent them.

Mintzberg identifies the following essential activities in strategic management:

1 **Manage stability**. Formal planning is the detailed working-out of the agreed strategy. Most of the time managers should be implementing strategies, not planning them, and obsession with change is dysfunctional. Knowing when to change is more important.

2 **Detect discontinuity**. Environments do not change regularly, nor are they always turbulent. Strategists should realise that some small environmental changes are much more significant than others.

   a) Technological developments are hard to assess. Combined with cheap production processes, they can revolutionise some industries.

CASE EXAMPLE 1.7

Hoffmann-LaRoche, a Swiss-based pharmaceutical company, began as a small firm making dyes. It acquired the patents to vitamins when no one else wanted them, and borrowed and invested all it could into producing and selling them. It is now an industry leader.

   b) International developments are frequent causes of uncertainty. Spotting international trends that are important to the organisation must be accompanied by assessing of commercial and political risks.

2 **Know the business**. Strategic management involves an intimate feel for the business. This has to include an awareness and understanding of operations.

3 **Manage patterns**. 'A key to managing strategy is the ability to detect emerging patterns and to help them take shape'. Some emergent strategies must be uprooted, others nurtured.

4 **Reconciling change and continuity**. 'Crafting strategy requires a natural synthesis of the future, present and past'. Obsession with change and/or continuity can be counterproductive.

Central to the concept of emergent strategy is that it places front-line workers in a key position in terms of developing strategy. They are effectively 'boundary workers', acting as environmental scanners and spotting changes in the business's operating environment. The key is to ensure that structures and processes are in place to capture their knowledge and information.

3.3 Critical comment on emergent strategy

Those who favour prescriptive strategic approaches have a number of basic concerns about emergent strategy. Lynch (2015) summarises these:

- It is entirely unrealistic to expect board members at corporate level simply to sit back and let operating companies potter along as they wish. In addition, there will be experienced managers who have a unified vision of where they wish the group to progress.

- Resources of the group need to be allocated between the demands of competing operating companies; this allocation can only be undertaken at the centre and demands some central strategic overview.

- While there are political groups and individuals that need to be persuaded that a strategy is optimal, to elevate this process to the level of strategic management is to abdicate responsibility.

- In industries where long time-frames are involved for decision making, decisions have to be taken and adhered to, or the organisation would become completely muddled: for example, building a new telecommunications network may take years to implement. Experimentation may be appropriate in the early years but, beyond this, strategy has to be fixed for lengthy projects.

- Although the process of strategy selection and choice has to be tempered by what managers are prepared to accept, this does not make it wrong. Rational decision making based on evidence is more likely to be successful than hunches and personal whims. A debate should take place but be conditioned by evidence and logic.

■ Management control will be simpler and clearer where the basis of actions to be undertaken has been planned in advance.

TEST YOUR KNOWLEDGE 1.3

a Define 'emergent' strategy.
b How might an organisation 'craft' its strategy?
c According to Mintzberg, what are the key components of strategic management if using the emergent approach?

4   Other strategy models

4.1 Introduction

If there are limitations to the rational model, what other options are there for strategists? We have looked at emergent strategy and the idea of crafting strategy. We now consider a range of other models with varying views about the real choice and control available to managers.

■ **Complexity and chaos theory**. Writers such as Stacey (1992) argue that the world in which organisations exist is highly complex and unpredictable. It is inconceivable that managers can know all there is to know about this complexity, let alone predict its effects. However, it is possible that people's experience within a particular context can help them become sensitive to the patterns of complexity and uncertainty around them. When there are deviations from these patterns they are able to sense them intuitively. Strategic management should therefore be seen as more to do with building the capacity to be intuitive and taking action based on that.

■ **Institutional theory**. On the whole, managers think that they have more choice in developing strategies than they really do. Institutional theorists such as Scott (1995) argue that organisations exist in relation to other similar organisations: all accountancy firms are similar, all universities are similar, etc. Over time, similarities develop in the way people in those organisations see their organisations and the environment in which the organisation operates. They also have ways of doing things that tend to be similar. These ways of seeing the world and of doing things can be so institutionalised that it is difficult for people to question or change them. Indeed, they can come to be seen as the legitimate way to behave within an industry or profession, so organisational strategies tend to develop within institutionally similar cultural parameters.

■ **Ecological view**. A view still further removed from the idea that managers control the destiny of their organisation is that of the ecologists (Boeker, 1991). They argue that organisations build up ways of doing things, whether within institutional frameworks or not. They argue that the success of organisations depends on the extent to which these approaches coincide with the needs of the environment. If they do coincide, the organisation prospers; if they do not, the organisation suffers or even dies. It is like natural selection. The cultures of some organisations are well suited to the environments in which they operate; others less so.

The rational planning approach suggests that managers can make major changes in strategy – the implication of these other explanations is that this is unlikely. Most suggest that strategies are likely to develop incrementally in organisations – they are more likely to develop by adapting or building on existing strategies. Mintzberg's view of crafting suggests that this may be done proactively and the notion of 'logical incrementalism' has developed this. The institutional view suggests that incremental strategy development is more the result of strategies being constrained by institutional cultures. Ecologists argue that incremental development is inevitable and will, in time, lead to the decline, even demise, of most organisations.

It is important to understand these different explanations because each provides insights into the challenges that managers face. To cope with the variety and range of factors involved in considering strategy, managers have to simplify things. They reduce the complex to a manageable frame of reference on the basis of their personal experience or their organisation's past experience which is embedded in its culture.

4.2 Strategy and objectives

Andrews (1987) sees strategies as patterns of management decisions. He does not accept the validity of separating objectives from the strategies designed to achieve them. Corporate strategy is:

- the pattern of decisions in a company that determines and reveals its objectives, purposes or goals;
- produces the principal policies and plans for achieving those goals, and defines the range of business the company is to pursue, the kind of economic and human organisation it is or intends to be; and
- reveals the nature of the economic and non-economic contribution the organisation intends to make to its shareholders, employees, customers and communities.

This implies:

- There is a certain *consistency* in the types of decision taken or the choices made. Crudely put, decisions determine strategy, rather than the other way round.
- Strategy arises out of the *general management* process whereby senior managers direct and control the business.
- Objectives and strategies are interdependent. The interdependence of purposes (objectives), policies (strategies) and organised action is crucial to an individual strategy and the opportunity to obtain competitive advantage.

4.3 A behavioural approach?

Johnson et al. (2014) suggest that in strategic decision-making strategy needs to be understood as an outcome of the social, political and cultural processes of management in organisation. Planning contributes to, rather than accounts for, strategic decisions. Johnson et al. suggest the following phases in the strategic decision-making process as a description of what happens rather than a way of prescribing what *should* happen.

1 **Problem awareness**. The awareness of a strategic problem occurs at an individual level. It is reinforced by internal measures; a pattern of customer reaction and environmental changes. A trigger will occur when the formal information system highlights the problem, so that organisational activity takes over from the individual's conception of the problem.
2 **Problem diagnosis**. Information is needed to enable managers to build up a picture of the problem. There may be little formalised environmental analysis in this phase. Information may be used to rationalise management's existing view of the situation, rather than challenge it. Formal analysis is little used in practice. Problem diagnosis is rooted in managerial experience and, if there are conflicting views, resolved through social and political processes.
3 **Solution development**. A number of possible solutions are developed and one is selected. Memory search involves using solutions similar to those that have been used in the past. Passive search involves waiting for a solution to suggest itself. They may begin with a vague idea that is further refined and probed by internal discussion.
4 **Solution selection**. A screening process eliminates unacceptable plans, but the screening process involves bargaining, diplomacy and judgement rather than formal evaluation. 'Unacceptable' might mean unacceptable in terms of organisational politics, rather than in terms of business sense. Many strategic decisions originate from management subsystems. Senior managers provide some sense of direction and their authorisation is often sought. However, junior managers might filter strategic information and ignore certain options.

Johnson et al. appear less averse to the planning approach to strategy than Mintzberg, but instead of assuming a rational objectivity, they anchor plans in the organisation's behaviour.

4.4 Incrementalism

Most versions of the rational model advocated by practitioners place considerable emphasis on the determination of objectives or ends. Once the ends are determined, all possible means of securing them are explored and their consequences analysed. The course of action with the greatest net benefits is then chosen. Others became aware that this model could not readily be realised. In practice, managers have limited time, information and skills. They also have their own habits and reflexes. An example is Lindblom (1959), who attempted to discredit rational approaches before formulating his own preferred alternative.

Lindblom suggested that in the real world, the rational model was not used as:

■ Managers do not in practice evaluate all the possible options open to them in a given situation but choose between relatively few options.
■ Strategy making tends to involve small-scale extensions of past policy – incrementalism – rather than radical shifts following a comprehensive rational search.
■ Like Andrews, he suggests that it is not always possible to distinguish ends from means.
■ Strategic policy-making necessitates seeking accommodation or compromises with interested groups – a process Lindblom described as 'partisan mutual adjustment'. Policy-making was seen as the outcome of political bargaining.
■ Strategy making often does not proceed according to any coherent plan but rather proceeds disjointedly. Lindblom used the term *disjointed incrementalism*.

Lindblom thought his incremental model was preferable to the rational model. He argued that strategy making involving small-scale extensions of past practices was more likely to be successful. It would avoid major errors and was more likely to be acceptable because consultation, compromise and accommodation were built into the process. Comprehensive rational planning was impossible and was likely to result in disaster if actively pursued.

Critics argue that incrementalism is not a good prescriptive model – strategists should aspire to do better. Incrementalism is not sufficient where radical new approaches are needed, and it has an inherent conservative bias. Lindblom suggested that it was possible to achieve a radical shift in policy over a period as a result of a series of incremental shifts. He partially conceded the case for some forward planning in later versions of his model. Incrementalism does not seem to highlight the role of corporate culture (strategy as perspective, perhaps) on decision-making, as it filters out unacceptable choices.

Logical incrementalism builds on Lindblom's ideas. Logical incrementalism is not just muddling through: 'it is a purposeful, effective, proactive management technique for integrating both the analytical and behavioural aspects of strategy formation' (Quinn and Ghoshal, 1995). Strategy is best described as a learning process by which managers have to deal with major internal or external events. It is impossible to predict the long-term consequences of decisions made in situations of crisis or change. For these reasons, managers deliberately keep their decisions small-scale, so that they can be tested. However, unlike 'muddling through', which appears simply reactive, the logical incremental model suggests a conscious process of decision-making. It suggests the following:

■ Managers have an outline notion about where the organisation should be. Perhaps this relates to pursuing a vision which we shall discuss below.
■ Strategies should be tested in small steps as there is too much uncertainty about actual outcomes, although they are directed in the context a framework.
■ Precise objectives discourage experimentation by business units.

The advantages of incrementalism are that it can map the environment closely. However, incremental change may not be enough, as the number of strategic options considered may be insufficiently radical to cope with environmental shift. To varying degrees, the rational, and perhaps the incremental, model both have their part to play.

4.5 The significance of competition

An important feature of the environment of any non-monopoly business is competition. Business strategy seeks to alter the strength of an organisation in relation to its competitors. What counts is performance in relative terms.

> 'A good business strategy is one by which a competitor can gain significant ground on its competitors at an acceptable cost' (Ohmae, 1982, pp.37–8).

Ohmae says that the purpose of any strategy is relative competitive success. The implication for a business is that merely 'seeking an environmental fit' can never be enough as that environment is inhabited by organisations whose interests are possibly antipathetic to its own.

Business strategy must be directed towards the competition, shaping the environment rather than merely reacting to it. Ohmae suggests four ways of doing this:

1 **Readjust current resources**. Identify the key factors for success and concentrate resources on these activities.
2 **Relative superiority**. A relative advantage can still be achieved by exploiting the competitors' actual or potential weaknesses or the particular features of one's own strengths.
3 **Challenge assumptions**. Aggressive initiatives challenge the accepted assumptions of doing business in a particular market (e.g. online banking challenges the need for branch networks).
4 **Degrees of freedom**. These involve altering the markets, or finding new ways of exploiting them (e.g. by segmentation or product differentiation).

In all cases, direct competition on the competitors' own turf is avoided. Successful strategy is the interplay of three Cs: *customers, competitors* and the *corporation*. Ohmae calls this the strategic triangle.

Michael Porter (1980) also defines strategy in competitive terms. Competitive strategy is 'the taking of offensive or defensive actions to create a defendable position within an industry and a superior return on investment'. Without going into depth here, Porter identifies five competitive forces in an industry and various states the industry is in. Porter holds that the state of the industry as a whole determines competitive success. He then gives a systematic analysis of how competitors should be identified and targeted, and suggests three generic strategies for dealing with the competition.

Implicit in Ohmae's and Porter's analysis are the assumptions that:

- the survival of a business is impossible without a competitive strategy;
- the actual strategy chosen will be unique to the organisation; and
- the marketplace is sometimes like a battlefield.

Others argue that concentrating exclusively on competitors is treating business strategy as analogous to a military campaign. Success in business derives from adding value of one's own, not diminishing that of competitors, and it is based on distinctive capability not destructive capacity.

A major problem facing any firm is sustaining competitive advantage over time; competitive advantage is not something that is built up once and for all. Porter suggests that over the past 20 years, firms have been learning to play to a new set of rules: benchmarking, outsourcing and the nurture of a few basic core competences. The assumption is that rivals can easily copy any position – hence, many companies are competing destructively with each other in a state of hyper-competition. Porter offers the following ideas:

1 **Operational effectiveness is not the same as strategy**. It is necessary but not sufficient; it involves doing things better than other firms. Porter suggests that managers' use of Total Quality Management is geared towards operational effectiveness – improvements here can be imitated.
2 **Strategy rests on unique activities**. Competitive strategy is about being different. It means choosing to perform activities differently or to perform different activities from rivals.
3 **A sustainable strategic position requires trade-offs**. These limit what a company does. Choosing a unique position is not enough to sustain competitive advantage, as competitors can aim to compete on the same basis or try to straddle two strategic positions. Trade-offs occur when:
   (a) activities are not compatible (e.g. an airline can offer a cheap, no-meals service or offer meals; doing both results in inefficiency);
   (b) where there will be inconsistencies in image and reputation; or
   (c) where an activity is over- or under-designed for its use (e.g. overqualified staff in low-skill positions).

While operational effectiveness is about being good at individual activities, strategy is about combining activities, and the way in which its activities fit and reinforce one another. Fit requires consistency between activity and overall strategy (if the generic strategy is low cost, all activities are low cost). Activities must reinforce each other. It is harder for rivals to imitate interlocked activities.

Strategy is about choices not blindly imitating competitors. Many firms operate inefficiently and so need to improve operational effectiveness. Caught up in the race for operational effectiveness, many managers simply do not understand the need to have a strategy.

4.6 Innovation and knowledge-based theories

Innovation and knowledge-based theories of strategy privilege the generation and sharing of new ideas through knowledge as being the most important aspects of strategy development. Such theories came to prominence in the 1990s. Innovation here does not just mean inventing new products or production processes; it means developing and exploiting organisational resources in a new way. In particular, the way that the knowledge of the organisation is used to generate new and radical solutions has become recognised as an important contributor to strategy development (Nonaka and Takeuchi, 1995).

According to those favouring innovation and knowledge theories, their advantage is that they begin to tackle a problem that has arisen with existing theories. The argument goes that the widespread study of theories like competitive advantage, for example, means that every company knows about such thinking, and therefore there is less chance for such theories to deliver new competitive advantage. By emphasising the new and evolving nature of knowledge and innovation, such theories help to overcome this difficulty. Lynch (2015) shows the way that companies involved in green strategy are willing to explore new ideas, share knowledge and build new business activities through an innovative approach to business strategy.

In the process of innovating, one important aspect is that of sharing knowledge and ideas. This has been made much easier in the past ten years as a result of the internet and telecommunications technology. This aspect has now developed into an important topic in strategy, with real potential to revolutionise strategic thinking.

 TEST YOUR KNOWLEDGE 1.4

a Explain the contribution of Porter's idea of competitive strategy to strategic management.
b What might the behavioural approach to strategy offer a company?
c Describe the essence of the incrementalist approach.

---

5 Strategic management in different contexts

To a greater or lesser extent, all these aspects are relevant to most organisations. However, it is likely that different aspects will be more important in some contexts, and in some organisations, than in others. For example, in retailing the need to understand customer needs and values and to consider these in relation to product and customer service is crucial, more so than it would be in a firm supplying commodity raw materials in an industrial setting. It would be wrong to assume that all aspects of strategic management are equally important in all circumstances. This section reviews some of the ways in which aspects of strategic management differ in different contexts.

Strategic management should also be considered not only in different organisational contexts, but also under different and changing economic conditions, such as stability or volatility, growth or recession, or, as in the UK at the time of writing, stagnation and austerity.

5.1 Organisational contexts

1 **The small business**
Small businesses are likely to be operating in a single market or limited markets, probably with a small range of products and services. With regard to positioning, small businesses will certainly need to attend closely to the environment, because they are so vulnerable to change. However, especially in small entrepreneurial and family businesses, the most important positioning issue will often be strategic purpose. This will not necessarily just be profit, but might include objectives such as independence, family control, handing over

to the next generation and maybe even a pleasant lifestyle. The range of strategic choices is likely to be narrower; it is rare for a small business to make an acquisition itself, although small businesses may have to decide whether to allow themselves to be acquired by another business. Some issues of strategy in action will be different – for example, strategic change processes will not involve the same challenges as for large, complex organisations. The firm may see **consolidation** as paramount and strategic relationships with funding bodies such as banks as the critical ones.

2 **The multinational corporation**

The multinational firm is likely to be diverse in terms of products and geographical markets. There may be subsidiaries and divisions, so structure and control at the corporate level are major strategic issues. Positioning in a complex global marketplace will be very important. Each significant geographical market may call for a separate analysis of the business environment. Likewise, operating in many different countries will raise positioning issues of culture: variations in national culture imply different demands in the marketplace and different managerial styles.

A major concern is the extent to which the centre adds or detracts from the value of its businesses. At the business unit level, many competitive strategic issues will be similar to those faced by smaller firms. For the parent company, a significant issue will be how business units are allocated resources. The coordination of operational logistics may become extremely important, and an important decision is the extent to which the multinational has to control such logistics centrally or devolve them to operating units. The scale and geographical reach of most multinationals point to significant issues for organisational structure and strategic change.

3 **The public and third sectors**

Competitive advantage will be important even in these contexts, but have a different flavour. The underlying values and ideology will be of central strategic significance. The *raison d'être* of the organisation is rooted in its values, and these will have a significant impact on the development of strategy. Third sector organisations, such as charitable not-for-profits, typically compete for funds from donors; public sector organisations, such as schools and hospitals, often compete on measures such as quality or service. This may mean high levels of lobbying and difficulties in clear strategic planning. The positioning issue of purpose is likely to be very important too. In the absence of a clear, focused objective such as profit, purpose in the public sector and not-for-profits can be ambiguous and contentious. Strategic choice issues may be narrower than in the private sector – for example, there may be constraints on diversification. Strategy-in-action issues often need close attention, with leadership and change typically being very challenging in large public-sector organisations.

4 **Professional service organisations**

Traditionally-based values are often of particular importance in professional service organisations where professional advice is sometimes seen as more important than revenue-earning capability. This was the case in medicine, accountancy, law and other professions. Private sector professional firms, like consultancies, may have a partnership structure in which the partners carry considerable power. In recent years many professions have come under pressure to be more 'professional' in their approach, increasing their concern with competitive strategy.

In short, while drawing on the same basic principles, strategy analysis is likely to vary in focus across different contexts.

5.2 Economic conditions

1 **Periods of stability and growth**

In periods of long-run stability, which usually display steady long-run growth, organisations have more time for planning and tend to focus more on revenue growth through research and development, innovation and new product development. Margins and profits are steady or growing; there is scope for investment, testing and launch of new products, and possibly of processes through new equipment or plant. Staffing levels can be comfortable, leaving staff some time to think, morale can be high and all is good with the world.

The danger, of course, is complacency, and an inability to detect the winds of change, if not in the overall economy, then within one's own sector as start-ups and other more agile organisations may start to eat into any competitive advantages that one's organisation may enjoy. Strategy may drift and not evolve at a pace that matches the economy/sector growth, group think may set in and contrarian thinkers may be dismissed. The strategy process, with an emphasis on the external environment, is still critical in good times as well.

2   Instability, recession and austerity

Conversely, in times of uncertainty, low or no growth and general austerity, which are often accompanied by public sector cuts, the focus of senior management shifts. The premise that we live in an increasingly VUCA world means that management has to adapt. It must see change as a constant and be agile and flexible in order to react to external macro forces driving change or disruption within the industry.

The 2008 recession has meant that cost control became the dominant strategic priority, with new product development put on hold, or adapted. In the past few years of austerity in the UK, product development in the grocery sector has switched from a steady stream of innovative new products to 'product re-engineering' – adapting pack sizes to fit key price points. At the same time, the sector has tried to defend margins as like-for-like sales fell and customers switched in droves to deep discounters such as Aldi and Lidl. Measures included driving out cost from the organisation in terms of management layers down to reduced staffing in store and cost saving tactics such as shelf-ready packaging.

Many organisations might face existential crises where they must implement a successful turnaround strategy or perish. Critical action in such situations demand a certain type of strategic leadership and focus mixed with accelerated change management skills.

Context matters, and when making strategy, the starting point should be an understanding of both the organisational as well as the macro-economic context. Whatever the context, competitive advantage may not be sustainable in the long run. As a result, the strategy process may become a hunt for a series of short-run 'transient competitive advantages'.

TEST YOUR KNOWLEDGE 1.5

a   How might the approach to strategy differ in a small firm when compared to a multinational company?

b   What will be the greatest influence over strategy in a third sector organisation?

c   How does the focus of strategy change in a recession compared to periods of economic growth?

CHAPTER SUMMARY

■ Planning is an everyday activity in which we are all engaged. We do this mostly intuitively although we may work more formally, for more important and complex tasks. Things get more complicated in organisations because they require many people to pull in the same direction while remaining ready to change direction.

■ Strategy is concerned with the long-term direction and development of an organisation. It is this that achieves advantage for the organisation by configuring resources within a changing environment to meet the needs of the market and stakeholder expectations.

■ Strategic decisions are made at a number of levels in organisations: (a) corporate level strategy is concerned with an organisation's overall purpose and scope; (b) business unit strategy with how to compete successfully in the market; and (c) operational or functional strategies with how resources processes and people can effectively deliver corporate and business strategies.

■ Strategic management covers the entire cycle of planning and control at a strategic level and comprises strategic analysis, choice of strategies, implementation of strategies and review and control processes.

■ There are a number of different explanations of how strategy is actually managed in organisations. These vary from those that emphasise high degrees of choice for managers to those that suggest managers have much less influence than they think. We described the rational planning model of the strategy process and saw that there are many good reasons to suppose this model may be flawed. Some say it is futile to distinguish between strategy and objectives; they are developed at the same time. The incrementalist model describes the tentative way in which many strategies are made in practice, not how they ought to be made. Mintzberg's emergent strategies model suggests that some strategies can be planned, but others almost develop by accident. Ohmae and Porter describe strategy almost exclusively in competitive terms, but unlike Porter, Ohmae assumes that strategy is a matter of intuition rather than rational analysis.

■ Context matters in how strategy is approached, both organisational context and its nature as well as the macro-economic climate, as the focus of senior management changes in terms of mission and goals, as well as strategy for growth (revenue generation) or recession (cost containment).

2 Developing strategy

■ INTRODUCTION

This chapter raises the question about how strategies are made in practice and, more specifically, the role of the Chartered Secretary in that process. Many of the issues raised here are developed further in the rest of the study text.

It is important to be clear from the beginning that the nature of the role of the Chartered Secretary in strategy making will vary from organisation to organisation and will be contingent on the nature of the organisation, the individual and his or her role, and the working environment. For that reason, no specific role is advocated or described here. There is a general assumption however, that the senior Chartered Secretary in the organisation will have access to, and influence over, strategy making. This may be in areas where they may deliver specialist guidance – governance, risk, etc. – or as a member of the top team accountable for the strategy. In either sense, he or she will be a strategist.

With this in mind, the chapter will consider:

- **Strategic leadership**. The overall management of the process that gives rise to organisational strategies. We consider this in the remainder of this section.
- **Strategic process**. This is a flow chart approach to framing the key elements of strategy making.
- **The strategists**. Who gets involved in these processes.
- **Strategic activities and methodologies**. What strategists do in developing strategies and some of the methodologies they use.

1 Strategy making

STOP AND THINK 2.1

What role does the Chartered Secretary or the secretarial function take in strategy making in an organisation with which you are familiar?

1.1 Strategic leadership

Strategy development may be strongly associated with a strategic leader, an individual (or group of individuals) on whom strategy is dependent. They are people whose position, personality or reputation mean that they are identified with and central to the strategy of their organisation.

The individual may be central because he or she is the owner or founder of the organisation. It may also be that the person remains central after a business is publicly quoted – such is the case with Rupert Murdoch at News Corp. It could be that an individual chief executive has turned a business around in times of difficulty and personifies the success of the organisation's strategy, as was the case with Michael O'Leary at Ryanair.

In any of these circumstances, strategy may be seen as the deliberate intention of that leader. How such an intention comes about can, however, be explained in different ways:

- **Strategic leadership as design**. It could be that the strategic leader has thought through the strategy analytically. This might be by using the sort of techniques associated with strategic analysis and evaluation.
- **Strategic leadership as vision**. It could be that a strategic leader determines or is associated with an overall **vision**, mission or strategic intent (see Chapter 7) that motivates others, helps create the shared beliefs within which people can work together effectively and which shapes more detailed strategy developed by others in an organisation (Bennis and Nanus, 1985).
- **Strategic leadership as command**. The strategy of an organisation might be dictated by an individual, perhaps an owner-manager, who is in direct control of all aspects of its business. This can mean speedy strategy adaptation and innovative, unorthodox strategies that are difficult for other companies to imitate. The disadvantage can, however, be excessive risk-taking or irrelevant strategies.

A strong message in this chapter is that effective **strategic leadership** is the foundation for using the strategic management process successfully. However, the challenge of strategic leadership is significant. For example, replacing Steve Jobs at Apple was difficult because of his special skills in identifying and nurturing creative new products that have significant market potential. Volberda et al. (2011) suggest that:

'If a strategic leader can create a strategic vision for the firm using forward thinking, she/ he may be able to energise the firm's human capital and achieve positive outcomes.' (p.398)

They imply that strategic leaders guide an organisation by deciding a vision and purpose, and creating goals that stretch the organisation to improve its performance. They will also facilitate the development of appropriate strategic actions and how to implement them.

According to Volberda et al., strategic leadership is the ability to anticipate, envisage and empower others to create strategic change. Multifunctional in nature, strategic leadership involves managing through others, managing an entire enterprise rather than a functional sub-unit and coping with change that continues to increase in the complex global environment. A commercial firm's ability to achieve a competitive advantage and earn above-average returns is compromised when strategic leaders fail to respond appropriately and quickly to changes in the complex global competitive environment and is one of the reasons some CEOs fail (Baraldi et al., 2007).

The primary responsibility for effective strategic leadership rests at the top, in particular with the CEO. Other strategic leaders include members of the board, the top management team and divisional managers. In truth, any individual with responsibility for the performance of a part of the organisation is a strategic leader. Regardless of their title and organisational function, strategic leaders have substantial decision-making responsibilities. We shall examine some of these strategy makers in the next section.

The styles used to provide leadership often affect the productivity of those being led. Researchers have studied top management leadership behaviour along a continuum of transactional and transformational leadership (Bass and Riggio, 2006).

- **Transactional leadership**. This entails engaging followers through an exchange between them and their leaders. This is typically done through the clarification and specification of what is expected of followers, as well as the leader's intervention to monitor and take action when expected standards are not met. This leadership behaviour can lead to an increase in productivity and innovation as it promotes a sense of fairness and reward for clearly specified objectives.
- **Transformational leadership**. This entails motivating followers to exceed the expectations others have of them, to continuously enrich their capabilities and to place the interests of the organisation above their own. Transformational leaders develop and communicate a vision

for the organisation and formulate a strategy to achieve that vision. They make followers aware of the need to achieve valued organisational outcomes. And they encourage followers to continuously strive for higher levels of achievement. Additionally, transformational leaders have emotional intelligence. Emotionally intelligent leaders understand themselves well, have strong motivation, are empathetic with others and have effective interpersonal skills. As a result, transformational leaders are especially effective in promoting and nurturing innovation in firms.

Schoemaker et al. (2013) suggest that successful strategic leadership requires mastery of the following six skills:

- **Anticipate.** Strategic leaders need to be able to anticipate ambiguous strategic threats and opportunities, and show constant vigilance throughout the strategic decision-making process. This requires them to establish effective networks with stakeholder groups and act upon the signals that are transmitted from them.
- **Challenge.** Strategic leaders constantly need to question the status quo and examine the merits of divergent points of view. This will involve a questioning approach to strategy and looking at the roots of organisational problems.
- **Interpret.** Strategic leaders need to do more than just reflect upon past strategic decisions, they need to be able to scrutinise details, synthesise different sources of information and identify information gaps.
- **Decide.** When making key strategic decisions, leaders need to look at and weigh the merits of multiple options, consider potential trade-offs, identify possible unintended consequences and consider the merits of piloting a strategy, in the first instance, to test the waters.
- **Align.** Strategic leaders need to garner buy-in from key stakeholder groups and should employ a proactive approach to engage and build trust with them. They should also make sure that they understand the nature and sources of stakeholder resistance, and devise strategies to address these concerns.
- **Learn.** Strategic leaders will build a culture of inquiry in their organisation and look to learn lessons from past strategic successes and failures. They will ensure that these lessons learned will be effectively documented and distributed within the organisation.

 **CASE EXAMPLE** 2.1

Renzo Rosso is the president and innovator behind Diesel, the Italian-based international fashion brand with more than 10,000 points of sale and more than 200 privately owned stores in over 50 countries. Rosso grew up in north-east Italy on a farm near a village of 2,000 inhabitants where there was only one car and one television. Rosso recalls: 'I think this experience of growing up in little town, of doing farm work, was important for me because I learned to respect the value of things. These sorts of experience give you a real sense of the value of money and, over the years, this has helped keep my feet on the floor.'

When Rosso was 15 years old, he decided to attend a newly established Italian industrial textile manufacturing and fashion school where he thought graduation would be easier. There he discovered that he loved the fashion business and, after graduating in 1975, he started making clothes for himself and friends. He dreamed of one day owning his own small business. In 1978 he joined forces with several other manufacturers in his region to form the Genius is Denim group, which created many successful brands still widely known today, including Katherine Hamnett, Goldie, Martin Guy and Diesel. In 1985 Rosso took total control of Diesel by buying out the other partners and becoming the sole force behind the brand. Rosso was determined to make his company a leader, a company that took chances and carved out a niche for itself in its field. He surrounded himself with creative, talented and innovative people, people who thought like him. By 2003, Diesel had worldwide revenues in excess of $760 million. While the luxury brand's primary product is denim, particularly jeans, it designs, manufactures and markets fashionable consumer products ranging from sunglasses to underwear.

Rosso is an idealistic, passionate man who has the motto: 'Diesel is not my company, it's my life'. Rosso describes himself as positive, simplistic and very demanding. Colleagues note that Rosso never looked or acted like a chief executive. He attended corporate meetings and interviews in simple faded jeans and cowboy boots. Rosso never apologised for his attire or his single-minded vision for Diesel, the company he founded and made into a multi-million-dollar fashion empire. His vision turned a small wholesale clothier into an international brand. The company is now part of the OTB (Only The Brave) Group, also owned by Rosso, where the aim is to build 'not the biggest, but the most alternative fashion group'.

Sources: Gail Amondson (2003) 'Diesel is smoking", *BusinessWeek*, 20 January; www.diesel.com; www.otb.net

2 The strategy process

As you work through the book and come across the wide variety of strategy models, concepts and frameworks, it may be helpful to keep in mind an overall structure or frame of reference for the strategy process. This is shown as Figure 2.1. Many of the strategy models can be inserted into this chart. Knowing where will guide the reader as to when to use them to best effect.

If we start with the premise that the strategy process is based on an assessment of:

a) where we are now;
b) where we want to get to; and
c) how we get there, with some reflection on the past and where we have come from, then the basic analytical approach is to undertake:

- an internal analysis to establish our strengths and weaknesses; and
- an external analysis to identify opportunities and threats. The strategy process attempts to make a best fit between internal resources and external opportunities, now and in the future.

This neatly leads us into a SWOT analysis. Note that the much-used SWOT (see page 95, Chapter 4) analytical tool is a second stage or 'synthesis' tool. Although it is based on past and current factors, it attempts to bring some forward movement to the strategy process. For a good SWOT analysis, it is important to go back to first principles to derive the core elements of our resources and how they are managed, and distinguish the main elements of the external environment, which can be split into:

- micro-environmental factors – the industry/sector conditions and the relative positioning of the competitors within, as key product, pricing and market decisions are made; and
- macro-environmental factors – the forces of change that will impact on all the players in an industry; strategy will determine who best responds to those forces of change.

Note the forward element – the future drivers of change, anticipated pricing decisions, etc. When used efficiently, SWOT and its derivatives enable us to think how we can deploy our strengths to exploit opportunities, and mitigate any weaknesses and threats – strategic 'fit'.

With help from some generic strategy positioning and growth models, we can derive and formulate some broad strategic options or choices for the organisation. These options have to be evaluated, and this takes us into two areas of consideration:

- **Investment appraisal** – what investment is required for each course of action, what the expected return on investment is, in what time frame and with what associated risks in terms of the key assumptions, plus a sensitivity analysis of the possible variance around the expected outcome. This is an assessment of the best, worst and most likely outcomes of a strategy. (Investment appraisal techniques are not covered in this book.)
- **Operational fit** – how well each of our strategic options fits with the organisation as it is and as it has developed. A conscious decision to distance the organisation from its past may be necessary. Whitbread moved from a 300-year history as brewers of beer and owners of pubs

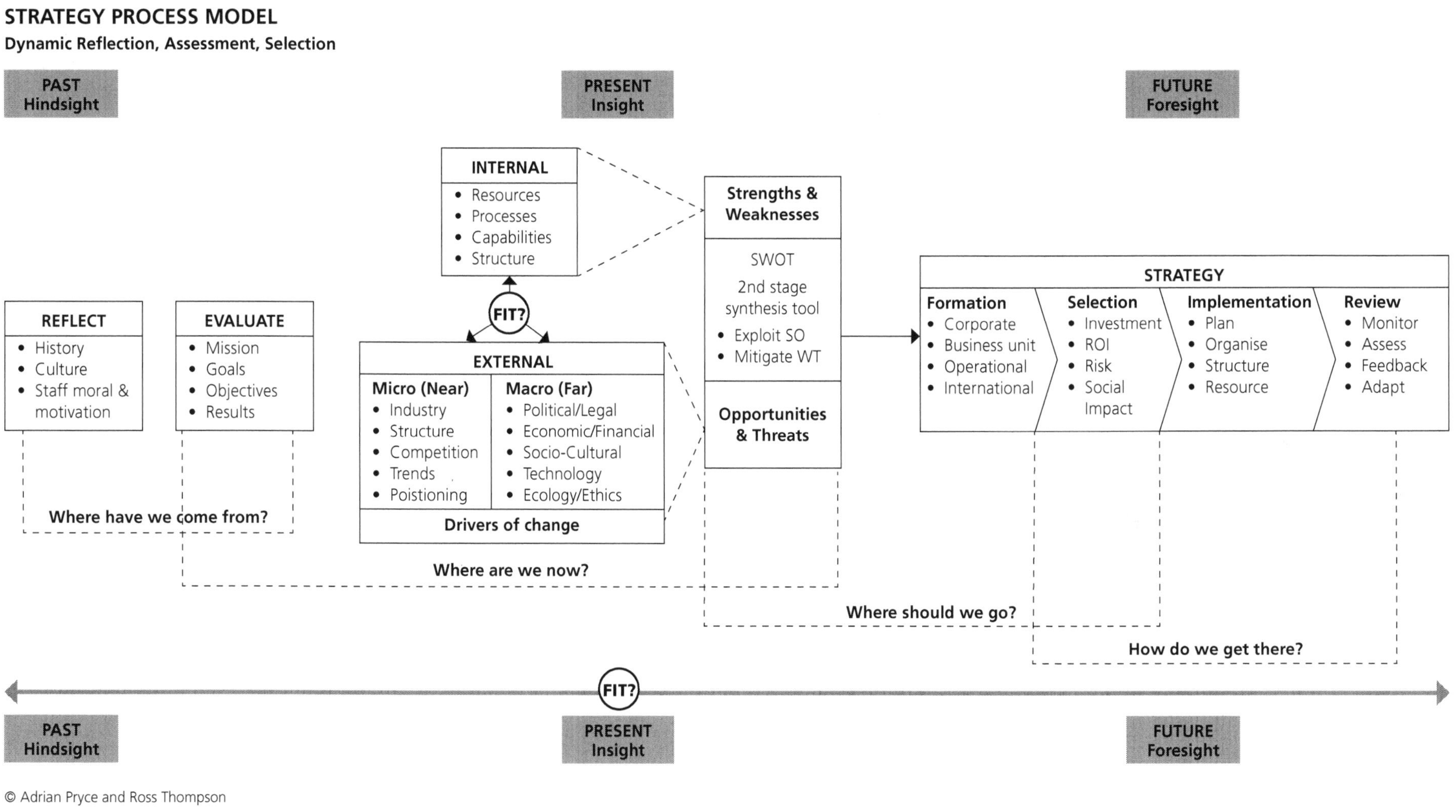
STRATEGY PROCESS MODEL
Dynamic Reflection, Assessment, Selection
PAST
Hindsight
PRESENT
Insight
FUTURE
Foresight
REFLECT
• History
• Culture
• Staff moral & motivation
EVALUATE
• Mission
• Goals
• Objectives
• Results
Where have we come from?
INTERNAL
• Resources
• Processes
• Capabilities
• Structure
FIT?
EXTERNAL
Micro (Near)
• Industry
• Structure
• Competition
• Trends
• Poistioning
Macro (Far)
• Political/Legal
• Economic/Financial
• Socio-Cultural
• Technology
• Ecology/Ethics
Drivers of change
Where are we now?
Strengths & Weaknesses
SWOT
2nd stage synthesis tool
• Exploit SO
• Mitigate WT
Opportunities & Threats
Where should we go?
STRATEGY
Formation
• Corporate
• Business unit
• Operational
• International
Selection
• Investment
• ROI
• Risk
• Social Impact
Implementation
• Plan
• Organise
• Structure
• Resource
Review
• Monitor
• Assess
• Feedback
• Adapt
How do we get there?
FIT?
PAST
Hindsight
PRESENT
Insight
FUTURE
Foresight
© Adrian Pryce and Ross Thompson

FIGURE 2.1 The strategy process

to become a leisure firm comprising a series of branded coffee, restaurant and hotel outlets. It was a conscious decision implemented over time.

Evaluation of the strategic choices will lead to a decision to adopt a particular option, after which the implementation phase begins. This will involve the staff, and needs to be effectively communicated to achieve their buy-in and enthusiasm. It may well lead to a new organisational structure. Once the chosen strategy is in play, the organisation should monitor its success or otherwise, and feed the results back into a dynamic model of strategy monitoring and evolution.

This truly is a 'big picture' approach, a foundation for strategic thinking. Many entrepreneurs pass through these steps intuitively, but many do not, and this can lie at the heart of organisational failure. This view of the strategy process is a necessary but insufficient approach to strategy formation; however, it still serves as a good framework to place the many strategy models, concepts and tools introduced in this book.

However, judgement must be used as to which models are most appropriate in any given context and time. Imagination, creativity and innovation are becoming increasingly important in the creation of competitive advantage. This text will introduce you to a wide range of models, which are appropriate to real world selection and usage. This need for selection will be reflected in the examination questions.

Often, strategy development is part of a formalised **strategic planning system**, which takes the form of a systematised, step-by-step, chronological set of procedures involving different parts of the organisation. For example, in a study of strategic planning systems of major oil companies, Grant (2013) noted the following stages in the cycle for a large corporation.

- **Initial guidelines**. The cycle's starting point is usually a set of guidelines or assumptions about the external environment and the overall priorities, guidelines and expectations of the corporate centre.
- **Business-level planning**. Business units or divisions then draw up strategic plans to present to the corporate centre. Corporate centre executives discuss these plans with the business managers and businesses revise their plans for further discussion.
- **Corporate-level planning**. The corporate plan results from the aggregation of the business plans. This coordination may be undertaken by a corporate planning department, which, in effect, has a coordination role. The corporate board then has to approve the corporate plan.
- **Financial and strategic targets**. These are extracted to provide a basis for performance monitoring of businesses and key strategic priorities on the basis of the plan.

STOP AND THINK 2.2

How does this compare with the strategy development process in an organisation with which you are familiar?

CASE EXAMPLE 2.2

The strategic planning process for an oil company is based on 20-year plans every four to five years on the basis of its scenario-planning process, and annual business plans with five to ten-year time horizons. The purpose is to enhance business unit strategies and coordinate strategy across the business.

Grant (2003) noted that some companies were much more formal and regularised than others. For example, the French Elf oil and lubricants business, which merged with Total in 2000, had more fixed planning cycles, less flexibility, and more specific objectives and targets relating to the formal plans. It had been part of the French government until 1994. Where there was more informality/flexibility (e.g. BP), companies placed greater emphasis on more general financial targets. Central corporate planning departments also played different roles. In some organisations they acted primarily as coordinators of business plans. In others they were more like internal consultants.

It is important to note that major strategic decisions may not be made within or as a direct result of such planning processes. As we saw in Chapter 1, there are two broad explanations of strategy development, which are not mutually exclusive.

- **Intended strategy**. Strategies come about as a result of careful deliberation typically associated with top management decisions. This is also linked to the idea that strategies are developed using the sorts of concepts and tools discussed in this study text. This is sometimes known as the rational/analytic or design view of strategy development.
- **Emergent strategy**. Strategies do not always develop on the basis of some grand plan but tend to emerge in organisations over time.

Nevertheless, even in the case of emergent strategy, a strategic planning system may play a role in how the organisational strategy is determined. For example, it might help to structure the analysis and thinking about complex strategic problems, to encourage questioning and challenging of received wisdom, and to encourage a longer-term view of strategy than might otherwise occur. But, as we have seen, Mintzberg (1994) and others have questioned the extent to which planning provides such benefits. Certainly, there has been a shift to line managers taking responsibility for strategy development and planning. Strategic planning is also becoming more project-based and flexible (Mankins and Steele, 2006). In this respect, strategic planning ceases to be a vehicle for the top-down development of intended strategy and more of a vehicle for the coordination of strategy emerging from below.

 TEST YOUR KNOWLEDGE **2.1**

   a   Distinguish strategy leadership as 'design' from strategy leadership as 'vision'.
   b   Explain what is meant by 'strategic leadership'.
   c   Outline the stages identified by Grant in the strategic management process.

3 The strategists

3.1 Top managers and directors

This section introduces the different people involved in strategy. It starts at the top management level, then considers a much wider range of potential 'actors', from strategic planners and consultants to middle managers.

The conventional view is that strategy is the business of top management. Chandler (1962) argued that it is essential that those in top management are clearly separated from operational responsibilities and focus on overall strategy. Otherwise, they are liable to get distracted from long-term issues by day-to-day responsibilities and to represent the interests of their departments or business units rather than those of the organisation as a whole.

In reality, the top management role involves much more than setting direction, and different members of the top team may play different roles.

The chief executive officer is often seen as the 'chief strategist', ultimately responsible for all strategic decisions. CEOs of large companies typically spend about a third of their time on strategy (Kaplan and Beinhocker, 2003). In this view, the CEO (managing director or equivalent top individual) owns the strategy and is accountable for its success or failure. Such clarity focuses attention but has dangers.

- Centralising responsibility on the CEO can lead to excessive personalisation. Organisations respond to setbacks simply by changing their CEO, rather than examining internal sources of failure.

■ Successful CEOs can become overconfident. Such overconfidence often leads to spectacular failures. Collins' (2001) research on American companies that outperformed their rivals over the long term found that their CEOs were typically modest, steady and long serving.

The top management team, often an organisation's executive directors, also share responsibility for strategy. Obviously, they can bring additional experience and insight and, in theory, should be able to challenge the CEO and increase strategic debate. In practice, they may be constrained by operational responsibilities that distract them, lack the independence for real challenge or suffer from 'groupthink' – the tendency to build strong consensus and avoid internal conflict (Janis, 1972).

Non-executive directors have no executive management responsibility and so should be able to offer an external and objective view on strategy. Although this varies according to national corporate governance systems (see Chapter 6), in a public company the chair of the board is typically non-executive. He or she will normally be consulted closely by the CEO on strategy. A key role for them also is to ensure that the organisation has a rigorous system in place for the making and renewing of strategy. It is therefore important that non-executives are authoritative and experienced and have sufficient independence from the top management executive team.

Johnson et al. (2014) suggest that there are at least three qualities senior managers need if they are to contribute effectively to high-strategy making:

1 Mastery of analytical concepts and techniques, as introduced in this study text.
2 Social and influencing skills, so that analysis is understood and accepted by senior colleagues.
3 Group acceptance as a player in strategic discussions. Boards and senior executive teams are social groups like any other, whose members have to win respect.

3.2 The role of the board

Garratt (1996) quotes an ancient Chinese saying: 'The fish rots from the head'. His point is that ultimately a strategy's success or failure depends on the performance of its board or leadership team. In the rest of this section the term 'board' is used, but much of what is said applies to leadership teams in the public and not-for-profit sectors. The board is ultimately accountable for both the choice and success of strategy. As board activities are made more and more transparent under national and international law, Garratt and other commentators believe that there is a need for a transformation in the way the directors view their role and their capability. Some commentators argue that there is little confidence that the interests of shareholders or stakeholders, whether they be staff, customers, suppliers, local communities or the physical environment, are being looked after satisfactorily. They believe that this is because of an overemphasis on managing, or being a professional, and an under-emphasis on directing – showing the way ahead and giving leadership at board level. A corporation needs effective management to keep its day-to-day operations running. But to ensure that it sustains itself in the long term, it needs effective directing too. If this is not recognised by the board, performance suffers.

Garratt argues that there are two key issues here.

Directing, not managing

It is the board's job to strike a balance between the external and internal pressures on the organisation to ensure its survival. The board must give a clear direction to the business and create the climate in which its people can align and attune to that direction. It is the board's job to ensure that members are committed to a common purpose, with similar values and behaviours, so that the organisation can function effectively and efficiently. There is a vast difference between 'directing' and 'managing' an organisation. Management is a hands-on activity, which thrives on crises and action. On the operations side of an organisation it is a crucial role. Direction is essentially about showing the way ahead, giving leadership. It is thoughtful and reflective. Both managing and directing are necessary for a healthy enterprise. It is essential that the board learn how to cope with the difficult, messy uncertainty of these issues in rigorous and self-disciplined ways. A 'directorial mind-set' is needed. But Garratt suggests that the dynamic balance between organisational efficiency and organisational effectiveness is not understood.

Handling four dynamic balances

The basic system in which a board must operate can be defined by four opposing forces that have to be balanced against each other. A key task of the board, under the ultimate responsibility of the chair, is to create sufficient space to maintain a continuous overview of these.

- **Organisational effectiveness**. The external, long-term perception in the customer's mind of the products or services being desirable and good value for money.
- **Organisational efficiency**. The internal, short-term focus on cost reduction and efficiency gain, just before it affects the customers' perception of organisational effectiveness in a negative way.
- **Board performance**. The external focus of the board on policy formulation in relation to the external macro-environment; and on strategic thinking about the competitive positioning and broad resource allocation of the enterprise in relation to its policies.
- **Board conformance**. The internal focus of the board on its performance to pre-set goals of accountability to its stakeholders and to its business performance through its people.

Each of these four forces has the potential to contradict the others and there are massive expectations demanding diversity, in terms of breadth and depth of experience, knowledge, attitudes and skills. Garratt resolves these dilemmas in terms of a set of board roles shown in Figure 2.2. Much of the work and concern of corporate governance is with conformance. This involves accountability to shareholders and other stakeholders, and the supervision of management. Performance involves driving the whole enterprise forward, allowing it to survive and grow by maintaining and developing its position. The strategic management process can be characterised as a combination of policy and strategic formulation.

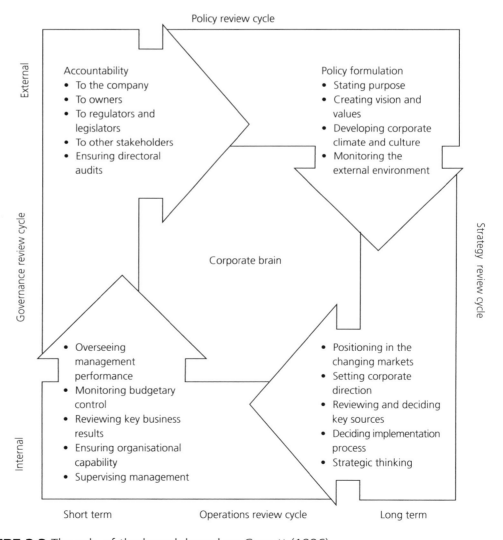

FIGURE 2.2 The role of the board, based on Garratt (1996)

STOP AND THINK 2.3

Think of a company you know well:

■ How effectively do you think its board is balancing its time between conformance and performance?
■ How effectively is it executing its strategic management role and what evidence do you have to support your view?

3.3 Other strategy makers

Strategic planners

Managers with a formal responsibility for contributing to the strategy process are common in large companies and increasingly widespread in both the public and not-for-profit sectors. Usually the strategist is not only making strategy, but also helping other departments to develop their own capabilities in strategy development. Strategic thinking and analytical skills are clearly very important, but so too is the ability to communicate clearly to various audiences and to work well with teams. Strategic planners do not take strategic decisions themselves but assist with information and analysis (see Part Two); managing the strategy process; and supporting top management on projects, such as acquisitions or organisational change (Chapter 13).

Middle managers

The conventional view of strategy making excludes middle managers from the process. Middle managers implement and are seen as lacking a long-term perspective, being largely involved in operations (Chandler, 1962). Yet Floyd and Wooldridge (2000) argue that involving middle managers in strategy formulation can lead to:

■ better strategic decisions, because middle managers have direct, up-to-date experience of the realities of the organisation and its market; and
■ improved implementation as they will be better at interpreting strategic intentions, have a stronger commitment to strategic goals and communicate the strategy more effectively to their teams.

Increased middle management involvement in strategy making results from decentralised organisational structures to increase accountability and responsiveness in fast-moving and competitive environments (Chapter 11). In knowledge-based work such as professional services (design, consulting or finance) the key source of competitive advantage is the knowledge of people actually involved in the operation of the business.

In the public sector, senior management/middle management have a parallel in the formal division between politicians and public officials. Just as directors are formally concerned with strategic 'direction', elected politicians were traditionally responsible for policy and public officials were supposed to do the implementation. However, the growing importance of specialised expertise and a reduction in the size of the public sector have effectively shifted influence to independent agencies and non-governmental organisations, which, within certain constraints, can make some decisions on their own.

Strategy consultants

External consultants are often used in the development of strategy in organisations. As well as specialist firms, most of the large general consultancies also have operations that provide services in strategy development and analysis. There are also smaller, niche consultancies and individual consultants who specialise in strategy. Schwarz (2004) has identified the roles consultants play in strategy development as:

■ **Analysing, prioritising and generating options**. This may involve challenging executives' preconceptions about their views of strategic issues.

- **Transferring knowledge**. In effect, consultants are carriers of knowledge and best practice within and between their clients.
- **Promoting strategic decisions**. Consultants may influence substantially the decisions that organisations eventually take. A number of major consultancies have been criticised in the past for undue influence on the decisions made by their client organisation, leading to major problems. For example, leading strategy consulting firm McKinsey was heavily associated with Enron's business model.
- **Implementing strategic change**. Consultants play a significant role in project planning, coaching and training associated with strategic change.

Consultants are often blamed for failures when in fact it is the client's poor management of the consulting process that is at fault. Many organisations select their consultants unsystematically, give poor initial project briefs and fail to act on and learn from projects at the end.

 **CASE EXAMPLE** 2.3

The German engineering company Siemens has professionalised its consultancy purchasing, for example by establishing a shortlist of just ten preferred management consulting suppliers.

The German railway company Deutsche Bahn and car company DaimlerChrysler both have central project offices that control and coordinate all consulting projects throughout their companies. As well as being involved in the initial purchasing decision, these central offices can impose systematic governance structures on projects, with clear responsibilities and reporting processes, as well as review and formal assessment at the project end.

3.4 Whom to include in strategy

There is, therefore, a potentially wide range of people to involve in any strategic issue: as well as the CEO and the top management team, non-executive directors, strategic planners, strategy consultants, middle managers and perhaps external stakeholders. This often raises practical dilemmas about who should be included on particular strategic issues. The paradox of strategy inclusion is that those with the most access to the CEO are often strategic planners and strategy consultants who have little responsibility for strategy implementation and little knowledge of business on the ground. Middle managers who have both the knowledge and the implementation responsibility may have least access to strategy discussions.

Strategy is not necessarily being made by the right people. Beinhocker and Kaplan (2002) suggest that the people involved should vary according to the nature of the issue (see Figure 2.3).

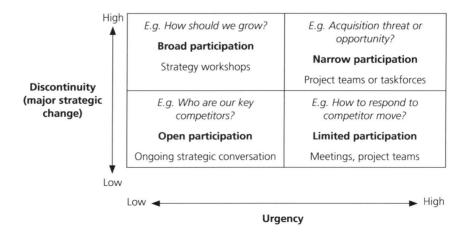

FIGURE 2.3 Whom to involve in strategy making (Johnson et al., *Exploring Corporate Strategy*, © Pearson Education Limited, 2002, 2014)

From *Exploring Strategy*, 9th edition, Johnson et al, Pearson Education Limited, © Pearson Education 2002, 2011

Highly urgent issues, and those involving significant strategic change (perhaps an acquisition), are often best approached by small special project teams, consisting of senior managers and perhaps planners and consultants. Issues which might imply equal discontinuity, but for which there is more time (e.g. growth options) can benefit from the participation of a broader group of managers, such as through a strategy workshop. For issues that are routine, but which still require speedy response (e.g. competitors' price moves), only limited participation is probably required, involving perhaps meetings between the relevant marketing and operations managers. The most open kind of participation would be in the continuing 'strategic conversation' of managers throughout the organisation, regarding, for example, key competitors or the long-run evolution of the market and business. So there are criteria that can guide managers about who to include according to the nature of the strategic issues in hand.

TEST YOUR KNOWLEDGE 2.2

a Identify the qualities senior managers need if they are to contribute effectively to high-level strategy making.

b What are the four dynamic balances advanced by Garratt?

c Distinguish between the 'conformance' and 'performance' role of the board.

3.5 The agency problem

The agency problem asserts that it cannot be taken for granted that an organisation's top management team will necessarily plan and implement a strategy that is in the shareholders' (and other stakeholders') best interests. Top managers may put their own interests first, and these may not coincide with the needs of the organisation. According to Masulis (1988), there are three main areas where potential conflicts might surface:

1   Managers may be risk adverse, and as such choose less risky investment projects. These projects may not provide the higher returns offered by riskier projects and may therefore not be in shareholders' best interests. Shareholders are able to manage this increased risk by maintaining a portfolio of share ownerships, thus spreading their risk.

2   Managers may have a preference for strategies with a short-term rather than long-term planning horizon. However, shareholders are more likely to see their investment as a long-term commitment.

3   Managers may be inclined to increase organisational costs by awarding themselves attractive remuneration and perquisite packages (perks). They may also be inclined to increase the staff headcount, increasing total salary costs, in order to increase their own prestige and status within the organisation.

Stakeholders may find it difficult to identify these behaviours in the top management team because of **information asymmetry**. This occurs because managers tend to have access to more complete information regarding the organisation which makes it difficult for other stakeholders to disprove the legitimacy of their decisions – for example, justifying an increase in the number of employees.

Top managers may therefore need to be audited and monitored to ensure that they do act in the best interests of the organisation. Control mechanisms include the use of internal audit departments and appraisal schemes. Managers may also have to be offered incentives to ensure they act according the interests of their organisation. Examples include the use of share options and performance related pay.

A particular problem lies with the incentivising of short-term management performance, which might come at the expense of overall long-term performance of the organisation. For example, a manager may be offered a bonus on the basis of cash flows. To do this, they might cut capital spending, leading to higher cash flows in the short term but lower ones in the longer term as production facilities become out of date and uncompetitive, thus reducing sales revenue. It is therefore sensible to ensure executive remuneration encourages organisational success over the longer term.

3.6 The role of the company secretary

The company secretary also plays an important role in the strategy process. Research by Kakabadse and Kakabadse (2014), which was commissioned by ICSA, identified the following key roles played by the company secretary:

- Company secretaries effectively help deliver strategic leadership by providing an independent bridge between the board and the chair.
- Company secretaries help ensure effective decision making by facilitating board dialogue, gathering and assimilating key information and aligning the interests of key parties.
- Company secretaries are also able to independently observe boards in action and flag areas of performance weakness and identify training needs.
- Company secretaries are frequently the longest-serving member of the board and, as such, constitute a vital repository of information regarding the organisation's history and its culture.

4 Key strategic actions

A number of key activities characterise effective strategy making or 'strategising'. These include strategic analysis, decision making to determine direction, resource allocation, strategy communication and a range of methodologies to support the process. These interact with each other although, as has been suggested, they rarely follow a logical sequence. For example, decisions are often made without great analysis, they are often reinterpreted in subsequent communications, and managing the firm's resources involves developing human capital – its people.

4.1 Strategic analysis

Part Two of this study text is concerned with strategic analysis. But strategy is not the outcome simply of rational analysis. Analysis is frequently ad hoc and incomplete, and costly in terms of resources and time. There are the costs of gathering information, particularly if using consultants, and there is a risk of 'paralysis by analysis', whereby managers spend too long perfecting their analyses and not enough time taking decisions and acting on them. Managers have to determine how much analysis they really need: 'quick and dirty' may be good enough. In addition, analysis is not always simply about providing the necessary information for good strategic decisions! The purpose may even be a deliberate attempt to postpone a decision. Analysis can also be symbolic, for example to rationalise a decision that has already been made, managers being asked to analyse an issue in order to get their support. Analyses can also be political, to promote the agenda of a particular manager or part of the organisation.

The implications of all this for strategists are that it is necessary to:

- **Design the analysis according to the real purpose**. The range and quality of people involved, the time and budget allowed and the subsequent communication of analysis results should all depend on underlying purpose, whether informational, political or symbolic. Prestigious strategy consulting firms are often useful for political and symbolic analyses. Involving a wide group of middle managers in the analysis may help build support.
- **Invest appropriately in technical quality**. For many projects, improving the quality of the technical analysis will make a valuable addition to subsequent strategic decisions. On other occasions, insisting on perfection can be counterproductive. For example, a SWOT analysis (see page 95) that raises lots of issues may be a useful means of allowing managers to vent their personal frustrations before getting on with the real strategy work. It may also be better to leave these issues on the table, rather than probing or challenging them and alienating these managers for the following stages.

Organisations typically face many strategic issues at any point in time. But these issues may not be appreciated to the same extent by all senior managers, or recognised by them at all. Some may be filtered out in the organisational hierarchy; others will be side-lined by more urgent pressures. The point is that strategic issues compete for top management attention and what gets management attention are not necessarily the most important issues (Ocasio and Joseph, 2005). Managers therefore have to 'sell' their particular strategic issues to top management and other important stakeholders.

Important aspects in seeking attention and support for strategic issue selling include:

- **Issue packaging**. The strategic importance of the issue needs to be underlined by linking it to critical strategic goals or performance measures and the presentation should be consistent with the cultural norms of the organisation. Clarity and succinctness help, as does packaging the issue with potential solutions.
- **Using formal or informal channels**. Managers need to balance formal and informal channels of influence. Formal channels include annual business reviews that the CEO carries out with each divisional head, annual strategy retreats (or workshops) of the top executive team, and the various reporting systems including finance, human resources and strategic planning. Informal channels might include ad hoc conversations with influential managers.
- **Sell alone or in coalitions**. A coalition adds credibility and weight to the issue. The ability to gather a coalition of supporters can be a good test of the issue's validity. But enlisting supporters may involve compromises or reciprocal support of other issues, so blurring the clarity of the case being put forward.
- **Timing**. A short-term performance crisis and the period before the handover to a new top management team are not good times to press long-term strategic issues.

Selling an issue is only the start, of course. Even after an issue has been successfully sold, and actions and resources agreed, managers should ensure that attention is sustained. Initial commitments in terms of top management attention and other resources need to be protected. As the strategic issue evolves over time, it may require more attention and resources than originally promised.

4.2 Determining strategic direction

Determining the strategic direction involves making decisions about the role and character the organisation seeks to develop over time. The strategic direction is framed within the context of the conditions strategic leaders expect their organisation to face in roughly the next three to five years and is therefore the outcome of the strategic analysis. The long-term strategic direction is likely to have two parts: a core ideology and a vision of the future (Part Three). Core ideology motivates employees through the organisation's purpose and values. The vision of the future serves as a guide to many aspects of a firm's strategic implementation process, including motivation, leadership, employee empowerment and organisational design. The strategic direction could include such decisions as entering new international markets and developing a set of new suppliers to add to the firm's value chain. Such decisions are difficult to take and implement.

 **CASE EXAMPLE 2.4**

Successors have faced a tough challenge following Jorma Ollila's time at Nokia, and their strategic decision-making has been criticised. Ollila had transformed Nokia from an average manufacturer of cables, tyres and rubber boots into a leading telecommunications company. The competitive landscape has become more dynamic over the years, putting pressure on Nokia's margins. Sustaining Nokia's dominant position was therefore an even more difficult task. A charismatic CEO might foster stakeholders' commitment to a new vision and strategic direction, but it is important not to lose sight of the organisation's strengths when making changes required by such a new strategic direction. Kallasvuo (Ollila's immediate successor), for example, needed to use Nokia's strengths to ensure continued positive performance.

But by 2012, Nokia was in crisis. It had ceded leadership of the global mobile phone market to Samsung, and its share price was less than 10% of its peak just five years earlier. The company's new CEO, Stephen Elop, reminded employees and investors of the company's history. Nokia had been through crisis and transition before. Elop insisted it would do so again. He argued that Nokia had been too slow, and must now make a dramatic move: 'I believe we have lacked accountability and leadership to align and direct the company through these disruptive times. We had a series of misses. We haven't been delivering innovation fast enough. We're not collaborating internally.'

CASE EXAMPLE 2.4 *continued*

Several days later, he announced that he was abandoning Nokia's own operating system in favour of Microsoft's. A senior Google executive commented on the Nokia–Microsoft alliance: 'Two turkeys do not make an eagle.'

Nokia's first phones with the new operating system were not an immediate success, and Nokia's losses deepened. By spring 2012, Stephen Elop was describing Nokia in terms of a famous Finnish long-distance runner, Lasse Virén, who had tripped during a race in 1972 but still won in the end: 'Like Virén we are off the grass, on the track and running again.' But Nokia's share price was still only one-fifth of what it had been at the time when the alliance had been announced. Many speculated that Nokia would not survive as an independent company at all. Indeed, in the summer of 2013, Nokia announced that its mobile phone business would be sold to Microsoft, with Stephen Elop returning to his original employer. A year later, Nokia announced that it would return to the consumer market as it launched a partnership with Foxconn to make a tablet device. Foxconn is the Chinese technology group that builds the iPad for Apple and will manufacture the Android-based tablet from designs and standards provided by Nokia, who will receive a licence fee for the use of its brand.

Key sources: J. Aspara, J.A. Lamberg, A. Laukia and H. Tikkanen, 'Strategic management of business model transformation: lessons from Nokia', *Management Decision*, 49(4) (2011), pp.622–47; *Financial Times*, 9 February 2011, 11 April 2011, 3 May 2012 and 18 November 2014.

Strategic issues are ultimately decided in many ways. Success and failure are not always rational. Strategic decision making is liable to biases, such as the influence of strategic issue selling, which suggests that people will exaggerate the case in favour of their own proposal. Similarly, there is the tendency to follow the lead of the most senior person in the decision-making process or to try to anticipate their view. Putting decisions in the hands of a team of managers, therefore, does not in itself guarantee rigorous and effective decision-making. Decision makers may make over-optimistic decisions or, conversely, can be risk-averse.

Eisenhardt's (1990) research on strategic decision making in fast-moving environments suggests four helpful guidelines for managers:

- **Build multiple, simultaneous alternatives**. Having several alternatives available at the same time encourages critical debate. This can help counter bias and is faster than taking proposals sequentially. Examining multiple, simultaneous alternatives is a practice adopted by Barclays Bank, for example, where proposals are never presented in isolation, but always alongside at least two other alternatives.
- **Track real-time information**. In fast-moving environments, a quick decision may be better than a delayed decision, and trend data are liable to become rapidly redundant. Fast decision-makers use real-time information from current operations, rather than statistical trends and forecasts. They tend to spend a lot of time in face-to-face meetings and on reviewing the most up-to-date indicators, such as weekly and even daily measures of sales, cash, stocks or work-in-progress.
- **Seek the views of trusted advisors**. Experienced managers in the organisation can provide fast feedback on what is likely to work based on their know-how. This is often both more reliable and more credible than lengthy analysis undertaken by junior managers or consultants.
- **Aim for consensus, but not at any cost**. Fast decision makers recognise that debates and disagreements cannot always be resolved to everybody's satisfaction and so seek consensus, but do not insist on it. Consensus can be too slow and often leads to mediocre choices. Eisenhardt's advice is that the CEO or senior strategist should, at a certain point, simply decide. The responsibility of other managers is then to accept that decision and implement it.

However, it is easy to exaggerate both the importance and the effectiveness of decision-making. Many decisions are not followed through and many strategies are emergent rather than consciously decided (see Chapter 1). As Eisenhardt's work suggests, intuition is not always a bad thing. Immersion in real-time information or the long experience of older middle managers can provide a strong feel for what should be done. Conflict in decision-making can also be useful in exposing biases.

4.3 Resource allocation processes

Bower (1972) and Burgelman (1983) argue that realised strategies emerge as a result of the way resources are allocated in organisations. A changing and uncertain environment, together with the cognitive limits of managers to cope with this, mean that strategy is better explained as the outcome of problems or issues being addressed as they arise. This explanation then emphasises the formal and informal processes by which this is done:

- **Negotiation across organisational level**. The nature of problems or issues and their resolutions are typically the outcome of negotiation across levels of an organisation. Most obviously this could be between a corporate centre and business units. Such issues usually start with a discrepancy. For example, between where top management wish a company to be in terms of its share price or a decline in market share or competitive position. In such a case, there is a need to make sense of the significance of that discrepancy and align expectations as to what needs to be resolved. The problem will then be worked on at the level most appropriate to the problem, for example, if it is a market-related issue, by the marketing department in a business. The key point is that a good deal of choice about what to focus on and what choices to make may lie far down in an organisation's subsystems.
- **The influence of the resource allocation process on the nature of the resolution of the problem**. All organisations have systems, routines and standards for deciding on proposed new ventures, products and services. These play a significant part in determining the type of solutions to problems that are advocated and to which resources are allocated. For example, many businesses have criteria for acceptability of new venture proposals based on measures of return (e.g. return on capital employed).

 **CASE EXAMPLE** **2.5**

The resource allocation process helps explain the major strategic changes at Intel in the 1980s. The top management of the firm were wedded to Intel as a memory company in the business of DRAMs (dynamic random access memories). Its major strategic switch to becoming a microprocessing company did not come about because of top management direction, but because the internal resource allocation routines within the firm favoured projects with greater profit margins. This resulted in the emerging microprocessor business being allocated more resources and therefore a basis for future investment and growth greater than DRAMs.

Source: Based on the case study on Intel by Jill Shepherd (Segal Graduate School of Business, Simon Fraser University, Canada) in Johnson et al. (2014).

Effectively managing the firm's portfolio of resources is therefore a significant strategic leadership task. The organisation's resources can be categorised as financial capital, human capital, social capital and organisational capital (Barney and Arikan, 2001). Effective strategic leaders recognise the importance of managing each type of resource, the integration of resources (for example, using financial capital to provide training opportunities through which human capital (people) is developed) and organising them into capabilities, and core competencies.

Exploiting and maintaining core competencies

As will be examined in Chapter 4, core competencies are capabilities that serve as a source of competitive advantage for a firm over its rivals. Typically, core competencies relate to an organisation's functional skills, such as manufacturing, finance, marketing and research and development (R&D). Intel, for example, has core competencies of competitive agility (an ability to act in a variety of competitively relevant ways) and competitive speed (an ability to act quickly when facing environmental and competitive pressures). Such capabilities are developed over time as firms learn from their actions and enhance their knowledge about specific actions needed – for example, a capability to fully understand customers' needs as they change. Core competencies are exploited effectively when they are developed and applied across different organisational units.

 **CASE EXAMPLE** 2.6

Richemont, the world's largest jewellery maker, purchased Net-A-Porter, an online fashion retailer. This step into e-commerce enabled Richemont to gain more insight into online buying behaviour for luxury items. Richemont can use this competence to market the sales for its watches, jewellery and fashion. Additionally, Net-A-Porter's product offering can be enriched by Richemont's product portfolio. By the end of 2014, Richemont had held talks with advisers over future options for Net-A-Porter, including not only an initial public offering but also a sale of the business.

Source: *Business Week*, April 2010, www.businessweek.com.; Reuters 21 November 2014

Firms must continuously develop and, if necessary, change their core competencies to outperform rivals. If they have a competence that provides an advantage but do not change it, competitors will eventually imitate that competence and reduce or eliminate the firm's competitive advantage.

Developing human and social capital

There is a growing body of evidence that demonstrates a positive link between the development of people – human capital – and organisational success. This reflects the view that success depends as much on intangible resources as more tangible ones such as finance.

 STOP AND THINK 2.4

To what extent are people a cost to an organisation or an asset in which to invest?

Human capital is the resource through which core competencies are developed and used. It refers to the knowledge and skills of an organisation's entire workforce. From this perspective, employees are viewed as a resource requiring continuous investment (Hatch and Dyer, 2004). The underpinning for the human capital view is the resource-based view of performance.

However, individuals must also invest their skills and expertise in the organisation and their position. In other words, commit or *engage* if human capital is to be used appropriately. In addition, therefore, to human capital, there must also be social and organisational capital: the valuable relationships among people and the processes and routines within the organisation.

HCM practices that encourage skills and abilities, such as careful selection and high investment in training, also inculcate a common set of core values, thus promoting the organisation's vision and organisational cohesion. They also contribute positively to the firm's efforts to form core competencies.

CASE EXAMPLE 2.7

'We're not doing this out of the goodness of our hearts. We're not training people for the sake of it. We are training people so that we can leverage that experience to drive sales. That's the strategy.' Matt Davies, CEO, Halfords

In May 2013, the new CEO of Halfords (a specialist retailer of leisure and car products), Matt Davies, took the opportunity, during a discussion of the company's preliminary results, to reveal the board's strategy to restore performance in the company to what he believed would be a permanently higher level. Davies took considerable care to describe the strategic challenges that explained Halfords' poor performance to date, and the human capital-centric means by which he intended to transform the company's performance.

With around 70% of its customers requiring some form of advice in order to make a purchase, Davies argued that Halfords was a speciality retailer. Yet Halfords' customer satisfaction rating measured poorly on expert service, and Halfords had left itself vulnerable to competition from business models that were not encumbered by high staff and product choice costs. In addition, more than 20% of Halfords' staff left the company in the first three months. 'All the time people are leaving and joining, leaving and joining; it's like a merry-go-round,' said Davies. He argued that this explained why Halfords had experienced declining like-for-like sales in 10 of the 13 quarters prior to him joining the company – and why his diagnosis of the strategic challenge that confronted Halfords focused on recruitment, on training and development, and on employee engagement. The treatment that Davies arrived at was simple. Halfords would invest around £50 million over the period to improve staff recruitment, training and retention processes. Davies funded Halfords' investment in human capital management (HCM) and additional investment in store refurbishment and digital strategy by cutting the company's dividend by 35%.

A great deal has happened to influence the business and share price performance of Halfords since Matt Davies gave his initial address to analysts in May 2013. There were many contributory factors to like-for-like sales growing at a rate of 6.8% when the company reported its interim results for fiscal year 2015, and in the appreciation of Halfords' share price from a closing low of 339.3p on the day Davies announced the dividend cut to over 460.0p the day before he announced his departure to Tesco. Yet he was also convinced that the investment he made in recruitment, in training and development, and in employee engagement was a major factor in the company's improved performance. For example, staff turnover at Halfords had fallen from around 21% to just over 10% in the first year of his HCM strategy; colleague engagement had risen from 64% to 80% over the same time-frame, and the company's NPS (net promoter score) had increased from around 55% in the previous year and was on its way to a score of above 75%.

Source: Based on a CIPD report, 'Valuing your talent,' www.valuingtalent.co.uk (2015).

Learning and building knowledge are also important for creating innovation in firms and innovation in turn leads to competitive advantage. Overall, firms that create and maintain greater knowledge usually achieve and maintain competitive advantages. However, as noted with core competencies, strategic leaders must guard against allowing high levels of knowledge in one area to lead to myopia and overlooking knowledge development opportunities in other important areas of the business (Miller, 2002).

External social capital is also increasingly critical to firm success as few organisations have all the resources they need to compete successfully against their rivals or achieve best in class standard. Social capital can develop in strategic alliances as firms share complementary resources (Chapter 10). However, resource sharing must be effectively managed to ensure that the partner trusts the firm and is willing to share the desired resources.

4.4 Communicating strategy

Deciding strategy is only one step: strategic decisions need to be communicated. Managers have to consider which stakeholders to inform (see Chapter 6) and how they should tailor their messages to each. Shareholders, key customers and employees are likely to be particularly central, all with different needs. For every new strategy there should be a communications strategy.

Employee communications are typically vital to ensure that the strategy is carried out in the first place. Unless people understand the strategy, it is unlikely to be implemented! Everyday interactions of lower-level managers and ordinary staff can undermine an intended strategy. For instance, a new strategy to improve customer service will fail if managers do not hire, train and reward their staff consistently.

In shaping a communications strategy for employees, Thatcher (2000) suggests four elements need to be considered:

- **Focus**. Communications should be focused on the key components of the strategy. Jack Welch's famous statement that General Electric should be 'either Number One or Number Two' in all its markets is remembered precisely because of its focus on the importance of being dominant wherever the company competed.
- **Impact**. Communications should have impact and a strong 'story-line' can help by encapsulating the journey ahead. Visual devices can be very important. Jeff Bezos at Amazon.com sketches a 'virtuous circle' to express how the growth strategy sets in motion a cycle in which lower costs produce improved customer experience, which in turn produces greater traffic, which would support a wider range of goods, and so on.
- **Media**. Choosing appropriate media to convey the new strategy is very important. Mass media such as e-mails, videos, intranets and senior manager blogs can ensure that all staff receive the same message promptly, so helping to avoid uncertainty. However, face-to-face communications are important too in order to demonstrate the personal commitment of managers and allow for interaction with the staff concerned. Thus senior managers may undertake road shows, carrying their message directly to various groups of employees with conferences or workshops at different sites.
- **Employee engagement**. It is often helpful to engage employees directly in the strategy so that they can see what it means for them personally and how their role will change. Interchanges through road shows and cascades can help, but some organisations use creative means to achieve more active engagement. For example, one British public sector organisation invited its entire staff to a day's conference introducing its new strategy, at which employees were invited to pin a photograph of themselves on a 'pledge wall', together with a handwritten promise to change at least one aspect of their work to fit the new strategy.

The process of communication is likely to change the strategy in various ways and staff response typically involves reinterpretation and may raise new issues. In a way, therefore, communication is not the end-point of a strategy making process, but feeds into the identification of new strategic issues for the next round of strategy making.

4.5 Methodologies

Strategists use a wide range of methodologies to organise and guide their strategy making activity. The theme of this study text is *Strategy in Practice*; it is important to consider methodologies as well as analytical concepts or techniques.

Strategy workshops

At the start of the strategy making activity there is often a strategy workshop (sometimes called a retreat, away-day or 'off-site'). This usually involves groups of senior executives working intensively for one or two days, often away from the office, on organisational strategy. Workshops can also be a valuable mechanism for involving a wider group of managers. Workshops are used typically to formulate or reconsider strategy, but are also used to address strategy implementation issues and to communicate strategic decisions to a larger audience. Workshops can be ad hoc or part of the regular strategic planning process. As well as facilitating strategy making, workshops can have a role in team building and the personal development of individual participants.

STOP AND THINK 2.5

What benefits/disadvantages might workshops have in comparison with other approaches to strategy development for an organisation?

Although strategy workshops can be a valuable part of an organisation's strategy making activity, they are prone to at least two problems:

- They are liable simply to reinforce managers' existing preconceptions. Especially where they are reduced to a routine part of the strategic planning cycle, and involving the usual group of senior managers, workshops may not be able to come up with new ideas that radically challenge the status quo.
- Workshops can become detached from subsequent action because they are separated from the routine of the organisation; it is difficult to translate workshop ideas and enthusiasm back into the workplace.

Strategy workshops, therefore, need to be designed for the purpose they are intended to serve. Clear objectives are strongly correlated with success and senior managers should seek to understand what they want from the workshop (or series of workshops) beforehand, and design them accordingly. Hodgkinson et al. (2006) recommend the following.

- **Insist on preparation**. Workshops are typically too short to allow much analysis and data may be difficult and time-consuming to access. It may be helpful to insist that participants bring key issues, analyses or data to the workshop and present on them briefly as input. Subsequent discussions are likely to be better grounded on firm facts, and awkward information is less easily dismissed.
- **Involve people from outside the senior executive team**. It may be useful to involve non-executive directors who bring an external and challenging view. Alternatively, middle managers can be included as they may have a more direct understanding of issues on the ground.
- **Involve outside consultants as facilitators**. Using consultants to facilitate workshop can free managers to concentrate on the discussion itself, help keep the discussion focused on the strategic issues and enable all participants to contribute equally to discussion.
- **Establish project groups**. Workshops can build on the cohesion on particular issues by commissioning groups of managers to work together on them.
- **Make top management commitment visible**. Senior managers need to signal commitment by both statements and actual behaviours – for example, as clear leaders in post-workshop actions.

Strategy projects

Both strategy making and strategy implementation are often organised in the form of projects or taskforces. These involve teams of people assigned to work on particular strategic issues over a defined period of time. Projects can be set up to explore problems or opportunities as part of the strategy development process: for example, they might be charged to explore new opportunities in overseas markets. Alternatively, they might be instituted to implement agreed elements of a strategy, for example, an organisational restructuring or the negotiation of a joint venture. Strategy projects should be managed like any other project, in particular, the need for a clear brief or mandate, clear objectives that are also the measure of the project's success, and the avoidance of 'scope creep' by which additional objectives are added as the project goes – a common danger.

Strategy projects may be organised as programmes and as portfolios. A programme contains a group of projects that address inter-related issues: for example, a set of projects examining new growth opportunities. The portfolio is an organisation's total set of projects, perhaps including several distinct programmes of projects. It is important that both programmes and overall portfolios have clear systems for governance, reporting and review.

Business cases and strategic plans

Strategy making activities, such as workshops or projects, are typically oriented to creating an output in the form of a business case or strategic plan. Keeping this end goal in mind provides a structure for the strategy making work: what needs to be produced shapes the strategising activities. A business case is usually focused on a particular proposal, perhaps an investment in new equipment. A strategic plan is more comprehensive, taking an overall view of the organisation's direction over a substantial period, usually three years and sometimes more. It is important that the business case or plan is consistent with the organisational culture in terms of style, format and detail.

A business case should aim to meet the following criteria:

- **Focused on strategic needs**. Identify the organisation's overall strategy and relate the case closely to it. The focus should be on a few key issues, with clear priority given to those that are both strategically important and relatively easy to address.
- **Supported by key data**. The team will need to assemble appropriate data, demonstrating appropriate returns on any investment. However, qualitative data should not be neglected, for example, recent cases of successes or failures in the organisation.
- **Demonstrated solutions and actions**. Issues attached to solutions tend to get the most attention. Discussion of how proposals will be acted on, who will be responsible and possible barriers should be identified. Alternative scenarios, risks and the feasibility of implementation should be recognised.
- **Provide clear progress measures**. Clear measures and review mechanisms add credibility.

Strategic plans have similar characteristics in terms of focus, data, actions and progress measures. Strategic plans are, however, more comprehensive, and they may be used for entrepreneurial start-ups, business units within a large organisation or for an organisation as a whole. Again, formats vary and it is important to follow one that fits the organisation's culture. However, a typical strategic plan has the following elements and models and frameworks to support them are the subject of the remainder of the study text.

- **Mission, goals and objectives statement**. This is the point of the whole strategy.
- **Environmental analysis**. This should cover macro-trends and more focused issues to do with customers, suppliers and competitors. The team should not stop at the analysis, but draw clear strategic implications (see Chapter 3).
- **Organisational analysis**. This should include the strengths and weaknesses of the organisation and its products relative to its competitors and include a clear statement of competitive advantage (see Chapter 4).
- **Proposed strategy**. This should be clearly related to the environmental and organisational analyses and support the mission, goals and objectives. Useful here are Chapters 7–10.
- **Resources**. Detailed analysis of the resources required, with options for acquiring them.

 **CASE EXAMPLE**   **2.8**

When the University of Notre Dame, Indiana, announced a campus-wide strategic planning initiative, the university's library service launched its own strategic planning review. Specifically, the Library Director established a taskforce of four members to work for ten weeks (alongside normal duties) to provide an initial assessment of the library's existing planning arrangements, which were thought to be weak. This assessment would be the basis for the library's new strategic planning exercise.

The membership of the taskforce included the Director's experienced executive assistant, the library's budget officer, the business reference librarian, currently studying for a MBA, and the taskforce leader, a maths librarian who had joined the library from a strategy consulting firm. The taskforce quickly established four stages to their work:

CASE EXAMPLE **2.8** *continued*

(a) Produce an operational definition of planning.
(b) Determine an appropriate planning framework for the library and its existing materials.
(c) Evaluate the existing materials in the light of this framework and assess the coherence of the whole.
(d) Recommend a future planning process.

The taskforce soon arrived at an operational definition of strategic planning through a search of the business literature and professional resources. They then examined various published frameworks for planning, finally comparing five of them systematically. They settled on one rather than trying to synthesise their own tailor-made version. They then searched for anything relevant to planning, from presentations given by the Library Director to formal vision and mission statements. Comparing against the chosen planning framework, they identified major gaps, such as the absence of an overall strategic plan. In evaluating these materials, the taskforce found that they were often inconsistent with each other and lightweight on implementation. In the end, the taskforce recommended that the library create a completely new strategic plan, with library-wide input.

The last step for the taskforce was to present the findings and recommendations to the library's senior management. The taskforce leader describes what went well and what went not so well in the presentation:

'In a one-hour session, we walked them through the four phases of work. We did well explaining . . . strategic planning and outlining a strategic planning framework. We should have taken more time to explain the definitions . . . this is a perpetual source of difficulty. Who can explain clearly the difference between a mission statement and a vision statement. . .? Nevertheless, we did well presenting our conclusions and recommendations and some in our audience were even enthusiastic about starting a thorough strategic planning process.'

Within a year, the Library Director had developed a strategic plan and won acceptance for it from the University's top management.

J. Ladwig (2005), 'Assess the state of your strategic plan', *Library Administration and Management*, 19(2), pp.90–3, cited in Johnson et al. (2001)

STOP AND THINK **2.6**

■ What were the key strengths of the taskforce and the process they engaged in?
■ What could have gone wrong?

TEST YOUR KNOWLEDGE **2.3**

a Outline Eisenhardt's (1990) advice on strategic decision-making.
b Explain what is meant by 'human capital'.
c Identify the key elements of a strategic plan.

 CASE QUESTIONS

1 Undertake a strategic analysis of Robin Hood's situation as if you were engaged as a consultant
2 Identify the strategic options available to Robin

3 Make a clear recommendation as to which strategic option to adopt and why.

CHAPTER SUMMARY

■ This chapter raises the question of how strategies are made in practice and the role of the company secretary in that process. The role of the company secretary in strategy making will vary from organisation to organisation, but there is a general assumption here that the company secretary in the organisation will have some access to and influence over strategy making. With this in mind, this chapter has considered: strategic leadership; the strategists; and strategic activities and methodologies.

■ Effective strategic leadership is a prerequisite to using the strategic management process successfully. Strategic leadership is the ability to anticipate events, envisage possibilities, maintain flexibility and empower others to create strategic change. The top management team may take a central role in this process.

■ An overview of the strategy process shows how strategic 'fit' is sought between internal resource factors and capabilities and the external market environment, with various steps that will be covered in this book

■ Often, strategy development is equated with formalised strategic planning systems, which take the form of systematised, step-by-step, chronological procedures involving different parts of the organisation.

■ CEOs, senior managers, non-executive directors, strategic planners, strategy consultants and middle managers are frequently involved in strategising. Middle manager involvement in strategy can suffer from the CEO access/ implementation responsibility paradox, but the degree of appropriate involvement none the less should depend on the nature of the issue. Typically, performance improves when the board is involved in shaping a firm's strategic direction, provided it is able to distinguish its role appropriately: focusing on directing rather than managing and on handling what Garrett calls 'the four dynamic balances'. The agency problem may, however, present an ongoing threat to the successful execution of strategy.

■ Strategy making activity involves analysing, issue selling, decision-making and communicating. Managers should not expect these activities to be fully rational or logical and can valuably appeal to the non-rational characteristics of the people they work with. Practical methodologies to guide strategising activity include strategy workshops, strategy projects and creating business cases and strategic plans.

Strategic analysis

■ **LIST OF CHAPTERS**

■ **OVERVIEW**

Taken together, Parts Two and Three are concerned with understanding the strategic position of the organisation. This means the factors that have to be taken into account at the outset of strategy development. These concern both the external factors and the internal factors. On the external side, many argue that environmental factors are what matters most to success: strategy development primarily should be about seeking attractive opportunities in the marketplace. Others argue that an organisation's specific strategic capabilities, resources or cultures should drive strategy. It is from these internal characteristics that distinctive strategies and superior performance can be built.

The theme of Chapter 3 is how managers can analyse the uncertain and increasingly complex world around them. This is addressed by considering various layers of influence from issues in the far environment or macro-environment to specific forces affecting their competitive position. However, the real challenge for strategists is to understand the interaction of these different forces and how these impact on the organisation.

Chapter 4 is concerned with understanding an organisation's strategic capability and how this underpins its competitive advantage or sustains excellence in providing value-for-money products or services. This is explained by considering four main issues: what is meant by 'strategic capability'; how this might provide competitive advantage for organisations; how managers might analyse capabilities; and how they might manage the development of such capabilities.

Chapter 5 takes an historical and cultural perspective on strategy. The business environment, the capabilities of an organisation and the expectations of stakeholders have historical roots. The theme of the chapter is that understanding history and culture helps managers develop the future strategy of their organisations. The chapter begins by explaining the phenomenon of strategic drift, which highlights the importance of history and culture in relation to strategy development. The chapter then examines the influence of the history of an organisation on its current and future strategy and goes on to consider how that history can be analysed. It then explains how cultural influences at different levels influence current and future strategy.

■ LEARNING OUTCOMES

After reading and understanding the contents of Part Two, considering the Case Examples and Test Your Knowledge questions, you should be able to:

- analyse the 'far' environment of organisations using PESTEL and systems maps;

- construct alternative scenarios based on key drivers in the environment;

- assess the attractiveness of industries and sectors as well as their potential for investment and change;

- recognise strategic opportunities by identifying market segments, strategic groups and critical success factors;

- distinguish the components of strategic capability, including resources, core competences and dynamic capabilities;

- recognise how strategic capabilities provide sustainable competitive advantage;

- assess strategic capability using value chain analysis, benchmarking and activity mapping;

- advise on the contribution of organisational knowledge to strategic capability;

- understand the significance of organisational structure and describe a range of structural forms;

- define organisational culture;

- understand the nature and importance of organisational culture; and

- understand the relationship between organisational and international cultures.

 PART 2 CASE STUDY

Walmart and Asda

In July 2012, Walmart took over Asda, Britain's fourth-largest grocery supermarket chain. Walmart is a firm founded in the US that operates in 18 countries outside the US. It has annual sales of $200 billion; more than twice its nearest rival.

Walmart's expansion had been built around keeping its costs down. This has been achieved by, among other things, excellent logistics, global sourcing and tight management control in the supermarkets. Clearly, this continued profitable expansion would depend on competences in reducing the opening costs of new outlets.

Asda is a long-established business that was founded in 1966. It has attached great importance to a high level of customer service and a distinctive brand. Recently, it has focused on sourcing local supplies and ethical trading with suppliers. Some years ago it codified the approach to retailing in the *Ten Golden Rules*, which govern the way they do business. Staff seem to stay in post at Asda and employee turnover is well below the industry benchmark. Customers too

seem loyal and it when a new Asda store opens in a town it is a popular event.

Not much changed in the short term. The company was pinning its hopes on non-food products and the prices that Asda's size could bring. The Walmart CEO, explained:

'The opportunity is in the soft side of the home and electronics. As you look at global sourcing, there is an opportunity to provide tremendous value to customers in Britain. The transition will happen incrementally as Asda buyers get more familiar with the opportunities that exist and as they have more exposure to Walmart stores. We're not talking about meat or produce: it's electronic goods, pillow cases.'

However, press comment has not been favourable. Several pointed out that its expansion outside the US has not always been successful and questioned its skills in acquiring new businesses. One analyst argued:

'Walmart has not yet succeeded in markets that it cannot drive a truck to and it has certainly had little impact as yet on the UK.'

Others pointed to problems that Walmart was

PART 2 CASE STUDY *continued*

experiencing in Germany. Joy explained that, as well as inheriting poor-quality properties:

'Germany is difficult. Building a supply chain that is willing to take costs out to pass on to the consumer does not happen overnight. It's also about convincing German management that a motivated staff really determines our success. We will continue to focus on Germany to bring it up to the standard it can operate at.'

Six of the Asda stores have received new mezzanine floors, which allow the chain to extend floor space without having to seek planning permission. Planning laws are now being changed to force retailers wanting mezzanines to apply for permission. Another 11 stores will get traditional extensions and four will be replaced. The chief executive, criticised what he saw as the UK's increasingly restrictive planning regime and said his stores made a 'tremendous contribution ... to local communities, providing the funds to transform difficult sites and offering a tremendous boost to town and district centres.'

The environmental campaign group Friends of the Earth said the new and bigger Walmart stores would be bad for local traders, local communities and farmers and questioned whether the group could truthfully say it was creating thousands of new jobs as it increasingly used internet trading, some of it from outside the UK.

3 The external environment

■ **INTRODUCTION**

The overall theme of Chapter 3 is how managers can analyse the VUCA world around them –the volatile, uncertain, complex and ambiguous world. This is addressed by considering various layers of influence from macro-environmental issues to specific forces affecting the competitive position. However, the challenge for a strategist is to understand the interaction of these different forces and how these impact on the organisation.

1 Environmental analysis

1.1 Importance and process

Businesses do not exist in a vacuum. They are part of an environment that can play a large role in determining their success. In the commercial world, opportunities arise from the environment in the form of new developments in technology, from changes in lifestyle and to the law. However, the environment is also the source of threats: for example, hostile shifts in market demand, new regulatory requirements or the entry of new competitors. Environmental change can be fatal for businesses. It is vital that strategists can analyse their environment in order to anticipate and, if possible, influence environmental change. Appraising the environment, the strategic capability of the organisation, the expectations of its stakeholders and the purpose and mission of the organisation, taken together, provide a basis for strategic analysis. We look specifically at issues to do with strategic purpose in Part Three.

 CASE EXAMPLE 3.1

BP is one of the world's largest oil and gas companies. It operates across the fields of exploration, production, refining, distribution and marketing. It has about 21,000 service stations worldwide, 50% of which are in the United States, 40% in Europe. The largest sources of its oil production are Russia (about 45%) and the US (20%); the US accounts for about a quarter of its natural gas production and Russia about 10%. Since 2005, BP has had a small alternative energy business, active in biofuels and wind power. In 2010, BP's Deepwater Horizon oil rig exploded, causing 11 deaths and an oil slick in the Gulf of Mexico covering 180,000 km². In 2012, the US government fined BP more than $4 billion for the disaster; many court cases are still pending.

Based on an example cited in Johnson et al. (2014)

It is vital that managers analyse their environments carefully in order to anticipate and, if possible, influence environmental change.

A difficulty that managers face when trying to understand the environment is uncertainty. They may claim that the volume and pace of technological developments mean more and faster change than ever before. A second difficulty is making sense of this change in a way that can contribute to strategic decision-making. Identifying many different environmental influences may be possible, but this is of little use if no picture emerges of the really important influences on the organisation. Regardless of whether change is faster and the changes more unpredictable, it is important to try to understand future external influences on an organisation, even though this may be difficult.

Managers seek to simplify this complexity by focusing on aspects of the environment that have been important in the past or that confirm their own views. This is a natural response when faced with complexity. One of the tasks of the strategic manager is to find ways in which he or she can avoid oversimplification while still achieving useful and usable analysis. These frameworks are associated with a series of steps summarised in Figure 3.1.

1 **Assess environmental influences**. It is useful to take an initial view of the nature of the organisation's environment in terms of how uncertain it is. Is it relatively static or does it show signs of change? In what ways? Is it simple or complex to understand? This helps in deciding what focus the rest of the analysis is to take and is a prelude to an audit of environmental influences. Here the aim is to identify which macro-environmental influences are likely to affect the organisation's development or performance.

2 **Identify competitive forces**. The second step focuses on the immediate environment of the organisation – for example, the competitive arena in which the organisation operates. The aim is to identify the key forces at work in the immediate or competitive environment and why they are significant.

3 **Analyse the organisation's competitive position**. That is, how it stands in relation to other organisations competing for the same resources, or customers, as itself. As we shall see, this may be done in a number of ways.

4 **Opportunities and threats**. The aim is to develop an understanding of opportunities that can be built on and threats which have to be overcome or circumvented. These need to be considered in terms of the resource base and competencies of the organisation and will contribute to strategic choice.

FIGURE 3.1 Steps in environmental analysis (based on Johnson et al., 2014)

This chapter provides frameworks for analysing changing and complex environments.

1.2 Organisational boundaries

Managers often claim that the volume and pace of technological and other developments mean more and faster change now than ever before. Whether or not change is in fact faster, it is important to seek to understand the external influences on an organisation, even though this may be difficult. But the problem for managers and strategists is that many of these changes are unpredictable. Consider, for example, the following in the UK:

- the travel industry was sent into recession by the events of 11 September 2001;
- the construction industry has been hugely affected by the recession and 'credit crunch' of 2008; and
- companies exporting to Europe have been depressed by the strength of the pound during 2014 and 2015.

 STOP AND THINK 3.1

What changes have there been in the environment in which your organisation operates?

You can probably identify your own examples fairly easily. What they are likely to have in common is that the changes were both brought about by external events, and the organisation may have been unable to control or influence them. This is significant if the greatest impact on the future of organisations arises from changes in the external environment, yet by far the major part of management time and effort is directed at the internal environment. Managers tend to be preoccupied with the near, the immediate and the internal. In part, this is because the external environment is difficult to understand – we shrink from the unfamiliar.

A willingness to look outside the boundaries of the organisation can therefore be an important source of success. Morgan (1988) argues that, to be successful, organisations must anticipate possible change and position themselves to deal with opportunities and challenges in a proactive rather than a reactive way. He refers to this as managing from the 'outside in'.

> Many organisations are preoccupied with 'inside out' management. They approach, understand, and act in relation to their environment in terms that make sense from internal divisions and perspectives, or in terms of what powerful members want to do. As a result, they often end up acting in fragmented and inappropriate ways.
>
> Some organisations, on the other hand, try to build from the 'outside in', in the sense that they try and 'embrace' the environment holistically, and shape internal structures and processes with this wider picture in mind. They use the views and needs of customers and other key stakeholders as a mirror through which they can see and understand their own strengths and weaknesses. And they use these insights to re-shape their activities and relations with the environment. (Morgan, 1988)

Morgan therefore emphasises the importance of understanding the external environment, and in this chapter we look at the important interdependence of the relationships that exist between organisations and their external environment. An organisation is part of a large and complex network of customers, suppliers, competitors and regulators. It is also subject to the vagaries of the economy, social trends and technological innovation. This can be represented thematically as three environments (see Figure 3.2).

- The *internal* environment comprises the staff, resources and facilities within the organisation. The internal environment is thought of as the one that managers can control! We discuss it in the next chapter.
- The *near* or *micro-* environment includes customers, clients, contractors, suppliers and competitors. Managers cannot control the near environment, but they can influence it.
- The *far* or *macro-* environment refers to factors that can be neither controlled nor influenced from within the organisation. We refer to these under the acronym PESTEL, indicating political/legal, economic, social, technological, environmental and legal factors, (you may have come across other versions). These are forces to which an organisation can only respond.

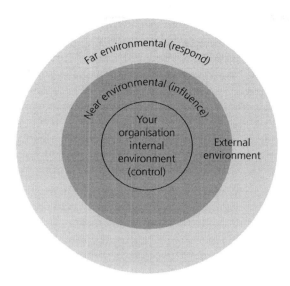

FIGURE 3.2 The three environments

An important point to make here is that, in practice, organisations set the boundaries between their internal and external environments in different ways.

 **CASE EXAMPLE** 3.2

AlphaPharm and BetaPharm are both pharmaceutical companies. They develop and sell proprietary pharmaceutical products to health services and clinicians on a global basis. They have similar turnover and profitability. But that is where the similarity ends.

AlphaPharm is a highly integrated company. It has three large research stations around the world, at which new molecules are synthesised and tested. It runs its own toxicological testing facilities in its own laboratories, and devises and manages its own global clinical testing programmes. It manufactures its products in its own factories and sells them through its own sales force in all major markets.

Although BetaPharm does carry out some laboratory synthesis itself, most of its new products are obtained from contract research carried out by a number of other small laboratories. All toxicological testing is carried out by a specialist commercial laboratory, and most clinical testing is run under contract by a number of collaborators. All products are manufactured on contract, and the products are sold through agencies or independent sales teams (including AlphaPharm in some markets).

These two companies are extreme examples. Even so, they do have some things in common: both companies – even AlphaPharm – use contractors to provide catering services, estate maintenance and security. On the other hand, information collection and collation, planning and marketing are carried out in-house by both organisations – even BetaPharm.

Based on a case example in Stapleton (2003).

There are many real examples where organisations operating in a similar sector have set their boundaries differently:

- Marks & Spencer control their own retail outlets, whereas branded goods manufacturers (such as Nestlé and Heinz) sell through retailers.
- BMW manufactures most of its engines in-house, whereas GM (General Motors) increasingly buys them in.

The key points are that organisations have choices about where they set their boundaries; these are not fixed and may change over time. The main choice is between carrying out activities in-house, outsourcing or using contractors. Each option has its advantages and disadvantages. In-house activities offer control and the benefits of experience. But the overhead structure of large organisations can lead to slower decision-making and reduced responsiveness. Large organisations are also susceptible to the political opportunism of managers pursuing their own agenda. On the other hand, outsourcing makes it easier to vary costs if conditions change. However, there is always likely to be less control over contractors, and outsourcing offers a reduced opportunity for cumulative learning. These are summarised in Table 3.1.

TABLE 3.1 Advantages and disadvantages of in-house and outsourced activities

In-house	Outsourced
Advantages ■ Control ■ Reliability ■ Flexibility ■ Accumulated experience ■ Quality control	■ Access to specialists ■ Flexibility in resource use ■ Reduction in fixed costs ■ Economies of scale ■ Potential for cost saving
Disadvantages ■ High overhead costs ■ Inflexible if requirements change ■ Limited economies of scale ■ Extended decision-making process ■ Lack of specialist skills	■ Loss of expertise in key areas ■ Need contract/project management skills ■ Loss of short-term flexibility ■ Loss of direct quality control

What follows from this is that an organisation's boundaries affect, even define, the strategic management task. There is no single or right solution, and organisations are constantly seeking the best balance between control, risk, short- and long-term flexibility and cost. Understanding that organisations can redefine their boundaries in their search for this balance is a key element of strategy making.

 TEST YOUR KNOWLEDGE 3.1

a Identify the steps in environmental analysis.
b Identify the three environments in which an organisation operates.
c Explain the advantages and disadvantages of outsourced activities.
d Identify the differences between the micro and macro environments

2   Analysing the 'far' environment

2.1 Uncertainty and 'megatrends'

The 'far' environment (what Johnson et al. describe as the macro-environment) is the highest layer. This consists of broad environmental factors that impact to a greater or lesser extent on almost all organisations. Here, a number of frameworks, such as PESTEL, can be used to identify how future trends in the environment might impinge on organisations. These can be used to construct scenarios of possible futures. Scenarios consider how strategies might need to change depending on the different views about how the business environment might change.

Since one of the main problems of business planning is coping with uncertainty, it is useful to consider how uncertain the environment is and why. The macro-environmental influences on organisations include economic conditions, ecology, government policy and action demographics and socio-cultural trends and developments. This is not an exhaustive list and environmental forces that are especially important for one organisation may not be for another; and, over time, their importance may change.

It is useful to consider what broad environmental influences have been particularly important in the past, and what changes are occurring which may make these more or less significant in the future for the organisation and its competitors. Megatrends are large-scale social, economic, political, ecological or technological changes that are typically slow to form, but which influence many other activities and views, possibly over decades. (Slaughter, 1993). A megatrend typically shapes other trends. Thus the megatrend towards ageing populations in the West influences other trends in social care, retail spending and housing. The megatrend towards rapid economic growth in Asia drives employment patterns in advanced economies and commodity prices worldwide. It is important to identify major megatrends, because they influence so many other things. Finlay (2000) points to the following patterns:

■ **Individualism and pluralism of outlook and behaviour.** These drive greater choice in product range (for example, supermarkets and types of table salt or the specialisation of the 'mass' media increasing the range of periodicals and TV channels).
■ **Decentralisation and the move to the 'knowledge age'.** Knowledge is viewed by many as more important than capital.
■ **Convergence of communication technologies.** These include telephony, television and the internet, together with user-driven content.
■ **Internationalisation and globalisation.** The decline in costs of transport and communications has made the growing integration of national economies feasible. This has been helped by the liberalisation of trade through blocs such as the EU. Johnson et al. (2008) discuss the forces that have increased the globalisation of some markets.
  – **Global market convergence.** Markets worldwide are converging for a variety of reasons. In some, customer needs and preferences are becoming more similar. For example, there is increasing homogeneity of consumer tastes in goods such as soft drinks, jeans and electrical items. Those operating in such markets may become global customers and may search for suppliers who can operate on a global basis. Marketing policies, brand names and identities may then be developed globally. This generates further global demand and expectations from customers, and may also provide marketing cost advantages for global operators.
  – **Cost advantages.** This is especially the case in industries that operate with large volume; standardised production is required for optimum economies of scale, as in some components to the electronics industry.
  – **Government influence.** Political changes in the 1990s meant that most trading nations function with market-based economies and their trade policies have tended to encourage free markets between nations. This has been further encouraged by technical standardisation of many products between countries, such as in the airline industry.
  – **Global competition.** This is therefore increasingly evident and encourages further globalisation. If the levels of exports and imports between countries are high, it increases interaction between competitors on a more global scale.

Although changes in the external environment make life difficult for managers and may pose threats to the organisation, they can also offer opportunities. Managers who can understand and monitor their external environment are therefore likely to be more effective. To be able to do this, it is important that you understand the factors that make up the external environment of your organisation.

2.2 PESTEL analysis

As suggested above, the priority an organisation gives to each of these trends will differ. A multinational corporation might be especially concerned with government relations and understanding the policies of national governments in its sector of operation. It is also likely to be concerned with labour costs and exchange rates, which will affect its ability to compete with rivals. A small retailer, on the other hand, may be primarily concerned with local customer tastes and behaviour. None of these forces will remain constant, and managers need to be aware of their changing impact.

PESTEL analysis, enables a comprehensive review of the influences on the possible success or failure of particular strategies. PESTEL stands for Political, Economic (including financial), Social/Cultural, Technological, Environmental (including Ecological and Ethical) and Legal. *Political* highlights the role of governments; *Economic* refers to macro-economic factors such as exchange rates, business cycles and economic growth rates; *Social* influences include changing cultures and demographics, for example, the ageing population in many Western societies; *Technological* influences refer to innovations such as the internet or nanotechnology; *Environmental* concerns 'green' issues, such as pollution and waste; finally, *Legal* embraces legislative constraints or changes, such as those on health and safety or restrictions on mergers and acquisitions.

For managers, it is important to analyse how these factors are changing now and how they are likely to change in the future, drawing out implications for the organisation. Many of these factors are linked. For example, technological developments may simultaneously change economic factors (for example, creating new jobs), social factors (influencing the use of leisure time) and environmental factors (reducing pollution and increasing sustainability).

Table 3.2 can be used as a checklist to consider and prompt analysis of the different influences. However, although a great deal of information can be generated in this way, it will be of limited value if it remains merely a listing of influences. It is important that the frameworks discussed in the rest of the section are used to inform and guide analysis.

TABLE 3.2 A PESTEL analysis of environmental influences

■ What environmental factors are affecting the organisation? ■ Which of these are the most important at present? ■ Which will be the most important in the next few years?	
Political ■ Taxation policy ■ Foreign trade regulations ■ Government stability	**Economic** ■ Business cycles ■ GNP trends ■ Interest rates ■ Money supply ■ Inflation ■ Unemployment ■ Disposable income ■ Energy availability and cost
Social ■ Population demographics ■ Income distribution ■ Social mobility ■ Lifestyle changes ■ Attitudes to work and leisure ■ Consumerism ■ Levels of education	**Technological** ■ Government support for research ■ Government and industry focus on technological effort ■ New discoveries/developments ■ Speed of technology transfer ■ Rates of obsolescence
Environmental ■ Pollution controls ■ Energy consumption controls ■ Land for growing airports	**Legal** ■ Competition legislation ■ Restrictions on mergers ■ Employment law

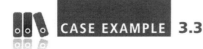 **CASE EXAMPLE 3.3**

The impact of the EU will differ according to the sector in which you work. If you work in an international commercial concern, EU legislation on competition and freedom of trade will be of major importance, as will the Eurozone. If your organisation operates primarily in its home market, you will nevertheless be faced by foreign competitors as markets become more open. If you are involved in the provision of public services, you will be affected by European legislation on minimum wages and working hours, you may have to comply with requirements to offer contracts to bidders from other European countries, and you are likely to be subject to a high level of regulation. The voluntary sector will also be required to comply, for example, with employee protection and minimum wage legislation.

As can be imagined, analysing these factors and their interrelationships can produce long and complex lists. It is useful to begin by considering two important questions:

- **What are the key drivers of change?** It may be possible to identify a number of key forces likely to affect the structure of *this* industry or market.
- **What are the differential impacts of key environmental influences?** PESTEL analysis may also help examine the *differential* impact of external influences on organisations, either historically or the likely future impact. This approach builds on the identification of key drivers by asking to what extent such influences will affect different organisations or industries differently.

These sorts of factors can be built into scenario planning which is discussed in Section 2.3.

STOP AND THINK 3.2

Take an organisation with which you are familiar and address the questions at the top of Table 3.2 to help you conduct a PESTEL analysis.

It is, therefore, necessary to step back to identify the key drivers for change. **Key drivers for change** are the high-impact factors likely to affect significantly the success or failure of strategy. These key drivers will vary by industry or sector. For example, a clothing retailer may be primarily concerned with social changes driving customer tastes and behaviour. A computer manufacturer is likely to be concerned with technological change (e.g. increases in microprocessor speeds). Public sector managers are likely to be especially concerned with social change (e.g. an ageing population), political change (e.g. changing government funding and policies) and legislative change (e.g. introducing new requirements). Identifying key drivers for change helps managers to focus on the PESTEL factors that are most important and which must be addressed as the highest priority. Many other changes will depend on these key drivers anyway (e.g. an ageing population will drive changes in public policy and funding). Without a clear sense of the key drivers for change, managers will not be able to take the decisions that allow for effective action.

2.3 Scenario planning

When the business environment has high levels of uncertainty arising from either complexity or rapid change, or (more usually) both, it is impossible and risky to develop a single view of how the environmental influences might affect an organisation's strategies. Preparing to cope with uncertainty is one of the biggest strategic challenges faced by organisations. There are few tools for coping with strategic uncertainty, especially over medium- to long-term horizons. **Scenario planning** allows for different possibilities and helps prevent managers from closing their minds to other options. Scenarios offer plausible alternative views of how the business environment of an organisation might develop in the future. They typically build on a PESTEL analysis and the key drivers for change, but do not offer a single forecast of how the environment will change.

CASE EXAMPLE 3.4

Scenario planning at Shell Oil Company

A key component of Shell's strategy making process is 'scenario planning'. Shell started using scenario planning back in the 1970s and achieved fame by anticipating and successfully navigating both Middle East oil shocks in that decade.

Shell believes that by asking 'what if?' questions, it will be able to make more informed business decisions. The goal is not to develop a 100% accurate forecast of the future, but rather to envision a series of possible futures that managers might have to deal with. Sometimes these scenarios try to

CASE EXAMPLE 3.4 *continued*

imagine what the world will look like decades into the future – no easy task. But with 40 years of experience of 'looking into their crystal ball', Shell is confident that these exercises have value. Shell is currently trying to give us a glimpse of what lies ahead in the next 50 years and, quite possibly, what the world might look like in the year 2100. As the world's population reaches 9 billion by the middle of this century, demand for energy could increase by 80%. Shell sees two possible futures. In one, there will be a continuation of the status quo, with present influential nations trying their best to maintain their influence and privileged access to resources. They call this a 'rigid' system and believe that it will stifle economic growth and social mobility. The other world they envision is one where power is diffused globally, with countries accommodating and compromising with one another. In this scenario there is dramatic growth in economic productivity offset by eroding social cohesion, and a degree of political uncertainty.

Shell believes that scenario planning deepens its partnerships with the companies it does business with, as well as its various stakeholders. Again, the goal is not to come up with a 100% accurate forecast of the future, but instead to challenge managers to ask more penetrating questions and to develop the competences that will allow them to better respond, and perhaps even anticipate, changes in the business environment.

Jeremy Bentham, a vice president at Shell, hopes that scenario planning will 'provide quantified insights and a language for Shell's executives to apply when grappling with increasingly unfamiliar and challenging conditions'. The results should be 'a more reflective, responsive, and resilient business'.

Sources: 'Pierre Wack', *The Economist*, 29 August 2008; 'Scenario planning', *The Economist*, 1 September 2008; Shell website: shell.com .

Scenario planning is an organised and formal way for companies to think about how environments will behave in the future. In order to be effective, scenario planning relies on several disciplines: politics, economics, psychology, sociology and demographics, to name just a few.

Scenarios typically start from the key drivers with the greatest uncertainty. Such key drivers could create radically different views of the future according to how they turn out. For example, in the oil business, key drivers might be technological change, oil reserves, economic growth and international political stability. It might be assumed that technological change and oil reserves are relatively certain, while economic growth and political stability are not. Scenarios could be constructed around different views about future political stability and economic growth and the interrelationship between them: high political instability and low economic growth are likely to go together. Constructing plausible alternative views of how the business environment might develop in the future therefore depends on knitting together interrelated drivers into internally consistent scenarios. In this analysis, therefore, two internally consistent and plausible scenarios could be proposed: one based on low growth and high instability, the other on high growth and low instability.

Scenario planning does not attempt to predict the unpredictable. The point is to consider plausible alternative futures. Sharing and debating alternative scenarios improves organisational learning by making managers more perceptive about the forces in the business environment and what is really important. Strategists may then evaluate and develop strategies for each scenario. They should then monitor the environment to see how it is actually unfolding and adjust their strategies accordingly. It is typically better to have two or four scenarios, avoiding an easy mid-point. It does not matter if the scenarios do not come to pass: the value lies in the process of exploration and contingency planning that the scenarios trigger.

TEST YOUR KNOWLEDGE 3.2

a   What are the key features of a PESTEL analysis?
b   What are the generic key drivers of change outlined by Johnson et al.?
c   Outline the process of scenario planning.

3 The 'near' or micro-environment – industry and sectors

3.1 The competitive environment

Section 2 looked at how forces in the far environment might influence the success of an organisation's strategies. But the impact of these general factors tends to surface in the more immediate environment through changes in the competitive forces surrounding organisations. The **competitive environment** consists of many factors that are particularly relevant to a firm's strategy. An important aspect of this for most organisations will be competition within their industry or sector. These include existing or potential competitors, customers and suppliers. Potential competitors may include a supplier considering forward integration, such as a car manufacturer acquiring a hire car company, or a firm in an entirely new industry introducing a similar product that uses a more efficient technology. Rutherford (1995) describes an 'industry' as 'a group of firms producing products that are close substitutes for each other'. This concept can be extended into the public services through the idea of a sector. Social services, healthcare or education also have many producers of the same kinds of services, which are effectively competing for resources.

From a strategic management perspective, it is useful for managers in any organisation to understand the competitive forces in their industry or sector since these will determine the attractiveness of that industry and the likely success or failure of particular organisations within it.

This section looks first at Porter's five forces framework for industry analysis and other techniques for analysing the dynamics of industries or sectors.

3.2 Identifying key competitive forces – five forces analysis

So far, we have looked at understanding broad aspects of the environment. However, organisations also have relationships with their near environments, with a particular focus on their competitive situation. Competition takes many forms: for customers and market share, for funds, for staff, etc. Some organisations are the sole providers of their product or service, but such monopolies are now largely restricted to public services or patented products. Most organisations, however, operate in a highly competitive environment, in which they are one of many similar organisations offering similar products or services and competing for the same customers (this applies to many not-for-profit organisations as well as commercial ones).

The near environment comprises all those organisations whose actions influence the organisation, and which in turn are influenced by its own actions. It therefore includes organisations that supply the organisation with services, materials or funds.

 STOP AND THINK **3.3**

Which other organisations most affect the work of your own organisation?

Your answer is likely to have included suppliers and customers. Most organisations have some key suppliers of goods and services and are in turn suppliers to other organisations. A doctor's practice, for example, 'supplies' or refers patients to a hospital, and a small business may supply specialist services to a bigger firm. You might also have included competitor organisations: obviously commercial companies compete for customers, but charities compete with each other for resources and influence, and public service organisations for funds.

In order to establish a view on the organisation's competitive position, a business needs to obtain and consider information about competitors. There are many frameworks by which this can be done, including looking at the differential impacts of competitive forecasts on competitors, core competences of competitors, the different missions of competitors and so on. The end result of a competitor analysis should be to indicate where each competitor is strong or weak and vulnerable. One approach to analysing competitors is the four-point list of the key elements of competitor analysis put forward by Greenley (1986).

- **The nature of competitors and any potential changes**. The organisation needs to watch its environment constantly and in particular note who is moving in and out.
- **The competitors' objectives and strategies**. These determine what they are doing and interpret their actions. This will enable the organisation to formulate effective competitive strategy and tactics.
- **The main strengths and weaknesses of each competitor**. These often determine the options open to a business or organisation.
- **The effects of competitors on your own organisation and its marketing operations**. This point is a reminder that while an organisation is analysing its competitors, they are likely to be doing the same.

The principal benefit of competitor analysis is to be able to understand how other organisations in the sector are meeting the challenge of satisfying their customers and managing their operations. This information can then be used to improve an organisation's current services or products, thereby offering better performance to customers or clients.

A long-established model that is widely used as a framework for analysing the structure and dynamics of the competitive environment of an industry sector is Porter's **five forces analysis**.

Michael Porter's work in the 1980s and 1990s on the economic structures of different industries has influenced the way many organisations seek to understand and influence their competitive environment. Although developed as a rational model for calculating the profitability of firms in different industries, it offers a useful analytical framework for many organisations seeking to understand their competitive position. It is important to recognise that his work applies to sectors and not to individual organisations although it can be extended to cover supply chains, competitive arenas and to a limited extent, geographical territories.

Porter (1980, 2008), argued there are five main forces affecting the profitability of industries:

1 industry structure, which reflects the intensity of rivalry between current competitors, and is affected by the:
2 threat of new entrants;
3 bargaining power of customers;
4 bargaining power of suppliers; and
5 threat of substitute products or services.

The forces are represented in Figure 3.3.

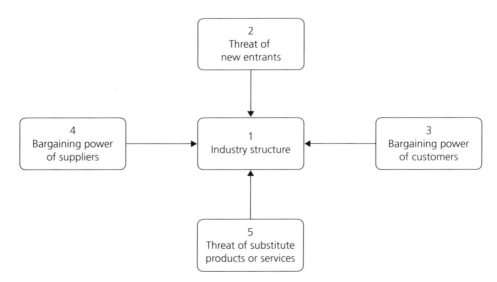

FIGURE 3.3 Forces governing competition in an industry (based on Porter, 1980)

To be of most value, a five forces analysis needs to be carried out at the strategic business unit (SBU) level. If the analysis is at a more generalised level, the variety of influences in the environment will be so great as to reduce the value of the analysis.

Exploring the five forces in more detail

■ **Competitive rivalry (industry structure)**. Porter suggests that the intensity of competition in an industry depends on:
  – **The number and strength of competitors**.
  – **The rate of industry growth**. If the total market is not expanding, companies must take market share from others to gain growth.
  – **Similarity of products**. Making it simple and easy for consumers to switch from one brand to another.
  – **The level of fixed costs**. High fixed costs require companies to maintain volume and so put downward pressure on prices.
  – **The level of exit barriers**. If economic, strategic and emotional factors prevent companies leaving an industry, even when suffering low or negative profitability, then competition is intensified.

The impact of these forces is illustrated in Table 3.3.

TABLE 3.3 Intensity of competition in two industries (based on an example in Stapleton, 2005)

Factors	Car manufacturer	Internet sales company
Number of competitors	Fewer companies, but increasingly global in nature	High, although the number and nature of competitors is changing frequently
Market growth	Growing slower than supply in main EU market, but subject to economic cycles	Fast but unstable
Product similarity	Easy for individuals to buy similar cars from other suppliers	Very easy for customers to buy from other sources
Fixed costs	High: plant must be kept utilised at all times	Low: investment mainly in people
Exit barriers	High: strong political and historical expectations of continued existence	Very few

■ **Threat of new entrants**. Threat of entry to an industry will depend on the extent to which there are *barriers to entry*, which most typically are:
  – **Economies of scale**. In some industries, economies of scale are extremely important: for example, in distribution (e.g. brewing) or in sales and marketing (e.g. fast-moving consumer goods industries).
  – **The capital requirement of entry**. The capital cost of entry will vary according to technology and scale. The cost of setting up a retail clothing business is minimal compared with the cost of entering capital-intensive industries such as chemicals.
  – **Access to distribution channels**. Brewing companies have traditionally invested in bars and pubs to guarantee the distribution of their products and make it difficult for competitors to break into their markets.
  – **Cost advantages independent of size**. These are to do with early entries into the market and the experience gained. It is difficult for a competitor to break into a market if there is an established operator who knows the market well, has good relationships with the key buyers and suppliers, and knows how to overcome market and operating problems.
  – **Expected retaliation**. If a competitor considering entering a market believes that the retaliation of an existing firm will be so great as to prevent entry or mean that entry would be too costly, this is also a barrier.
  – **Government policy**. Legal restraints on competition vary from patent protection, to regulation to control markets (e.g. over-the-counter pharmaceuticals and insurance), through to direct government action – for example, in relation to pension selling and other financial services provisions.
  – **Differentiation**. Organisations able to achieve strategies of differentiation provide their own barriers to competitive entry. For example, Marks & Spencer built a reputation for reliability and quality underpinned by staff training, product and quality specification and control at supplier level, and strong corporate values supportive of the quality image.

Barriers to entry differ by industry and by product/market, so it is impossible to generalise about which are more important than others.

TABLE 3.4 Threat of new entrants in two industries (based on an example in Stapleton, 2005)

	Car manufacturer	Internet sales company
Economies of scale	Very high	Low
Cost barriers	High	Low
Government policy	Very high	Low
Differentiation	Hard to establish new brands	Moderate
Switching costs	Moderate	Low
Distribution channels	Access very difficult	Access moderately difficult
Overall entry barriers	Very high – new entrants very unlikely	Very low – new entrants likely

 **CASE EXAMPLE** 3.5

Professional football clubs in the lower divisions in England have found it increasingly difficult to break into the Premiership league and sustain a position once promoted. One of the key reasons for this is the level of finance required to obtain the top players and fund the necessary ground improvements and expansion to compete at the higher level.

 STOP AND THINK 3.4

Think about the industry in which your business operates.

■ What barriers to entry, if any, exist?
■ To what extent are they likely to prevent entry in the environment concerned?
■ Is your company trying to prevent the competition of entrants or is it attempting to gain entry, and if so how?

■ **The bargaining power of customers and suppliers**. All organisations have to obtain resources and provide goods or services. But the relationship of buyers and sellers can have similar effects in constraining the strategic freedom of an organisation and influence the profit margins of that organisation.

Customer power is likely to be high when there is a concentration of buyers. This is the case in grocery retailing in the UK, where just a few retailers dominate the market. Supplier power is likely to be high when there is a concentration of suppliers rather than a fragmented source of supply or when 'switching costs' from one supplier to another are high, perhaps because a manufacturer's processes are dependent on the specialist products of a supplier, as in the aerospace industry.

With some organisations, supplies are intangible goods. For example, for professional services, such as consultancy or teaching, the availability of skilled staff is crucial. However, while this may be a significant constraint, the suppliers may not be organised to exert power.

■ **The threat of substitute products or services**. The threat of substitution may take different forms:
   – **Product-for-product substitution**. The substitution of letters by e-mail or fax, for example.

- **Substitution of need**. By a new product or service rendering an existing product or service superfluous.
- **Generic substitution**. This occurs where products or services compete for need; for example, retailers compete for available household expenditure.
- **Doing without**. As with the tobacco industry!

The availability of substitutes can place a ceiling on prices for a company's products or make inroads into the market and so reduce its attractiveness. The key questions are whether or not a substitute poses the threat of obsolescence or provides a higher perceived benefit or value and the ease with which buyers can switch to substitutes.

The value of Porter's five forces model as an analytical framework is in assisting the organisation to become more aware of events in its near, competitive environment – events that it cannot control but may be able to influence. It is possible that collaboration between organisations may be a more sensible route to achieving advantage than competing. Identifying opportunities for collaboration nonetheless requires an understanding of the structure of industries, and the frameworks above can be used for this purpose. Collaboration between potential competitors or between buyers and sellers is likely to be advantageous when the combined costs of buying are less through collaboration than the internal cost that would be incurred by the organisation operating alone.

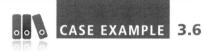

CASE EXAMPLE 3.6

In the developing area of disease management, pharmaceutical companies and health providers, such as hospitals, agree to share savings resulting from the optimal management of a defined medical condition. In the past, Salick (owned largely by Zeneca) did this for cancer treatment and Eli Lilly for diabetes programmes.

Johnson et al. (2014) have proposed the following key questions arising from five forces analysis:

- **What are the key forces at work in the competitive environment?** These will differ by type of industry. For example, for computer manufacturers the growing power of chip manufacturers and growth in competitive intensity might be regarded as most crucial.
- **Are there underlying forces?** Identified from PESTEL analysis or from an analysis of global forces, which are driving competitive forces? For example, the competitive strength of lower-cost high-tech manufacturers in the Asia Pacific region is an underlying and persistent threat to European and American producers.
- **Is it likely that the forces will change, and if so, how?**
- **How do particular competitors stand in relation to these competitive forces?** What are their strengths and weaknesses in relation to the key forces at work?
- **What can management do to influence the competitive forces affecting a SBU?** Can barriers be built to entry, or can power over suppliers or buyers be increased?
- **Are some industries more attractive than others?** Some industries are intrinsically more profitable than others because, for example, entry is more difficult, or buyers and suppliers are less powerful.

CASE EXAMPLE 3.7

Consolidating the steel industry

The five forces framework helps us to understand the changing attractiveness of an industry.

For a long time, the steel industry was seen as static and unprofitable. Producers were nationally based, often state-owned and frequently unprofitable – between the late 1990s and 2003, more than 50 independent steel producers went into bankruptcy in the US alone. But there has been a surge in confidence. During 2006, Mittal Steel paid £19.6 billion for European steel giant Arcelor, creating the world's largest steel company. The following year, Indian conglomerate Tata bought

CASE EXAMPLE **3.7** *continued*

Anglo-Dutch steel company Corus for $13 billion. However, these acquisitions were made just before the onset of the recession in 2008 and further turmoil in the world steel industry.

New entrants

In the last two decades, China has become a major force in the world steel industry. Between the early 1990s and 2011, Chinese producers increased their capacity seven times. Although the Chinese share of world production reached over 45% by 2011, most of this was directed at the domestic market. However, China was the world's largest steel exporter in 2013, and in that year the Chinese companies Hebei and Baosteel were ranked number three and number four in the world (World Steel Association, 2014).

Substitutes

Steel is a nineteenth-century technology, increasingly substituted for by other materials such as aluminium in cars, plastics and aluminium in packaging, and ceramics and composites in many high-tech applications. Steel's own technological advances sometimes work to reduce need: thus steel cans have become about one-third thinner over the last few decades.

Buyer power

Key buyers for steel include the global car manufacturers, such as Ford, Toyota and Volkswagen, and leading can producers such as Crown Holdings, which makes one-third of all food cans produced in North America and Europe. Such companies buy in volume, coordinating purchases around the world. Car manufacturers are sophisticated users, often leading in the technological development of their materials.

Supplier power

The key raw material for steel producers is iron ore. The big three ore producers — Vale, Rio Tinto and BHP Billiton — control 70% of the international market. Iron ore prices had multiplied four times between 2005 and 2008, and, despite the recession, were still twice 2005's level in 2012.

Competitive rivalry

World steel production increased by about 50% between 2000 and 2008, then dropped about 10% in 2009, before recovering to increase again by 30% and reach a new record in 2013. Despite acquisitions by companies such as Mittal and Tata, the industry is fragmented. The top five producers still accounted for only 17% of world production in 2013, up only 3% since 2000. The world's largest steel company, Arcelor Mittal, accounted for just 6% of production. Over-capacity in the European steel industry was estimated at 25% in 2012, but when Arcelor Mittal tried to close down its Florange plant, the French government threatened to nationalise it. After a cyclical peak in 2008, the world steel price was down 40% by 2012 – returning to essentially the same price as in 2005.

Source: Based on figures in World Steel Association (2014) and an example in Johnson et al. (2014).

The five forces framework has to be used carefully. When using it, it is important to bear the following three issues in mind:

- **Defining the 'right' industry**. Most industries can be analysed at different levels. For example, the airline industry has several segments, such as domestic and long haul, and different customer groups, such as leisure, business and freight. The competitive forces are likely to be different for each and can be analysed separately. It is often useful to conduct industry analysis for each distinct segment. The overall picture for the industry as a whole can then be assembled.
- **Converging industries**. Industry boundaries are continuously changing. Many industries, especially in high-tech areas, are converging. This means the activities, technologies, products and customers of previously separate industries begin to overlap or merge.

CASE EXAMPLE 3.8

Technological change has brought convergence between the telephone and photographic industries. For example, smartphones include camera and video functions. For a camera company like Kodak, phones are increasingly a substitute, and Apple or Samsung may be regarded as direct competitors.

- **Complementary products/accessories**. This category refers products that a consumer may need to purchase alongside an original purchase. For example, when buying a personal computer it is normal to also purchase a number of accessories such as software, cases etc. Some analysts argue for a 'sixth force', organisations supplying complementary or accessory products or services, known as 'complementors'. These are players from whom customers buy complementary products that are worth more together than separately. Thus Dell and Microsoft are complementors insofar as computers and software are complementary products for buyers. Microsoft needs Dell to produce powerful machines to run its latest-generation software. Dell needs Microsoft to work its machines. Complementors have opportunities for co-operation. It makes sense for Dell and Microsoft to keep each other in touch with their technological developments, for example. This implies a significant shift in perspective. While Porter's five forces see organisations as battling against each other for industry share, complementors may cooperate to increase the value of the whole 'cake'. In some case, complementors demand a high share of the available value for themselves. Microsoft has been much more profitable than the computer manufacturers and its high margins may have depressed the sales and margins available to companies like Dell. The potential for co-operation or antagonism with such a complementary 'sixth force' needs to be included in industry analyses.

3.3 Industry structure

A five forces analysis might reveal the existence of a number of industry market structures. According to Johnson et al. (2014), there are four main types of structure:

- **Monopolistic industries.** In this type of industry, there is only one firm and therefore no competitive rivalry. The firm is thus able to assert considerable bargaining power over both its buyers and suppliers, leading to high levels of profitability. A slight variation of this structure is a **monopolistic competition** structure, whereby one firm dominates its rivals to such an extent that it exerts monopolistic power. An example occurs in the social media industry, where Facebook is able to exert monopolistic power via the harnessing of network effects. Network effects accrue because Facebook has been able to build a dominant position as its customers also recruit new users in the form of their friends and family.
- **Oligopolistic industries**. This is where the industry is highly concentrated. An industry may be considered oligopolistic if a small number of firms hold a large aggregate market share. An example occurs in auditing services for multinational companies, where four accounting firms dominate the industry: Deloitte, Ernst and Young (now known as EY), KPMG and PricewaterhouseCoopers (known as PwC). Oligopolies are termed **duopolies** where dominance is achieved by just two firms. Both types of structure can be highly profitable for member firms, as there is a clear incentive towards minimising competitive rivalry in order to ensure healthy profit margins and maintaining a tight focus on product/service differentiation.
- **Hyper-competitive industries**. These industries are characterised by the frequency and high level of competitive activity by member firms. Examples of such activities include: price cutting and deep discounting, intensive marketing campaigns and guerrilla marketing campaigns. As a result, this type of industry can be very unprofitable.
- **Perfectly competitive industries**. In this structure, there are usually many competitors, and barriers to entry are low. Products and services offered tend to be similar and largely undifferentiated, meaning that buyers frequently base their purchase decisions largely upon price alone. There is usually the presence of considerable product and service information which helps buyers to identify the best value products and services. Profit margins therefore tend to be small.

CASE EXAMPLE 3.9

Industry structure matters. Understanding the industry structure gives us insights into the nature of competition, or as Porter refers to in his five forces model, 'competitive rivalry'. A quick test of this is to calculate the 'Concentration Ratio' of the top four companies in an industry. Take the UK grocery market, for instance. It is worth £100 billion in annual sales turnover, and comprises approximately 90,000 outlets owned by around 50,000 firms. However, the top four companies – Tesco, Sainsbury's, Morrison's and Asda – control an 80% share of the market between them.

Knowing this leads us to think in terms of an oligopolistic situation, with each of the big firms having approximately a 20% share. Further analysis reveals that Tesco at its peak had a 32% share of the market, leaving 48% for the other three – an average of 16% market share each. This highlights the considerable power of Tesco as number one, at roughly twice the size of its nearest competitor.

From Tesco's perspective, it competes with thousands of firms, but in reality it has limited its market analysis to a 'competitor set' of similar full service multiple grocers. What has been fascinating in the UK grocery sector is the strength of Waitrose and M&S in terms of premium food on the one hand, and the advance of the deep discounters Aldi and Lidl on the other. This has caused Tesco to reassess its competitor set to defend market share in its premium and value ranges.

3.4 Industry lifecycle

Analyses of industry structure can easily become too static; as we have seen, competitive forces change over time. The key drivers for change are likely to alter industry structures, and scenario planning can be used to understand the possible impacts. The power of the five forces typically varies with the stages of the industry lifecycle. The **industry lifecycle** concept suggests that industries are small in their development stage, then go through a period of rapid growth (the equivalent to adolescence in the human life cycle), culminating in a period of 'shake-out'. The final two stages are first a period of slow or even zero growth ('maturity'), before the final stage of decline ('old age'). Klepper (1996) and McGahan (2000) both argue that each stage has implications for the five forces.

The *development stage* is experimental, with few players exercising little direct rivalry and highly differentiated products. The five forces are likely to be weak, though profits may be scarce because of high investment.

High growth exhibits little rivalry as there is plenty of market opportunity for everybody. Buyers may be keen to secure supplies and lack sophistication about what they are buying, so diminishing their power. Barriers to entry may be low, as existing competitors have not built up much scale, experience or customer loyalty. The power of suppliers may be high if there is a shortage of components or materials that fast-growing businesses need for expansion.

Shake-out begins as the growth rate starts to decline, so that increased rivalry forces the weakest out of the business.

In the *maturity* stage, barriers to entry tend to increase, as control over distribution is established and economies of scale and experience comes into play. Products or service tend to standardise. Buyers may become more powerful as they become more confident in switching between suppliers. For major players, market share is typically key to survival, providing leverage against buyers and cost advantages

Decline can be a period of extreme rivalry, especially where there are high exit barriers, as falling sales force remaining competitors into intense competition. Figure 3.4 summarises some of the conditions that can be expected at different stages in the lifecycle.

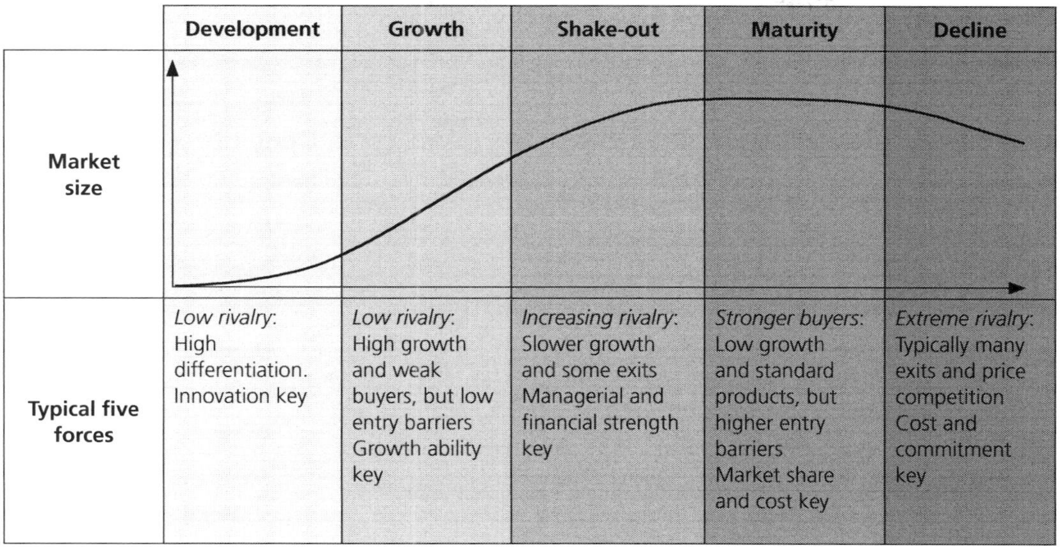

	Development	Growth	Shake-out	Maturity	Decline
Market size	*(curve rising through Development, Growth, peaking at Shake-out/Maturity, then declining in Decline)*				
Typical five forces	*Low rivalry:* High differentiation. Innovation key	*Low rivalry:* High growth and weak buyers, but low entry barriers Growth ability key	*Increasing rivalry:* Slower growth and some exits Managerial and financial strength key	*Stronger buyers:* Low growth and standard products, but higher entry barriers Market share and cost key	*Extreme rivalry:* Typically many exits and price competition Cost and commitment key

FIGURE 3.4 The industry life cycle

From *Exploring Strategy*, 9th edition, Johnson et al, Pearson Education Limited, © Pearson Education 2002, 2011

It is important not to put too much faith in the inevitability of lifecycle stages. One stage does not follow predictably on another: industries vary widely in the duration of their growth stages, and others can rapidly 'de-mature' through innovation. The telephony industry, based for nearly a century on fixed-line telephones, de-matured rapidly with the introduction of mobile and internet telephony. McGahan (2000) warns of the 'maturity mind-set', which can leave many managers complacent and slow to respond to new competition. In fast-moving industries, five forces analyses need to be reviewed regularly.

3.5 Analysing the organisation's competitive position

An industry or sector may be at too high a level to provide for a detailed understanding of competition. The five forces can impact differently on different kinds of players. For example, Ford and Porsche may be in the same broad industry (automobiles), but they are positioned differently: they face different kinds of buyer power and supplier power at the very least. It is often useful to disaggregate. Many industries contain a range of companies, each of which has different capabilities and competes on different bases. These competitor differences are captured by the concept of **strategic groups**. Customers too can differ significantly. Distinguishing between strategic customers and ultimate consumers, and between different market segments, can capture such customer differences.

Strategic groups

Strategic groups are organisations within an industry or sector with similar strategic characteristics, following similar strategies or competing on similar bases. These characteristics are different from those in other strategic groups in the same industry or sector. For example, in the grocery retailing industry, supermarkets, convenience stores and corner shops each form different strategic groups. There are many different characteristics that distinguish between strategic groups but these can be grouped into two major categories. First, the scope of an organisation's activities (e.g. product range, geographical coverage and range of distribution channels used); second, the resource commitment (e.g. brands, marketing spend and extent of vertical integration).

Which of these characteristics are especially relevant for a given industry needs to be understood in terms of the history and development of that industry and the forces at work in the environment.

CASE EXAMPLE 3.10

Figure 3.5 provides a strategic grouping of the worldwide car industry. The firms in each group are representative; not all firms are included. Four strategic groups have been identified. In the top left-hand corner are high-end luxury car-makers who focus on a very narrow product market. Most of the cars produced by the members of this group cost well over £100,000. Some cost many times that amount. The Ferrari SP America costs roughly £3 million and the Lamborghini Aventador £325,000. Players in this market have a very exclusive clientele and face little rivalry from other strategic groups. At the other extreme, in the lower left-hand corner is a strategic group that has low-price/quality attributes and targets a narrow market. These players, Hyundai and Kia, limit competition from other strategic groups by pricing their products very low. The third group (near the middle) consists of firms high in product pricing/quality and average in their product-line breadth. The final group (at the far right) consists of firms with a broad range of products and multiple price points. These firms have entries that compete at the lower end of the market (e.g. the Ford Focus).

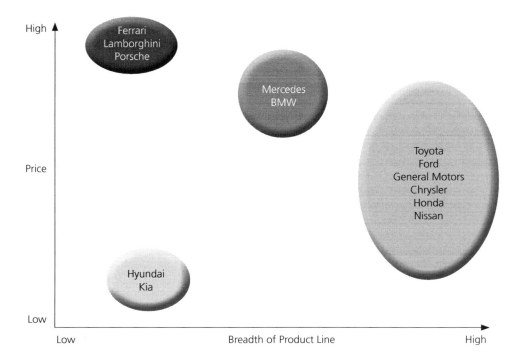

FIGURE 3.5 The world automobile industry: strategic groups (based on Dess, Lumpkin and Eisner, 2014)

Market segmentation

This seeks to identify similarities and differences between groups of customers or users. This is important because not all users are the same: they have different characteristics and needs, behave differently, and so on. Markets are therefore thought of in terms of market segments and identifying which organisations are competing in which market is an important exercise for a strategist.

When undertaking a **market segmentation** analysis, the following should be considered:

■ There are many bases of market segmentation. Table 3.5 summarises some of these. It is important to consider which bases of segmentation are most important. For example, in industrial markets, segmentation is often thought of in terms of the industrial classification of buyers: 'we sell to the car industry'. However, segmentation by buyer behaviour (or purchase value) might be more appropriate in some markets. Indeed, it is useful to consider different bases of segmentation in the same market to help explain the dynamics of that market and suggest strategic opportunities.

■ It is important to assess the attractiveness of different market segments and relative market share within them.

■ Organisations are most likely to achieve competitive advantage by developing and building strategies based on their own unique competences. It may therefore be important for a business to try to identify market segments suited to its particular competences.

TABLE 3.5 Some bases of market segmentation (Johnson et al., 2014)

Type of factor	Consumer markets	Industrial/organisational markets
Characteristics of people/ organisations	Age, sex, race Income Family size Life-cycle stage Location Lifestyle	Industry Location Size Technology Profitability Management
Purchase/use situation	Size of purchase Brand loyalty Purpose of use Purchasing behaviour Importance of purchase Choice criteria	Application Importance of purchase Volume Frequency of purchase Purchasing procedure Choice criteria Distribution channel
Users' needs and preferences for product characteristics	Product similarity Price preference Brand preferences Desired features Quality	Performance requirements Assistance from suppliers Brand preferences Desired features Quality Service requirements

STOP AND THINK 3.5

What does Coca-Cola compete against?

■ Pepsi in the cola market?
■ All other soft drinks?
■ Tea and coffee?
■ Tap water?

As Michael Porter's five forces framework underlines, reducing industry rivalry involves competitors finding differentiated positions in the marketplace. Kim and Mauborgne (2005) propose two concepts that help us to think about the relative positioning of competitors in the environment: the strategy canvas and 'Blue Oceans', is covered in Chapter 9.

3.6 Exploiting opportunities

The concepts and frameworks discussed above should help in understanding the factors in the environments of an organisation. However, as this chapter has stressed, the critical issue is the implications that are drawn from this understanding, and then using these to guide strategic decisions and choices. The crucial next stage, therefore, is to draw from the environmental analysis specific strategic opportunities and threats for the organisation. Identifying these opportunities and threats is extremely valuable when thinking about strategic choices for the future (Chapter 10). Opportunities and threats form one half of the strengths, weaknesses, opportunities and threats (SWOT) analysis that shape many companies' strategy formulation (see Chapter 4). In responding strategically to the environment, the goal is to reduce identified threats and take advantage of the best opportunities.

Considering the concept of strategic gaps, six types of opportunity are particularly important.

- **Opportunities in substitute industries**. Organisations face competition from industries that are producing substitutes. But substitution also provides opportunities. For example, software companies substitute electronic versions of reference books and atlases for the traditional hard copy versions. For the customer, these have easier search facilities and are more likely to be up to date.
- **Opportunities in other strategic groups or strategic spaces**. It is also possible to identify opportunities by looking across strategic groups. For example, deregulation of markets (say, in electricity generation and distribution) could create new market gaps. Locally based smaller-scale generation of electricity may become viable, possibly linked to waste incineration plants.
- **Opportunities in targeting buyers**. The nature of the buyers can be complex, with the strategic customer critically important. There may be several people involved in the overall purchase decision. There may be opportunities in targeting neglected strategic customers or neglected influencers of purchasing decisions. It might, for instance, be worth targeting health and safety executives at a customer organisation: they might be willing to pay more for a safe product or service than the buyers in the purchasing department who are more focused on cost.
- **Opportunities for complementary products and services**. This involves considering the potential value of complementary products and services. For example, in book retailing the overall book-buying experience requires much more than just stocking the right books. It also includes providing an ambience conducive to browsing and perhaps providing a coffee bar as a complementary service.
- **Opportunities in new market segments**. Looking for new market segments may provide opportunities, but product/service features may need to change. If the emphasis is on emotional appeal, the alternative may be to provide a no-frills model that costs less and would appeal to another potential market. For example, the Body Shop, operating in the highly emotional cosmetics industry, challenged the accepted viewpoint by producing purely functional products, without elaborate packaging or heavy advertising. This created new market space by attracting the consumer who wanted quality skincare products without the frills.

3.7 Game theory

It is also necessary for organisations to consider the nature of competitor reactions to their strategies. According to Johnson et al. (2014), game theory suggests that organisations should be especially alert to the presence of two particular reactions as follows:

1   Where the competitive response might alter the original assumptions behind the strategy. For example, a price reduction in one product line might lead to a competitor cutting pricing in another competing product line.
2   Where competitors interpret an organisation's strategy as a signal. For example, a particular strategy might signal to the competition how strongly the organisation is prepared to defend its market share in the industry. Firms therefore need to be alert to the signals that may be transmitted by their strategies and consider all of the various possible competitor interpretations.

Game theory suggests that organisations should attempt to get into the minds of their competitors and consider using scenario analysis to unveil potential reactions to their various strategic moves.

TEST YOUR KNOWLEDGE 3.3

a   Outline the elements of Porter's five forces analysis.
b   Define market segmentation.
c   Explain the nature of strategic groups.

CASE QUESTIONS

1   Use an appropriate framework to analyse the 'far' environment for Walmart.

2   Explain how scenario planning might be used to help the strategic planning at Asda or Walmart.

CHAPTER SUMMARY

- The ability to sense changes in the environment is important because perceived changes signal the possible need to change strategy. They reveal opportunities and warn of threats.
- Environmental influences can be thought of as layers around an organisation, with the outer layer making up the far environment, the next layer making up the industry, sector and strategic groups and market segments. The inner layer comprises the inner resources of the organisation (we look at these in Chapter 4).
- Clarifying the nature of the environment helps provide an initial view on appropriate ways of understanding the influences of that environment. In simple, static conditions, historical analysis and forecasting may be sensible. In more dynamic conditions, scenario planning may be important. As the environment becomes more complex, the design of organisation structure and development of a learning culture is important.
- The far environment can be analysed in terms of the PESTEL factors, from which key drivers of change can be identified. Alternative scenarios about the future can be constructed according to how the key drivers develop.
- Five forces analysis provides a means of identifying the forces that determine the nature of the competitive environment, especially in terms of barriers to entry, the power of buyers and suppliers, the threat of substitutes and other reasons for the extent of competitive intensity. It can also be used to examine the benefits of collaboration within industries.
- Profitability is influenced by the structure of the industry. The main structural forms are: monopolies, monopolistic competition, oligopolies, duopolies, hypercompetitive industries and perfectly competitive industries.
- Game theory suggests that firms need to be alert to the potential competitor reactions to their chosen strategies.
- Industries and sectors are dynamic, and their changes can be analysed in terms of the industry lifecycle. In the middle layer of the environment, strategic group analysis and market segment analysis can also help identify strategic gaps or opportunities.

4 Strategic capability and competences

■ CONTENTS

■ INTRODUCTION

In Chapter 3, we discussed how organisations seek to position themselves in their competitive environment. In this chapter, we shift the emphasis from the external to the internal context of strategy – the resources that an organisation possesses, or needs to possess, as the basis for its strategy. We shift from the industry sector to the organisation, by looking at: the organisation's capabilities and its important networks of relationships; how relevant these are to the objectives of the organisation; any new capabilities and relationships that may be needed over time and how these should be built or acquired.

1 Sources of strategic capability

1.1 The resource-based view

Chapter 3 outlined how an organisation's external environment can create both strategic opportunities and threats. Two firms may compete in the same industry and both may have strengths in a variety of areas: marketing, operations, logistics and so on. However, one of these firms may outperform the other by a wide margin over a long period of time. How can this be? It is not the environment that distinguishes between them, but it could be their internal strategic capabilities.

The importance of strategic capability is the focus of this chapter. There are three key concepts that underpin what follows.

1 Organisations are heterogeneous and have different capabilities.
2 It can be difficult for one organisation to obtain or copy the capabilities of another.
3 If an organisation is to achieve competitive advantage, it will do so on the basis of capabilities that its rivals do not have or have difficulty in obtaining.

These help to explain how some organisations are able to achieve superior performance compared with others. They have capabilities that permit them to produce at lower cost or generate a superior product or service at standard cost in relation to other organisations with inferior capabilities. These concepts underlie what has become known as the **resource-based view** of strategy (Wernerfelt, 1984; Barney, 1991): the view that the competitive advantage and superior performance of an organisation is explained by the distinctiveness of its capabilities.

However, resources are not productive in themselves; they need to be converted into capabilities by being managed and coordinated. It is these resultant capabilities that, if hard to imitate, are the main source of competitive advantage. Strategy, from the resource perspective, is therefore about choosing among and committing to long-term paths of capability development.

Grant (2013) summarises the relationship between resources, capabilities and competitive advantage, as shown in Figure 4.1.

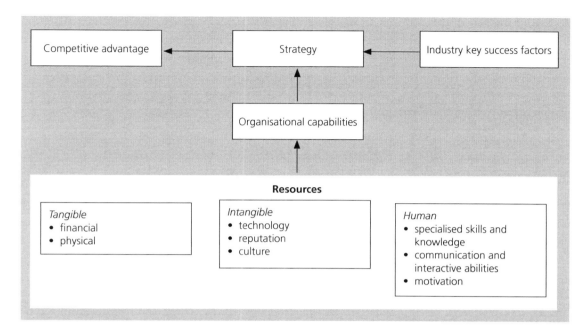

FIGURE 4.1 The relationship between resources, capabilities and competitive advantage (Grant, 1998)

1.2 Capability, resources and competences

A range of terms and concepts is used to explain the importance of strategic capability, so it is important to understand how the terms are used.

Organisational capabilities can be defined as the resources and competences that an organisation needs in order to survive and prosper. **Resources** are the tangible and intangible assets of the organisation. These may be physical assets such as plant, people and finance, or non-physical assets such as information, reputation and knowledge as well as the skills and knowledge of employees.

In detail, an organisation's resources can be considered under the following four broad categories:

- **Physical resources**. The machines, buildings or production capacity. Their age and condition will determine how useful they are.
- **Financial resources**. Capital, cash and suppliers of money (shareholders, bankers, etc.).
- **Human resources**. These include the demographic profile and skills.
- **Intellectual capital**. This includes patents, brands, business systems and customer databases. In a knowledge-based economy, intellectual capital is likely to be a major asset of many organisations.

How an organisation uses these resources matters at least as much as what resources it has. There would be no point in having state-of-the-art equipment, valuable knowledge or a valuable brand if they were not used effectively. The efficiency and effectiveness of physical or financial resources, or the people in an organisation, therefore depend not just on their existence but on how they are managed, co-operation between people, their adaptability, their innovatory capacity, the relationship with customers and suppliers, and experience and learning about what works well and what does not. The term **competence** is usually used to refer to the skills and abilities by which resources are deployed effectively through an organisation's activities and processes.

STOP AND THINK 4.1

Think about an organisation that you know. Identify its range of capabilities, and the resources and competences upon which these are based.

1.3 Threshold capabilities and core competences

A distinction needs to be made between organisational capabilities that are at a threshold level and those that might help the organisation to achieve competitive advantage and superior performance. **Threshold capabilities** are needed for an organisation to meet the necessary requirements to compete in a given market. These could be threshold resources, or the threshold competences required to deploy these to meet customers' requirements and support particular strategies. Threshold levels of capability will change over time as critical success factors change in the industry or market segment, and through the activities of competitors and new entrants.

CASE EXAMPLE 4.1

The increasing demands on suppliers by modern multiple retailers mean that those suppliers need a sophisticated IT infrastructure simply to stand a chance of fulfilling retailer requirements. However, retailers do not simply expect suppliers to have the required IT infrastructure, but to be able to use it effectively so as to guarantee the required level of service. Suppliers to major retailers did not require the same level of IT and logistics support 15 years ago. But the retailers' drive to reduce costs, improve efficiency and ensure availability of merchandise to their customers means that their expectations of their suppliers have increased markedly in that time and continue to do so. So there is a need for those suppliers to review and improve continuously their logistics resource and competence base just to stay in business.

Different market segments may require different thresholds. For example, some businesses have found it hard to compete in market segments that require large quantities of standard products as well as those that require added value specialist products. The first requires high-capacity and fast-throughput plant, standardised highly efficient systems, and a low-cost labour force; the second needs a skilled labour force, flexible plant and a more innovative capacity. The danger is that an organisation fails to achieve the threshold capabilities required for *either* segment.

While threshold capabilities are important, they do not of themselves create competitive advantage or the basis of superior performance. These depend on an organisation having distinctive or unique capabilities that competitors will find difficult to imitate. This could be because the organisation has unique resources that critically underpin competitive advantage, and that others cannot imitate or obtain – Virgin's long-established brand, for example. It is, however, more likely that an organisation will achieve competitive advantage because it has distinctive, or core, competences. **Core competences** (Hamel and Prahalad, 1990) are the skills and abilities by which resources are deployed through an organisation's activities and processes, to achieve competitive advantage in ways that others cannot imitate or obtain. Section 2 discusses in more depth the role played by unique resources and core competences in contributing to long-term competitive advantage.

	Resources	Competences
Threshold capabilities	**Threshold resources** • Tangible • Intangible	**Threshold competences**
Capabilities for competitive advantages	**Unique resources** • Tangible • Intangible	**Core competences**

FIGURE 4.2 Strategic capabilities and competitive advantage

From *Exploring Strategy*, 9th edition, Johnson et al, Pearson Education Limited, © Pearson Education 2002, 2011

 CASE EXAMPLE 4.2

In 1984, Michael Dell started Dell Inc. with an investment of $1,000. By 2006, Dell had attained annual revenues of $56 billion and a net income of $3.5 billion. Dell achieved this meteoric growth by differentiating itself through the direct sales approach that it pioneered. Its user-configurable products enabled it to satisfy the diverse needs of its corporate and institutional customer base. Figure 4.2 summarises the Dell recipe for success by integrating its tangible resources, intangible resources, and organisational capabilities.

Dell continued to maintain this competitive advantage by further strengthening its activities and interrelationships that are critical to satisfying the largest market opportunities. They achieved this by: (1) implementing e-commerce direct sales and support processes that accounted for the sophisticated buying habits of the largest markets; and (2) matching their operations to the purchase options by adopting flexible assembly processes, while leaving inventory management to its extensive supplier network. Dell has sustained these advantages by investing in intangible resources such as proprietary assembly methods and packaging configurations that help to protect against the threat of imitation.

Based on an example in Dess et al. (2014)

In an ideal world, organisations would like to achieve sustainable or long-term competitive advantage, as posited by Michael Porter. The reality is that sooner or later, advantage is eroded; therefore, current strategic management thinking led by Professor Rita Gunter McGrath refers to a transient advantage economy where companies need to build in an agility to establish and exploit a series of short-term transient competitive advantages.

STOP AND THINK 4.2

a Explain the resource-based view of the firm.
b Distinguish between capabilities and competences.
c Explain what is meant by the term 'core competence'.

2   Strategic capabilities for competitive advantage

2.1 Introduction

If the aim is to achieve competitive advantage, then a key question for strategists concerns which capabilities might provide competitive advantage in ways that can be sustained over time. It is important to emphasise that if an organisation seeks to build competitive advantage, it must have capabilities that are of value to its customers. This may seem obvious but some managers may argue that a distinctive capability of their organisation is of value simply because it is distinctive. Barney (1991) argued that capabilities for achieving and sustaining competitive advantage are characterised by *value, rarity, inimitability and non-substitutability* – the **VRIN criteria**.

2.2 Value

Strategic capabilities are valuable when they create a product or a service that is of value to customers, and if they generate higher revenues or lower costs or both.

There are three components here:

1   **Taking advantage of opportunities and neutralising threats**. To be valuable, capabilities need to provide the potential to address the opportunities and threats that arise in the organisation's environment. For example, IKEA's cost-conscious culture, size and its intricate configuration of interlinked activities lower its costs compared to competitors, and addresses opportunities of low-priced furniture that competitors do not.

2   **Value to customers**. This may seem obvious, but in practice it is often ignored or poorly understood. For example, managers may seek to build on capabilities that they may see as valuable, but which do not meet customers' needs. Having capabilities that are different from those of other organisations is not *of itself* a basis of competitive advantage.

3   **Cost**. The product or service needs to be provided at a cost that still allows the organisation to make the returns expected. The danger is that the cost of developing or acquiring the capabilities to deliver what customers especially value will render products or services unprofitable.

Managers should consider carefully which of their organisation's activities are especially important in providing such value.

2.3 Rarity

Competitive advantage might be achieved if a competitor possesses a unique or rare capability. This could take the form of unique resources. For example, some libraries have unique collections of books unavailable elsewhere; a company may have a powerful brand; retail stores may have prime locations. For service organisations unique resources may be intellectual capital particularly talented individuals. There are three important points to bear in mind about the extent to which rarity might provide sustainable competitive advantage:

■   **Ease of transferability**. Rarity may depend on who owns the competence and how easily transferable it is. For example, the competitive advantage of some professional service organisations is built around the competence of specific individuals such as the CEO of a business. But since these individuals may leave or join competitors, this resource may be a fragile basis of advantage. More durable advantage may be found in competences that exist for recruiting, training, motivating and rewarding such individuals in the first place so ensuring that are less likely to defect.

■   **Sustainability**. Rarity could be temporary. If an organisation is successful on the basis of a unique set of competences, then competitors will seek to imitate or obtain those competences for themselves.

■   **Core rigidities**. Rare capabilities may also become rigid and difficult to change. Managers may be so wedded to these bases of success that they perceive them as strengths of the organisation and 'invent' customer values associated with them.

2.4 Inimitability

It is unusual for competitive advantage to be explained by differences in the tangible resources of organisations, since over time these can usually be imitated or traded. Advantage is more likely to be determined by the way in which resources are deployed to create competences in the organisation's activities. For example, as suggested above, an IT system itself will not improve an organisation's competitive standing: it is how it is used that matters. Indeed, what will probably make most difference is how the system is used to bring together customer needs with activities and knowledge both inside and outside the organisation. It is therefore to do with linking sets of competences. So, extending the earlier definition, core competences are likely to be the skills and abilities to *link activities or processes* through which resources are deployed so as to achieve competitive advantage. In order to achieve do so, core competences need to be difficult for competitors to imitate – or unique.

 **CASE EXAMPLE** 4.3

Monster.com entered the executive recruiting market in the US by providing, in essence, a substitute for traditional bricks-and-mortar headhunting firms. Although Monster.com's resources are rare and valuable, they were subject to imitation by new rivals. There are very low-entry barriers for firms wanting to try their hand at recruitment. Many job search firms have emerged in recent years. It would be extremely difficult for a single firm to attain a sustainable advantage in this industry.

Figure 4.3 summarises how this might be achieved. The three main reasons are complexity, culture and history, and causal ambiguity.

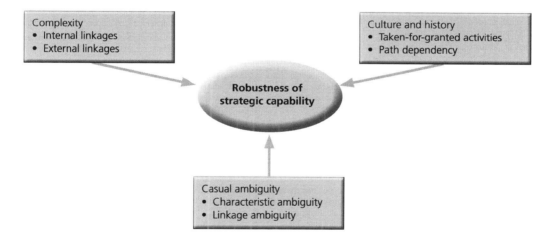

FIGURE 4.3 Criteria for inimitability

From *Exploring Strategy*, 9th edition, Johnson et al, Pearson Education Limited, © Pearson Education 2002, 2011

Complexity

The core competences of an organisation may be difficult to imitate because they are complex. This may be to do with *internal linkages*: the ability to link activities and processes that, together, deliver customer value. It is unlikely that it would be able to replicate. Organisations can make it difficult for others to imitate or obtain their bases of competitive advantage by developing activities together with the customer on which the customer is dependent. This external interconnectedness is sometimes referred to as co-specialisation.

CASE EXAMPLE 4.4

An industrial lubricants business moved away from just selling its products to customers by coming to agreements with them to manage the applications of lubricants within the customers' sites against agreed targets on cost savings. The more efficient the use of lubricants, the more both parties benefited.

Similarly, software businesses can achieve advantage by developing computer programs that are distinctively beneficial to specific customer needs.

Culture and history

Core competences may become embedded in an organisation's culture, so coordination between various activities occurs 'naturally' because people know their part in the wider picture or it is simply taken for granted that activities are done in particular ways. For example, in the lubricants business the experience in rapid changes in production-runs and the close links between sales personnel, production and despatch were not planned or formalised: they were the way the firm had come to operate over the years. It is likely that such competences have developed over time and in a particular way. The origins and history by which competences have developed are referred to as path dependency, are specific to the organisation and cannot be imitated.

CASE EXAMPLE 4.5

Southwest Airlines Co., headquartered in Dallas, Texas, is a major US airline and the world's largest low-cost carrier. The loyalty and trust that Southwest Airlines employees feel towards their firm, and its founder and Chairman Emeritus Herb Kelleher, are resources that have been built up over a long period of time and that are difficult to imitate.

Causal ambiguity

Another reason why competences might be difficult to imitate is that competitors find it difficult to discern the causes and effects underpinning an organisation's advantage. This is called causal ambiguity. Causal ambiguity may exist in two forms:

1 **Characteristic ambiguity**. Where the significance of the characteristic itself is difficult to discern or comprehend, perhaps because it is based on tacit knowledge or rooted in the organisation's culture.
2 **Linkage ambiguity**. Where competitors cannot discern which activities and processes are dependent on which others to form linkages that create core competences.

For example, what is the root of 3M's innovation process? You can study it and draw up a list of possible factors, but it is a complex process that is hard to understand and would be difficult to imitate. Often, causally ambiguous resources are organisational capabilities, involving a complex web of social interactions that may even depend on particular individuals.

CASE EXAMPLE 4.6

When Continental and United tried to replicate the successful low-cost strategy of Southwest Airlines, the planes, routes and fast gate turnarounds were not the most difficult aspects to copy. Those were all easy to observe and, at least in principle, easy to duplicate. However, they could not replicate Southwest's culture of fun, family, frugality and focus since no one can clearly specify exactly what that culture is or how it came to be.

2.5 Non-substitutability

The organisation may also be at risk from substitution. Substitution can take two forms:

1 **Product or service substitution**. A product or service as a whole might be a victim of substitution. For example, increasingly e-mail systems have substituted for postal systems. No matter how complex and culturally embedded were the competences of the postal service, it could not avoid this sort of substitution.
2 **Competence substitution**. Substitution might, however, not be at the product or service level but at the competence level. For example, task-based industries have often suffered because of an over-reliance on the competences of skilled craft workers that have been replaced by expert systems and mechanisation.

For example, internet booksellers such as Amazon compete as substitutes for bricks-and-mortar booksellers such as W.H. Smith. The result is that resources such as premier retail locations became less valuable. Similarly, several pharmaceutical firms have seen the value of patent protection erode in the face of new drugs that are based on different production processes and act in different ways, but can be used in similar treatment regimes.

In summary, resources and capabilities must be rare and valuable as well as difficult to imitate or substitute in order for a firm to attain competitive advantages that are sustainable over time. Table 4.1 illustrates the relationship among the four criteria of sustainability and shows the competitive implications.

A final point: whereas in more stable conditions competitive advantage might be achieved by building capabilities that may be durable over time, in more dynamic conditions competitive advantage requires the building of capacity to change, innovate and learn in order to build dynamic capabilities.

TABLE 4.1 Criteria for sustainable competitive advantage

Is a resource or capability:				
Valuable?	Rare?	Difficult to imitate?	Without substitutes?	Implications for competitiveness
No	No	No	No	Competitive disadvantage
Yes	No	No	No	Competitive parity
Yes	Yes	No	No	Temporary competitive advantage
Yes	Yes	Yes	Yes	Sustainable competitive advantage

Source: Dess et al., 2008, adapted from J.B. Barney, 1991, 'Firm resources and sustained competitive advantage', *Journal of Management*, 17, pp.99–120.

2.6 Organisational support

In a later development of his work, Barney (1997) amended VRIN to VRIO (the 'O' standing for 'Organisation'), to encompass this idea of organisational support and encompassing non-substitutability in inimitability. Providing value to customers and possessing capabilities that are rare and difficult to imitate provides the potential for competitive advantage. However, an organisation must also be suitably organised to support these capabilities, which includes having appropriate organisational processes and systems in place.

This implies that to take full advantage of capabilities, an organisation's structure and management control systems need to support and facilitate the exploitation of these. Some of the potential competitive advantage can be lost if a company is not organised in a way that it can fully take advantage of valuable, rare and/or inimitable capabilities.

2.7 Organisational knowledge

Organisational knowledge is the collective experience accumulated through systems, routines and activities of sharing across the organisation. As such it is closely related to what has been discussed as the competences of an organisation. As organisations become more complex and larger, the need to share what people know becomes more of a challenge and information systems are providing more sophisticated ways of doing this. As we have explained in this chapter, it is less likely that organisations will achieve competitive advantage through their physical resources and more likely that it will be achieved through the way they do things and their accumulated experience. Knowledge about how to do things that draws on that experience becomes crucially important.

Two points should be highlighted here:

- **Explicit and tacit organisational knowledge**. Organisational knowledge may take different forms. Nonaka and Takeuchi (1995) distinguish between two types of knowledge:
  - **Explicit knowledge**. Knowledge that is articulated, stored and transmitted through systems and procedures.
  - **Tacit knowledge**. Knowledge embedded in individual experience; shared through personal contact with others.

There are limits to what computer-based knowledge management systems can achieve imposed by the complex nature of the knowledge itself. Explicit knowledge comes as words and numbers and can be readily stored and transmitted. Tacit knowledge, on the other hand, relates to anything from the subtle aspects of running a tricky process to a deep understanding of cultural values. Nonaka argues that it has little to do with data processing. Stored in the minds of specialists and middle managers, it has great strategic value. Non-imitable competitive advantage is much more likely to exist where knowledge is lodged in the experience of groups of individuals. Yet this is often the group that re-engineering and other planned changes have sought to replace with digital media.

 CASE EXAMPLE 4.7

For over a quarter of a century, Tocris Bioscience has been established as a leading supplier of innovative, high-performance life science research reagents. The organisation has strong ties with large pharmaceutical companies, patent lawyers and academics in the field. This is because pharmaceutical firms often hold patents on chemicals that Tocris needs to synthesise, so rights have to be negotiated. The company needs to maintain close links with universities not only because they represent important clients, but also to update its own employees' knowledge and build an external recruitment pool by making top-performing research chemists aware of its activities.

Findings from interviews with all 60 employees suggested that building client relationships was an art that took several years to master. While these relationships are central to the firm's success, in view of its young, highly qualified and mobile workforce, they also constitute a threat. To counter the threat of poaching by clients and other partners, the company has developed a strong culture, which employees describe as a family or a home away from home. Its site in Bristol, which houses state-of-the-art laboratories, has a distinctive campus feel. In this environment, employees describe themselves as friends as well as colleagues, and they engage in lively debates over lunch and at social gatherings after work. This social structure is as evident in the workplace as it is outside working hours, and helps to ensure that knowledge is shared and turned into the intellectual capital that is Tocris' stock in trade.

- **Communities of practice**. The sharing of knowledge and experience in organisations is an essentially social and cultural process relying on communities of practice (Wenger and Snyder, 2000) developing and sharing information because it is mutually beneficial. This may happen through formal systems such as the Internet but it is also highly dependent on social contact and trust. Indeed, exchange of knowledge is more likely to occur in cultures of trust without strong hierarchical or functional boundaries. Jose Santos (unpublished) has argued that in dispersed and diverse organisations, the various knowledge processes (creation and sharing) must be managed explicitly. This means understanding the nature and complexity of the knowledge and the contexts in which it resides if we are to avoid the pitfalls of managing dispersed teams and the waste of the 'not invented here' syndrome (Figure 4.4).

		Same	Distant
Context	*Diverse*	Strict Co-location	Dispersion & Diversity
	Same	Co-location & Co-setting	Virtual Co-location
		Same	*Distant*
		Location	

FIGURE 4.4 Knowledge management in the global context (Jose Santos, INSEAD)

Organisations have tried to improve the sharing of knowledge by setting up IT-based systems. However, there has been an increasing realisation that, while some of this knowledge can be codified and built into computer-based systems, it is very difficult to codify knowledge where its value is especially dependent on knowledge sharing. Both organisational knowledge and learning need to be thought of in terms of the dynamic capabilities to adapt to changing conditions. The links between knowledge, experience and social interaction also need to be considered in relation to cultural aspects of strategy addressed further in Chapter 5.

TEST YOUR KNOWLEDGE 4.2

a Explain what is meant by rarity as a capability.
b Explain what is meant by causal ambiguity.
c Define the two types of organisational knowledge.

3 Assessing strategic capability

3.1 Value chain analysis

Value chain analysis views the organisation as a sequential process of value-creating activities. This approach is useful for understanding the building blocks of competitive advantage. It describes the activities within and around an organisation and relates them to its competitive strength of the organisation. Value analysis (Miles, 1961) was originally introduced as an accounting tool to shed light on the 'value added' by separate steps in complex manufacturing processes to determine where cost improvements could be made or value creation improved. Porter (1985) linked these steps to an analysis of an organisation's competitive advantage.

The basis of the approach is that organisations are more than a collection of machines, money and people. These resources are deployed into activities and organised into routines and systems that ensure that products or services are produced that are valued by the final consumer or user. Porter argued that understanding strategic capability must start with identifying these separate value activities. Figure 4.5 shows the value chain within an organisation.

Primary activities are directly concerned with the creation or delivery of a product or service and can be grouped into five main areas.

1 **Inbound logistics**. These include materials handling, stock control, transport, etc.
2 **Operations**. Transform these various inputs into the final product or service: machining, packaging, assembly, testing, etc.
3 **Outbound logistics**. These include warehousing, transport, etc. In the case of services, they may be more concerned with arrangements for bringing customers to the service is a fixed location.
4 **Marketing and sales**. These provide the means whereby consumers/users made aware of the product or service and are able to purchase it.

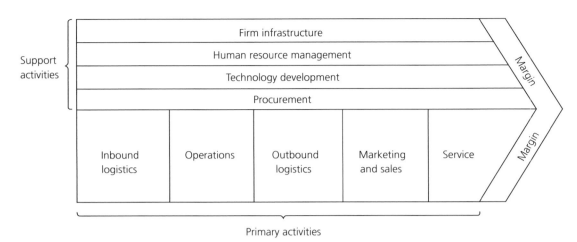

FIGURE 4.5 The value chain (Porter, 1985)

5   **Service**. Those activities that enhance or maintain the value of a product or service, such as installation, repair, training and spares.

Support activities help to improve the effectiveness or efficiency of primary activities. They can be divided into four areas:

1   **Procurement**. The processes for acquiring the various resource inputs to the primary activities.
2   **Technology development**. All value activities have a 'technology' even if it is simply know-how.
3   **Human resource management**. Recruiting, managing, training, developing and rewarding people.
4   **Infrastructure**. The systems of planning, finance, information management etc. and the routines within the culture (Chapter 5).

Porter's value chain forces us to think more deeply about the organizational structure, processes and capabilities, and the flow of value added elements, and to look for linkages between primary and support activities. For instance, in the case of Tesco, the Tesco Club Card is a marketing and sales tool, but Tesco's significant IT support systems means it has gained significant competitive advantage from its ability to analyse purchasing data of individual customers.

The value chain is therefore about more than just supply chain management. In addition, most organisations are part of a wider value system – a value network that is linked to customer and supplier value chains. The **value network (or system)** is the set of inter-organisational links and relationships necessary to create a product or service. Indeed, it is often this that underpins excellence in creating value for money. Much of the value creation occurs in the supply and distribution chains, and this whole process needs to be analysed and understood. For example, the quality of a car when it reaches the final purchaser is not only influenced by the activities undertaken within the manufacturing company itself. The quality of components and the performance of the distributors also determine it.

 **CASE EXAMPLE** 4.8

A value system for Ugandan chilled fish fillet exports

A fish factory in Uganda barely made any profit. Fish were caught from small motorboats owned by poor fishermen from local villages. Just before they set out, they would collect ice and plastic fish boxes from the agents who bought the catch on their return. The boxes were imported, along with tackle and boat parts. All supplies had to be paid for in cash, in advance, by the agents. Sometimes ice and supplies were not available in time. Fish landed with insufficient ice achieved half of the price of iced fish, and sometimes could not be sold to the agents at all. The fish factory had always processed the fillets in the same way – disposing of the waste back into the lake. Once a week, some foreign traders would come and buy the better fillets; they did not say to whom they sold them, and sometimes they did not buy very much.

CASE EXAMPLE **4.8** *continued*

By mapping the value chain, it was clear that there were opportunities for capturing more value along the chain and reducing losses. Together with outside specialists, the fish factory and the broader fishing community developed a strategy to improve their capabilities. They became a flourishing international business, named the Lake Victoria Fish Company, with regular airfreight exports around the world.

Source: Ian Sayers, Senior Adviser for the Private Sector, Division of Trade Support Services, International Trade Centre, Geneva (cited in Johnson et al. (2014).

The value chain can help with the analysis of the strategic position of an organisation in two ways:

1   **As generic descriptions of activities**. These can help managers understand if there is a cluster of activities providing benefit to customers located within particular areas of the value chain. Perhaps a business is especially good at outbound logistics linked to its marketing and sales operation and supported by its technology development. It might be less good in terms of its operations and its inbound logistics. The value chain also prompts managers to think about the role different activities play. For example, in a local, family-run sandwich bar, is sandwich making best thought of as 'operations' or as 'marketing and sales', given that its reputation and appeal may rely on the social relations and banter between customers and sandwich makers? Arguably it is 'operations' if done badly but 'marketing and sales' if done well.
2   **In terms of the cost and value of activities**. Value chain analysis can be used as a way of identifying what to focus upon on in developing a more profitable business model.

STOP AND THINK 4.3

Draw up a value chain for a business in terms of the activities within its component parts. What are the strategic implications of your analysis?

3.2 Benchmarking

Benchmarking can be used as a way of understanding how an organisation's strategic capability, in terms of internal processes, compares with those of other organisations. Benchmarking can be described as the process of identifying, understanding and adapting exemplar practices from within the same organisation or from other organisations to help improve performance.

A number of benefits can arise from adopting benchmarking of activities. These include:

■   setting performance goals that can be demonstrated to be achievable;
■   accelerating and managing change;
■   improving processes;
■   focusing on the external environment; and
■   generating an understanding of world-class performance.

There are several approaches to benchmarking:

■   **Historical benchmarking**. Organisations may consider their performance in relation to previous years in order to identify any significant changes. The danger is that this can lead to complacency since it is the rate of improvement compared with that of competitors that is really important.
■   **Industry/sector benchmarking**. Insights about performance standards can be gleaned by looking at the comparative performance of other organisations in the same industry sector or between similar service providers against a set of performance indicators. Some public

sector organisations have, in effect, acknowledged the existence of strategic groups by benchmarking against similar organisations rather than against everybody: for example, local government services and police treat 'urban' differently from 'rural' in their benchmarking and league tables. An overriding danger of industry norm comparisons is, however, that the whole industry may be performing badly and losing out competitively to other industries that can satisfy customers' needs in different ways. Another danger with benchmarking within an industry is that the boundaries of industries are blurring through competitive activity and industry convergence. For example, supermarkets are entering retail banking and their benchmarking needs to reflect this (as does the benchmarking of the traditional retail banks).

■ **Best-in-class benchmarking**. Compares an organisation's performance against 'best-in-class' performance (wherever that is found) and therefore seeks to overcome the limitations of other approaches. It may also help challenge managers' mind-sets that acceptable improvements in performance will result from incremental changes in resources or competences. It can therefore encourage a more fundamental reconsideration of how to improve organisational competences.

 CASE EXAMPLE 4.9

Southwest Airlines were trying to improve their 40-minute refuelling time for their aircraft. As well as benchmarking within the industry, the airline looked across industry. By adopting practices from the fastest refuellers in the world – Formula 1 motor racing – the airline can now refuel its aircraft in just 12 minutes.

Source: Murdoch (1997)

The importance of benchmarking is, then, not so much in the detailed mechanics of comparison but in the impact that these comparisons might have on behaviours. It can be usefully regarded as a process for gaining momentum for improvement and change.

The process also has its limits. It works well for high-performance companies, yet for moderate performers, the exercise may only generate confusion. Issues to watch out for include:

■ **Measurement distortion**. Benchmarking can lead to a situation where you get what you measure and this may not be what is intended strategically. It can therefore result in changes in behaviour that are unintended or dysfunctional.

 CASE EXAMPLE 4.10

The university sector in the UK has been subjected to rankings in league tables on research output, teaching quality and the success of graduating students in terms of employment and starting salaries. This has resulted in academics feeling obliged to orient their published research to certain types of academic journals that may have little to do directly with the quality of the education in universities.

■ **Surface comparisons**. Benchmarking compares inputs (resources), outputs or outcomes; it does not identify the reasons for the good or poor performance of organisations since the process does not compare competences directly. For example, it may demonstrate that one organisation is poorer at customer service than another but not show the underlying reasons. However, if well directed, it could encourage managers to seek out these reasons and hence understand how competences could be improved.

3.3 SWOT analysis

The key 'strategic messages' from both the environment (Chapter 3) and this chapter can be summarised in the form of an analysis of strengths, weaknesses, opportunities and threats – **SWOT**.

The well-known SWOT analysis is every student's favourite security blanket, often thrown into a report or assignment with little thought as to its power, despite its apparent simplicity. Therein lies the danger of all strategy models. Very often, the simpler they are, the deeper the thinking and reflection that needs to occur to apply them. This is also the case with SWOT, which stands for:

- Strengths
- Weaknesses
- Opportunities
- Threats.

Often attributed to Albert Humphrey at the Stanford Research Institute in the 1960s, a SWOT analysis can be conducted for a company, product, place, industry or person. In organisational strategy, the strengths and weaknesses must be derived from an analysis of the organisation's resources, capabilities and competences, whereas opportunities and threats should be derived from an analysis of the external environment. It is for this reason that SWOT should be seen as a **second stage** analytical tool – what we might call a 'synthesis' tool, which brings internal and external factors together and helps ensure strategic 'fit' between the two for strategic and operational effectiveness.

A SWOT analysis summarises the key issues from an analysis of the business environment and the strategic capability of an organisation. Rather than just listing these in terms of perceptions, the idea is to undertake a more structured analysis, so as to contribute to the formulation of strategy – providing a basis upon which to generate strategic options and assess future courses of action. The goal is to identify the extent to which the current strategy of an organisation and its more specific strengths and weaknesses are relevant to, and capable of, dealing with the changes taking place in the business environment. It can also be used to assess whether there are opportunities to exploit further the unique resources or core competences of the organisation.

The procedure is:

- Identify the key changes in the organisation's environment following the analyses outlined in the previous section. It is helpful if the list does not exceed seven or eight key points that represent the opportunities and threats.
- Undertake the same process for the resource profile and competences of the organisation, following the analysis outlined in this section to identify the organisation's strengths and weaknesses. It is useful to keep the total list to no more than eight points. It is important to avoid over-generalising this analysis and to keep to quite specific points: a statement such as 'poor management' means very little and could be interpreted in any number of ways. If it really means that senior managers have not been good at managing change in the organisation, that is a more specific and more useful point.

When this is completed, the analysis should look something like that shown in Table 4.2 and should provide some useful strategic insights. This example is a SWOT analysis completed by an internal organisational development team within an organisation in the communications sector. Some issues could be either opportunities or threats, depending on the extent to which the organisation can capitalise on its strengths. An analysis of perceived weaknesses should also recognise that their importance varies depending on the types of strategy the organisation is likely to pursue.

 STOP AND THINK 4.4

Conduct a SWOT analysis for an organisation that is familiar to you.

TABLE 4.2 Sample SWOT analysis

STRENGTHS	WEAKNESSES
■ Consultancy skills ■ Diversity of background experience and skills ■ Much experience in delivering to meet 'bottom line' business need ■ Capability in team and individual development ■ Change and transition expertise ■ Knowledge of learning technology ■ Design and implementation of leadership development programmes ■ Good understanding of the business ■ Good sector experience	■ Admin support ■ Lack of large-scale organisation change experience ■ 'Business' experience (i.e. line experience) ■ Global 'teamwork' ■ Not sufficiently visible! ■ Multi-cultural imbalance
OPPORTUNITIES	THREATS
■ Leadership development and cultural intelligence ■ Team development opportunities in new structure ■ Commissioning/partnering external with external contractors ■ We have wide skill base which we must be able to focus as required	■ Credibility with top management ■ Capability of senior management to support ■ Pressure on numbers ■ Lack of 'multiculturalism'/global mind ■ Infrastructure support in the company ■ Lack of funding

The SWOT analysis is thus a useful tool for understanding and decision-making for all sorts of situations in organisations. It complements and draws from the PESTEL framework for external analyses. Adaptations of the SWOT framework include the TOWS matrix, shown in Figure 4.6. Clearly an organisation would want to leverage its strengths to address the opportunities identified, and eliminate or diminish its weaknesses to mitigate external threats.

A SWOT analysis is only really helpful, however, if it is comparative. It should help focus discussion on future choices and the extent to which an organisation is capable of supporting these strategies. There are, however, limitations:

■ **Strengths may not lead to an advantage**. A firm's strengths and capabilities, no matter how unique or impressive, may not enable it to achieve a competitive advantage in the marketplace. The skills of a highly creative product designer would offer little competitive advantage to a firm that produces low-cost commodity products. Indeed, the additional expense of hiring such an individual could erode the firm's cost advantages. If a firm builds its strategy on a capability that cannot by itself create or sustain competitive advantage, it is essentially a wasted use of resources.

■ **SWOT's focus on the external environment is too narrow**. Strategists who rely on traditional definitions of their industry and competitive environment often focus their sights too narrowly on current customers, technologies and competitors. Hence they fail to notice important changes on the periphery of their environment that may trigger the need to redefine industry boundaries and identify a whole new set of competitive relationships. For example, the *Encyclopaedia Britannica*'s competitive position was severely eroded by a non-traditional competitor – initially CD-based encyclopaedias that could be used on home computers.

■ **SWOT gives a single view of a moving target**. A key weakness of SWOT is that it is primarily a static assessment that may focus too much of a firm's attention on one moment in time. Essentially, this is like studying a single frame of a film. You may be able to identify the principal actors and learn something about the setting, but it does not tell you much about the plot! Competition among organisations is played out over time. As circumstances, capabilities and strategies change, a static analysis does not reveal the dynamics of the competitive environment.

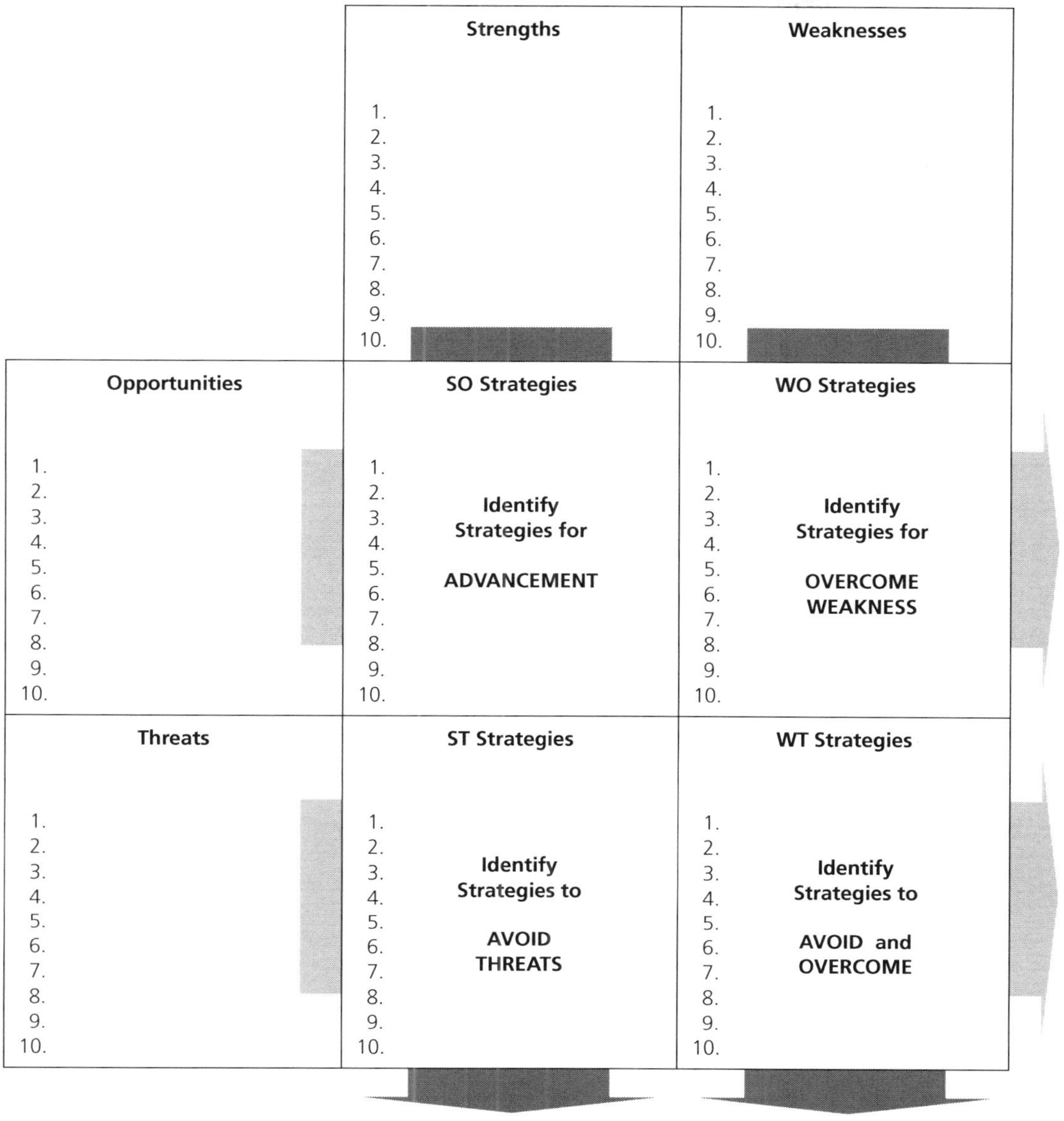

	Strengths	Weaknesses
	1. 2. 3. 4. 5. 6. 7. 8. 9. 10.	1. 2. 3. 4. 5. 6. 7. 8. 9. 10.
Opportunities 1. 2. 3. 4. 5. 6. 7. 8. 9. 10.	**SO Strategies** 1. 2. 3. 4. 5. 6. 7. 8. 9. 10. **Identify Strategies for ADVANCEMENT**	**WO Strategies** 1. 2. 3. 4. 5. 6. 7. 8. 9. 10. **Identify Strategies for OVERCOME WEAKNESS**
Threats 1. 2. 3. 4. 5. 6. 7. 8. 9. 10.	**ST Strategies** 1. 2. 3. 4. 5. 6. 7. 8. 9. 10. **Identify Strategies to AVOID THREATS**	**WT Strategies** 1. 2. 3. 4. 5. 6. 7. 8. 9. 10. **Identify Strategies to AVOID and OVERCOME**

FIGURE 4.6 TOWS example

- **SWOT over-emphasises a single dimension of strategy**. Sometimes firms become preoccupied with a single strength and ignore other factors needed for competitive success. For example, Food Lion, a large grocery retailer, paid a heavy price for its excessive emphasis on cost control. The resulting problems with labour and negative publicity led to its eventual withdrawal from several markets.

SWOT analysis has much to offer, but only as a starting point. By itself, it rarely helps a firm develop competitive advantages that it can sustain over time. Thus for business strategists, and strategy students, the use of SWOT and its derivatives come with a health warning: SWOT should be used as a second stage synthesis tool and its simplicity should not mask the need for deep thinking about the organisation. This is especially true of long-established managers, whose knowledge of their organisation may be based on outdated assumptions or 'group think'. It is for this reason that a strategist should approach the strategy process, and SWOT, much like a management consultant, challenging all internal assumptions and looking for fresh evidence to support them.

3.4 McKinsey's 7S model – ensuring strategic harmony throughout your organisation

A popular and long-lasting strategy model is McKinsey's 7S model, which was developed in the early 1980s by two of McKinsey's consultants, Tom Peters and Robert Waterman. Tom Peters went on to fame with his book *In Search of Excellence*. The 7S model is based on alignment between seven internal aspects of the organisation that together enable a strategy to succeed.

This model can help in a variety of ways, including:

- undertaking a gap analysis of an organisation's current situation and future desired state;
- benchmarking one organisation with another;
- improving company performance;
- exploring impact of future changes; and
- identifying weaknesses and strengths in delivering a strategy.

The McKinsey 7S model combines seven 'hard' and 'soft' elements:

Hard elements	Soft elements
Strategy	Shared values
Structure	Skills
Systems	Style
	Staff

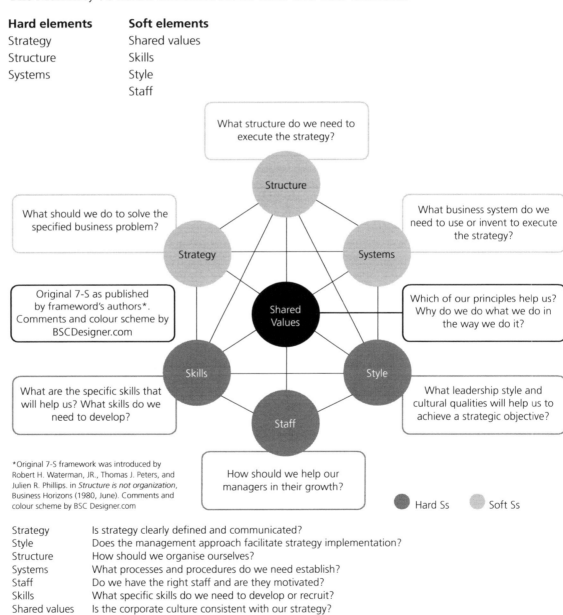

Strategy	Is strategy clearly defined and communicated?
Style	Does the management approach facilitate strategy implementation?
Structure	How should we organise ourselves?
Systems	What processes and procedures do we need establish?
Staff	Do we have the right staff and are they motivated?
Skills	What specific skills do we need to develop or recruit?
Shared values	Is the corporate culture consistent with our strategy?

FIGURE 4.7 The McKinsey 7S model

Hard elements can be influenced by management relatively easily, whereas soft elements can be difficult to define, identify and manage, and are heavily influenced by corporate culture. All the elements are inter-related, however, as can be seen in Figure 4.7. It is normal to depict the model around the 'Shared values' element. These are considered central to the organisation, all arising from why the organisation was created, what its purpose is and what it stands for.

For an organisation to perform well, all seven elements must be aligned. As with all strategy models, it does not tell us the right answer, but prompts us to ask the right questions. A useful application of the 7S model is to undertake a 'gap analysis' – for example, to benchmark your own organisation against a competitor by giving a score to each factor to produce a visual depiction of your organisation compared to others, thus identifying where priorities should be given. Figure 4.8 gives an example.

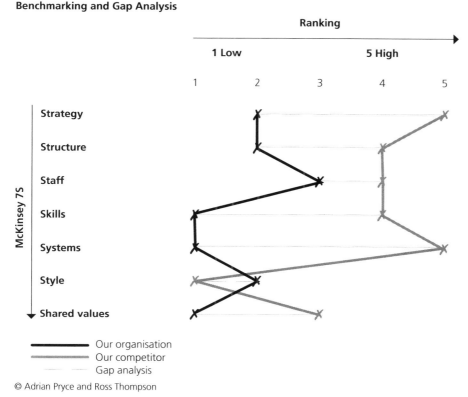

FIGURE 4.8 Gap analysis

The model can be applied to almost any organisation or team. Any difficulties in implementing a strategy will often be caused by an inconsistency between the 7S factors. Once this inconsistency is identified, it can then be worked on and resolved.

McKinsey's 7S model has the benefit of simplicity yet depth, addressing tangible and intangible elements of an organisation and the inter-connectedness of these. It can be used at any point in the strategy process, and as a comparative tool across time, projects and organisations for benchmarking purposes. Used in conjunction with Kaplan's Balanced Scorecard model (see Chapter 12), the McKinsey 7S model can be a powerful tool to link strategy with operational tactics.

Its limitations are that it contains no external environment (input)/throughput (output) element, no performance variables and no feedback loops. Other similar models that the reader may wish to look into include Galbraith's Star Model (developed in the 1960s), the Weisbord Six Box Model (1970s) and the Burke-Litwin Model (1990s).

TEST YOUR KNOWLEDGE 4.3

a   Explain the purpose of value chain analysis.
b   What is meant by the term value network/system?
c   Identify the limitations of SWOT analysis.
d   Identify and explain the 'hard' and 'soft' elements of the McKinsey 7S model

With reference to the organisation you chose in Stop and Think 4.1, which of the capabilities might be especially important in terms of achieving competitive advantage and why?

4   Managing strategic capability

4.1 Developing strategic capabilities

This section considers what managers might do, in addition to these assessments, to manage and improve the strategic capability of their organisation.

There is a range of ways in which managers might develop strategic capabilities:

- **Adding and changing capabilities**. Capabilities could be added or changed so that they reinforce outcomes against critical success factors. For example, could faster ways be found of responding to customer needs?
- **Extending capabilities**. Managers might identify strategic capabilities in one area of the business, perhaps customer service in one geographic business unit of a multinational, that are not present in others. They might then seek to extend this throughout all the business units. That said, Maritan and Brush (2003) argue that the capabilities of one part of an organisation might not be easily transferred to another because of the problems of managing change (see Chapter 13).
- **Stretching capabilities**. Managers may see the opportunity to build new products or services out of existing capabilities. Indeed, building new businesses in this way is the basis of related diversification (see Chapter 11).
- **Creating 'something from nothing'**. Strategic capabilities may be built by exploiting resources, skills and knowledge that have been ignored or rejected by others. For example, social networks ignored by others have been used for building technology businesses and information systems. Designers experiment with different configurations to create new systems drawing from their and others' experience.
- **Ceasing activities**. Activities not central to delivering value to customers could be stopped, outsourced or reduced in cost. This is what new industry entrants in the airline industry, such as Ryanair or EasyJet, did to create new business models for low-cost airlines.
- **External capability development**. There may be ways of developing capabilities by looking externally. For example, managers may seek to develop or learn new capabilities by acquisition or by entering into alliances and joint ventures (see Chapter 9).

4.2 People and strategic capability

One of the lessons of this chapter is that strategic capability often lies in the day-to-day activities that people undertake in organisations, so developing the ability of people to recognise the relevance of what they do in terms of the strategic capability of the organisation is significant.

- **Targeted training and development**. For strategic purposes, it may be important to target the development of competences that can provide competitive advantage. For example, an engineering business, while acknowledging the abilities its personnel had in the technical aspects of engineering products, recognised that these were attributes that competitors had too, and that there was a need to develop people's abilities to innovate more around value-adding customer service.
- **Talent management practices**. These might be employed to develop particular competences. For example, an oil company that sought to build its competitive advantage on developing

close customer relationships in markets for industrial oils did so by ensuring that senior field managers with an aptitude for this were promoted and sent to different parts of the world that needed to be developed in such ways.

- **Organisational learning**. In fast-changing conditions, successful firms are those that have grown the dynamic capabilities to readjust required competences continually. In effect their competence becomes that of learning and development. In this context the characteristics of what has become known as a 'learning organisation' may become especially important (see Chapter 9). Since this may require the acceptance that different, even conflicting, ideas and views are valuable and that experimentation is the norm, managers need to consider how to protect and foster such behaviour. For example, it may be that those within the organisation who show most ability to contribute to such learning are the least powerful, perhaps quite junior in the hierarchy. They may need the protection of more powerful people.

4.3 Cost efficiency

Managers often regard the management of costs as a key strategic capability. Customers can benefit from cost efficiencies in terms of lower prices or more product features for the same price. The management of the cost base of an organisation could also be a basis for achieving competitive advantage.

If cost is to be managed effectively, attention has to be paid to key cost drivers:

- **Economies of scale**. These may be especially important in manufacturing organisations, since the high capital costs of plant need to be recovered over a high volume of output – for example, motor vehicles, chemicals and metals. In other industries, such as drinks and tobacco and food, scale economies are important in distribution or marketing.
- **Supply costs**. Location may influence supply costs, which is why, historically, steel and glass manufacturing were close to raw material or energy sources. In some instances, ownership of raw materials was a unique resource, giving cost advantage. Supply costs are of particular importance to organisations that act as intermediaries, where the value added through their own activities is low and the need to identify and manage input costs is critically important to success. For example, retailers pay a great deal of attention to trying to achieve lower costs of supply than their competitors.
- **Product/process design**. Efficiency gains in production processes have been achieved by many organisations through improvements in capacity-fill, labour productivity, yield (from materials) or working capital utilisation. Understanding the relative importance of each of these to maintaining a competitive position is important. For example, in terms of managing capacity-fill: an unfilled seat in a plane, train or theatre cannot be 'stocked' for later sale. So marketing special offers (while protecting the core business) and having the IT systems to analyse and optimise revenue are important capabilities.
- **Experience**. There is evidence that experience may provide competitive advantage in particular in terms of the relationship between the cumulative experience gained by an organisation and its unit costs — described as the experience curve (see Figure 4.9). The experience curve suggests that an organisation undertaking any activity develops competences in this activity over time and therefore does it more efficiently. Unit costs should decline year on year as a

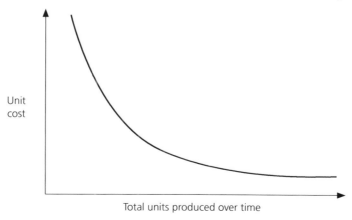

FIGURE 4.9 The experience curve

result of cumulative experience. In high-growth industries this will happen quickly, but even in mature industries a decline in costs should occur.

- **First-mover advantage**. The organisation that moves down the experience curve by entering a market first should be able to reduce its cost base because of the accumulated experience it builds up over its rivals.

However, for many organisations the management of costs is becoming a threshold strategic capability. Customers do not value product or service features at any price. If the price rises too much, they will sacrifice value and opt for lower price. So the challenge is to ensure that an appropriate level of value is offered at an acceptable price. This means that everyone is forced to keep costs as low as possible, consistent with the value provided. Not to do so invites customers to switch products or invites competition. In addition, competitive rivalry will continually require costs to be driven down, because competitors will be trying to reduce their cost so as to under-price their rivals while offering similar value.

4.4 Limitations in managing strategic capabilities

One lesson that emerges from an understanding of strategic capabilities is that the most valuable bases of strategic capability may lie in aspects of the organisation that are difficult to discern or be specific about. So, how is it possible to manage that which it is not always easy to be clear about? For example, some of the capabilities of an organisation may be lodged in activities that top management are not directly managing. It is important to understand what managers might be able to do and what they cannot do in terms of how much they understand and how much they value bases of strategic capability. Ambrosini (2003) argues that there may be different circumstances:

- **Competences are valued but not understood**. Managers may know that there are activities in their organisation that have a positive impact and may value them, but may not understand just how such positive impact arises. For example, the delivery of value may be dependent on highly specialised skills as in a cutting-edge high-tech firm, or on complex linkages far down in the organisation. The lesson here is that managers may have to be careful about disturbing the bases of such capabilities, while ensuring that they monitor the outputs and benefits created for customers.
- **Competences are not valued**. Managers may know that activities and processes exist in the organisation but not recognise their positive impact or value such activities. There are dangers here that managers take the wrong course of action. For example, they may cut out areas of activity that create actual or potential competitive advantage, perhaps because they are intent on cutting costs. It would be wise to understand the value-creating capabilities more clearly using value chain analysis before taking such decisions.
- **Competences are recognised, valued and understood**. Here managers may be able to nurture and further develop such competences. for example, by ensuring that overall company policies support and enhance them. The danger can be that top management may seek to preserve such capabilities by over-formalising or codifying them such that they become 'set in stone'.

 TEST YOUR KNOWLEDGE 4.4

a Identify two ways in which managers might develop strategic capability.
b What might an organisation do to ensure the contribution of people to the development of strategic capability?
c Explain how managing costs efficiently might contribute to the development of strategic capability.

CASE QUESTIONS

1	Provide a SWOT analysis for Asda and highlight the limitations of the approach.	**2**	Identify and explain the nature of the strategic capabilities of either Asda or Walmart.

CHAPTER SUMMARY

- Strategic capability is concerned with whether the organisation has adequate, suitable resources and competences to prosper.
- Strategic capabilities comprise both resources and competences. If organisations are to achieve competitive advantage, they require resources and competences that are both valuable to customers and difficult for competitors to imitate. These are known as core competences. The sustainability of competitive advantage depends on strategic capabilities being of value to customers, rare, inimitable or non-substitutable. In dynamic conditions, it is unlikely that such strategic capabilities will remain stable.
- Ways of assessing organisational capabilities include:
  - analysing an organisation's value chain and value network to understand how value to a customer is created and can be developed;
  - benchmarking to understand the relative performance of organisations and challenge the assumptions that managers have about the performance of their organisation; and
  - carrying out a SWOT analysis to gain an understanding of strengths, weaknesses, opportunities and threats that an organisation faces. SWOT is a second stage analytical tool that builds on prior analyses of internal resources and the external environment.
- The McKinsey 7S model is a good benchmarking tool that forces managers to think about all the components, both hard and soft, of a successful strategy.
- Managers need to think about how and to what extent they can manage the development of the strategic capabilities of their organisation by stretching and adding to such capabilities, and through the way they manage people in their organisation.

5 Strategy and organisational culture

■ CONTENTS

■ INTRODUCTION

As organisations seek to compete in ever-changing environments, they need to adapt and develop to take advantage of new opportunities. To do this effectively means more than knowing which levers to pull or which structural form to take. It also requires a deep understanding of what makes the organisation work – its culture. The challenge is to understand what culture is, how it is created and changed, and what choices are available to you.

1 Culture and history

So far, we have considered the influences of the environment and organisational capabilities on the development of strategy. It is equally important to understand how these organisational responses to the environment and strategic capabilities have come about, and how the past influences current and future strategy. The theme of this chapter is that the strategic position of an organisation has historical and cultural roots and that understanding those roots helps managers develop the future strategy of their organisations.

Many organisations have long histories. The large Japanese Mitsui Group was founded in the seventeenth century and managers in the UK retailer Sainsbury's still refer to the founding principles of the Sainsbury family in the nineteenth century. In the public sector, the police, universities and the National Health Service are strongly influenced by their historical legacies, which have become embedded in their cultures.

Johnson et al. (2014) argue that historical and cultural perspectives can help strategists to understand both the opportunities and the constraints that organisations face. The capabilities of an organisation may have historical roots and have been built up over time in ways unique to that organisation. In so doing, they may become part of the culture of an organisation – a taken-for-granted way of doing things. They may, therefore, both be difficult for other organisations to copy or to change. So, understanding the historical and cultural bases of such capabilities also informs the challenges of strategic change (Chapter 13).

This chapter highlights the importance of history and culture in relation to strategy development and identifies important challenges managers face in managing that development and how each can be analysed.

1.1 What is organisational culture?

STOP AND THINK 5.1

A number of years ago, I asked an executive to tell me what he thought organisational culture meant. He gave me essentially the same answer that a Supreme Court Justice once gave in attempting to define pornography: 'I can't define it, but I know it when I see it' (cited in Robbins and Judge, 2015, p.496).
    How would you define organisational culture?

Most of us understand what is meant by **organisational culture**. Although we may not always be conscious of it, culture has a pervasive influence over people's behaviour and actions. However, it is a difficult concept to define or explain precisely. There is no real consensus on its meaning or its application to the analysis of work organisations. A popular and simple way of defining culture, used by Deal and Kennedy (1982) among others, is: 'How things are done around here'. In this section, we propose more specific definitions and review several issues that emerge from these.

The concept of culture has developed from anthropology and there seems to be some agreement in the definitions in the literature that organisational culture refers to a system of shared meaning that members hold which distinguishes the organisation from other organisations. This system of shared meaning is a set of key characteristics that the organisation values; these form the basis for the shared understanding that members have about the organisation, how things are done in it and the way members are supposed to behave.

CASE EXAMPLE 5.1

Contrasting cultures

Organisation A

This organisation is a manufacturing firm. Managers are expected to document all decisions; and 'good managers' are those who can provide detailed data to support their recommendations. Decisions that incur risk or involve change are not encouraged. Managers of failed projects are openly criticised and penalised. Management is concerned with high productivity, regardless of the impact on employee morale or turnover. There are exhaustive rules and regulations that employees are required to follow and managers supervise employees closely. Work activities are designed around individuals. There are distinct departments and lines of authority, and employees are expected to minimise formal contact with other employees outside their functional area or line of command. Performance evaluations and rewards emphasise individual effort, although seniority tends to be the primary factor in determining pay raises and promotions.

Organisation B

This organisation is also a manufacturing firm but here management encourages and rewards risk-taking and change. Decisions based on intuition are valued as much as those that appear rational. Management prides itself on experimenting with new technologies and its success in regularly introducing innovative products. Failures are treated as 'learning experiences'. The company prides itself on being responsive to the changing needs of its customers. There are few rules for employees to follow, and supervision is loose because management believes that its employees are hardworking and trustworthy. Management is concerned with high productivity, but believes that this comes through treating its people appropriately. The company is proud of its reputation as being a good place to work. Jobs are designed around work teams, and team members are encouraged to interact with others across functions and authority levels. Teams have goals, and bonuses are based on achievement of these outcomes. Employees are given considerable autonomy in choosing the means by which the goals are attained.

A more precise definition of culture is 'the collection of traditions, values, policies, beliefs, and attitudes that constitute a pervasive context for everything we do and think in an organisation' (McLean and Marshall, 1993). Culture is reinforced through the system of rites and **rituals**, patterns of communication, the informal organisation, expected patterns of behaviour and perceptions of the psychological contract.

Schein (1985) suggests a view of organisational culture based on distinguishing three levels of culture: artefacts, values and basic assumptions.

1   **Artefacts**. The most visible level of the culture; the constructed physical and social environment. This includes physical space and layout, written and spoken language, and the overt behaviour of group members.
2   **Values**. Ideas about how to deal with a new task, issue or problem are based on convictions. If the idea works, the value can transform into a belief. Values and beliefs become part of the process by which group members justify actions and behaviour. These values and beliefs may be espoused and explicit, or simply replicated in behaviour.
3   **Basic underlying assumptions**. When a solution to a problem works repeatedly it comes to be taken for granted. Basic assumptions are unconsciously held learned responses. They are implicit assumptions that guide behaviour and determine how group members perceive, think and feel about things.

Schein suggests that the basic assumptions are the essence – what culture really is – and values and behaviours are observed manifestations of this cultural essence. His model is shown in Figure 5.1.

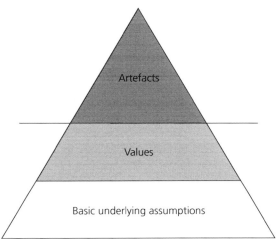

FIGURE 5.1 Components of culture (Schein, 1985)

An important point here is that culture is a descriptive term. Organisational culture can be likened to the organisation's 'personality'. It is concerned with how employees perceive the characteristics of an organisation's culture and not with whether they like them or not. Research on organisational culture has sought to measure how employees see their organisation, whether it encourages teamwork, rewards innovation or, instead, stifles initiative.

1.2 Strategic drift

Case example 5.2 illustrates what Johnson et al. (2014) and others have referred to as **strategic drift**, which is the tendency for strategies to develop incrementally on the basis of historical and cultural influences, but fail to keep pace with a changing environment. The reasons and consequences of strategic drift are important as it helps explain why organisations often run out of steam. As we saw in Chapter 1, organisational strategies tend to change gradually. As well as the emergent nature of strategy, there is a tendency for strategies to develop on the basis of what the organisation has done in the past, especially if that has been successful. This is shown in Figure 5.2 (page 108).

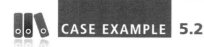

CASE EXAMPLE 5.2

Kodak, the manufacturer of photographic film and cameras, was one of the world's most valuable brands. Based in Rochester, New York State, Kodak had 90% share of film and 85% share of camera sales in the US by 1976. By 1999, profits were nearly $2.5 billion on a turnover of around $16 billion. But by 2011, Kodak's traditional photography business had been almost entirely eroded – first by digital cameras and then by smartphones – and in 2012, Kodak filed for bankruptcy protection. In 2014 it was still loss-making, with a turnover of around $2 billion.

Initially known for its innovative technology and marketing, Kodak had developed digital camera technology by 1975, but did not launch digital cameras until the late 1990s, by which time it was too late. How did Kodak miss such a fundamental shift in the market?

According to Steve Sasson, the engineer who invented the first digital camera, the response to his invention in Kodak was dismissive, because it was filmless photography. There were similar responses to early internal intelligence reports on digital technology: a former Kodak executive recalls writing a report in 1979 detailing fairly accurately how different parts of the market would switch from film to digital, starting with government reconnaissance, then professional photography and finally the mass market, all by 2010.

The Kodak response was to use digital to enhance the film business. For example, in 1996, Kodak launched a film system using digital technology to provide users with a preview of shots taken and to indicate the number of prints required. It flopped.

Executives in the film division carried the most weight in the company, and they were over-confident about Kodak's brand strength. They also misjudged the speed of the change in customer buying preferences. For example, they believed that people in fast-developing markets such as China would buy lots of film, but many moved from no camera at all to digital.

Rosabeth Moss Kanter of Harvard Business School also pointed to the Kodak culture: 'Working in a one company town did not help… Kodak's bosses in Rochester seldom heard much criticism…' Moreover, 'executives suffered from a mentality of perfect products, rather than the hi-tech mind-set of make it, launch it, fix it.' They also moved slowly: 'Even when Kodak decided to diversify, it took years to make its first acquisition.' Kodak's attempts to diversify by developing the thousands of chemicals that its researchers had created for use in film for the drug market also failed. In 1989, the Kodak board needed to choose a new CEO and opted for a long-serving executive in the traditional film business, rather than a candidate more associated with digital technology. As late as 2007, a Kodak marketing video announced that 'Kodak is back' and 'wasn't going to play grab ass anymore' with digital.

In 2014, the company was in the midst of a two-year restructure, streamlining its complex infrastructure, making large cost reductions and exiting non-core businesses – including the spin-off of its consumer imaging and document imaging businesses that now operate under new ownership. Kodak describes itself as 'leaner, financially stronger and ready to grow'.

Sources: *The Economist*, 'The last Kodak moment?' 14 January 2012; New York Times, 9 December 1989; Chunka Mui, 'How Kodak failed', Forbes, 18 January 2012; www.kodak.com.

Phase 1: Incremental change

In most successful businesses there are usually long periods of relative continuity during which established strategy remains largely unchanged or changes very incrementally. There may be good reason for this as the environment could be changing gradually and the organisation is simply keeping in line with those changes through incremental change. But there may be a natural unwillingness on the part of managers to change a strategy significantly if it has been successful in the past, especially if it is built on capabilities that have been shown to be the basis of competitive advantage, as can be seen in the Kodak example. In addition, managers may have learned how to build variations around their successful formula, in effect experimenting without moving too far from their capability base – an example of the 'logical incrementalism' discussed in Chapter 1. The challenge for managers, however, is for how long and to what extent relying on incremental change to build on the past is sufficient. When should they make more fundamental strategic changes? How are they to detect when this is necessary?

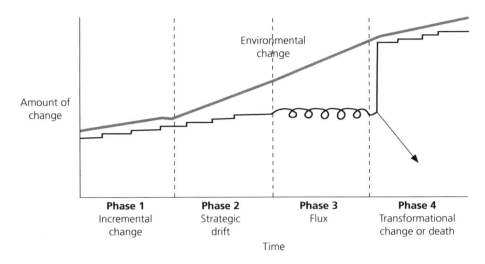

FIGURE 5.2 Strategic drift

From *Exploring Strategy*, 9th edition, Johnson et al, Pearson Education Limited, © Pearson Education 2002, 2011

Phase 2: Strategic drift

While an organisation's strategy may continue to change incrementally, it may not change in line with the environment. Phase 2 shows environmental change accelerating, but it is not always sudden. For Kodak, there was the growing share of its digital rivals, accompanied by the growth of smartphones. These changes, however, had been taking place for a number of years. The problem that gives rise to strategic drift is that, as with many organisations, Kodak's strategy was not keeping pace with these changes. If strategic drift continues, there may be a downturn in financial performance or a loss in market share. Even the most successful companies may drift in this way becoming victims of the very success of their past.

Phase 3: Flux

A period of flux may be triggered by the downturn in performance. Strategies may change, but in no very clear direction. There may also be management changes, often at the very top, as the organisation comes under pressure from its stakeholders, not least shareholders. There may be internal rivalry as to which strategy to follow, quite likely based on differences of opinion as to whether future strategy should be based on historic capabilities or whether those capabilities are becoming redundant. Indeed, this happened at Kodak due to the power wielded by the traditional film division. All this may result in a further loss of confidence in the organisation: perhaps a further drop in performance or share price, or a further seepage of customers' loyalty.

Phase 4: Transformational change or death

The outcome will be one of three possibilities: the organisation may die; it may get taken over by another organisation; or it may go through a period of transformational change, as is happening at Kodak. This may involve multiple changes related to strategy, such as a change in products or market focus, changes of capabilities on which the strategy is based, changes in the top management and perhaps the way the organisation is structured. Transformational change does not take place frequently in organisations and is usually the result of a major downturn in performance. Johnson et al. (2014) argue that this may sometimes be too late. Competitive position may have been lost, shareholder value has probably already been destroyed and many jobs will have been lost too.

The time when 'making a difference' really matters most is in phase two when the organisation is beginning to drift. In a study of 215 major UK firms, Johnson et al. (2009) identified that just eight had effected major transformational change without performance decline. The problem is that drift is not easy to see before performance suffers. As Johnson et al. (2014) put it:

'... in understanding the strategic position of an organisation so as to avoid the damaging effects of strategic drift, it is vital to take seriously the extent to which historical tendencies in strategy development tend to persist in the cultural fabric of organisations.' (p.166)

This then is the vital link between culture and strategy and the rest of this chapter explores this in more detail. The challenge is also how to manage change in such circumstances and this is examined in Chapter 13 on managing strategic change.

1.3 The influence of the past

Culture develops over time and in response to a complex set of factors. Handy (1993) has identified a number of key influences that are likely to play an important role in the development of any corporate culture (see section 4 for more detail). He argues that the reason and manner in which the organisation was originally formed, its age and the philosophy and values of its owners and first senior managers will affect culture. A key event in the organisation's history such as a merger or major reorganisation, or new chief executive or set of top managers, may bring about a change in culture as well as its structural form. Describing corporate history can be an effective induction tool and help integrate acquisitions and new employees by infusion with the organisation's culture and identity.

Top managers can also have considerable influence on the nature of corporate culture. An example is the key role played by Richard Branson at Virgin. But all members of staff help to shape the dominant culture of an organisation, irrespective of what senior management believe it should be. Culture is also determined by the staff employed and whether they truly accept management philosophy and policies or only pay lip service to them.

Management style may also have its roots in history. This may be not only in terms of the values of the founder, which indeed may have a strong influence, but also in the interplay between past ways of doing things and the lessons learned from the organisation's evolving environment. However, management style may not always have such a beneficial effect. The evolution of management style may be not in line with the needs of a changing environment, but over-influenced and bound by the past. Capabilities that are rooted in tradition may become entrenched. The capabilities that were once the bases of competitive advantage and success will then become core rigidities, leading to strategic drift (explained in Section 1.2).

 **CASE EXAMPLE** 5.3

Tesco is one of the most successful international retailers. In its early days it was a family firm run by Jack Cohen, who was renowned for his blunt and authoritative style. This gave rise to internal conflicts and between suppliers and Tesco. The historic conflict has evolved into productive challenge and rivalry between managers and different parts of the firm that, arguably, have substantially contributed to its innovation and success. Others might point out that this could also have contributed to the accounting scandal that hit Tesco in September 2014, when the supermarket chain stunned investors with the news that it had misstated its half-year profit guidance by £250 million – a figure that was subsequently revised to £263 million.

Johnson et al. (2009); BBC Business News 24 March 2015

There are other reasons why understanding history can help in understanding the strategic position of an organisation and in the management of strategy. Johnson et al. (2014) point to the following factors.

Managers' organisational experience

Managers may have spent many years in an organisation or in an industry. The experience on which they base their decisions may be heavily influenced by that history. How can managers stand back from that history to understand the influence it has?

Avoiding 'recency' bias

Managers can give too much weight to recent events or performance, forgetting past patterns, resulting in either undue optimism or undue pessimism. Understanding the current situation in terms of the past can provide useful lessons. For example, have there been historical trends that may repeat themselves? An historical perspective may help managers see what gave rise to events that were seen as surprises in the past and learn from how their organisation dealt with them.

Misattribution of success?

Is it clear where current bases of success originate, how they developed and how this might inform future strategy development? The danger is that there may be a misattribution of causes of success, which may lie elsewhere. Such misattribution could in turn lead to the reinforcement of wrong behaviours.

 CASE EXAMPLE 5.4

The future strategy of an engineering firm stressed the importance of actively managing the innovation of new products and services because managers saw that its current growth was coming from such an innovation, whilst the rest of its offering was showing no growth. However, a study of the origins of innovatory products in the firm showed that the limited extent to which they occurred was largely due to what appeared to be chance, or as a result of technologies inherited from acquisitions relevant to the business's core activities. Historically, there was no evidence of innovation being internally planned or proactively managed. In this case, the historical perspective raised important questions about what the firm saw as its capabilities for managing future innovation.

'What if?' questions

History can also encourage managers to imagine what might have happened had there been other influences in the environment, different responses from customers or competitors, or different initiatives or leadership within their organisation. It makes the present more evidently a product of circumstances and thus less fixed. So potentially it opens up the possibilities for changes in the future.

Detecting and avoiding strategic drift

If managers sensitise themselves to the influence of the history of their organisation they stand a better chance of seeing current strategy. Managers are more likely to be able to question the extent to which the strategy they are seeking to develop is usefully informed by that history as distinct from being driven or captured by it.

History, then, is important in terms of how it influences current strategy for better or worse. If the tendency for strategic drift is to be understood, the history of organisations needs to be taken seriously by strategists. History becomes 'encapsulated in culture'. Understanding an organisation's culture is one way of understanding the historical influences that can be very powerful. The next section explains how culture can be analysed.

 TEST YOUR KNOWLEDGE 5.1

a   Define organisational culture.
b   Explain what is meant by strategic drift.
c   Explain why the past is important to strategy development.

2 Understanding culture

2.1 Cultural frames of reference

Cultural influences on behaviour exist at several levels, as Figure 5.3 shows. This section discusses these and examines how organisational culture can be analysed and characterised in order to understand the influences of culture on organisational strategy.

As well as the organisation's culture, Johnson et al. (2014) argue that are three other cultural frames of reference that have an impact on the individual in the organisation.

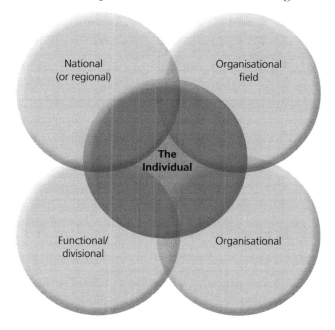

FIGURE 5.3 Cultural frames of reference

From *Exploring Strategy*, 9th edition, Johnson et al, Pearson Education Limited, © Pearson Education 2002, 2011

National and regional cultures

Attitudes to work, authority and other important factors differ from one country to another. Powerful cultural forces concerned with history, religion and even climate have shaped such differences over many centuries. it may also be important to understand subnational (usually regional) cultures. For example, attitudes to some aspects of employment and supplier relationships may differ at a regional level even in a relatively small and cohesive country like the UK, and quite markedly elsewhere in Europe (for example, between northern and southern Italy). We explore national cultures later in the chapter.

The organisational field

The culture of an organisation is also shaped by work-based groupings, such as an industry or profession. This organisational field is a community of organisations that interact more frequently with one another than with those outside the field and which have developed a degree of shared meaning. Such organisations may share a common technology, set of regulations or education and training, and thus tend to cohere around a set of assumptions, norms and routines held in common. For example, there are many organisations in the organisational field of justice, such as lawyers, police, courts, prisons and probation services. The role of each is different and they may differ in their views about justice, but all are committed to the principle of justice.

Organisational subcultures

Some aspects of culture pervade the whole organisation. However, there may be subcultures that relate directly to the structure, such as functional groups – finance, marketing, operations, etc. Different divisions may pursue different types of strategy or hold different values, and these may foster different cultures. Aligning strategy and organisational culture is a critical feature of successful organisations.

2.2   Types of culture

There are a number of ways in which to classify different types of organisational culture. For example, developing the ideas of Harrison, Handy (1993) describes four main types of organisational culture: power culture; role culture; task culture; and person culture. These are shown in Figure 5.4. This model links organisational culture to structure.

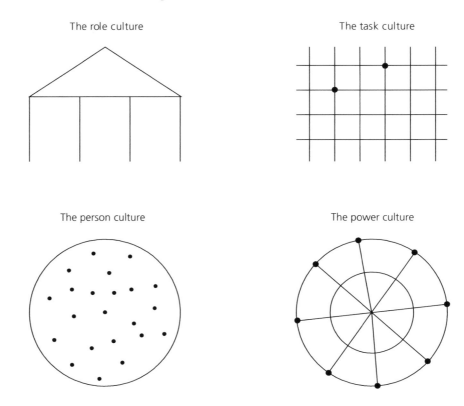

FIGURE 5.4 Harrison and Handy's cultural types

- **Power culture**. This depends on a central power source with lines of influence from the central figure extending throughout the organisation. A power culture is frequently found in small entrepreneurial organisations and relies on trust, empathy and personal communication for its effectiveness. Control is exercised from the centre by appointing key individuals. There are few rules and procedures and little bureaucracy. It is a political organisation with decisions taken largely through the balance of influence.
- **Role culture**. This is often stereotyped as a bureaucracy and works by logic and rationality. It is characterised by Handy as a temple. Role culture rests on the strength of strong organisational 'pillars' – the functions of specialists in, for example, finance, purchasing and production. The work of and interaction between the specialists is controlled by procedures and rules, and coordinated at the top by a small group of senior managers. Job description is often more important than the individual and position is the main source of power.
- **Task culture**. This is job- or project-oriented. In structural terms, the task culture can be likened to a net, some strands of which are stronger than others, and with much of the power and influence at the interstices. An example is the matrix organisational form. Task culture seeks to bring together the right resources and people, and uses the unifying power of the group. Influence is widely spread and based more on expert power than on position or personal power.
- **Person culture**. This has the individual as the central focus and any structure exists to serve the individuals within it. When a group decide that it is in their interests to share office space, equipment or clerical assistance, for example, the resulting organisation has a person culture. Examples are groups of barristers, architects, doctors or consultants. Although it is found in only a few organisations, many individuals have a preference for the person culture – for example, university professors and specialists. Management hierarchies and control mechanisms are possible only by mutual consent. Individuals have almost complete autonomy and any influence over them is likely to be on the basis of personal power.

From an examination of hundreds of business organisations and their environments, Deal and Kennedy (1982) categorise corporate cultures according to two determining factors in the marketplace:

1   the degree of risk associated with the organisation's activities; and
2   the speed at which organisations and their employees receive feedback on the success of decisions or strategies.

These factors give rise to four generic types of culture: the tough-guy, macho culture; the work-hard/play-hard culture; the bet-your-company culture; and the process culture (see Figure 5.5).

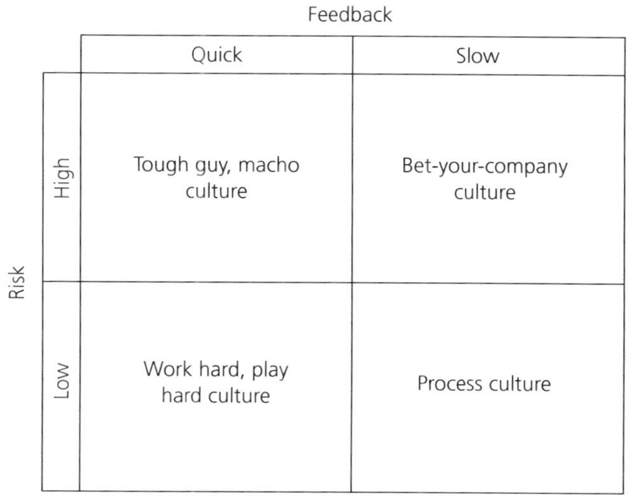

Feedback

	Quick	Slow
High	Tough guy, macho culture	Bet-your-company culture
Low	Work hard, play hard culture	Process culture

Risk

FIGURE 5.5 Deal and Kennedy's model of organisational culture (Deal and Kennedy, 1982)

- **Tough-guy, macho culture**. This involves an organisation of individualists who frequently take high risks and receive quick feedback on the efficacy of their actions. Examples cited include police departments, surgeons, construction, management consulting and the entertainment industry. Financial stakes are high and there is a focus on speed. The intense pressure and frenetic pace often results in early burnout. Internal competition and conflict are normal; stars are temperamental but tolerated. A high staff turnover can create difficulties in building a strong cohesive culture.
- **Work-hard/play-hard culture**. This is characterised by fun and action where employees take some risks, all with quick feedback. There is a high level of relatively low-risk activity. Examples include sales organisations such as estate agents, mass consumer companies such as McDonald's, and retail stores. Organisations tend to be highly dynamic and the primary value centres on customers and their needs. It is the team that produces and the culture encourages meetings, promotions and conventions to help maintain motivation. However, although a lot gets done, volume can be at the expense of quality.
- **Bet-your-company culture**. Here there are decisions with high risks and stakes but slow feedback, so it may be years before employees know if decisions were successful. Examples include oil companies, pharmaceutical businesses and architectural firms. The focus is on the future and the importance of investing in it. There is a sense of deliberateness throughout the organisation typified by the ritual of the business meeting. There is a hierarchical system of authority with decision-making from the top down. The culture leads to high-quality inventions and scientific breakthroughs, but moves only very slowly and is vulnerable to short-term fluctuations.
- **Process culture**. This is a low-risk, slow-feedback culture where employees find difficulty in measuring what they do. Typical historical examples include banks, insurance companies, financial services and the Civil Service. The individual financial stakes are low, and employees get relatively little feedback on their effectiveness. Their work and output seems to disappear into a void. Lack of feedback forces employees to focus on *how* they do something not *what* they do. People tend to cover their backs, and bureaucracy results in attention to minor detail, formality and technical perfection. Process cultures can be effective when there is a need for order and predictability.

2.3 Analysing culture – the cultural web

Johnson et al. (2014) offer the cultural web as another way of representing the prevailing paradigm of an organisation through analysing and observing the way in which the organisation actually behaves, seeking clues about the taken-for-granted assumptions. It is like trying to describe an iceberg by observing the parts of the iceberg that show above the water and, from this, inferring what the submerged part of the iceberg must look like.

Figure 5.6 outlines some of the issues that might help build up an understanding of culture through the elements of the cultural web.

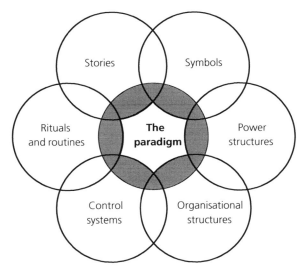

FIGURE 5.6 The cultural web

From *Exploring Strategy*, 9th edition, Johnson et al, Pearson Education Limited, © Pearson Education 2002, 2011

- **Rituals and routines.** The routine ways that members of the organisation behave towards each other, and towards those outside organisation, make up 'the way we do things around here'. The rituals of organisational life are the special events through which the organisation emphasises what is particularly important and reinforces culture. Examples include relatively formal organisational processes – training programmes, promotion and assessment procedures, sales conferences, and so on. An extreme example is the ritualistic training of army recruits to prepare them for the discipline required in armed conflict. However, rituals can also be thought of as relatively informal processes, such as drinks in the pub after work.
- **Stories.** Told by members of the organisation to each other, to outsiders, to new recruits, and so on, they embed the organisation's history and indicate important events and personalities. They typically concern successes, disasters, heroes, villains and mavericks that deviate from the norm. They distil the essence of an organisation's past and legitimise types of behaviour.
- **Symbols.** Logos, offices, cars and titles, or the type of language and terminology commonly used, become a shorthand for the nature of the organisation. For example, in long-established or conservative organisations it is likely that there will be many symbols of hierarchy or deference to do with formal office layout, differences in privileges between levels of management, the way in which people address each other. In turn, this formalisation may reflect difficulties in changing strategies within a hierarchical or deferential system.
- **Power structures.** These are also likely to be associated with the key assumptions. The most powerful groupings within the organisation are likely to he closely associated with this set of core assumptions and beliefs. For example, accountancy firms may offer a range of services, but typically the most powerful individuals are qualified chartered accountants with experience in the audit practice. Power may be based not just on seniority. In some organisations, power could be lodged within other levels or functions, for example, with technical experts in a high-tech firm.
- **Control systems.** Alongside measurements and reward systems, they emphasise what it is important to monitor in the organisation, and to focus attention and activity upon. Reward systems are important influences. For example, an organisation with individually based bonus schemes related to volume could find it difficult to promote strategies requiring teamwork and an emphasis on quality rather than volume.

- **Organisational structure**. This is likely to reflect power structures and, again, delineate important relationships and emphasise what is important in the organisation. Formal hierarchical, mechanistic structures may emphasise that strategy is the province of top managers and everyone else is 'working to orders'. Highly devolved structures may signify that collaboration is less important than competition and so on.
- **Paradigm**. The paradigm of the organisation encapsulates and reinforces the behaviours observed in the other elements of the cultural web. The cultural web is a useful concept for understanding the underlying paradigm of an organisation.

 STOP AND THINK 5.2

Use the cultural web to analyse the culture of your own organisation or one with which you are familiar.

Most organisations often make visible, public statements of their values, beliefs and purposes – for example, in annual reports, mission or values statements and business plans. There is a danger, however, that these will be seen as accurate descriptions of the organisational culture. This is only partly true as statements of values and beliefs are often statements of the aspirations of a particular stakeholder such as the CEO, rather than accurate descriptions of the actual culture.

The detailed 'map' produced by the cultural web is a rich source of information about an organisation's culture, but it is useful to be able to characterise the culture that the information conveys. Sometimes this is possible by means of graphic descriptors. For example, managers who undertook a cultural analysis in the NHS summed up their culture as 'The National Sickness Service'.

 TEST YOUR KNOWLEDGE 5.2

a   Outline Harrison and Handy's model of culture.
b   In which types of organisation might you expect to find each of Deal and Kennedy's cultural types?
c   Explain what is meant by 'paradigm' in the context of culture.

3   The importance of culture

3.1 Culture's role

Organisational culture can be regarded as a common perception held by the organisation's members. But acknowledging that organisational culture has common properties does not mean that there cannot be subcultures within any given culture. Most large organisations have a dominant culture and numerous sets of subcultures.

A **dominant culture** expresses the core values that are shared by a majority of the organisation's members. When we talk about an organisation's culture, we are usually referring to its dominant culture – a macro-view of culture that gives an organisation its distinct personality.

 CASE EXAMPLE 5.5

Corporate culture at Nike

Nike has an enviable brand worldwide, and is increasingly admired as an innovator. One of the most important parts of maintaining that reputation is building an extremely committed workforce. Employees appear to preach the company's values. Workers quote the company's maxims like the Ten Commandments – for example, 'Be a sponge' and 'If you have a body, you're an athlete.'

CASE EXAMPLE 5.5 *continued*

The company is intensely aware of its own history and story, and works to keep employees conscious of it. Nike keeps a Winnebago to use as a conference room in the middle of its Innovation Kitchen because cofounder Phil Knight, according to legend, first sold shoes out of a similar vehicle. That helps embed a sense of value, history and shared culture in what employees are doing. So too, oddly enough, does an emphasis on secrecy and mystery.

Secrecy can have a profoundly negative effect on corporate culture, leading to resentment and leaks, but Nike has found a way to turn it to their advantage. The attitude of secrecy about projects becomes part of an internal story – that their work has value that's worthy of being kept under wraps.

Nelson Farris, Nike's head of corporate education, describes what the company expects from its employees. 'Figure out where you want your career to go, and when you see something that would help you get there, ask us for it,' he said. That attitude helps create intensely loyal employees.

The attitude of mystery and innovation features prominently in Nike's marketing and public image as well. Culture is strongest when there's little disconnect between what the public expects and what happens within a company. That way, employees are inclined to deliver what people have come to want.

Source: Based on M. Niesen (2013) 'At Nike, workers quote the company's maxims like the Ten Commandments', www.businessinsider.com/nikes-corporate-culture-2013-2#ixzz3WLRtLw7x.

Mullins (2014) highlights several aspects of the importance of culture as follows.

Culture and work ethic

Culture can influence people's attitudes and behaviour at work. For example, a report from the Chartered Management Institute found that one in three managers felt that in their organisation there was a culture of not taking time off for sickness, and nearly half felt they would not be treated sympathetically if they took sick leave (Worrall and Cooper, 2007). Bunting (2004) maintains that it is through work that we seek to satisfy our craving for a sense of control, mastery and security, and that clever organisations exploit this by designing corporate cultures that meet the emotional needs of their employees. The culture of the organisation is also important in determining the behaviour of managers. Brodbeck (2004) refers to a blame culture existing in many organisations that are a very unhealthy environment in which to work. For example, an organisation may see low reports of errors as a healthy sign, but in reality this is because individuals are worried about reporting mistakes.

Culture and organisational control and performance

A number of writers have referred to culture as a means of organisational control. For example, Cartwright (1999) sees culture as a system of management authority. When accepted by employees, cultural values increase the power and authority of management in three ways. Employees identify themselves with their organisation and accept its rules when 'it is the right thing to do'; they internalise the organisation's values when they believe they are right; and they are motivated to achieve the organisation's objectives. Willmott (1999) argues that organisation culture goes further than other mechanisms of control, such as leadership and structure, and attempts to control both the behaviour and identities of individuals.

Culture and organisational performance

Culture is also seen as an important ingredient of effective organisational performance. In their study of highly successful companies, Goldsmith and Clutterbuck (1998) identified that from eight characteristics built into the day-to-day culture of the world's top companies, a key element of high-performing companies is a challenge culture. All the companies are very demanding of the people who work for them, but this is balanced by a nurturing culture that shows that the companies also care for their employees. A growing body of research has shown that culture can affect strategy formulation and implementation as well as a firm's ability to achieve high levels of excellence (Cummings and Worley, 2005). However, Hilton (2011) believes that there is a stronger link and that companies succeed because of their culture. Most management systems, such as risk management, neglect the importance of culture and treat business as a mechanical operation, when in fact its outcomes depend fundamentally on the way people behave and interact. Companies succeed because of their culture; they decline because of their culture.

A guide to management and leadership

It is the role of management to act as an integrating activity and to coordinate, guide and direct the efforts of members towards the achievement of goals and objectives. The process of management, however, does not take place in a vacuum but within the context of the organisation. Effective management of human resources is dependent therefore not only on the nature of the industry or business, but also on the characteristic features of the individual organisation – and its culture. The pervasive nature of culture in terms of common values, beliefs and attitudes has a significant effect on organisational processes, such as decision-making, design of structure, group behaviour, work organisation, motivation and job satisfaction, and management control. Excellent leaders are not merely aware of the organisation's basic assumptions, they also know how to take action and mould and refine them. This process of cultural management appears to have been achieved through the skilful use of artefacts, stories, myths and symbolic actions to reinforce desired patterns of thought and behaviour.

Covert culture

Companies and institutions have both an overt and covert culture that influences both business and organisational behaviour. The covert set can be quite dysfunctional and costly. Egan (1993) distinguishes between the 'preferred culture', which serves the business, and the 'culture-in-use'. This culture-behind-the-culture carries the *real* beliefs, values and norms that drive patterns of behaviour within the company. These remain unnamed, undiscussed and unmentionable, and they lie outside ordinary managerial control.

Culture and change

The pervasive nature of organisational culture means that if change is to be brought about successfully, it is likely to involve changes to culture. Stewart (1999) argues that there is now widespread recognition that organisational change is not just, or even mainly, about changing the structure, but requires change to the culture too. However, changing the ethos and culture of an organisation is not easy. In practice, organisations usually appear to alter their underlying ethos only on a gradual basis, and the complexity of environmental pressures may itself hinder rapid change. Culture is often deep-rooted, and commitment to the objectives and policies of the organisation, as well as people's cognitive limitations and their uncertainties and fears, may cause a reluctance to accept a change in behaviour. The nature of strategic change is discussed in chapter 13.

3.2 Strong and weak cultures

It is possible to differentiate between strong and weak cultures. In a **strong culture**, the organisation's core values are both intensely held and widely shared. The more members who accept the core values and the greater their commitment to those values, the stronger the culture. The argument is that, consistent with this definition, a strong culture will have a great influence on the behaviour of its members because the high degree of sharing and intensity creates an internal climate of high behavioural control. There is also evidence that it is linked to lower levels of labour turnover. Peters and Waterman (1982) argue that these factors are also correlated with success.

 STOP AND THINK **5.3**

It is not a coincidence that employees at Disney theme parks appear to be almost universally attractive, clean and with bright smiles. That is the image Disney seeks. The company selects employees who will maintain that image. And once on the job, a strong culture, supported by formal rules and regulations, ensures that Disney theme park employees will act in a relatively uniform and predictable way.

How strong is the culture where you work?

One specific result of a strong culture should be lower employee turnover. A strong culture demonstrates high agreement among members about what the organisation stands for. Such unanimity of purpose builds cohesiveness, loyalty and organisational commitment. These qualities, in turn, lessen the likelihood that employees will leave the organisation.

A strong organisational culture increases behavioural consistency. In this sense, a strong culture can act as a substitute for formalisation. High formalisation in an organisation creates predictability, orderliness and consistency. The point is that a strong culture achieves the same end without the need for written documentation. The stronger an organisation's culture, the less management need be concerned with developing formal rules and regulations to guide employee behaviour. Those guides will be internalised by employees when they accept the organisation's culture.

3.3 The influence on strategy

Mark Fields, President of Ford Motor Company in 2006, famously argued that 'culture eats strategy for breakfast' – emphasising the influence of culture on the strategy of the business. It is the taken-for-granted nature of culture that makes it central to strategy and its management, and Johnson et al. (2014) argue that there are three primary reasons for this:

- **Cultural 'glue'.** The taken-for-granted nature of culture has benefits. Josephine Rydberg-Dumont, President of IKEA, argues that, because all her company's employees cohere around the founding principles and values, it reduces the need for constant supervision. In addition, since one of these values is to question the status quo, it also supports innovation.
- **Captured by culture.** Organisations may, however, be 'captured' by their culture. When faced with a changing business environment, managers are more likely to attempt to deal with the situation by searching for what they can understand and handle. The result is likely to be incremental strategic change and eventual strategic drift, as explained above. Culture is thus an unintended driver of strategy.
- **Difficulty in managing culture.** It is difficult to manage that which is hard to observe, identify and control. Analysing culture to reveal it is, therefore, important.

The likely effect of culture on strategy is shown in Figure 5.7.

Faced with declining performance, managers first try to improve implementation of the existing strategy. This might be through trying to lower costs, improve efficiency or tighten controls. If this is not effective, a change of strategy may occur, but in line with the existing culture. For example, managers may seek to extend the market for their business, but assume that it will be similar to their existing market, and therefore set about managing the new venture. But abandoning the existing paradigm can be very challenging and culture may become a liability.

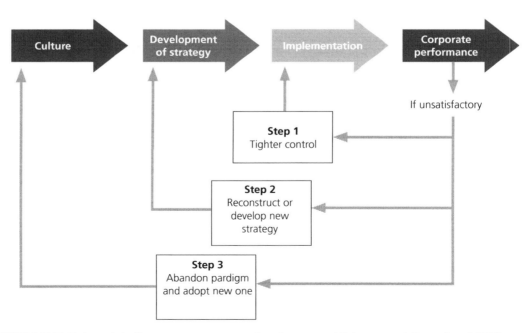

FIGURE 5.7 Culture's influence on strategy development (Grinyer and Spender, 1979)

3.4 Culture as a liability

Although we have discussed the significance of strong cultures, this has been treated in a non-judgemental manner. We have not said that it is good or bad, only that it exists. Many functions of a strong culture, as outlined above, can be valuable for strategists and the organisation. A strong culture enhances organisational commitment and increases the consistency of employee behaviour. These are clearly benefits to an organisation. From an employee's standpoint, culture is valuable because it reduces ambiguity. It tells employees how things are done and what is important. But we should not ignore the potentially dysfunctional aspects of culture, especially a strong one, on an organisation's effectiveness. A strong culture may act as a liability.

Consider the following:

 **CASE EXAMPLE** 5.6

Hewlett-Packard, once known as a premier computer manufacturer, has been rapidly losing market share and profits as the dysfunction of its top management team has trickled down, leaving employees disengaged, uncreative, unappreciated and polarised.

Source: Bandler and Burke (2012).

Barriers to change

Culture is a liability when the shared values are not in agreement with those that will further the organisation's effectiveness. This is most likely to occur when the organisation's environment is rapidly changing. When the environment is undergoing rapid change, the organisation's entrenched culture may no longer be appropriate. So consistency of behaviour is an asset to an organisation when it faces a stable environment. It may, however, burden the organisation and make it difficult to respond to changes in the environment. This helps to explain the challenges that IBM and Kodak, have had in recent years. These companies have strong cultures that worked well for them in the past. But these strong cultures became barriers to change when 'business as usual' was no longer effective. For many organisations with strong cultures, practices that led to previous successes can lead to failure when those practices no longer match up well with environmental needs.

Barriers to diversity

Hiring new employees who differ from the majority of the organisation's members creates a paradox. Management wants new employees to accept the organisation's core cultural values to fit in or be accepted. But at the same time, management wants to acknowledge and support the differences that these employees bring to the workplace. Strong cultures put considerable pressure on employees to conform. They limit the range of values and styles that are acceptable. In some instances, for example where senior managers have made disparaging remarks about minorities, a strong culture that condones prejudice can undermine formal corporate diversity policies. Organisations seek out and recruit diverse individuals because of the strengths these people bring to the workplace. Yet these diverse behaviours and strengths are likely to diminish in strong cultures as people attempt to fit in. Strong cultures, therefore, can be liabilities when they effectively eliminate those unique strengths that people of different backgrounds bring to the organisation. Moreover, strong cultures can also be liabilities when they support institutional bias or become insensitive to people who are different.

Barriers to mergers and acquisitions

Robbins (2015) argues that, historically, the key factors in making merger or acquisition decisions were related to financial advantages or product synergy. In recent years, cultural compatibility has become the primary concern. While a favourable financial state or product line may be the initial attraction of an acquisition candidate, whether the acquisition works seems to have more to do with how well the two organisations' cultures match. Consultants A.T. Kearney (2003) revealed that 58% of mergers failed to reach the value goals set by managers. The primary cause of failure was conflicting organisational cultures.

 **CASE EXAMPLE** 5.7

The 2001 merger of America Online (AOL) and Time Warner was one of the largest in corporate history. The merger is widely seen as a disaster and after two years the share value had fallen by 90%. Culture clash is argued to be the cause of the AOL/Time Warner's problems. One commentator described the merger as like the marriage of a teenager to a middle-aged banker – the cultures were vastly different: 'There were open collars and jeans at AOL; Time Warner was more buttoned down.'

Time Inc.'s merger with Warner Communications in 1990 had also been difficult. Time's culture was conservative and paternalistic, while Warner's was a 'high-risk, high-reward' culture of deal making. Employees from the two companies did not trust each other, and the combined Time Warner never saw the synergies predicted.

Culture therefore performs a number of functions within an organisation. It:

- has a boundary-defining role, creating distinctions between one organisation and others;
- conveys a sense of identity for organisation members;
- helps to generate commitment to something larger than one's individual self-interest;
- enhances social system stability – culture is the social glue that helps hold the organisation together, by providing appropriate standards for what employees should say and do; and
- serves as a sense-making and control mechanism that guides and shapes the attitudes and behaviour of employees.

 **TEST YOUR KNOWLEDGE** 5.3

a   What influence does culture have on an organisation?
b   What is a 'dominant' culture?
c   What might be the advantages and disadvantages to an organisation of a strong culture?

3.5 Corporate culture and organisational success

The culture coalition, led by the Financial Reporting Council (FRC) and comprising a number of leading professional bodies, argues that a healthy corporate culture is vital to the long-term success of organisations and needs be consistently strong and focused in order to help defeat the inevitable business and managerial challenges that they will undoubtedly face. The coalition's report (2014) identified the following specific points:

- **Recognise the value of culture.** A healthy corporate culture is a valuable asset, a source of competitive advantage and vital to the creation and protection of long-term value. It is the board's role to determine the purpose of the company and ensure that the company's values, strategy and business model are aligned to it. Directors should not wait for a crisis before they focus on company culture.
- **Demonstrate leadership.** Leaders, in particular the chief executive, must embody the desired culture, embedding this at all levels and in every aspect of the business. Boards have a responsibility to act where leaders do not deliver.
- **Be open and accountable.** Openness and accountability matter at every level. Good governance means a focus on how this takes place throughout the company and those who act on its behalf. It should be demonstrated in the way the company conducts business and engages with and reports to stakeholders. This involves respecting a wide range of stakeholder interests.
- **Embed and integrate.** The values of the company need to inform the behaviours which are expected of all employees and suppliers. Human resources, internal audit, ethics, compliance, and risk functions should be empowered and resourced to embed values and assess culture effectively. Their voice in the boardroom should be strengthened.

- **Assess, measure and engage.** Indicators and measures used should be aligned to desired outcomes and material to the business. The board has a responsibility to understand behaviour throughout the company and to challenge where they find misalignment with values or need better information. Boards should devote sufficient resource to evaluating culture and consider how they report on it.
- **Align values and incentives.** The performance management and reward system should support and encourage behaviours consistent with the company's purpose, values, strategy and business model. The board is responsible for explaining this alignment clearly to shareholders, employees and other stakeholders.
- **Exercise stewardship.** Effective stewardship should include engagement about culture and encourage better reporting. Investors should challenge themselves about the behaviours they are encouraging in companies and to reflect on their own culture

4 Creating and sustaining culture

4.1 How a culture starts

An organisation's culture does not just arrive. Once established, it rarely fades away. What forces influence the creation of a culture? What reinforces and sustains these forces once they are in place?

The culture of an organisation develops over time and in response to a complex set of factors (Handy, 1993).

History

The reason, and manner in which the organisation was originally formed, its age, and the philosophy and values of its owners and first senior managers will affect its culture. A key event in the organisation's history such as a merger or major reorganisation, or a new generation of top management, may bring about a change in culture. Corporate history can be an effective induction tool to assist a growth programme, and to help integrate acquisitions and new employees.

Primary function and technology

The nature of the organisation's 'business' and its primary function have an important influence on its culture: the range and quality of products and services provided, the importance of reputation and the type of customers. The primary function of the organisation will determine the nature of the technological processes and methods of undertaking work, which in turn also affect culture.

Strategy

A business organisation may pursue profitability, but to what extent is emphasis placed on long-term survival or growth and development? How much attention is given to avoiding risks and uncertainties? How much concern is shown for broader social responsibilities? The organisation must give attention to objectives in all key areas of its operations. The combination of objectives and resultant strategies will influence culture, and may itself be influenced by changes in culture.

Size

Larger organisations have more formalised cultures. Increased size is likely to result in separate departments and possibly split-site operations. This may cause difficulties in communication and inter-departmental rivalries, with the need for effective coordination. A rapid expansion or decline in size and rate of growth, and resultant changes in staffing, will influence structure and culture.

Location

Geographical location and its physical characteristics can have a major influence on culture – for example, whether an organisation is located in a quiet rural location or a busy city centre can influence the types of customers and the staff employed. Examples of organisations included by geographical location include hotels and restaurants.

Management and leadership

Top executives can have considerable influence on the nature of corporate culture – for example, the key roles played by Sir Richard Branson (Virgin) and Anita Roddick (founder of The Body Shop).

 **CASE EXAMPLE** 5.8

The source of IKEA's culture is its founder, Ingvar Kamprad, who grew up in a poor farming area in Sweden where people worked hard and lived frugally. Kamprad combined the lessons he learned as a youngster with his vision of creating a better everyday life for people by offering them affordable, functional and well-designed furniture. He named his company IKEA by combining his initials with the first letters of Elmtaryd and Agunnaryd, the farm and village where he grew up. IKEA's success stems from Kamprad's vision and his continued influence as an active senior adviser to the company.

4.2 Sustaining culture

Once a culture is in place, there are practices within the organisation that act to maintain it by giving employees a set of similar experiences. Many human resource practices reinforce the organisation's culture, ensuring that those recruited fit in with the culture, rewarding those who support it and penalising those who challenge it.

■ **Recruitment and selection**. Hire people who fit the company's culture, even if this involves overlooking some technical skills for a better cultural fit. Look carefully at the characteristics of your recruiters and consider your selection decision in the light of culture.
■ **Training and organisational development**. Develop practices that enable new people to understand the values, abilities, expected behaviour and social knowledge in order to participate fully as an employee, and to create strong bonds among members.
■ **Reward system**. Culture is an organisation's informal reward system, but it needs to be intricately connected to formal rewards. This means rewarding the behaviours (for example, team work) that are to be encouraged. More unusual examples include staff meetings where the seating arrangements reflect the level of sales and when payments of large commissions are made in front of other staff.

The process of developing organisational cultures is shown in Figure 5.8.

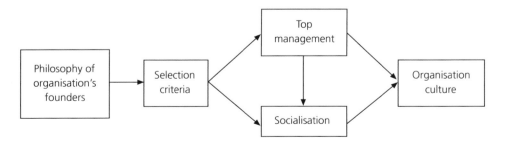

FIGURE 5.8 How organisational cultures develop

Top management

The actions of senior managers also have a major impact on the organisation's culture. Through what they say and how they behave, senior executives establish norms that filter through the organisation as to whether risk-taking is desirable; how much freedom managers should give their subordinates; what is appropriate dress and what actions will pay off in terms of pay rises, promotions and other rewards.

Socialisation

New employees are not fully indoctrinated in the organisation's culture and, for that reason, are potentially likely to disturb the beliefs and customs that are in place. The organisation will, therefore, want to help new employees adapt to its culture. This adaptation process is called **socialisation**.

CASE EXAMPLE 5.9

At Starbucks, the global coffee chain, all new employees go through 24 hours of training. The programme covers everything necessary to make new employees 'brewing consultants'. They learn the Starbucks philosophy, the company jargon (including phrases such as 'half-decaf double tall almond skim mocha'), and even how to help customers make decisions about beans, grind and espresso machines. The aim is employees who understand Starbucks' culture and who project an enthusiastic and knowledgeable interface with customers.

The most critical socialisation stage is at the time of entry into the organisation when it seeks to mould the outsider into an employee. Those employees who fail to learn the essential or pivotal role behaviours risk being labelled 'rebels', and may ultimately lead to their expulsion. But the organisation will be socialising every employee, though maybe not as explicitly, throughout his or her entire career in the organisation. This further contributes to sustaining the culture.

Robbins (2015) sees socialisation as a process made up of three stages:

1 pre-arrival
2 encounter
3 metamorphosis.

The first stage encompasses all the learning that occurs before a new member joins the organisation. In the second stage, the new employee sees what the organisation is really like and confronts the possibility that expectations and reality may diverge. In the third stage, relatively long-lasting changes take place. This three-stage process impacts on the new employee's work productivity, commitment to the organisation's objectives and eventual decision to stay with the organisation. Figure 5.9 depicts this process.

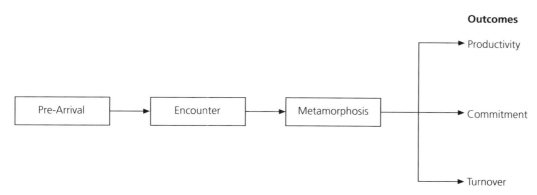

FIGURE 5.9 A socialisation model

TEST YOUR KNOWLEDGE 5.4

a Outline how organisational culture develops.
b Explain how culture might become a liability.
c Explain the part played by socialisation in developing culture.

5 Organisational culture and national culture

5.1 Introduction

As we saw earlier in the chapter (section 2.1), differences in national cultures, must be taken into account if accurate predictions are to be made about the full range of cultural influences on strategy making.

STOP AND THINK 5.4

Does national culture override an organisation's culture? Is an IBM facility in Germany, for example, more likely to reflect German ethnic culture or IBM's corporate culture?

The research indicates (Laurent, 1983) that national culture has a greater impact on employees than does their organisation's culture. German employees at an IBM facility in Munich, therefore, will be influenced more by German culture than by IBM's culture. As influential as organisational culture is to understanding the behaviour of people at work, national culture is even more so. This has to be qualified to reflect the self-selection that goes on at the hiring stage. IBM, for example, may be less concerned with hiring the 'typical German' for its German operations than in hiring an Italian who fits within the IBM way of doing things.

5.2 Cultural convergence and variance

It has been assumed that there are indeed significant differences in organisations across the world that can be attributed to culture. However, one should be wary of overstating this since some academic research now points to a somewhat different conclusion. Some of the work of the Aston School points to a *convergence* of organisational culture. For example, the work of Hickson et al. (1979) suggests that there is a relationship between factors such as size/technology and structure, which transcends culture. A bureaucracy is a bureaucracy in all societies and bureaucratic structures are more likely to occur in particular sectors of the economy. On a more general level, many commentators suggest that industrial or post-industrial societies would in any case become more similar as they developed in the future.

The contrary argument, that culture does matter when studying organisational behaviour, is perhaps more prevalent at present. Geert Hofstede (1980) conducted a large-scale research study of IBM subsidiaries across the world. Arguing that culture is collective programming that does indeed affect behaviour, Hofstede initially identified four dimensions of culture: power distance; uncertainty avoidance; individualism; and masculinity subsequently adding two more: long term orientation; and indulgence.

1 **Power distance**. This is essentially used to categorise levels of inequality in organisations, which Hofstede claims will depend on management style, the willingness of subordinates to disagree with superiors and the educational level and status accruing to particular roles. Countries that displayed a high level of power distance included France, Hong Kong, Iran and Spain. Countries as diverse as Australia, Germany, Italy, the UK and the US were characterised as low power distance societies.

2 **Uncertainty avoidance**. This refers to the extent to which members of a society feel threatened by unusual situations. High uncertainty avoidance is said to be characteristic of France,

Germany, Spain and many of the Latin American societies. Low-to-medium uncertainty avoidance was displayed in Ireland, the Netherlands and Scandinavia. In this case the UK is also said to be low-to-medium, together with Australia, Canada and the US.

3 **Individualism**. This describes the relatively individualistic or collectivist ethic evident in a particular society. Thus, France, Spain, the UK and the US display high individualism. This contrasts with Greece, Hong Kong, India and Portugal, all of which are low individualism societies.

4 **Masculinity**. The final category suggested by Hofstede, this refers to a continuum between 'masculine' characteristics, such as assertiveness and competitiveness; and 'feminine' traits, such as caring, a stress on the quality of life and concern with the environment. High masculinity societies included the Germany, Italy, Japan, the UK and the US. More feminine (low masculinity) societies included the Netherlands and Scandinavia.

Hofstede's work is by no means beyond criticism. The dimensions consist of generalised categories and no allowance is made for regional differences. By concentrating on one organisation, Hofstede restricts the scope of his work. Some may find the definitions of terms such as 'masculinity' and 'femininity' unconvincing and confrontational. Nonetheless, Hofstede's work represents an attempt to understand work-related differences and to account for these by reference to preferred management styles.

Another Dutch writer, Fons Trompenaars (1993), has also attempted to make a direct link between cultural variance and workplace behaviour. Trompenaars identifies seven areas in which cultural differences may affect aspects of organisational behaviour.

1 **Relationships and rules**. Here societies may be more or less *universal*, in which case there is relative rigidity in respect of rule-based behaviour, or *particular*, in which case the importance of relationships may lead to flexibility in interpretation of situations.

2 **Individual or collective**. Societies may be more oriented to the *individual* or *collective*. The collective may take different forms; the corporation in Japan, the family in Italy or the Catholic Church in Ireland. There may be implications here for such matters as individual responsibility or payment systems.

3 **Emotions**. It may also be true that societies differ to the extent it is thought appropriate for members to show emotion in public. *Neutral* societies favour a stiff upper lip while overt displays of feeling are more likely in *emotional* societies.

 STOP AND THINK 5.5

Trompenaars cites a survey in which 80 employees in various societies were asked whether they would think it wrong to express distress openly at work. The numbers who thought it wrong were:

Japan   80
Germany   75
UK   71
Hong Kong   55
US   40
Italy   29

Where might other cultures fit?

4 **Diffuse/specific**. In diffuse cultures, the whole person would be involved in a business relationship and it would take time to build such relationships. In a specific culture such as the US the basic relationship would be limited to the contractual. This distinction clearly has implications for those seeking to develop new international links.

5 **Long term orientation**. Every society has to maintain some links with its past while dealing with the present and the future. Societies priortise these two existential goals differently. Societies who score low on this dimension prefer to maintain traditions and norms while viewing societal change with suspicion. Those who score high take a more pragmatic approach, encouraging thrift and education as a way to prepare for the future.

6 **Indulgence**. Indulgences stands for a society that allows relatively free gratification of basic and natural human drives related to enjoying life and having fun. On the contrary restraint stands for a society that suppresses gratification of needs and regulates it by means of strict social norms.

7 **Environment**. Finally, it is suggested that there are differences in attitudes to the environment. In Western societies, individuals are typically masters of their fate. In other parts of the world, however, the world is seen as more powerful that individuals.

Trompenaars' work is based on lengthy academic and field research in a wide range of organisations over a number of years. It is potentially useful in linking the dimensions of culture to aspects of organisational behaviour for managers and leaders working internationally.

The price of a failure to take these matters into account can be high, as Case Example 5.10 shows.

 CASE EXAMPLE 5.10

Project management can be important in the implementation of strategy. In a study of how project management is viewed in China and the UK, researchers have found significantly different conceptions between managers in China and those in the UK. These findings inform an understanding of some underlying differences of the wider concept of management itself. Variations include relationship with the company, views of teamwork, relationships with clients and subcontractors, conflict resolution and attitudes to uncertainty.

Source: Ping Chen and David Partington, 'An interpretive comparison of Chinese and Western conceptions of relationships in construction project management work', *International Journal of Project Management*, 22(5) (2004), pp.397–406.

 TEST YOUR KNOWLEDGE 5.5

a   Outline Hofstede's four dimensions of culture.
b   What criticisms can be levelled at Hofstede's work?
c   Contrast Britain and France using Trompenaars' seven dimensions.

 CASE QUESTIONS

1   Using a framework of your choice, compare and contrast the culture of Walmart and Asda.
2   Using your understanding of the impact of international culture, explain why Walmart may have had difficulties in markets outside the US.

CHAPTER SUMMARY

■ The theme of this chapter has been that an organisation's history and culture contribute to explaining and, to some extent, predicting behaviour and strategy development. In addition to individual and group factors, the culture in which people work has an important bearing on employee attitudes and behaviour. Such factors may also result in strategic drift.

■ Employees also form an overall subjective perception of an organisation based on such factors as degree of risk tolerance, team emphasis and support of people. This overall perception becomes, in effect, the organisation's culture or personality. These favourable or unfavourable perceptions then affect employee performance and satisfaction, with the impact being greater for stronger cultures.

Just as people's personalities tend to be stable over time, so too do strong cultures. This makes strong cultures difficult for managers to change. When a culture becomes mismatched to its environment, management will want to change it. We shall look at the issues in a later chapter. The result, at least in the short term, is that managers should treat their organisation's culture as relatively fixed.

- How is an organisation's culture established and sustained? The original culture is derived from the founder's philosophy. This, in turn, strongly influences the criteria used in selection. The actions of the current top management set the general climate of what is acceptable behaviour and what is not. How employees are to be socialised will depend both on the degree of success achieved in matching new employees' values to those of the organisation's in the selection process and on top management's preference for socialisation methods.

- One of the more important managerial implications of organisational culture, aside from the impact on strategy development, relates to recruitment decisions. Hiring individuals whose values do not align with those of the organisation are likely to lead to employees who lack motivation and commitment and who are dissatisfied with their jobs and the organisation.

- Managers should not overlook the influence socialisation has on employee performance. An employee's performance depends to a considerable degree on knowing what he should or should not do. Understanding the right way to do a job indicates proper socialisation. Furthermore, the appraisal of an individual's performance includes how well the person fits into the organisation. These qualities differ between jobs and organisations. As a result, proper socialisation becomes a significant factor in influencing both actual job performance and how others perceive it.

- Differences in national culture can be significant, and form part of the field of cultural influences on the individual.

Strategic purpose

■ OVERVIEW

Part Two looked at the influence of the internal and external environment on an organisation's strategic position. However, a fundamental decision that has to be taken in strategic management concerns the purpose of the strategy that is to be followed. This is the focus of Part Three, which looks at choices that may be made about purpose, together with the influences on purpose of the expectations of the organisation's stakeholders. We begin by looking at the role of the governing body of an organisation and the significance of other stakeholders in determining strategic direction and issues of risk and reputation management. An underlying issue raised by this part is the extent to which the strategic purpose of an organisation should be determined in response to a particular stakeholder group, for example shareholders in the case of a commercial enterprise, or to broader stakeholder interests – at the extreme, society and the social good. This theme is considered in relation to corporate governance and the regulatory framework within which organisations operate. Here, the concern is how these influence strategic purpose by supervising executive decisions and actions. This raises issues of accountability: to whom are strategists accountable?

The purpose of Chapter 6 is to look at the relationship between corporate governance and organisation strategy.

In Chapter 7, we look in more depth at the various elements of purpose. How in practice do organisations express this and what are the benefits and issues associated with each approach? What is the difference between a vision and a mission? What are the key components of effective strategic objectives?

Chapter 8 looks at the ethical stance of organisations, how they may choose to go beyond their obligations to their stakeholders and examines issues of corporate social responsibility, ethics and sustainability. Here, the question is which purposes an organisation should fulfil. How should managers respond to the expectations society has of their organisations, in terms of corporate social responsibility and in terms of the behaviour of individuals within organisations – including themselves?

■ LEARNING OUTCOMES

After reading and understanding the contents of Part Three, considering some of the Case Examples and Test Your Knowledge questions, you should be able to:

■ apply the concept of the governance chain to organisations;

■ understand the relationship between stakeholders and governance;

■ recognise the importance of determining, challenging and balancing conflict in the risk appetite of differing stakeholders;

■ apply the outcomes of stakeholder analysis to manage the influence of different stakeholders and stakeholder groups;

■ understand the nature and sources of reputation and advise on ensuring a coherent approach to reputation and risk;

■ recognise the significance of the hierarchy of purpose;

■ advise on appropriate ways to express the strategic purpose of an organisation: values, vision, strategic intent, mission and objectives;

■ define ethics and taking an ethical perspective in strategy development;

■ critically review the role of ethics in the organisation;

■ understand the different ethical stances taken by organisations;

■ advise on ethical decision-making and conflicts of interest amongst stakeholders;

■ advise on the link between sustainability and strategy.

 PART 3 CASE STUDY

Strategy at Anglia Symphony Orchestra

Developing a new strategy for the Anglia Symphony Orchestra (ASO) seems likely to prove complex and challenging. A major review has been prompted by a critical report from the Arts Council, the orchestra's main funding body. Commenting on 'poor audience reaction to new initiatives' introduced by the Conductor, the report argued that the organisation needed 'clearer artistic and audience focus'. The report called for a change in strategic leadership, recommending 'that the CEO should take overall responsibility for the artistic direction'. The Conductor defended his previous decisions, arguing that he had been criticised for having programmes that were both too conservative and too adventurous. He suggested the confusion over strategic focus was partly due to a 'clash of ideals' with the previous marketing director, who had quite different views about the repertoire and customer preferences and 'went off in her own direction'.

Other individuals had expressed concerns about the orchestra's artistic direction, including members of the management, board and the orchestra itself. The

musicians' representative, for example, expressed the need for a change from 'churning out Tchaikovsky', but felt they had now gone too far the other way, playing lesser-known repertoire which was neither the orchestra's strength, nor popular with their audiences. There were also differences of opinion about how far the orchestra should focus on a single venue – Norwich – and how far it should tour the region.

The CEO responded to the widespread disquiet with an announcement that he intended to appoint an Artistic Director who would 'own' future artistic policy. In the meantime, the chairman commented: 'We haven't got an artistic strategy and are struggling to find one.' He has produced a strategic framework document that has been discussed with the orchestra because 'it was terribly important that it was owned by everybody'. The board of directors sought to contribute their views too and so an Artistic Sub-committee was formed. When the Artistic Director was appointed some months later, however, he decided that it was impractical to involve a committee in repertoire issues and instead worked with the conductor on artistic planning.

PART 3 CASE STUDY *continued*

Because of the number and diversity of stakeholder groups seeking to contribute to the artistic strategy, the process was drawn out, with several interpersonal conflicts along the way. Six months after his appointment, the Artistic Director still believed the big issue was 'to get the policy together', and at the board's away-day in early 2011, he announced: 'I've been here for one year and I don't think I've made any impression at all.' At the same meeting, the chairman said: 'We're accused of losing coherence in what we do and who we are. We are failing to serve the community of which we are a part. A compromise between what the Conductor wants and what's financially possible is what happens. It's impossible to create good concerts and certainly a long term strategy.' He concluded: 'We need agreement, even if it's not exactly to everyone's liking.'

Adapted from S. Maitlis and T. Lawrence, 'Orchestral manoeuvres in the dark: discourse and politics in the failure to develop an artistic strategy', Proceedings of the EIASM Workshop on Microstrategy and Strategising, Brussels, 2001.

6 The governing body and strategy

■ INTRODUCTION

The purpose of this chapter is to look at the relationship between corporate governance and organisational strategy. It examines the main options for governing organisations and the how this reflects the purpose and power of key stakeholders. It looks at how organisations manage these stakeholders and in particular their appetites for risk and the impact that this might have on reputation – itself a strategic issue for many organisations.

1 Corporate governance and strategy

1.1 The nature of corporate governance

The overall purpose of a commercial organisation is to maximise the long-term return to the owners – its shareholders. We may therefore ask: who is really responsible and accountable for fulfilling this purpose? Our focus here is on the link between governance and strategy. In that sense **corporate governance** can be defined as the relationship among various participants in determining the direction and performance of organisations.

Corporate governance has become increasingly important in strategic management. The chief executive can influence every aspect of an organisation, including the way that it treats its key stakeholders. The primary participants in commercial firms are typically the shareholders, the management (led by the CEO) and the board of directors. This relationship is illustrated in Figure 6.1. But stakeholders may include other groups such as employee representatives and customers. It is also the chief executive and other executive directors who take strategic decisions on behalf of the stakeholders.

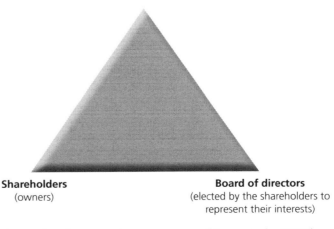

Management
(headed by the chief executive officer)

Shareholders
(owners)

Board of directors
(elected by the shareholders to represent their interests)

FIGURE 6.1 The key elements of corporate governance (Dess et al., 2008)

The corporate governance relationship with strategy arises from the opportunities given to senior managers to influence the future purpose of the organisation. Connecting stakeholder interests with management action is a vital part of strategy. The senior officers are usually the directors of the organisation. However, they may also include senior representatives of workers and senior outside advisers with no daily responsibility for strategy development. In some European countries such as Germany, the Netherlands and Sweden, this latter group would constitute a supervisory board that oversaw the work of the directors.

Many public bodies will also have corporate governance structures. These are likely to cover the major issues of the not-for-profit sector, including the monitoring of the quality of public services and the value-for-money obtained by taxpayers and charity givers.

For most organisations, corporate governance goes beyond selecting, remunerating and reviewing the conduct of the senior officers. It will also include a review and approval process for the main corporate strategies that have been developed by the officers. Typically, such a procedure might take place on an annual basis.

 CASE EXAMPLE 6.1

The major international oil company British Petroleum (BP) conducts particular monitoring during the year to test the confidence in or risks to the achievement of the performance objectives and the observance of the strategy and policies.

Source: www.BP.com

Corporate governance policies have been tightened up in the wake of a number of corporate scandals in recent years. Well-documented failures in corporate governance have contributed to calamitous strategic choices in many leading companies, even resulting in the complete destruction of global companies, such as the energy giant Enron in 2001 and the leading investment bank Lehman Brothers in 2008. With the survival of whole organisations at stake, governance is increasingly recognised as a key strategic issue. The serious consequences of major scandals in this area have led to considerable tightening of corporate governance in recent years.

 CASE EXAMPLE 6.2

News Corporation (the media company controlled by the Murdoch family) had made, by 2013, payments of $340 million to settle the legal claims of people whose mobile telephones had been hacked. There was one particularly notorious example: the hacking of the mobile of the UK schoolgirl, Milly Dowler, who had disappeared and was found dead.

Source: *Press Gazette*, 7 February 2013, 'Phone hacking scandal: News Corp costs rise to $340 million'.

 CASE EXAMPLE 6.3

Sports Direct, the UK based sport's retailer, faced serious criticisms regarding the working conditions in its stores and distribution centres in 2016. A Business Committee report found evidence that workers were not being paid the national working wage and were being penalised for taking routine work breaks and short term absences.

Source: *Sky News*, 22 July 2016

1.2 The governance chain

Managers and stakeholders are linked together by the governance chain. This extends the illustration in Figure 6.1 of the roles and relationships of different groups involved in the governance of an organisation. In large, publicly quoted organisations, these chains can be complex. There are extra layers of management internally, while being publicly quoted introduces more investor layers as well. Individual investors (the ultimate beneficiaries) often invest in public companies through collective funds, such as pension funds, which then invest in a range of companies on their behalf. Trustees typically control funds, with day-to-day investment activity undertaken by investment managers. So, the ultimate beneficiaries may not even know which companies they have a financial stake in and have little power to influence the companies' boards directly.

The relationships in such governance chains can be understood in terms of the *principal-agent model* (Eisenhardt, 1989). Here 'principals' pay 'agents' to act on their behalf. For example, company boards are principals with senior executives their agents in managing the company. The issue for strategy in practice is that there are many layers of agents between ultimate principals and the managers at the bottom, with the reporting mechanisms between each layer liable to be imperfect. In large companies, board members and other managers driving strategy are likely to be very remote from the ultimate beneficiaries of the company's performance. The result may be that decisions are taken that are not in the best interests of the final beneficiaries. This is just what has happened in the case of many of the corporate scandals of recent years.

 **CASE EXAMPLE** 6.4

Enron was one of the world's leading electricity, natural gas, pulp, paper and communications companies. Based in Houston, Texas, it employed around 21,000 people with reported revenues of $101 billion in 2000. However, at the end of 2001 it was revealed that its reported financial condition was sustained mostly by accounting fraud. When Enron sought Chapter 11 protection in late 2001, it was the biggest bankruptcy in US history and cost 4,000 employees their jobs. The scandal also caused the dissolution of Arthur Andersen, a Big Five accounting firm.

Many of Enron's recorded assets and profits were inflated, fraudulent or non-existent. Later investigations revealed that some executives were hiding losses for the company. Chief Financial Officer Andrew Fastow led the team that manipulated the deals to provide himself, his family and friends with hundreds of millions of dollars in guaranteed revenue, at the expense of the shareholders. A group of Enron employees had been expressing concerns as early as 1998, but Arthur Andersen confirmed that it was comfortable with the accounting. In October 2002, the Securities and Exchange Commission opened a formal inquiry into Enron, which started a devastating trail of events at Arthur Andersen exposing its accounting fraud at WorldCom. J.P. Morgan Chase, Citigroup, Merrill Lynch, Credit Suisse, First Boston, Canadian Imperial Bank of Commerce, Bank America, Barclays Bank, Deutsche Bank; and Lehman Brothers were also named as players in the series of fraudulent transactions. Sixteen of Enron's top executives were convicted in connection with the case.

Source: Based on a case by Rajshree Prakash, University of Lancaster Management School, cited in Johnson et al. (2014), p.136.

 STOP AND THINK 6.1

What issues do the Enron case and others like it raise for strategy in practice in organisations, particularly the way purpose is determined?

In this context, the governance chain helps highlight important issues that affect the management of strategy:

- **Responsibility to whom?** A fundamental question in large corporations is whether executives should regard themselves as solely responsible to shareholders, or as trustees of the assets of the corporation acting on behalf of a wider range of stakeholders. Practice varies across the world.

- **The shareholders.** If managers see themselves as primarily responsible to shareholders, what does this mean in terms of the governance chain? Final beneficiaries are often far removed from the managers, so for many managers, responsibility to such beneficiaries is notional. Strategists face a difficult choice, even if they espouse primary responsibility to shareholders. Do they develop strategies they believe to be in the best interest of a highly fragmented group of unknown shareholders or to meet the needs and aspirations of the investment managers, for example? A similar problem exists for public sector managers. They may see themselves as developing strategies for the public good, but they may face direct scrutiny from an agency acting on behalf of the government. Is the strategy to be designed for the general public good or to meet the scrutiny of the agency? Managers and doctors in the NHS, for example, are dedicated to the well-being of their patients. But how they manage their services has been governed by the targets placed upon them by a government department, which presumably also believes it is acting in the public good.

- **The role of institutional investors.** The role of institutional investors differs according to governance structures around the world. However, a common issue is the extent to which they do or should actively seek to influence strategy. Historically, in the UK, investors have exerted their influence simply through buying and selling shares rather than engaging with the company on strategic issues. However, investors are becoming more actively involved in strategies (Davies et al., 2006). Johnson et al. suggest that there is evidence that institutional investors that seek to work proactively with boards to develop strategy do better for their beneficiaries.

- **Scrutiny and control.** Given recent concerns about governance, there has been an increase in scrutiny and control of the activities of 'agents' in the chain to safeguard the interests of the final beneficiaries. There are increasing statutory requirements as well as voluntary codes placed on boards to disclose information publicly and regulate their activities. Nevertheless, managers are still left with a great deal of discretion as to what information to provide to whom and what information to require of those who report to them. For example, how specific should a CEO be in explaining future strategy to shareholders in public statements such as annual reports? Are the typical accountancy measures (such as return on capital employed) the most appropriate, or should measures be specifically designed to fit the needs of particular strategies or particular stakeholder/shareholder expectations? How managers answer these questions depends both on what they decide the strategic purpose of the organisation is and their view about to whom they see themselves responsible.

A key point is that strategists and managers need to be aware that the governance chain typically operates imperfectly as a result of:

- a lack of clarity concerning the end beneficiaries;
- unequal division of power between the different 'players' in the chain, with different levels of access to information available to them;
- potentially agents in the chain pursuing their own self-interest; and
- using measures and targets reflecting their own interests rather than those of end beneficiaries.

In such circumstances it is not surprising that governance structures are changing around the world and there have been reforms to corporate governance. These are well known to chartered secretaries. Dess et al. (2014) focus on three important mechanisms to ensure effective corporate governance: an effective and engaged board of directors, shareholder activism, and proper managerial rewards and incentives. In addition to these internal controls, a key role is played by various external control mechanisms. These include the auditors, banks, analysts, an active financial press and the threat of hostile takeovers.

 STOP AND THINK 6.2

Reflect on how these changes are affecting and influencing the strategy of organisations known to you.

1.3 Types of governance structure

The governing body of an organisation is typically a board of directors. The primary statutory responsibility of a board is to ensure that an organisation fulfils the wishes and purposes of the primary stakeholders. However, who these stakeholders are varies. In the private sector in some parts of the world it is shareholders, but in other parts of the world it is a broader or different stakeholder base. In the public sector, the governing body is accountable to the political arm of government? possibly through some intermediate agency such as a funding body. These differences lead to differences in the way firms and other organisations operate, how the purposes of an organisation are shaped and how strategies are developed as well as the role and composition of boards (Clarke and Clegg, 2000).

Johnson et al. (2014) argue that there are two broad governance structures: the shareholder model and the stakeholder model.

Shareholder mode of governance

In this case, shareholders have the prime right to the wealth generated by the corporations. There is dispersed shareholding, though a large proportion of shares is held by financial institutions. In principle, trading shares provides the regulatory mechanism for maximising shareholder value, as dissatisfied shareholders can sell their shares, resulting in a drop in share price and threats of takeover for underperforming firms.

The shareholder model is epitomised by the economies of the UK and US. The arguments for the shareholder model include:

- **Higher rates of return for investors**. Managers are not distracted by the needs of other stakeholders;
- **Reduced risk for shareholders**. This is because they can diversify their risk by using the stock market to buy shares in many different companies and to sell the shares of companies that appear to be in financial danger.
- **Increased innovation and entrepreneurship**. Since the system facilitates higher risk taking by investors, the shareholder model should promote entrepreneurship, innovation and higher growth. It is easier to attract capital investment where investors know that they can easily diversify their shareholdings and trade their shares.
- **Better decision-making**. The separation of ownership and management arguably makes strategic decisions more objective in relation to competing demands and constraints of financial, labour and customer markets. If the shareholders are well spread, no single shareholder is likely to exercise undue control.

The disadvantages include:

- **Diluted monitoring**. Dispersed shareholdings prevent close monitoring of management. This may result in the managers sacrificing shareholder value to pursue their own agendas;
- **Corporate reputation and top management greed**. The lack of management control allows for the huge compensations the managers reward themselves in the form of salary, bonuses and stock options. In the US, CEOs have 530 times more compensation than their employees, in comparison with the UK at 130 times and Japan, where the comparable figure is closer to a multiple of just ten; and
- **Short-termism**. Lack of control of management may lead to managers taking decisions to benefit their own careers (for example, to gain promotion). This, combined with the threat of takeovers, may encourage managers to focus on short-term gains at the expense of long-term projects.

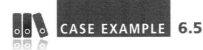 **CASE EXAMPLE 6.5**

Google and Facebook have deliberately adopted a dual-class shareholder structure, where the original founders and their associates have larger voting rights. This protects these companies' commitment to long-term innovation and prevents short-termism in decision-making.

Stakeholder mode of governance

An alternative model of governance is the stakeholder model. This is founded on the principle that wealth is created, captured and distributed by a variety of stakeholders. This may include shareholders, but could include other investors, such as banks, as well as employees or their union representatives. As such, management need to be responsive to multiple stakeholders, who themselves may be formally represented on boards. We discuss the stakeholder view in greater depth in the next section.

Germany and Japan are often cited as examples of the stakeholder model. In Germany (as well as France and the Netherlands) there is a two-tier board system: the supervisory board and the management board. The supervisory board is a forum where the interest of various groups is represented, including shareholders and employees but also typically bankers, lawyers and stock exchange experts. Strategic planning and operational control are vested with the management board, but major decisions like mergers and acquisitions require approval of the supervisory board.

The advantages for the stakeholder model of governance are as follows:

- **Less reckless risk taking**. Apart from the argument that the wider interests of stakeholders are taken into account, it is also argued that employee influence in particular is a deterrent to high-risk decisions and investments.
- **Closer monitoring of management**. With investors having greater access to information from within the firm, and given that power may reside with relatively few block investors, intervention may also be easier in case of management failure.
- **Long-term horizons**. It is argued that the major investors – banks or other companies, for example – are likely to regard their investments as long term, thus reducing the pressure for short-term results as against longer-term performance.

There are also disadvantages of the stakeholder model of governance:

- **Weaker decision making.** Close monitoring by powerful stakeholders could lead to interference, slowing down decision processes and the loss of management objectivity when critical decisions have to be made.
- **Uneconomic investments.** Lack of financial pressure from shareholders could mean that long-term investments are made in projects where the returns may be below market expectations.
- **Reduced innovation and entrepreneurship.** Because investors fear conflicts of interests with other stakeholders, they will be less likely to provide capital for risky new opportunities.

These advantages and disadvantages are usefully summarised by Johnson et al. in Table 6.1.

TABLE 6.1 Benefits and disadvantages of governance systems (Johnson et al., 2008, p.142)

	Shareholder model	**Stakeholder model**
Benefits	For investors: ■ Higher rate of return ■ Reduced risk For the economy: ■ Encourages entrepreneurship ■ Encourages inward investment For management: ■ Independence	For investors: ■ Closer monitoring of management ■ Longer-term decision horizons For stakeholders: ■ Deterrent to high-risk decisions
Disadvantages	For investors: ■ Difficult to monitor management For the economy: ■ The risk of short-termism ■ The risk of top management greed	For management: ■ Potential interference ■ Slower decision making ■ Reduced independence For the economy: ■ Reduced financing opportunities for growth

A further strategic issue of these different governance types is that there are implications for the financing of businesses. In the shareholder model, equity is the dominant form of long-term finance and commercial banks provide debt capital, so relationships with bankers are essentially contractual. This means that the company itself has a higher degree of influence over strategic decisions since the banks are not seeking a strategic involvement with the company. However, if strategies start to fail, the organisation can become increasingly dependent on the bank as a key stakeholder. This often happens in small, family-owned businesses. In the extreme, banks may exercise their power through exit (that is, by withdrawing funds), even if this liquidates the company. In contrast, in some stakeholder systems, banks often have significant equity stakes or are part of the same parent company. They are less likely to adopt an arm's-length relationship and more likely to seek active strategic involvement.

Yoshimori (1995, in De Wit & Meyer) split countries into three broad groupings of governance – monistic, dualistic and pluralistic:

- **Monistic** – prevalent in Anglo-Saxon countries with the corporate unitary board as the centre of power and control of the organisation is highly shareholder oriented and the primary focus is on shareholder value creation.
- **Dualistic** – this is the dominant model in Germany and other parts of the continent where the corporate governance concept distinguishes between those who are leading the firm (the executive board) and those who exercise control (the supervisory board), so that power is split in order to better serve all stakeholder interests.
- **Pluralistic** – this is seen in Japan, where it is assumed that the organisation belongs to all the stakeholders, which, under the Keiretsu system, may include banks, local authorities, suppliers, sub-contractors and distributors, but with a primary focus on the interests of employees.

Until the credit crunch in 2007–08, there had been a growing dominance worldwide of the Anglo-Saxon monistic model, albeit with some elements of stakeholder management. Since then, there has been more discussion regarding the merits of each – e.g. in the UK, where after the June 2016 Brexit referendum, the Conservative government talked of curtailing the power of boards and strengthening worker representation on them, or at least on remuneration committees.

Table 6.2 shows a comparison of the three systems.

TABLE 6.2 Comparison of three corporate governance systems

	Germany	US	Japan
Purpose	Corporate interests 'stakeholder value'	'Shareholder value'	Corporate interests 'stakeholder value'
Governance principles	Cooperative with dividend-based remuneration	Directorship with stock options	Seniority and little sharing of profits
Governance practice	Dualistic, dominated by institutions and banks	Monistic, capital market-oriented	Pluralistic, dominated by institutions and banks
Participation of stakeholder	Firm as a social institution (of employees, banks, politicians and so on)		Banks and Keiretsu partner

Source: Witt (2000), p. 160; Yoshimori (1995).

TEST YOUR KNOWLEDGE **6.1**

a   Explain what corporate governance is when considering strategy.
b   Distinguish the shareholder model and stakeholder model of corporate governance.
c   Explain the advantages of the stakeholder model.
d   Distinguish between the monistic, dualistic and pluralistic models of governance.

2   Stakeholder expectations

2.1   What is a stakeholder?

The governance framework of an organisation tends to provide a broad framework for understanding the political context in which strategy is both formulated and implemented. For this to work, a board or leadership team needs to be able to understand the expectations of its stakeholders and the extent to which they are likely to show an active interest in the strategy of the organisation or seek to influence it.

We need to go back a little and define and explore the notion of a stakeholder. Stakeholders are people or groups who have a legitimate interest in the activities of companies and other organisations in society. A **stakeholder** is defined by Freeman (1984, p.25) as:

'Any group or individual who can affect or is affected by the achievement of the firm's objectives.'

This definition encompasses customers, employees, managers, shareholders and suppliers, as well as local communities, the state (in the form of citizens, institutions and taxpayers) and those who share the environment. These stakeholders can be grouped into 'internal', 'market' and 'external'.

 CASE EXAMPLE 6.6

At McDonald's, the stakeholders include the shareholders, the managers and the employees. They also include the McDonald's franchisees: independent companies and individuals who operate many of the McDonald's restaurants around the world under the parent brand name. Franchisees have a significant influence on McDonald's headquarters and its strategy, because the franchisees have to deliver aspects of this strategy. In fact, stakeholders can be an area of competitive advantage, if managed well.

Source: Lynch (2015).

 STOP AND THINK 6.3

Select an organisation that you know well as an employee or as a user of its products and services
    Who are the stakeholders?
    What are their main 'stakes' or interests?

You have probably identified managers and employees and a wide range of other stakeholders. The interests and the balance of power among the stakeholders will vary according to the type of organisation and over time.

Different stakeholders have different interests, and these interests may be in conflict. We can easily recognise the potential for conflict, for example, between the interests of employees in security of employment and increasing earnings and those of shareholders who may be seeking short-term cost reductions. For example, McDonald's shareholders will want to ensure that profits are high in order to pay reasonable share dividends. By contrast, McDonald's employees may want higher wages, which will reduce profits.

An organisation's culture and structure (Chapters 5 and 11) will determine how conflicts or trade-offs such as these are resolved, and in reality the interests of one stakeholder group often have a dominant position. Commercial organisations are conventionally considered to be shareholder-led, although directors and senior managers are likely to have the dominant interests. Some service industries may be regarded as being customer-led, whereas public and voluntary services are often staff-led.

Some stakeholder interests are protected by law. Owners and shareholders are generally protected by property and company law, and employees have statutory rights in many countries. The interests of other stakeholders, however, are protected, if at all, only by regulation, contract or management discretion. In EU countries, measures have been taken in recent years to adjust this imbalance: consumer protection legislation is intended to achieve just that; and environmental legislation and regulation constrain companies' activities to the benefit of local communities and the environment in general.

This has not always been the accepted view: the belief was that a firm's responsibility was to its shareholders. And some managers still hold this view. Even if an organisation accepts that its obligations extend beyond its financial stakeholders, however, it is likely to find that the interests of these stakeholders are not identical and at times may be in direct opposition. This creates a problem for managers: how can they balance or reconcile the conflicting interests of stakeholders? As if this was not difficult enough, organisations do not simply respond to each stakeholder individually; but to the interaction of multiple influences from the entire stakeholder set. Thus, explanations of how organisations respond to their stakeholders require an analysis of the complex array of multiple and interdependent relationships existing in stakeholder environments. This problem lies at the heart of management and sets the context in which organisations and their managers operate. Two tools that can help are stakeholder mapping and analysis.

2.2 Analysing stakeholder groups

The preceding sections have emphasised that the decisions managers have to make about the purpose and strategy of their organisation are influenced by the expectations of stakeholders. This is challenging because there are likely to be many stakeholders, especially for a large organisation, with different, perhaps conflicting, expectations. So who are the stakeholders? As we have seen, all organisations have:

- **internal stakeholders**: directors, employees, managers and trustees;
- **market stakeholders**: competitors, customers, distributors and suppliers
- **external stakeholders**: those who are indirectly affected by the organisation, who might include professional services such as banks, members of the community or the general public as well as national, regional and local government, and, most vocal of all, protest groups and non-governmental organisations (NGOs).

Figure 6.2 illustrates the main categories of stakeholder for a commercial organisation.

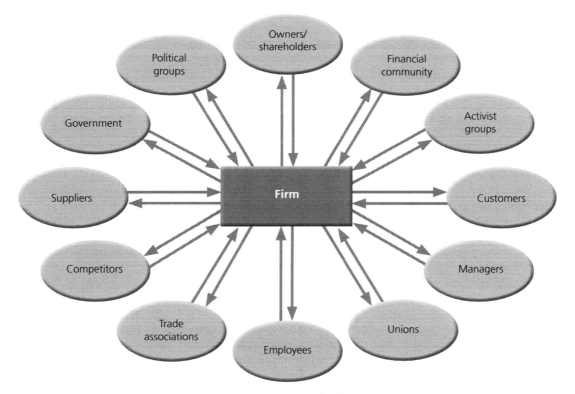

Source: Adapted from R.E. Freeman, *Strategic Management: A Stakeholder Approach*, Pitman, 1984. Copyright 1984 by R. Edward Freeman, cited in Johnson et al. (2014).

FIGURE 6.2 Stakeholders of a large organisation

Stakeholders in the voluntary sector include funders or donors, whereas in the public sector they include the general public in their capacity as citizens (through elected representatives), as taxpayers (funders) and as beneficiaries of public services (customers). All organisations depend on a source of funds. In a commercial organisation, the source is shareholders or banks. Public sector organisations are funded by taxpayers, channelled through government organisations or agencies. And voluntary organisations are funded by donors, grants or trading income.

Since the expectations of stakeholder groups differ, there are often conflicts about the importance or desirability of many aspects of strategy. In most situations, a compromise will be needed.

 STOP AND THINK 6.4

Identify the potential stakeholder conflicts inherent in the list of stakeholders in Table 6.2.

Some of the typical stakeholder expectations that exist are shown in Table 6.3.

TABLE 6.3 Stakeholders and their expectations (Lynch, 2015)

Stakeholder	Expectations	
	Primary	**Secondary**
Owners	Financial return	Added value
Employees Customers	Pay Supply of goods and services	Work satisfaction, training Quality
Creditors	Creditworthiness	Payment on time
Suppliers	Payment	Long-term relationships
Community	Safety and security	Contribution to community
Government	Compliance	Improved competitiveness

Global organisations may have added complications as they are operating in multiple arenas. For example, an overseas division is part of the parent company but is also part of a local community, which has different expectations. These two worlds may not sit comfortably alongside each other.

The stakeholder map such as that in Figure 6.2 is little more than a listing of the groups having an influence on the organisation and its strategy. An analysis of stakeholders is therefore useful, particularly when related to an assessment of specific strategic developments. What will the different people and groups think, and how will they be affected?

Stakeholder analysis identifies stakeholder expectations and power and helps to establish political priorities. It consists of making judgements on:

■ the *interest* each stakeholder group has in impressing its expectations on the organisation's choice of strategies; and
■ whether they have the *power* to do so.

We can, therefore, classify stakeholders in relation to the power they hold and the extent to which they likely to show interest in the organisation's strategies. The resulting matrix indicates the type of relationship that the organisation needs to establish with each stakeholder group (Table 6.4). As such, it is a useful analytical tool both in assessing the political ease or difficulty of particular strategies and in planning the political dimension of strategic changes.

TABLE 6.4 Stakeholder mapping (Johnson et al., 2014)

		LEVEL OF INTEREST	
		Low	**High**
POWER	**Low**	Minimal effort	Keep informed
	High	Keep satisfied	Key players

- **Key players**. Clearly, the acceptability of strategies to the key people should be a major consideration during the formulation and evaluation of new strategies.
- **Keep satisfied**. Often the most difficult relationship to plan is with stakeholders in this segment (institutional shareholders often fall into this category). Although they might, in general, be relatively passive, a disastrous situation can arise if their level of interest is underrated and they suddenly reposition and frustrate the adoption of a new strategy. Strategists may need to raise the level of interest of powerful stakeholders so that they can fulfil their expected role.
- **Keep informed**. Similarly, the needs of these stakeholders need to be addressed properly, largely through information. They can be important allies in influencing the attitudes of more powerful stakeholders: for example, through lobbying.

Stakeholder analysis helps to assess:

- whether the levels of interest and power of stakeholders properly reflect the corporate governance framework within which the organisation is operating;
- whether actions need to be taken to reposition certain stakeholders. This could be to lessen the influence of a key player or to ensure that there are more key players who will champion the strategy;
- who are the key 'blockers' and facilitators of change, and how blockers will respond to education or persuasion, and how facilitators might help;
- the extent to which stakeholders will need to be helped or encouraged to maintain their level of interest or power to ensure successful strategy implementation. For example, public endorsement by powerful suppliers or customers may be critical to the success of a strategy. Equally, it may be necessary to discourage some stakeholders from repositioning themselves. This is what is meant by 'managing stakeholders' – keeping them satisfied and informed.

Stakeholder groups are not usually homogeneous but may contain subgroups with different expectations and power. When using stakeholder mapping, there is clearly a balance to be struck between describing stakeholders too generically, thereby hiding important issues of diversity, and too much subdivision, making the situation confusing and difficult to interpret.

The role and the individual currently undertaking that role need to be distinguished. It is useful to know if a new individual in that role would shift the positioning. A change might change this situation.

2.3 Power and political priorities

The previous section was concerned with understanding stakeholder expectations and highlighted the importance of power, which is, in most organisations, unequally shared between the various stakeholders. For the purposes of this discussion, **power** is the ability of individuals or groups to persuade, induce or coerce others into following certain courses of action. This is the mechanism by which one set of expectations will influence strategic development or seek compromise with others.

There are many different sources of power. On the one hand, there is power that people or groups derive from their position within the organisation, the resources or know-how they control, and through the formal corporate governance arrangements. Stakeholders' power is summarised in Table 6.5.

The relative importance of these sources will vary over time. Indeed, major changes in the business environment can significantly shift the power balance between organisations and their stakeholders. For example, consumers' knowledge of different companies' offerings through internet browsing has increased their power considerably as they compare different offerings and reduce their traditional loyalty to a particular supplier. Deregulation has required public service organisations to adopt more customer-focused strategies.

TABLE 6.5 Sources and indicators of power

Sources of power	
Within organisations	**For external stakeholders**
■ Hierarchy (formal power), e.g. autocratic decision making ■ Influence (informal power), e.g. charismatic leadership ■ Control of strategic resources, e.g. strategic products ■ Possession of knowledge and skills, e.g. computer specialists ■ Control of the human environment, e.g. negotiating skills ■ Involvement in strategy implementation, e.g. by exercising discretion	■ Control of strategic resources, e.g. materials, labour, money ■ Involvement in strategy implementation, e.g. distribution outlets, agents ■ Possession of knowledge or skills, e.g. subcontractors, partners ■ Through internal links, e.g. informal influence
Indicators of power	
Within organisations	**For external stakeholders**
■ Status ■ Claim on resources ■ Representation ■ Symbols	■ Status ■ Resource dependence ■ Negotiating arrangements ■ Symbols

Since there is a variety of different sources of power, it is useful to look for indicators of power, which are the visible signs that stakeholders have been able to exploit sources of power. Indicators of power include: the status of the individual or group (such as job grade or reputation); the claim on resources (such as budget size); representation in powerful positions; and symbols of power (such as office size or use of titles and names). It should be remembered, however, that the distribution of power will vary in relation to the strategy under consideration. For example, a corporate finance function will be more powerful in relation to developments requiring new capital or revenue commitments than in relation to ones which are largely self-financing or within the financial authority of separate divisions or subsidiaries.

A similar understanding of the power held by external stakeholders can be useful. The indicators of power here are slightly different:

■ The status of an external stakeholder can often be inferred by the speed with which the company responds.
■ Resource dependence in terms of the relative size of shareholdings or loans, or the proportion of a company's business tied up with any one customer, or a similar dependence on suppliers.
■ Symbols are also valuable clues about power. For example, the level of person in the company who deals with a particular supplier.

These questions raise some difficult ethical issues for managers and leaders in deciding the role they should play in the political activity that is part of strategic change. For example, are managers 'honest brokers' who balance the conflicting expectations of stakeholder groups? Are they really only answerable to one stakeholder – the shareholders? Are they the real power, structuring strategies to suit their own purposes and managing stakeholder expectations to ensure acceptance of these strategies? The corporate governance arrangements of the organisation answer these questions only at the most general level. Balancing the conflicting interests of different stakeholders is strongly determined by the ethical stance of the organisation and individual managers. This is discussed in more detail in Chapter 8.

In practice, it may be necessary to subdivide a stakeholder group into more than one group because there are important differences in expectations or power within that group. Most stakeholder groups consist of large numbers of individuals (e.g. customers or shareholders) and hence can be thought of as largely independent of the expectations of individuals within that group. But some stakeholder groups consist of a small number of individuals or even single individuals (e.g. the chair of the company). It is essential that the analysis properly acknowledges the extent to which the mapping of the role (e.g. chair) is concerned with the particular individual that occupies it. It is useful to know if a new individual in that role would shift the positioning. Misjudgements can be made if proper care is not paid to this.

Political priorities can be established from stakeholder analysis by:

- plotting a map showing how stakeholders would line up in relation to a new strategy;
- plotting a second map showing how you would like stakeholders to line up if the strategy is to succeed; and
- comparing these two maps and looking for the mismatches will establish the political priorities. These may simply involve maintaining stakeholders in their current position.

2.4 Stakeholders in the public sector

This discussion has focused on commercial organisations, but similarly complex issues arise in the public services. This can be illustrated by the emphasis on the public as customer. This emphasis has had value in focusing attention on those for whom the services are provided. Yet the word 'customer' cannot encompass the variety of relationships between government and the public. Who is the customer of a school: child, parent, future employers? Many services are provided not on demand, as for a customer in the private sector, but as an assessment of need.

Elcock (1995) identifies five categories of user:

1 **Citizens**. They have the right and duty to participate in the government of their communities.
2 **Subjects**. They must obey government but who receive and expect protection from the threat of harm.
3 **Clients**. They receive and accept advice and services, but who have only a limited influence over what is provided.
4 **Customers**. They purchase goods and services through commercial transactions and have the right to expectations of quality and service. Whereas in the commercial sector customers can take their business elsewhere, in the public sector the choice may be limited, and so too is the opportunity for redress.
5 **Consumers**. They receive goods and services on a market or non- market basis, have the same rights as customers, and may also be consulted about the goods and services that they receive.

STOP AND THINK 6.5

As part of the development of its new strategy, a communications company invited customers and suppliers alike to experience an event as part of a change programme. They heard the CEO speak of the company's strategic intent and the part that they could play in achieving it.

Why might the company have done this?

TEST YOUR KNOWLEDGE 6.2

a What do you understand by the term 'stakeholder'?
b Distinguish between internal and external stakeholders.
c Prepare a simple stakeholder map of an organisation with which you are familiar.

3 Risk, reputation and strategy

3.1 Business risk and governance

As we have discussed in the previous section, the board of a commercial organisation has a responsibility to govern the company in the interests of the shareholders and other stakeholders. A part of this responsibility is to decide the purpose and strategic direction, to approve detailed strategic plans put forward by management, and to monitor and review the implementation of those plans. An important objective of a commercial company is to make a profit, and the company's strategies should be directed towards this.

A business must take risks to make profits. **Risk** refers to the possibility that something unexpected or unplanned will happen. In many cases, risk is seen as the possibility that something bad might happen. There is 'upside' risk too. This is the possibility that actual events might turn out better than expected. In a business context, an example is the possibility that sales volumes will be higher than planned or that working days lost through industrial action will be fewer than anticipated.

STOP AND THINK 6.6

What may be the consequences of failing to consider business risks or establish an effective business risk management system?

But how much risk should an organisation tolerate, and would it be able to withstand shocks in the business environment if an unexpected event or development were to occur?

CASE EXAMPLE 6.7

Northern Rock reported a loss of £232.4 million for 2010. It was the bank's near-collapse in the autumn of 2007 that signalled the onset of the financial crisis in the UK. Many banks had very successfully made good profits for years but the crisis saw them criticised for the financial difficulties in which they found themselves as a result of reckless business strategies and failing to recognise the nature of the business risks they were taking. Although there were failures in the regulation of the banking industry, much of the blame for the crisis was attributable to poor governance, and in particular inadequate attention to risk management.

Risk taking refers to a business's willingness to seize a venture opportunity, even though it does not know whether the venture will be successful – to act boldly without knowing the consequences. To be successful, businesses usually have to take on riskier strategic alternatives at some point, even if it means forgoing the methods or approaches that have worked in the past. To obtain high financial returns, firms take such risks as assuming high levels of debt, committing significant resources, introducing new products or services into new markets, and investing in unexplored technologies.

Excessive risk taking can result in the insolvency and collapse of a company and is one aspect of poor governance. The key point here is that the board must take business risk into account when making strategic business decisions. It should choose policies that are expected to be profitable, but should limit the risks to a level that it considers acceptable. It should also be satisfied that in their decision-making, managers take risk as well as expected returns into account.

3.2 Risk management

Even though risk taking involves taking chances, it is not gambling. The best-run companies investigate the consequences of various opportunities and create scenarios of likely outcomes – at the minimum the best, worst as well as the expected or most likely outcome. Risk is a measure of the potential variance around the expected outcome. A key to managing entrepreneurial risks is to evaluate new venture opportunities thoroughly enough to reduce the uncertainty surrounding them.

 **CASE EXAMPLE 6.8**

Companies that 'do their homework' – that is, carefully evaluate the implications of bold actions – reduce the likelihood of failure. Graybar Electric Co. took a risk when it invested $144 million to revamp its distribution system. It consolidated 231 small centres into 16 supply warehouses and installed the latest communications network. Graybar is now considered a leader in facility redesign, and its sales have increased steadily since the consolidation.

Source: Dess et al., (2012).

The Cadbury Report (1992) described **risk management** as 'the process by which executive management, under board supervision, identifies the risk arising from business ... and establishes the priorities for control and particular objectives'.

Risk management involves making decisions about upside as well as downside risks. For example, businesses make decisions to acquire other businesses. Every such investment is risky. Returns could be lower or higher than expected so that in deciding whether or not to undertake an investment, the risks as well as the potential returns should be considered. Shareholders would like to see their company earning high returns, but might be unwilling to see the management taking excessive investment risks in trying to achieve those returns.

'Desire to take on risk' refers to the amount and type of risk to which the board would like the company to have exposure. According to Coyle (2010), this suggests a number of important concepts for strategists:

- **Risk appetite**. The level of risk that an organisation is willing to take in the pursuit of its objectives.
- **Risk capacity**. The maximum risk exposures that the company can accept without threatening its financial stability.
- **Risk tolerance**. The amount of risk that the board allows the organisation to accept.

The Walker Report (2009), which investigated the banking crisis, recommended that more attention be given to these issues through the strategic planning cycle by approving and monitoring appropriate limits to exposure. The board should review risk appetite regularly, and decisions should be taken about the scale of risk that is desired or acceptable. Risk tolerance could be expressed numerically, such as the maximum loss that the board is willing to accept on a particular venture if events turn out adversely. Risk tolerance could also be expressed in terms of a total ban on certain types of business activity or behaviour.

Brian Coyle (2014) suggests that there are four basic elements to a risk management system.

1 **Risk identification**. An organisation needs a procedure for reviewing and identifying the risks it faces. Risks change over time, so risk reviews should therefore be undertaken regularly.
2 **Risk evaluation**. The evaluation of risks calls for procedures to assess the potential size of the risk. The expected losses that could occur from adverse events or developments depend on:
   a) the probability that an adverse outcome will occur; and
   b) the size of the loss in the event of an adverse outcome.
   Where a risk is high, measures should be taken to protect the organisation so that the remaining exposure to risk is within the company's tolerance level and consistent with its risk appetite. Risk Identification and evaluation is considered in more detail in section 3.3.

3 **Risk management measures**. The measures taken to deal with each risk are decided by management, which is accountable to the board for the measures they take. In broad terms, business risks can be dealt with by avoiding them or by taking steps to limit the exposure:

a) Some risks can be avoided. For example, a car manufacturer might be concerned about the risk of losses at a subsidiary specialising in car repairs, due to the strength of competition in the car repair industry. It could decide to avoid the risk by selling the subsidiary.

b) Many risks have to be accepted as an inevitable feature of business. For significant risks, a company should decide what measures might be necessary to reduce the risk to acceptable proportions. Business risks may be reduced through measures such as a diversification of product range (to avoid over-reliance on a single product), joint ventures (to share new venture risks) and cost reduction measures (to reduce the risks from competition).

It is a board responsibility to make sure that risks are reviewed regularly and that managers take suitable measures to deal with them.

4 **Risk control and review**. Control systems should be established by executive management to monitor risks. There should be a system for identifying situations that are getting out of control or where significant events have developed or are developing.

3.2 Types of business risk

The nature and severity of business risks vary from one organisation to another. Risks also change over time: some become less significant, and new risks emerge.

Coyle (op. cit.) argues that business risks can be categorised or identified in different ways, and it is helpful to look at the following sources of risk.

■ **Reputation risk**. The risk of loss in customer loyalty or customer support following an event that damages the company's reputation. We explore this in more detail below.

 **CASE EXAMPLE** 6.9

In 2010 it was reported that sales of some models of car produced by Toyota had fallen sharply following the recall of millions of vehicles to rectify a design fault that caused unintended acceleration. There were also suspicions that the company had tried to cover up the scale of the problem. Sales of the cars had been affected by the damage to the company's reputation. In 2015 the VW motor group suffered major reputational damage (as well as potential liability for financial claims) when it was revealed that the emissions tests for its vehicles were not satisfactorily accurate.

■ **Competition risk**. The risk that business performance will differ from expected performance because of actions taken (or not taken) by business rivals. The firm therefore needs to carefully consider potential competitor reactions to its strategies.

■ **Business environment risks**. These are risks of significant changes in the business environment from political and regulatory, economic, social and environmental, and technology factors (the so-called PESTEL factors). For example, business performance may be affected by the introduction of new regulations, political upheaval in a country, economic decline or growth, environmental issues, unexpected changes in social habits or technological change.

■ **Business risk.** This is the risk arising from the variability of the firm's operating income. It is caused only by business-related factors such as variability in sales volumes, selling prices and the costs of inputs (supplies).

■ **Financial risks**. These are risks that stem from the level of debt that an organisation may be carrying. As the organisation takes on additional debt, it increases its gearing (the ratio of debt to equity capital), which in turn increases the probability of the organisation being unable to service its loan requirements (interest payments and capital repayments). Financial conditions may also change, with adverse changes in interest rates or exchange rates, higher losses from bad debts or changes in prices in financial markets (such as changes in share prices) all increasing financial risk. The ultimate financial risk is therefore insolvency.

■ **Strategic risks**. The risks of taking decisions on strategy that will result in exposures to excessive business risk and so could lead to losses or even business collapse.

Each industry and each company within an industry faces different risks. The questions that management should ask are:

■ What risks does this company face?
■ How can these risks be measured? It may be possible to assess the risk in a business in terms of unpredictable variations in key factors such as sales demand or market prices. High volatility is associated with high business risk.
■ For each of these risks, how would the company be affected if the worst outcome came about, or if a fairly bad outcome happened?
■ What is the likelihood of a bad outcome for that risk item?
■ What is the company's risk appetite or risk tolerance?
■ What should the company be doing to manage the risk, either by avoiding it altogether or planning to deal with the problems that will arise in the event of a bad outcome?

3.3 Managing risk

Once risks have been identified, the organisation can employ a number of frameworks to enable it to control and manage risks. The severity–probability matrix (see Figure 6.3) allows risks to be plotted on a matrix based on the severity of the risk identified (in terms of potential damage and disruption to the organisation) and the likelihood or probability of the risk occurring. Following this exercise, risks can be classified as low, medium or high.

RISK ASSESSMENT MATRIX				
Severity / Probability	Catastrophic (1)	Critical (2)	Marginal (3)	Negligible (4)
Frequent (A)	High	High	Serious	Medium
Probable (B)	High	High	Serious	Medium
Occasional (C)	High	Serious	Medium	Low
Remote (D)	Serious	Medium	Medium	Low
Improbable (E)	Medium	Medium	Medium	Low
Eliminated (F)	Eliminated			

FIGURE 6.3: The severity–probability matrix

In order to plot identified risks on the matrix, the organisation will have to assign probabilities to the risks and also an indication of their potential severity. Once this task is completed, the organisation can devise specific strategies in order to control and manage each risk. For example, it may be acceptable simply to monitor low risks, whereas medium and high risks may need specific interventions in order to reduce the potential threats they pose. Organisations may employ a range of strategies to reduce such risks, including:

■ use of insurance contracts;
■ the establishment of a corporate sinking fund or internal insurance facility;
■ employment of a risk management team to actively devise ways to reduce the potential severity of risks; and
■ attempting to remove the risk threat entirely, for example, by exiting the area of business activity that is exposed to the risk.

Risk matrices have a number of advantages:

- They are relatively simple to construct and understand.
- They may promote effective discussion within organisations about risk management.
- The simple layout promotes a high degree of consistency in the way risks are measured.

Risk matrices also have a number of disadvantages:

- It may not be possible or appropriate to use quantitative data in order to assign probabilities of risk likelihood and severity.
- If qualitative measures are used, these may be highly subjective and potentially unreliable.
- Risk matrices usually make no mention of the time frame in which risks are being considered.
- Risk matrices usually do not take account of the volatility of risks.

3.4 Reputation management

Whereas some assets, like copyrights, licences and leases, may be assessed, **intangible assets** are more difficult to account for or imitate. They are typically embedded in unique routines and practices that have evolved and accumulated over time. These include human resources (e.g. experience and capability of employees, trust effectiveness of work teams, managerial skills), innovation resources (e.g. technical and scientific expertise, ideas) and reputation resources (e.g. brand name, reputation with suppliers for fairness and with customers for reliability, and product quality). These can be key resources, and a source of competitive advantage when considering the resource-based view of the firm (see Chapter 4).

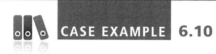
CASE EXAMPLE 6.10

You might not think that motorcycles, clothes, toys and restaurants have much in common. Yet Harley-Davidson has entered all of these product and service markets by capitalising on its strong brand image – a valuable intangible resource. It has used that image to sell accessories, clothing and toys, and has licensed the Harley-Davidson Café in New York City to provide further exposure for its brand name and products.

Reputation has been defined by Louisot (2010) as the excess value over the total physical assets, which can only be derived from the financial market's evaluation of the company's shares. Yet a number of drivers may have an impact on the long-term reputational standing of any organisation, and these apply to not-for-profit entities as well as to local authorities and public or private healthcare providers.

Managing reputation is therefore an essential part of the strategic role of the board, who must take into account all stakeholders, whose perception of the organisation will determine its reputation. Louisot further suggests that risks or uncertainties, both positive and negative, must be managed in a holistic, systemic approach, as there is no such thing as reputation risks; rather, all risks may impact on reputation.

Organisations, often with a push from public opinion, consumer associations or even trading partners are being made more and more aware of a major exposure the risk to reputation (image, brand). This is the risk that an organisation's reputation can be tainted, either by real mismanagement or simply in the public's or its economic partners' perception. Such degradation may have different origins – defamation, dramatic accidents, questioning of management's wisdom, product defect and ill-organised or untimely product recall, to quote but a few.

Then two questions arise:

- What is reputation and how can it be managed?
- What are the main risks to reputation, and can they be mitigated?

In organisations, **reputation** reflects the perception that the different stakeholders have of the organisation, basing their evaluation of its performance on the available information. Reputation is thus a subjective assessment resulting from a number of factors, among which trust will be a key ingredient. Therefore, managing or building a reputation over time will require an effort to be applied to all the components involved. However, it will revolve around efficient communication and long-term solid relationships inside and outside the organisation. Reputation can constitute a major competitive advantage. The benefits of effective reputation management summarised below are derived from a book by Larkin (2003) most of which have strategic implications:

- improving relations with shareholders;
- creating a more favourable environment for investment and for access to capital;
- recruiting and retaining the best employees; attracting the best partners, both upstream (suppliers and subcontractors) and downstream (customers);
- reducing barriers to development in new markets;
- securing premium prices for products and/or services;
- minimising threats of litigation and of more stringent regulation;
- reducing the potential for crises; and
- reinforcing the organisation's credibility and the trust of stakeholders.

Reputation has always mattered, but globalisation, linked to the acceleration of the circulation of information, best illustrated by the internet, has made it a much more fluid commodity that needs to be managed carefully.

Larkin identifies the core principles that contribute to effective reputation management, based on managing the organisation's relationship with its stakeholders:

- a sense of distinctiveness in the minds of the stakeholders (market segmentation);
- a focus on a core theme (e.g., nurturing and caring, a 'magical experience', reliability, innovation);
- an effort at consistency in performance and communication;
- an effort at integrity and authenticity in dealings, including communication, with all stakeholders; and
- a commitment to transparency as a prerequisite for effective financial and social performance, encouraging contact with and support from stakeholders.

Reputation is the result of long-term trust-building through consistent efforts, but the world is growing less trusting and the different stakeholders may, as we have seen, have diverse, indeed contrary, interests in the organisation. Reputation can be ruined overnight by an ill-managed event which results in a crisis. The challenge is that such perils can come from any direction.

- **Economic**. For example, a sudden shift in consumers' taste – the company is perceived as unresponsive and out of touch.
- **Natural**. For example, a flood – the company is perceived as ill-managed. Why was a plant built in a flood-prone area?
- **Operational**. For example, a fire – the company was ill-managed in allowing a fire-hazardous plant to be built; or pollution – the company has allowed unsafe practices, damaging to health, safety or the environment.
- **Unfair employment practices**. For example, there are discrepancies between the company's published values and the reality.
- **Governance**. For example, there are lapses in governance standards or ethics, or unfair competition practices – the company behaves in a way inconsistent with its published charter of values.
- **Human**. For example, involuntary product or service failure may mean that the company is threatened with litigation.

These perils illustrate that damage to reputation may result from any other risk with which the organisation is confronted, and that such damage is directly linked to the way the incident/ accident is managed and to the capacity of the organisation to react to and deal with the event. In other terms, the key to managing reputation risks is sound risk management, coupled with straightforward communication on the problem the organisation is facing.

TEST YOUR KNOWLEDGE 6.3

a What is the responsibility of the board for business risk?
b Explain what is meant by 'risk appetite' and 'risk tolerance'.
c What is the difference between 'business risk' and 'internal control risk'?

CASE QUESTION

1 Critically review the role of the governing body in strategy-making at the ASO.

2 Explain how stakeholder analysis and management might help the CEO with the formulation of the new strategy.

CHAPTER SUMMARY

- The purpose and strategy of an organisation will be influenced by the expectations of its stakeholders. The influence of some key stakeholders will be represented formally within the governance structure of an organisation. This can be represented in terms of a governance chain, showing the links between ultimate beneficiaries and the managers of an organisation.
- There are two generic governance structures: the shareholder model and the stakeholder model. These vary by country.
- Different stakeholders exercise different influence on organisational purpose and strategy, dependent on the extent of their power and interest. Managers can assess the influence of different stakeholder groups through stakeholder analysis.
- Yoshimori (1995) talks about three broad types of corporate governance – monistic, dualistic and pluralistic – and gives the advantages and disadvantages of each.
- Businesses must accept risks in order to make a profit. The board should decide how much business risk the company is prepared to accept in order to achieve its objectives and has a responsibility for ensuring that business risks to which the company is exposed, or might be exposed, are considered acceptable. Risk appetite is the amount of exposure to business risk the board wants to take so that targets for financial performance can be achieved. Risk tolerance is the amount of risk that the board is willing to accept. Risk tolerance may be measured quantitatively, so that actual exposures to business risk can be compared with a target or tolerance limit. The board should review risk appetite and risk tolerance regularly.
- Risks arise from unexpected changes or developments in the business environment that are outside the control of management. Unexpected changes can be positive or negative. Examples of risks are reputation risk, business risks, business environment risk, financial risks in the business environment (such as interest rate risk and foreign exchange rate risk) and liquidity risk. The basic elements of a risk management system are procedures for identifying risks, evaluating the risks that have been identified and assessing their significance, taking measures to manage the risk that are consistent with board policy on risk appetite and risk tolerance, control of the system and regular reviews of the effectiveness of the system.
- Organisations may use risk matrices such as the severity–probability matrix to identify risks and then rank them in terms of their potential threat. From this analysis, strategies to manage the most potent risks can be devised.

Expressing organisational purpose

■ **CONTENTS**

1 Strategy and purpose
2 Elements of purpose
3 Statements of purpose – benefits and issues

■ **INTRODUCTION**

Chapter 6 looked at how stakeholders influence the overall purpose of an organisation. However, it is managers who will need to form a view about this purpose and find a way of expressing it. It may be that an explicit statement of such a purpose is a formal requirement of corporate governance or expected of the organisation by one or more stakeholders, or it may be that managers themselves decide such a statement is useful. This chapter will look at the different ways in which such purpose may be expressed explicitly through statements of corporate values, vision, mission and objectives.

1 Strategy and purpose

1.1 Thinking about purpose

The conventional view of organisations is that they exist to pursue particular aims and objectives – that is to say, they are goal seeking. It is this that gives them coherence and explains their activities. In Chapter 1, for example, where the concepts of business strategy and planning were defined, we saw that strategy is one of the ways that enable the organisation to achieve its purpose. Looked at another way, it is impossible to develop strategy if the organisation's purpose is unclear.

 STOP AND THINK 7.1

What is the purpose of the organisation for which you work?
  How clear is it?

 CASE EXAMPLE 7.1

In spring 2012, Sir Stelios Haji-Ioannou, founder of easyJet, took his former company to court as part of his campaign to curb what he saw as its excessive growth. Although he had stepped down from a management role, Sir Stelios and his family were still major shareholders, with 38% ownership, and they had become fierce critics of the company's growth strategy. According to Sir Stelios, easyJet's current management were investing in growth at the expense of dividends for shareholders. At stake

CASE EXAMPLE 7.1 *continued*

in the clash between founder and managers were crucial issues about the purpose of business – long-term growth or immediate dividends – and who has the right to control strategy – owners or management.

Source: Johnson et al. (2014).

In practice, complaints of 'a lack of strategic direction' are common, even in organisations that have laboured long and hard to produce a **mission statement** (we shall look at these below). All too often, strategic aims are either very general or unrealistic – to be number one in the industry is an almost universal aim (Kellaway, 2000). Purpose is often simplified to 'profit maximisation' by writers such as Porter (1980) or 'survival' by Williamson (1991), or some other simplifying assumption. Even where there is a clearly expressed and specific purpose, embodied in a mission statement, there are problems about purpose. For example, an organisation may act opportunistically to exploit chances where it believes it has a competitive advantage. If these are only short term and are not consistent with the strategic direction, then goals may become confused.

CASE EXAMPLE 7.2

The purpose at Yahoo! might be summarised as to 'grow the business profitably'. But this would miss key elements of the Yahoo! business purpose. The reason for such a simplification in the definition is that purpose is complex and multifaceted, involving not only profit and survival, but also the motivations of the people involved and the relationship of the organisation with society and the community. Yahoo! is an example of a company where its purpose of growth remains elusive and it requires complex new products and services to be successful.

1.2 The hierarchy of purpose

Employees and managers throughout the organisation must therefore strive towards common goals and objectives. By specifying desired results, it becomes much easier to move forward. If no one knows what the firm is striving to accomplish, they have no idea of what to work towards. As an old nautical expression puts it, 'No wind favours the ship that has no charted course.'

However, there is often confusion about terminology. What one organisation calls a goal may be referred to by another as an objective and as a target by yet another. Many talk about corporate **mission** or vision: are these strategies, objectives or something entirely different?

Purpose will be unique to each organisation. Yet, however complex and singular, the general principles underlying the development of purpose need to be understood and clarified if the subsequent development of strategy is to be meaningful. Organisations tend to express priorities best through stated goals and objectives that form a **hierarchy of purpose**, or goals, which include its vision, mission and strategic objectives. Figure 7.1 depicts the hierarchy of goals and its relationship to two attributes: general versus specific and time horizon. At the top of the hierarchy is a description of why the organisation exists; below are broad statements of what it is trying to do; and lower down there are increasingly specific statements of how things will be done. A pharmaceutical company, for example, might describe what it is trying to achieve as follows:

- we are trying to reduce human pain by curing or preventing disease (why we exist);
- we produce pharmacological products that address the symptoms or causes of disease (what we do); and
- we synthesise chemicals, test them for efficacy and safety, and market them to doctors and health authorities throughout the world (how we do it).

Alternatively, we can move up the hierarchy, achieving objectives, which allows aims or goals to be realised, which in turn contributes to the organisation's mission and vision. Different organisations (and writers) use different terms to describe these different levels, but they should still move logically from broad, general mission and aims to specific, measurable targets.

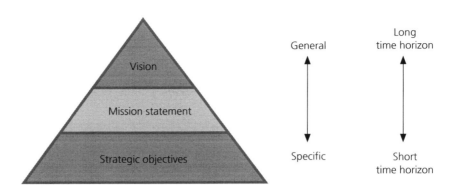

FIGURE 7.1 Hierarchy of purpose

It is important to recognise that how you describe a particular activity or event will depend on the context in which it is being discussed. For example, in the context of an organisation's long-term strategy, a proposed marketing event may be no more than one target towards the objective of a successful campaign. However, if you are the manager discussing the next few months' priorities with colleagues, the same event may be your major goal. Thus words such as 'vision', 'values', 'mission', 'objectives', 'aims' and 'goals' are used in conflicting ways. The terminology offers scope for confusion. If in doubt, check that you know what the other person means!

Purpose is often explored or defined solely in terms of business organisations. But many other not-for-profit organisations, such as government institutions, charities and public services, also generate value-adding activities that have a clear purpose and need strategies to attain that purpose. An exploration of purpose therefore needs to be broad enough to include such bodies. Whether an organisation is a private company or public body, it will need to develop its purpose and develop a common understanding of the main elements.

1.3 Corporate values

Increasingly, organisations have been keen to develop and communicate a set of corporate values that define the way that the organisation operates (Lencioni, 2002). Of particular importance are an organisation's **core values** – the underlying 'principles' that guide an organisation's strategy. For example, the emergency services have an overriding commitment to saving life which employees are committed to, so that they may break strike action or risk their own lives to attend emergencies when life is threatened. Collins and Porras (2002) argue that the long-run success of many American corporate businesses, such as Disney, General Electric and 3M, can be attributed in part to strong core values.

 **CASE EXAMPLE   7.3**

Values – Google

Ten things we know to be true. We first wrote these 'ten things' when Google was just a few years old. From time to time we revisit this list to see if it still holds true. We hope it does – and you can hold us to that.

1 Focus on the user and all else will follow.
2 It's best to do one thing really, really well.
3 Fast is better than slow.
4 Democracy on the web works.
5 You don't need to be at your desk to need an answer.
6 You can make money without doing evil.
7 There's always more information out there.
8 The need for information crosses all borders.
9 You can be serious without a suit.
10 Great just isn't good enough.

Source: www.google.com.

There are disadvantages to public statements of corporate values if an organisation fails to live up to them in practice, whether they are part of the public or commercial sector.

It is also important to distinguish between the core values expressing the way the organisation is, as distinct from those to which the organisation aspires. Unless this distinction is clear there is room for considerable misunderstanding and cynicism about statements of corporate values. In either case such statements may be concerned with aspects of **corporate social responsibility**, which will be discussed in the next chapter.

We shall now look at some of the key elements of purpose.

TEST YOUR KNOWLEDGE 7.1

a How might organisations express their purpose?
b Explain what is meant by the hierarchy of purpose.
c What benefits and problems arise from having clear corporate values?

2 Elements of purpose

2.1 Strategic vision

Whereas corporate values may be a backcloth and set boundaries within which strategies are developed, a statement about vision is typically concerned with what the organisation aspires to be. Its purpose is to set out a view of the future so as to enthuse, gain commitment and stretch performance.

STOP AND THINK 7.2

Does your organisation have a vision?
 If it is not currently written down, how would you describe it?

So a vision is a goal that is 'massively inspiring, overarching, and long term' (Lipton, 1995). It concerns what the organisation aspires to be and represents a destination that is driven by and evokes passion. A vision may or may not succeed; it depends on whether everything else happens according to a firm's strategy. As Mark Hurd, Hewlett-Packard's CEO, pointed out, *'Without execution, vision is just another word for hallucination'* (Hardy, 2007).

Lynch (2014) identifies five main reasons to develop a strategic vision.

1 Most organisations compete for business and resources. They have ambitions that go well beyond the immediate future and purpose needs to include this vision. Even not-for-profit organisations or those in the public sector usually compete for funds and often seek to increase the range of services that they offer; such organisations will also benefit from a picture of where they expect to be in the future.
2 The organisation's mission and objectives may be stimulated in a positive way by the strategic options that are available from a new vision.
3 There may be major strategic opportunities from exploring new development areas that go beyond the existing market boundaries and organisational resources. These require a vision of the future that deserves careful exploration and development.
4 Simple market and resource projections for the next few years will miss the opportunities opened up by a whole new range of possibilities, such as new information technology, new materials and lifestyle changes. Virtually every organisation will feel the impact of these significant developments. Extrapolating the current picture is unlikely to be sufficient.
5 Vision provides a challenge for managers.

Vision is therefore a backdrop for the development of the purpose and strategy of the organisation. To be clear, it is not the same as purpose: vision is the future picture, with purpose being the more immediate and broader role and tasks that the organisation chooses to define based on the current situation. However, it may be that the vision will lead to the purpose: for example, the Yahoo! vision of a wide-ranging internet service company led to the specific purpose of acquiring two companies, Flickr and Tumblr, in the last few years.

It is the leadership's role to develop and implement a vision. In a survey of 1,500 senior leaders, 870 of them CEOs from 20 countries, respondents were asked what they believed were a leader's key traits. Ninety-eight per cent responded that 'a strong sense of vision' was the most important. Similarly, when asked about the critical knowledge skills, the leaders cited 'strategy formulation to achieve a vision' as the most important skill. In other words, managers need to have not only a vision but also a plan to implement it. Unfortunately, 90% reported a lack of confidence in their skills and ability to conceive a vision (Quigley, 1994).

One of the most famous examples of a vision is Disneyland's: 'To be the happiest place on earth.' Other examples are:

- 'Restoring patients to full life' (Medtronic);
- 'Our vision is to be the world's best quick service restaurant' (McDonald's); and
- 'To become the operating system of music' (Spotify).

Although such visions cannot be accurately measured by a specific indicator of how well they are being achieved, they do provide a fundamental statement of an organisation's values, aspirations and goals. Such visions go well beyond narrow financial objectives, of course, and strive to capture both the minds and hearts of employees.

There is a problem with this concept of vision. It has little meaning unless it can be successfully shared with those working in the organisation, since it is they who will have to realise it. In addition, as the boundary between organisations blurs, there will increasingly be groups of workers associated with many companies and organisations, such as part-time workers, contracted suppliers and other flexible workers, who may not feel committed to such a vision.

Clearly, vision statements are not a cure-all. Sometimes they backfire and erode a company's credibility. Visions fail for many reasons, including those discussed by Lipton (op. cit.).

- **The walk doesn't match the talk**. An idealistic vision can arouse employee enthusiasm, which may be dashed if employees find that senior management's behaviour is not consistent with the vision. Often, vision is a slogan or campaign of new buzzwords and empty platitudes like 'devotion to the customer' or 'teamwork' that are not consistently backed by management action.
- **Irrelevance**. Visions created in a vacuum unrelated to environmental threats or opportunities or an organisation's resources and capabilities often ignore the needs of those who are expected to buy into them. Employees may reject visions that are not anchored in reality.
- **Not the Holy Grail**. Managers often search for the one elusive solution that will solve their firm's problems. They may have tried other management fads only to find that they fell short of their expectations. A vision simply cannot be viewed as a magic cure for an organisation's problems.
- **Too much focus leads to missed opportunities**. Clearly, one of the benefits of a sound vision statement is that it can focus efforts and excite people. However, the downside is that in directing people and resources towards a grandiose vision, the consequences can be devastating.

 **CASE EXAMPLE** 7.4

In 1992, Kun-Hee Lee, chairman of South Korea's Samsung Group, created a bold strategy to become one of the ten largest car makers by 2010. Seduced by the clarity of the vision, Samsung bypassed staged entry through a joint venture or initial supply contract. Instead, Samsung borrowed heavily to build a state-of-the-art research and design facility and erect a greenfield factory, complete with cutting-edge robotics. Samsung Auto suffered operating losses and crushing interest charges from the beginning. And within a few years the business was divested for a fraction of the initial investment.

Sull (2005)

■ **An ideal future irreconcilable with the present**. Although visions are not designed to mirror reality, people have difficulty identifying with a vision that paints a rosy picture of the future but does not account for the often-hostile environment in which the firm competes or that ignores some of the organisation's weaknesses.

2.2 Mission

A mission aims to provide employees and stakeholders with clarity about the overall purpose and raison d'être of the organisation. It is therefore to do with building understanding and confidence about how the strategy of the organisation relates to that purpose. Organisational mission is thus the foundation on which strategy is built. Missions have two principal elements. First, there is a focus on organisational purpose, as suggested by questions such as 'What are we here to do?' and 'Why was this organisation established?' Google's mission, for example, is to organise the world's information and make it universally accessible and useful.

Second, these purposes are shaped by values: the beliefs about the manner in which these purposes should be achieved. Below is an example that embodies the idea of mission being about both purpose and values.

 CASE EXAMPLE 7.5

The Co-operative movement in the UK is a good example of the role of 'mission' to an organisation. The Co-operative Wholesale Society and Co-operative Retail Society are business organisations but their mission is not simply profit. They are owned by their suppliers/customers rather than external shareholders and have, since their foundation, had a wider social concern. The Co-op has explicit social objectives. In some cases, it will retain stores, which, although too small to be as profitable as a large supermarket, provide an important social function in the communities that host them.

The Co-op is also a good example of a distinction between the mission, ethos and behaviour of an organisation as distinct from its senior management. The Co-op is trying to recover from its near collapse in 2013, when a large £1.5 billion hole was revealed in its finances, and its chairman was exposed in a drugs scandal. The crisis saw bondholders take control of the bank, relegating its long term owner, the mutual Co-operative Group, to a minority holding.

Many organisations present their purposes and values in the form of a mission statement, which seeks to encapsulate the mission in a format that can be used both internally and externally. An organisation's statement mission statement differs from its vision in that it encompasses both the purpose of the company as well as the basis of competition and competitive advantage.

As Hudson (1999) observes, the *process* of preparing a mission statement can be valuable:

'Mission statements have an important role to play, particularly when it comes to reviewing future strategy. They need to be written and agreed, but their power as a management tool should not be over-emphasised. By contrast, working on the mission and taking actions to bring together the beliefs in the organisation with its strategy can be a powerful lever for increasing the organisation's effectiveness.' (p.95)

So perhaps engaging people in the process of developing the mission is a valuable way of building commitment. As such, mission statements have an *internal* and an *external* role, as shown in Figure 7.2.

Ethical stance

		Legal minimum	Ideological
Drivers of strategy	Internal managers	Secretive	Evangelical
	External stakeholders	Regulations and procedures	Political

FIGURE 7.2 The role of mission statements (Johnson and Scholes, 2002)

Within the organisation, they provide:

- **Unity of direction**. Set a sense of direction. They focus members' attention and give an opportunity to coordinate effort in achieving them. Without such clarification, each manager may interpret situations differently and find it difficult to act in unison.
- **Basis of plans and decisions**. Good mission statements help in the production of good plans. They help set priorities. Some objectives may be more vital to a company's success than others. Identifying these 'must-do' objectives separates them from others that can be postponed if resources are unavailable.
- **Motivation**. As we have argued, the process of preparing a mission statement and following this with goal- and objective-setting, encourages employees to consider and commit themselves to the ends of the organisation and offer the individual a sense of personal achievement.
- **Basis of control**. Through clarifying the performance that is expected, objectives become the basis for control. They are the criteria by which comparisons between outcomes and plans are made. Therefore, they need to be set against the backdrop of the overall mission.

It can be useful to ask yourself (and other staff members) how clear you are about what the organisation exists to do and how the commitment of staff is harnessed to its purpose. Is there a mismatch between what the organisation says it exists to do and how the staff feel about this? If so, does that affect the organisation's performance? If you are a manager, it can be stressful to be in the middle of such a mismatch, or to motivate staff if the organisation loses its sense of direction.

Declarations of mission are often addressed to wider audiences. They signify legitimacy to stakeholders from investors to customers and suppliers. It is intended that these interest groups then regard the organisation in a favourable light and accept its function. The Body Shop is a global business that incorporates the values of its founder, Anita Roddick. Strong, clear statements of the company's aims cover not only what business it is in, but also how it wishes to carry it out and whom it prefers to recruit as employees or suppliers.

Mission statements are formal documents that are often displayed in a number of places such as in an organisation's annual report, in publicity material, etc. There is no standard format, but usually have the following characteristics:

- **Brevity**. They should be easy to understand and remember.
- **Flexibility**. They must accommodate change.
- **Distinctiveness**. They should make the company seem different.

Effective mission statements incorporate the concept of stakeholder management, suggesting that organisations must respond to multiple constituencies if they are to survive and prosper. Customers, employees, suppliers and owners are the primary stakeholders, but others may also play an important role. Mission statements also have the greatest impact when they reflect an organisation's enduring, overarching strategic priorities and competitive positioning. Mission statements also can vary in length and specificity. The two mission statements below illustrate these issues. Compare these two. Which do you think works best?

 **CASE EXAMPLE 7.6**

Amazon.com's mission statement is 'to be Earth's most customer-centric company, where customers can find and discover anything they might want to buy online'.

The *principal* aims of Birkbeck College, London are to:

- provide part-time higher education courses which meet the changing educational, cultural, personal and career needs of adults; in particular, those who live or work in the London region;
- enable adult students from diverse social and educational backgrounds to participate in our courses;
- maintain and develop excellence in research and provide the highest quality research training in all their subject areas; and
- make available the results of research, and the expertise acquired, through teaching, publication, partnerships with other organisations and the promotion of civic and public debate.

The key supporting objectives are to:

- offer their students an integrated range of flexible, research-led courses across all levels of provision;
- achieve and maintain strong research cultures in support of interdisciplinary work in each school and faculty;
- ensure the College provides an inclusive working and learning environment for its students and staff so that all may develop to their full potential;
- develop the College's capacity to respond rapidly to new and changing opportunities in higher and further education;
- strengthen the College's financial position by accumulating reserves to ensure its long-term viability; and
- develop sustainable partnerships within the London region and beyond.

While some organisations produce detailed mission statements, others prefer brief phrases. Matsushita, for example, whose brands include Panasonic and Technics, adopted the management slogan: 'Take Action for Progress'.

There is a tendency for organisations to give their purpose in a few sentences. For example, an organisation will summarise its purpose as the maximisation of shareholder wealth, the achievement of growth targets, the delivery of market share or similar statements. Hamel and Prahalad (1989) have even argued that purpose should be summarised in a few words under the heading of 'strategic intent'. However, the purpose of the organisation deserves more thought than a single statement about profitability or some other phrase. The complexity of the topic is usually handled by identifying and concentrating on the essentials for that organisation. Such a process takes time and is best described as a process of shaping the purpose of the organisation. It is multifaceted, with a number of important elements.

The Ashridge Mission Model was devised by Campbell (1991) to help develop and evaluate the effectiveness of a mission statement. The model is shown in Figure 7.3.

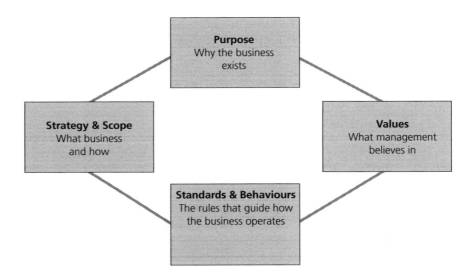

FIGURE 7.3 The Ashridge Mission Model (Campbell, 1991)

STOP AND THINK **7.3**

Using English Heritage's Mission Statement as an example, assess it using the model.

- **Mission statement**. 'To make sure that the historic environment of England is properly maintained and cared for. By employing some of the country's very best architects, archaeologists and historians, we aim to help people understand and appreciate why the historic buildings and landscapes around them matter. From the first traces of civilisation, to the most significant buildings of the twentieth century, we want every important historic site to get the care and attention it deserves.'
- **Purpose**. Does it say why the organisation exists?
- **Company values**. Does it convey what the company believes in? Are employee's personal values expressed?
- **Standards and behaviours**. Are the standards and behaviours that underpin the value system evident?
- **Strategy**. Does the statement give an impression of a distinctive competence or the competitive position?

STOP AND THINK **7.4**

Does your organisation have a mission statement? If not, prepare one using the guidelines above.
   If it does, think of an organisation you know well or an organisation like a health authority, a school or large shop and draft its mission statement.

2.3 Strategic objectives

Statements of vision tend to be quite broad and can be described as a goal that represents an inspiring, overarching and emotionally driven destination. Missions tend to be more specific and address questions concerning the organisation's reason for being and the basis of its competitive advantage.

The terms 'goals' and 'objectives' are often used interchangeably. Mintzberg (1994) sees an objective as a goal expressed in a form by which its attainment can be measured. An operational goal may be to 'cut costs'. The objective could be to 'reduce the budget by 5%'.

Strategic objectives are statements of specific outcomes that are to be achieved. They operationalise the mission statement; they help to provide guidance on how the organisation can fulfil or move towards the higher goals in the goal hierarchy – the mission and vision. They therefore tend to be more specific and cover a more specific time-frame. They are often expressed in precise financial terms – for instance, the level of sales, profits or share valuation in one, two or three years' time. Organisations may also have quantifiable market-based objectives, such as market share, customer service, repeat business and so on. Sometimes objectives focus on the basis of competitive advantage: for example, low-cost airlines such as Ryanair set objectives on turnaround time for their aircraft, because this is at the core of their distinctive low-cost advantage. Organisations are increasingly also setting objectives referred to as 'the **triple bottom line**', by which is meant not only economic objectives such as those above, but also environmental and social objectives to do with organisations' corporate responsibility to wider society.

It is also possible to distinguish corporate objectives and unit objectives as different 'levels' of objectives, with different characteristics.

- **Corporate objectives**. These are often expressed in financial terms. They could be the expression of desired sales or profit levels, rates of growth, dividend levels or share valuations. Increasingly, organisations use corporate objectives of a non-financial nature, such as employee welfare or technological advance, but these are usually accompanied by financial objectives. They are frequently formal statements of how the organisation intends to address stakeholder expectations and usually comprise formal statements of objectives to be met on behalf of a variety of stakeholders, including customers, suppliers, employees and the wider community.
- **Unit objectives**. These are likely to have the following characteristics:
  - They relate to the individual units of the organisation, for example a division, or of one company within a holding company.
  - They may be financial objectives stated in the same way as corporate objectives but at a unit level. They are more operational in nature than corporate objectives.
  - Multiple objectives might well be more common at the unit level than at the corporate level.
- A good objective should be couched in terms that are quantitative, both in measuring the outcome and the length of time before achievement. Furthermore, since objectives represent formal agreements over means and ends, they should be written. In summary, the tests of a good objective are threefold:
  - Is the desired result clearly stated?
  - Is it possible to measure whether the result has been achieved?
  - Is the time scale made clear?

Problems that arise with objectives include:

- **Conflict**. Managers are usually faced with multiple objectives that may be in conflict. Conflict may be direct. For example, when choosing outputs managers have to balance efficiency and effectiveness, or work speed and quality. On the other hand, conflict may be indirect, as when activities compete for a constraint, such as when several customers ask for delivery simultaneously.
- **Measurability**. Achieving some tasks is difficult to measure. Managers have to combine such tasks as ensuring that short-term schedules are achieved with other aspects such as developing staff, improving quality, and so on. There is the related problem of *massaging* objectives so they appear good at the period end.
- **Means–ends confusion**. Difficulties arise when the objective becomes an end in itself and its contribution to the wider effort is forgotten. This is especially true if achieving the objective is the basis of reward to an individual, department or organisation. There have been many cases of stakeholders or leaders demanding improvements in particular aspects of performance and forgetting that these may be achieved at the expense of equally vital objectives or constraints. For example, in the public sector, targets are a well-tried means of creating organisational focus, mobilising people and providing a concrete measure of success. The problem arises when, instead of the target being simply a way of calibrating the delivery of substance, meeting the target itself becomes the goal.

■ **Change**. Each objective contributes to the general plan of the organisation. But this raises the question of what happens when circumstances change. In unstable environments, no sooner is the plan created than it is out of date. Pursuing an objective may become irrelevant. Such situations need continual review.

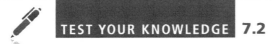

TEST YOUR KNOWLEDGE 7.2

a Explain what is meant by a 'vision statement'.
b Explain why visions may fail.
c Describe the difference between a mission statement and strategic objectives.

3 Statements of purpose – benefits and issues

3.1 The precision of mission and objectives

As suggested in the previous section, some argue that objectives are not helpful unless they are capable of being measurable and achievable. Others argue that open statements may be just as helpful as closed statements. Mission statements are certainly difficult to make in closed terms. Their role is to focus strategy rather than deciding when it has been 'achieved'. There may also be some objectives that are important but difficult to quantify or express in measurable terms. An objective such as 'to be a leader in telecommunications' may be highly relevant in today's technological environment, but it may become absurd if it has to be expressed in some measurable way. It is nonetheless valid as a statement of purpose. The aim of being a leader in telecommunications is there not as a detailed blueprint from the corporate centre but as an indication of a broad direction that becomes real as groups and individuals respond and progress it via their own priorities.

There are times when specific objectives are required, for example, when urgent action is needed in a crisis or at times of major transition and it becomes essential for managers to focus attention on a limited number of priorities. If the choice is between going out of business and surviving, there is no room for latitude through vaguely stated requirements and control.

Table 7.1 lists several firms' strategic objectives, divided into financial and non-financial categories. While most of these strategic objectives are directed towards generating greater profits and returns for the owners of the business, others are directed at customers or society at large.

TABLE 7.1 Strategic objectives (from company documents and annual reports (Dess et al., 2014)

Strategic objectives (financial)
■ Increase sales growth from 6% to 8% and accelerate core net earnings growth from 13% to 15% per share in each of the next five years. (Procter & Gamble)
■ Generate internet-related revenue of $1.5 billion. (AutoNation)
■ Increase the contribution of Banking Group earnings from investments, brokerage, and insurance from 16% to 25%. (Wells Fargo)
■ Cut corporate overhead costs by $30 million per year. (Fortune Brands)
Strategic objectives (non-financial)
■ We want a majority of our customers, when surveyed, to say they consider Wells Fargo the best financial institution in the community. (Wells Fargo)
■ Reduce volatile air emissions 15% by 2015 from 2010 base year, indexed to net sales. (3M)
■ Our goal is to help save 100,000 more lives each year. (Varian Medical Systems)
■ We want to be the top-ranked supplier to our customers. (PPG)

For objectives to be meaningful, they need to satisfy several criteria. They should be SMART:

- **Specific**. This provides a clear message as to what needs to be accomplished.
- **Measurable**. There must be at least one indicator (yardstick) that measures progress against fulfilling the objective.
- **Appropriate**. It must be consistent with the vision and mission of the organisation.
- **Realistic**. It must be an achievable target given the organisation's capabilities and opportunities in the environment. In essence, it must be challenging but achievable.
- **Timely**. There needs to be a time frame for accomplishing the objective.

When objectives satisfy these criteria, there are several benefits for the organisation:

- They help to channel employees throughout the organisation towards common goals. This helps the organisation concentrate and conserve valuable resources and work collectively in a more timely manner.
- Challenging objectives can help to motivate and inspire employees throughout the organisation to higher levels of commitment and effort. A great deal of research has supported the notion that individuals work harder when they are striving for specific goals rather than being asked simply to 'do their best'.
- There is the potential for different parts of an organisation to pursue their own goals rather than overall organisational goals. Although well intentioned, these may work at cross-purposes to the organisation as a whole. Meaningful objectives thus help to resolve conflicts when they arise.

3.2 Effective purpose statements

Some critics regard vision, mission and values statements as liable to become bland and too wide-ranging (Bartkus et al., 2000). Objectives can seem attractively precise by contrast. However, vision, mission and values statements provide a longer-term view of the organisation and its underlying strategy. While objectives are useful for guiding and monitoring performance in the short term, visions, missions and values can offer more enduring sources of direction and motivation. However, it remains crucial to make vision, mission and values statements meaningful.

Lencioni (2002) identified three principles that are helpful in creating meaningful vision, mission and values statements:

- **Focus.** Statements should focus attention and help guide real decisions. Effective vision, mission and values statements should define what is excluded from the organisation's strategy as much as what is included. At Apple, the visionary founder Steve Jobs regarded as crucial the ability to say 'no' to non-core activities. Statements should also be practical decision-making tools. Google's value of 'fast' can guide choices between strategic options with different levels of complexity: Google's product development managers will cut product features that slow down its essential search and advertising functions, even if they might be nice to have.
- **Motivational.** Statements should motivate employees to do their best. It is important that they are not so bland as to be applicable to nearly all organisations, but rather are distinctive and authentic to the particular organisation in question. To motivate, they should stretch organisational performance to higher levels, but at the same time, the targets must be credible. Apple's vision of making computers available to everybody inspired Steve Jobs' employees in the early years of the company.
- **Clear.** In order to motivate employees in their day-to-day work, visions, missions and values should be easy to communicate, understand and remember. It is often useful to be crisp and simple. Founder Mark Zuckerberg identified three of Facebook's values as 'move fast', 'be bold' and 'be open': these are clear, memorable and actionable.

As well as being associated with identity and providing a guide to strategy, it is also clear that statements of purpose are an important component of corporate reputation, as Case Example 7.7 suggests.

CASE EXAMPLE 7.7

The global energy company BP under the leadership of John Browne had been applauded for developing an explicit code of social responsibility emphasising efficient and sustainable energy, energy diversity, concern for climate change, local development where it operates and high levels of safety. This stance was publicised in an advertising campaign promoting the slogan 'Beyond Petroleum'. And John Browne stated: 'Our commitment to responsibility has to be expressed not in words, but in the actions of the business, day in and day out, in every piece of activity and every aspect of behaviour' (in *Business Strategy Review*, vol. 17, no. 3 (2006), pp. 53–6).

It was, therefore, a major disaster, not only to the local community but also to BP, when, twice in five years – 2005 and 2010 – accidents brought death, injury and major pollution to parts of the southern US.

In 2005, an explosion at BP's Texas City oil refinery killed 15 workers and BP was fined £12 million for 300 safety violations at the plant. The press were very critical, as the disaster had happened in the same year as BP profits soared and Browne received £6.5 million in pay and shares. The criticism was that BP's top management had emphasised cost cutting over safety. They did not listen to people lower down in the organisation; they reported a staff survey that rated 'making money' as the top priority and 'people' as the lowest. Too many jobs have been outsourced to cheaper contractors, and so it went on.

In January 2007, John Browne left BP 18 months early to be succeeded by Tony Haywood, who had been in charge of BP's exploration and production division. Passed over was John Manzoni, the board director with the responsibility of refineries.

In 2007, an independent investigation concluded that:

'BP has not provided effective process safety leadership and has not adequately established process safety as a core value across all its five U.S. refineries … BP tended to have a short-term focus and its decentralised management system and entrepreneurial culture have delegated substantial discretion to US refinery plant managers without clearly defining process safety expectations, responsibilities or accountabilities … The company did not always ensure that adequate resources were effectively allocated to support or sustain a high level of process safety performance.'

The company relied excessively on monitoring injury rates that 'significantly hindered its perception of process risk'. Incidents and near misses were probably under-reported and, when spotted, root causes often not identified correctly.

On 20 April 2010, the Deepwater Horizon drilling rig exploded in the Gulf of Mexico, killing eleven workers and causing an oil spill that soon became the worst environmental disaster in US history. On 2 May President Obama made his first trip to the Gulf Coast and said that BP was responsible for the leak and for paying for its clean-up.

'We're dealing with a massive and potentially unprecedented environmental disaster …The oil that is still leaking from the well could seriously damage the economy and the environment of our Gulf states. And it could extend for a long time. It could jeopardise the livelihoods of thousands of Americans who call this place home.'

An estimated 4.9 million barrels of oil leaked into the Gulf until the well was finally capped on 15 July. BP announced that it will place $20 billion in a fund to compensate victims of the oil spill and says it will not pay a shareholder dividend this year. BP's chief executive Tony Hayward, who was criticised over his handling of the spill, negotiated an early exit from his post. An investigation carried out by BP acknowledged that it was responsible in part for the disaster, but it also blamed two other companies working on the well.

Adapted from a case example by Johnson et al. (2014) and www.bbc.co.uk.

STOP AND THINK 7.5

To what extent might the negative publicity around the Texas City and Gulf disasters affect BP's strategy?

A danger is that stakeholders may see the various statements that we have examined here as rhetorical, manipulative or merely wish-driven. Although there is much prescriptive theory persuasively recommending the mission approach, there is rather less empirically valid research. A key problem is how to isolate and measure the extent of its impact. It is possible to show that it can change attitudes (if successful), but the relative significance of its long-term impact on behaviour, performance and the bottom line remain a matter of debate. As a result, some are sceptical and argue that a mission (statement) is neither a necessary nor a sufficient condition for commercial success.

TEST YOUR KNOWLEDGE 7.3

a Describe the issues associated with precision in statements of purpose.
b List the main benefits of mission statements.

CASE QUESTIONS

1 Advise the CEO why the ideas inherent in the hierarchy of purpose might help develop a more effective strategy for the ASO.

2 Explain how a mission statement might help the ASO to develop clarity of direction.

CHAPTER SUMMARY

■ An important managerial task is to decide how the organisation should express its strategic purpose. This chapter has addressed the need for consistency amongst an organisation's vision, mission and strategic objectives. Collectively, these form an organisation's hierarchy of goals.

■ Visions should evoke powerful and compelling mental images of the organisational goals. Mission statements take these further by expressing the purpose of the organisation, its scope of operations and the basis of its competitive advantage in the case of commercial firms.

■ Neither visions nor missions are very specific. Strategic objectives are more specific and are vital to ensuring that the organisation is striving towards fulfilling its vision and mission.

■ Although statements of purpose provide a focus, as a sense of identity and reputation and are a valuable communication tool, they may also be perceived as manipulative and little more than a wish list.

8 Business ethics, social responsibility and good corporate citizenship

■ **CONTENTS**

■ **INTRODUCTION**

This chapter looks at two particular aspects of purpose – business ethics and corporate social responsibility, which together many call good corporate 'citizenship'. Each of these reflects the position of organisations in a broader environment – the expectations that others in society have for organisations as well as the founders or primary stakeholders. Ethics is concerned with what is viewed as right or wrong and is considered at the individual level (in as far as this has an impact on strategy) as well as the overall ethical stance of the organisation. The chapter also considers the growth in significance of ways in which organisations seek to exceed their minimum obligations to stakeholders – corporate social responsibility – also known as corporate citizenship.

1 Business ethics

1.1 Introduction

Underlying the discussion of corporate governance (Chapter 6) is the issue about whether the purpose of an organisation and its strategy is for the benefit of a primary stakeholder, such as the shareholders of a company, or for the benefit of a wider group of stakeholders. In turn, this raises the question of society's expectations of organisations, the impact these have on an organisation's purpose and hence its strategy. Since the growth of large corporations at the end of the nineteenth century, companies have increasingly come to be seen more as public property with non-owners having a legitimate interest in influencing the decisions that managers make. There has also been a growing concern by some commentators from inside business (e.g. Roddick, 1992) and outside (e.g. McIntosh et al., 2003) that the goals and activities of business should be concerned with:

■ conducting business in an ethical manner;
■ treating people who come into contact with the business, such as suppliers and customers, fairly;
■ being socially responsible; and
■ taking care of the environment.

■ Governments have increasingly taken this view too, and are beginning to legislate accordingly.

This chapter considers:

■ the overall notion of business ethics;
■ corporate social responsibility – the role that businesses and other organisations might take in society;
■ the ethics of the behaviour and actions of people in relation to the strategy of their organisations; and
■ the notion of sustainability.

The issues covered by business ethics and corporate social responsibility are wide-ranging. They cover macro-issues (pollution reduction, the responsible exploitation of raw materials and corporate fraud) and micro-issues (fair pay, sexual harassment and cheating on expenses). These are issues that cover every business activity. For example:

- In marketing, many countries have banned or restricted tobacco advertising and set up commissions to monitor advertising and sales promotions to ensure honest representation.
- In research and development, pharmaceutical firms have established committees to oversee the ethical aspects of drugs testing.
- In finance and accounting, standards have been established about public accountability.

1.2 The scope of business ethics

The relationship of ethics to business is complex. For example, there are widespread beliefs about how customers or employees should be treated. However, we can see from examples around the world, and even between firms in the same sector or area, that practices vary significantly. **Business ethics** are therefore a function of:

- the *values* of individuals working in organisations;
- the *corporate culture* created by top management;
- *codes of conduct* operating in individual organisations;
- the *social norms* of the society within which the organisation is located;
- the prevailing *laws*.

For example, in some societies, bribery is an essential part of getting business done, while in others it is considered unacceptable behaviour. The dilemma occurs when employees of an organisation in a country where bribes are unacceptable must do business in a country where bribes are expected. Standards also change over time. The West decries the use of child labour in other countries, yet it was commonplace in nineteenth-century Europe.

Mahoney (1998) identifies three strands of business ethics.

1 **Stakeholder theory**. Identifies the various groups in society to whom the organisation is responsible.
2 **Corporate accountability**. Corporations are accountable for their actions to the general public. Companies that transgress socially acceptable standards can expect to be punished, usually by the imposition of fines. In some cases, board members can be held responsible and prosecuted as individuals, for example in the case of the bankruptcy of Enron, the US energy company.
3 **Social responsibility**. Corporations take responsibility for society at large and, through their actions; attempt to make the world a better place in which to live.

The implication of ethical issues and business is shown in Case Example 8.1.

 CASE EXAMPLE 8.1

Al Jazeera is a news network based in Qatar. It is seen as politically independent. In 2009, Al Jazeera showed a five-part series on lawsuits brought against multinational companies. The topics covered in the series varied from environmental dumping in Ivory Coast to killings of labour union activists in Colombia.

The latter focuses on Chiquita's links to the killings and disappearances carried out by paramilitary groups in Colombia. Chiquita has admitted making payments to paramilitaries and was fined US$25 million by the US government for funding a terrorist organisation. The company has defended its payments by claiming that the paramilitaries threatened to kill its employees, but paramilitary commanders have denied this and alleged that Chiquita made payments in order to provide security for their banana plantations. The company has now sold its subsidiary in Colombia, but it has been sued by family members who lost their relatives in the killings.

Al Jazeera (2009), f/english.aljazeera.riet/programmes/peopleandpower/
2009105120095191271847849.html, (accessed 21 July 2009).

1.3 The emergence of corporate social responsibility

The term corporate social responsibility has emerged in recent years. It is useful to consider briefly where the idea came from and how it has developed.

Corporate social responsibility (CSR) emerged as an area of general concern for companies in the 1960s (Ackerman, 1975), reflecting increasing pressures on companies to assume a greater responsibility for redressing the harmful impacts of their operations, a role traditionally performed by society as a whole. It was seen as a method of self-regulation distinct from both government legislation and managerial ethics. Companies experienced public scrutiny regarding a variety of issues, including discrimination against women and minorities, and, at the same time, the growth of the Green Movement focused a spotlight on the impact of commercial activity on the natural environment. CSR was therefore a way in which the business community reacted to the concerns raised by various groups rather than something imposed on business externally.

By the 1980s, governments had introduced legislation on many of the issues that had led to the emergence of CSR in the 1960s. For example, most European and North American countries had passed laws forbidding gender or racial discrimination in employment. But our current interest in ethical issues and responsible business stems from growing public and corporate concern about a number of disasters and scandals. In Bhopal, India, in 1984 there was a leakage of toxic pesticide at the Union Carbide Plant. This resulted in an estimated 2,500 deaths and 200,000 injuries. The case of the American companies Enron and WorldCom and the practices of some of their managers and the large pay rises given to managers in poor performing firms in the financial sector have given more recent cause for concern.

Griseri and Seppala (2010) argue that the most recent wave of interest in CSR has been marked by two new developments:

- The debate is now more about how to make substantial commitments rather than whether to make them at all. This shift is illustrated by a number of concrete and specific initiatives on corporate social responsibility, including ethical sourcing, social audits, stakeholder dialogue and ranking companies in relation to socially responsible investing criteria (e.g. the Dow Jones Sustainability Index and the FTSE4Good Index).
- In Europe not only businesses but also governments have engaged in the debate and launched initiatives on corporate social responsibility. This contrasts with the 1960s when corporate social responsibility was mainly a North American phenomenon.

TEST YOUR KNOWLEDGE 8.1

a Explain what is meant by 'business ethics'.
b Trace the emergence of corporate social responsibility.

2 Corporate social responsibility

2.1 The nature of corporate social responsibility

The size and globalised nature of many companies mean that they have a significant influence on society. Furthermore, the widely publicised corporate scandals and failures of the last two decades have raised concerns about the role they play. The regulatory environment and the corporate governance arrangements for an organisation determine its minimum obligations towards its stakeholders. However, such legal and regulatory frameworks set only minimum obligations, and stakeholders typically expect greater responsibility on the part of organisations.

CSR is a commitment by organisations to behave ethically and contribute to economic development while improving the quality of life of the workforce and their families, as well as of the local community and society at large (source: World Business Council for Sustainable Development). CSR is therefore concerned with the ways in which an organisation exceeds its minimum legal obligations.

In practice, CSR generally refers to business decision making linked to ethical values, compliance with legal requirements, and respect for people, communities and the environment.

Business in the Community, a voluntary group of UK companies that promotes CSR (cited in Coyle, 2010), has set out five principles that companies should apply:

1 Treat employees fairly and with respect.
2 Operate in an ethical way and with integrity.
3 Respect basic human rights.
4 Sustain the environment for future generations.
5 Be a responsible neighbour in their communities.

CSR is therefore consistent with a stakeholder approach to corporate governance by companies. Several issues come together in a CSR approach to conducting business:

■ an ethical approach to conducting business;
■ concern for all stakeholders;
■ concern for social and environmental issues; and
■ a recognition that a company must be profitable to survive and succeed in the long term.

Although CSR is commonly associated with ethical values and social and environmental issues, it is important to recognise that companies must carry on business in a way that is financially viable and profitable. CSR recognises social, environmental and economic issues (sometimes known as SEE), and is concerned with how companies can integrate the requirements of each into their business strategies and activities.

According to Carroll (1991), CSR involves the expectations that society has of business. As the expectations placed on companies evolve over time and across countries, social responsibility becomes a continuous process of the accommodating corporate behaviour to society's expectations. Any corporate activity should be assessed against the expectations placed on companies. Carroll also argued that CSR encompasses the entire range of expectations placed on companies, including economic, legal, ethical and philanthropic responsibilities.

■ **Economic responsibilities**. The primary responsibility of companies is to produce goods and services in a way that is profitable to their owners. Companies also offer employment and career opportunities and in this way form the basic economic unit of modern society. All the other responsibilities are underpinned by this economic role of business in society.
■ **Legal responsibilities**. While assuming their fundamental economic role, companies are expected to comply with the laws and regulations that reflect society's values and norms. Legal expectations apply to companies as juristic entities that can act as persons for some purposes, but also to individuals in their role as employees irrespective of the responsibilities they have in an organisation.
■ **Ethical responsibilities**. Businesses are also expected to abide by the ethical norms of society. Carroll argues that because these norms are not written in law, they are more ambiguous than legal requirements and therefore more difficult for companies to anticipate and follow. Nevertheless, there is an inherent link between legal and ethical responsibilities because ethical expectations can be seen to underpin and predict the emergence of new laws and regulations. For example, social movements, including those promoting women's rights and the natural environment, have advocated values that have been later codified into law.

FIGURE 8.1 Strategic management style (Carroll, 1969)

■ **Philanthropic responsibilities**. Business may engage in activities that go beyond the expectations of society. These include voluntary work, sponsorship of philanthropic projects and donations to public and non-profit organisations such as sports clubs. Even though lack of engagement in discretionary activities is not perceived as irresponsible, it is quite common for companies to carry out such roles in society, particularly in local communities.

Carroll presented the four different types of responsibilities in the form of a pyramid as shown in Figure 8.1, but the responsibilities are neither consecutive nor cumulative, nor are they mutually exclusive. It is therefore possible that a company satisfies the ethical expectations placed on it, but fails to meet its legal responsibilities lower down the pyramid. Moreover, any single action by an organisation may embody or conflict with more than one of the responsibilities. For example, a decision to pull out from a repressive regime may meet the ethical expectations placed on a company, but be against its economic interests. Carroll's four-part model is therefore useful in distinguishing and clarifying the motives and contradictions behind corporate behaviour, but does not predict corporate behaviour or indicate priorities for decision-making. The model can therefore be seen as successfully encompassing a range of concerns and definitions of social responsibility and, to an extent, bridging the gap between those in favour of CSR and those with misgivings. However, Carroll's model has some limitations for example, it does not indicate what to do when different types of expectations conflict. But it is useful in terms of categorising aspects of business activity.

 STOP AND THINK 8.1

How far can expectations of corporate social responsibility go?

Where should one draw the line between what is a reasonable requirement of corporate social responsibility and what is not?

These questions go to the heart of the CSR debate: opponents suggest that CSR is a voluntary concept, while adherents sometimes speak as if businesses have to comply with ethical requirements to obtain a 'licence to operate'.

2.2 The ethical stance

Different organisations take differing stances on CSR. Figure 8.2 outlines four basic types used by Johnson et al. (2014) to illustrate these differences. They represent a progressively more inclusive 'list' of stakeholder interests and a greater breadth of criteria against which strategies and performance will be judged. The stances are discussed further below.

The *laissez-faire view* suggests that organisations should be left alone to get on with things. Proponents argue that the only responsibility of business is to make a profit and provide for the interests of shareholders (Friedman, 1970). They believe that it is for government to protect society through legislation and regulation; organisations need do no more than meet these minimum obligations. Expecting companies to exercise social duties beyond this will only confuse decision-making and undermine the accountability of managers to their shareholders. In any case, society benefits from the profits reinvested. This stance may be taken by executives who are persuaded of it ideologically or by small businesses that do not have the resources to do anything more than comply with regulations.

Enlightened self-interest recognises the potential long-term financial benefit to the shareholder of well-managed relationships with other stakeholders. The justification for social responsibility is that it makes good business sense. For example, a good reputation in the eyes of customers and suppliers is important to an organisation's long-term financial success. Helping to improve the quality of marginal suppliers in the developing world is likely to create a stronger overall supply chain (Porter and Kramer, 2011). Managers with this enlightened self-interest stance take the view that organisations have not only responsibilities to society, but also relationships with other stakeholders. Therefore communication with stakeholder groups is likely to be interactive. Managers may well also set up systems and policies to ensure compliance with best practice (e.g. ISO 14000 certification), monitor their social responsibility performance and take more of a proactive social role.

	Laissez-faire	Enlightened self-interest	Forum for stakeholder interaction	Shaper of society
Rationale	Legal compliance: make a profit, pay taxes and provide jobs	Sound business sense	Sustainability or triple bottom line	Social and market change
Leadership	Peripheral	Supportive	Champion	Visionary
Management	Middle-management responsibility	Systems to ensure good practice	Board-level issue; organisation-wide monitoring	Individual responsibility throughout the organisation
Mode	Defensive to outside pressures	Reactive to outside pressures	Proactive	Defining
Stakeholder relationships	Unilateral	Interactive	Partnership	Multi-organisation alliances

FIGURE 8.2 Corporate social responsibility stances

From *Exploring Strategy*, 9th edition, Johnson et al, Pearson Education Limited, © Pearson Education 2002, 2011

A forum for stakeholder interaction (Hummels, 1998) explicitly incorporates multiple stakeholder interests and expectations as influences on organisational purposes and strategies. The argument is that the organisational performance should be measured in a pluralistic way, not just through the financial bottom line. Such organisations adopt the principle of sustainability in strategy, one that ensures a better quality of life by attending to environmental protection, social responsibility and economic welfare. Social responsibility here can be measured in terms of a 'triple bottom line' – social and environmental benefits as well as profits. Companies in this category might retain uneconomic units to preserve jobs, avoid manufacturing or selling 'anti-social' products, and be prepared to bear reductions in profitability for the social good. Sustainability will typically have board-level champions.

Shapers of society regard financial considerations as of secondary importance or as a constraint. Shapers seek to change society and social norms. Public sector organisations and charities are typically committed to this kind of stance. There are also social entrepreneurs who found new organisations that earn revenues but pursue a specific social purpose. For example, Traidcraft UK is a public limited company with a chain of retail shops that fights poverty by promoting 'fair trade'. For shapers of society, the social role is the *raison d'être* of the business. Financial viability is important only in terms of providing the means for continuing the social mission.

 **CASE EXAMPLE** 8.2

H&M is the world's second-largest clothing retailer. It has 3,150 stores worldwide, operating in 54 countries. It sells about 550 million items of clothing per year. It has traditionally been a leader in 'fast-fashion', the retailing of cheap fashion items designed to be worn only a few times before disposal.

Fast-fashion is a voracious industry. There are 30–50 trend-driven fashion seasons a year. Eighty billion garments are made annually by the majority of the 40 million garment workers. A garment worker in Bangladesh earns an average monthly wage of $40, where a pair of underpants costs about one penny to make

Fast-fashion is a target of international campaign groups such as the 'Clean Clothes Campaign', which in 2012 organised mass 'faint-ins' in prominent stores such as Gap, Zara and H&M across Europe, to draw attention to how under-nourished women workers frequently faint at work in Third World garment factories.

CASE EXAMPLE **8.2** *continued*

In 2012, H&M launched its new 'Conscious' range of clothing, making use of a large proportion of recycled materials and more environmentally friendly virgin materials such as hemp. The company explained the motivation: 'Our vision is that all business operations shall be run in a way that is economically, socially and environmentally sustainable.' This was accompanied by a Sustainability Report with some impressive statistics: for example, 2.5 million shoes were made during 2011 using lower-impact water-based solvents

Asked whether she could offer guarantees for the sustainability of the company's products across its ranges, H&M's Head of Sustainability, Helena Helmersson, responded: 'I don't think guarantee is the right word. A lot of people ask for guarantees: 'Can you guarantee labour conditions? Can you guarantee zero chemicals?' Of course we cannot when we're such a huge company operating in very challenging conditions. What I can say is that we do the very best we can with a lot of resources and a clear direction of what we're supposed to do. H&M does not own any factories itself. We are dependent on the suppliers – it is impossible to be in full control.'

Between April 2010 and 2015, H&M's share price increased by more than half, well ahead of the local Stockholm market index. Sales too have increased by nearly a third over the same five years.

Sources: Guardian, 7 April 2012; Ecouterre, 21 September 2012; www.hm.com; H&M Conscious Actions and Sustainability Reports.

STOP AND THINK **8.2**

Where would you place H&M in terms of the four stances on social responsibility?

Whichever ethical stance an organisation takes, this should become an integral element of corporate strategy. It helps a company to decide what kind of company it wishes to be: an important element in defining its organisational purpose.

2.3 Social auditing

Table 8.1 provides some questions against which an organisation's actions on CSR can be assessed. **Social auditing** is a way of ensuring that issues of CSR are systematically reviewed and has been championed by a number of organisations. This takes several forms, ranging from social audits undertaken by independent external bodies, through aspects of the social agenda that are now mandatory in company reporting (e.g. some environmental issues) to voluntary social accounting by organisations themselves.

STOP AND THINK **8.3**

How does your organisation fare on the dimensions set out in Table 8.1?
    Which others might you include?

TABLE 8.1 Issues of corporate social responsibility (adapted from Johnson et al., 2014)

Internal issues	External issues
Employee welfare – providing medical care, assistance with mortgages, extended sickness leave, assistance for dependents, etc.	**Environmental Issues** – reducing pollution below legal limits even if competitors are not doing so
Working conditions – enhancing working surroundings, social and sporting clubs, above minimum safety standards, etc.	**Markets and marketing** – deciding not to sell in some markets. Advertising standards.
Job design – designing jobs to the increased satisfaction of workers rather than for economic efficiency	**Suppliers** – 'fair' terms of trade; 'blacklisting' certain suppliers
Intellectual property – respecting the private knowledge of individuals and not claiming corporate ownership	**Community activity** – sponsoring local events and supporting local good works
	Human rights – respecting human rights concerning child labour and trade union rights

Clutterbuck and Snow (1991) revealed several areas of concern regarding how organisations were addressing issues such as those listed above. Although a large number of companies had produced guidelines on some or all of the issues, a significant number had no programme with which to put them into effect. The authors concluded that companies in Britain had generally increased their awareness and level of activity in some aspects of social responsibility, but they seemed to limit their involvement to a relatively narrow range of issues. Most organisations also failed to seek out best practice elsewhere, and this, they suggested, indicated that social responsibility considerations were not pursued as keenly as commercial activities, even where they were included as part of the purpose of the organisation.

As we have argued, extending this can be viewed as the obligation of managers to choose and act in ways that benefit both the interests of the organisation *and* those of society as a whole. This raises three issues that need to be clarified:

■ **Who is included?** While there is a growing consensus that all organisations should do their best to avoid detrimental impact on the natural environment, there is less agreement about who and what else ought to be included in the 'society as a whole'. Consumer rights have become well established in advanced economies, taken seriously by leading companies and underpinned by legislation. Few companies are concerned with disadvantaged people even though the disadvantage may be an indirect outcome of their activities. A supermarket may drive local shops out of business. Although many gain from the switch, some customers will find difficulty in reaching the new store. This is not seen as the company's problem.

■ **Complexity of decisions**. It is often difficult to select the best course of action for an organisation itself. Assessing the impact of any action on the wider society is a far more exacting task. What chance do managers have of getting it right? A firm may decide not to close a plant in a region where unemployment is high, deciding that community interests demand that it be given 'a last chance'. This may save jobs in the short term but may put other areas of the business at risk. Furthermore, it may reinforce a local habit of relying on outdated skills and employment patterns. When the plant is eventually closed, the catastrophe could be worse.

■ **Winners and losers**. Part of the decision-making problem is the choice of who benefits from its outcomes. CSR, may not come free. It is an example of managers choosing to benefit some groups at the expense of others.

 **CASE EXAMPLE** **8.3**

In 2008, Wal-Mart told 1,000 Chinese suppliers that it would hold them to strict environmental and social standards. It has encouraged companies to cut down on packaging – if suppliers do this, more can be fitted into delivery trucks, and carbon emissions and spending on petrol are reduced. If producers make concentrated laundry detergent, this saves on both packaging and shelf space.

Coyle (2015)

2.4 Sustainability and sustainable development

The concept of sustainability (also called **sustainable development** or sustainable business) is linked to CSR but focuses more on the environmental aspects of CSR than the economic and social aspects. However, there is no generally accepted definition of what it means. The Brundtland Report 1987 (prepared for the World Commission on Environment and Development) defined sustainable development as 'development that meets the needs of the present without compromising the ability of future generations to meet their own needs'. However, although this definition might seem broadly acceptable, Coyle points out that there are difficulties with what it means in practice.

- There can be disagreement about the meaning of 'needs of the present'. Presumably these are more than the bare minimum needs for survival, because in much of the world consumption is well above survival level and affluent societies do not accept the need to reduce consumption to levels in other countries of the world.
- Similarly, it is not clear what the needs of future generations are. If they are just survival needs, there must be an inherent assumption that at some time in the future economic wealth must decline in the more affluent societies.
- It is not clear over what period the needs of future generations should be considered and measured. In theory, society's long-term needs should be recognised. However, governments and companies are likely to plan over much shorter time-scales. Since companies plan for the future and report their performance within fairly short time-frames, reporting for sustainable development by companies is likely to focus on relatively short-term measures of sustainability.
- Should sustainability be measured collectively for all people in all societies of the world, or should sustainability be measured in terms of individual countries or regions?

In general terms, sustainability is concerned with conducting business operations in a way that can be continued into the foreseeable future, without using natural resources at such a rate or creating such environmental damage that the continuation of the business becomes impossible.

Environmental sustainability is now embraced by many competitive and successful multinational companies and is becoming a central part of their cultures and management processes. And, as noted earlier, environmental impacts are being audited and accounted for as the 'third bottom line'. According to one 2004 company report, 'If we aren't good corporate citizens as reflected in a Triple Bottom Line that takes into account social and environmental responsibilities along with financial ones – eventually our share price, our profits, and our entire business could suffer' (Vogel, 2005). In the next section we shall look at this issue in more depth.

Hilton (2015) suggests that not only are an increasing number of businesses building their brand on sustainability, but also this has risen up the agenda of pensions funds. This has occurred out of pressure for higher levels of shareholder engagement from the Kay Report, the stewardship code and guidance from the pensions regulator. The emphasis on stewardship stems from a belief that constructive engagement with management by shareholders leads to improved long-term performance and higher returns.

Another strand in pension fund thinking is the role of sustainability in shaping society for the longer term. Saker Nusseibeh, CEO of Hermes, the manager responsible for the BT pension schemes, has floated the idea that the fiduciary duty of trustees should take into account a view of the world in which their members will live when the pensions are being paid. For example, he suggests that pension funds should not press for excessive pay-outs from electricity companies today, if doing so undermines their ability to invest and therefore makes it more likely that there will be power shortages in 20 years' time.

In 2014, the National Association of Pension Funds published the results of a public opinion survey, which found that, although pension fund members had little idea how their money was invested, they were strongly in favour of it being invested ethically. The members also understood that the ethical stance and engagement would cost money to implement, but they expressed a willingness to accept that. This was particularly noticeable among younger members. How the wishes of members will be fed through the system to have an effect on investment outcomes is a difficult point. Hilton (op. cit.) argues that this lies behind the suggestion that pension funds and sponsoring companies should work closely together to promote sustainability. Both stand to benefit if sustainability takes hold as the guiding principle for business models.

'They do ... have common interests and there is an interesting thread leading from corporate responsibility, through shareholder responsibility, to corporate sustainability and pension fund efficiency.' (p.11)

2.5 Corporate social responsibility and corporate strategy

Lynch (2015) has made some specific connections between CSR considerations and strategic management at different levels:

- **The national and international level**. The role of the organisation in society and the country. Political, economic and social issues such as those explored in Chapter 3 will impact here: laissez-faire or planned, the role and power of trade blocks and state social policies, etc. The organisation is entitled to have a view on these matters and to seek to influence society, if it so desires.
- **The corporate level**. Ethical and corporate issues over which the organisation has some direct control. Matters such as the preservation of the environment, contributions to political parties and representations to the country's legislative parliament are all examples of direct corporate activities that need to be resolved.
- **The individual manager and employee level**. Standards of behaviour that organisations will wish to set for individual managers and workers. Some of these matters may not be strategic in nature, in the sense that they are unlikely to affect the future direction of the organisation overall but rather will affect the future of individuals. However, there may well be some general policies on, for example, religious, ethnic and equality issues that involve both the individual and fundamental matters relating to the direction of the organisation. These general matters of policy deserve to be treated at the highest possible level, and therefore come within the ambit of strategic management.

There are differing views about the extent to which companies benefit commercially from CSR policies. In 2004, the Association of British Insurers examined CSR and its impact on company performance. The key findings were as follows:

- Some studies had found that companies with active CSR policies benefited financially. The evidence was not conclusive but suggested that companies might benefit in areas such as corporate reputation, consumer acceptance, employee loyalty and environmental management.
- The benefits of CSR for companies were not uniform across all companies or sectors.
- The strategic risk aspects of CSR were as important as the effect on short-term profitability. Companies should recognise CSR risks in their strategic planning and management because they can have important implications for brand value and market acceptability. There was now a greater awareness of the importance of risk as well as returns, including risk to reputation. Social, cultural, demographic and technological changes meant that social and environmental risks were now more significant than in the past.

The potential benefits of CSR policies for companies may be divided broadly into these categories:

- **Reduction in reputational risk**. Reputational risk is difficult to quantify. It is the risk that a company's reputation with the general public (and customers), or the reputation of its product 'brand', will suffer damage. Damage to reputation can arise in many different ways:

incidents that damage reputation are often reported by the media. There appears to be a link between public attitudes towards a company and the way in which the company presents itself as an organisation concerned with social, ethical and environmental issues. There is a risk to a company's reputation, depending on the CSR policies it adopts. A company's reputation can be damaged by adverse publicity and public comment from incidents such as a serious environmental spillage or a serious accident. Reputational risk exists for many large companies, not just the obvious examples of companies in mining and extracting, pharmaceuticals and food.

 CASE EXAMPLE 8.4

In the UK, the rail system operator Railtrack failed to recover from the damage to its reputation from the safety concerns of the public following the Hatfield rail crash in 2001. The company collapsed in the following year.

Managing reputational risk and protecting a company's name or brands against reputational damage is now regarded as a key policy objective for companies with well-known brands.

- **Reputation and public relations**. Companies that might suffer losses from damage to their reputation need to be vigilant and alert for any incident that could create adverse publicity. CSR policies may therefore be used to create favourable publicity, and PR consultants may be used to publicise ethical or socially responsible activities by companies, including sponsorship of charity events or involvement in community activities. It may therefore be argued that some CSR policies that companies attempt to publicise are little more than attempts to promote the company and so are similar in many ways to advertising, except at a lower cost.
- **Commercial and financial benefits**. Many companies can also see commercial and financial benefits from CSR policies. As environmental and social regulations are extended, and governments introduce stricter laws on environmental protection and health and safety, new commercial opportunities for environmentally friendly technologies and environmentally friendly products have emerged. Developing new technologies and new products can take a long time and require substantial investment, but companies might need to make these investments in order to survive in the long term. The development of renewable energy technology and environmentally friendly cars are perhaps well-known examples. Many companies have also improved their technology for reducing waste or toxic emissions, in order to avoid fines and penalties.

 CASE EXAMPLE 8.5

In 2010 the retailer Marks & Spencer announced a new list of ethical and environmental commitments up to 2020, and its intention to become one of the world's most environmentally friendly retailers by 2015. An initial list of 100 five-year ethical and environmental targets had been announced in 2007, including the aim of becoming carbon neutral and eliminating landfill waste, and the company expected to achieve its targets. It had also expected to commit £40 million in expenditure each year to this initiative, but in 2009 it had saved over £50 million. For example, it had achieved a 20% reduction in fuel costs by using aerodynamic lorries for its deliveries. Its new targets for 2020 included sourcing all food, clothing and home items from sustainable or ethical sources such as the Fairtrade scheme and trying to persuade its clothing suppliers, especially in India, to pay a living wage to its employees, but without adding to costs for the consumer.

Cited in Coyle (2015)

---

3 Social business and creating shared value

3.1 The social business and social enterprise

The financial crash of 2007–08 and the subsequent recession and prolonged period of austerity in the UK has seen the rise of the **social business** or **social enterprise**, a fast-growing phenomenon which is also experiencing rapid growth in many other parts of the world.

A social business was defined by Nobel Peace Prize laureate Professor Muhammad Yunus as a business that:

- is created and designed to address a social problem in some way;
- is a non-loss, non-dividend company;
- is financially self-sustainable; and
- has its profits reinvested in the business with the aim of increasing social impact.

The phrase 'social business' is sometimes used interchangeably with 'social enterprise'. There are differing opinions as to exact definitions. Some talk about a spectrum, ranging from profit-first corporations to non-profits or charities, with social enterprises closer to non-profits and social businesses closer to for-profits (see Figure 8.3).

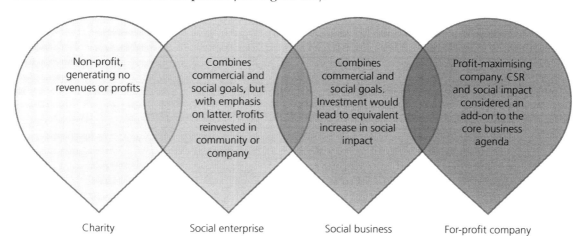

FIGURE 8.3 Types of social business (source: ClearlySo)

In the UK, social enterprises are often incorporated as a 'community interest company' (CIC), a new type of company registration. A community interest company must have a social mission, and also its constitution includes an 'asset lock' so that assets of the company cannot be distributed or used other than in support of the social mission. If a CIC closes, then any net assets are required to be transferred to a registered charitable organisation selected upon the formation of the CIC.

Social businesses and enterprises can have a social impact in many ways, from diverting profits to social causes, through delivering social services as part of its operation, to training and employing the social beneficiaries in the production of goods and services and thus revenue generation.

A changing emphasis between people, planet and profit

While environmentalism has come a long way since its origins in the 1960s, in terms of awareness of global warming and the need to save the planet from future catastrophes, the social component of the so-called 'triple bottom line' (economic, social and environmental benefits) has seen much less attention. The recession has focused attention on the current human impact of the Great Depression, and for many this has assumed priority alongside future environmental problems.

When national governments assumed the liabilities of failing banks, they shored up the financial system at the cost of significant debt and deficit problems for many governments, who were, in turn, forced to cut the size of the public sector, with a consequent impact on social services. At the same time, socially motivated organisations emerged to fill many of the gaps, bringing private sector approaches to solving social problems.

In the UK, for example, the public sector has withdrawn from direct provision of many social services, in many cases becoming the commissioners of such services rather than deliverers. The new providers that sprang up were social businesses, often incorporated as social enterprises, many as spin-offs or subsidiaries of charities – but with a different, harder financial edge. Many of these organisations were management buy-outs from the public sector, feather-bedded with initial three-year contracts and one-off lump sum grants, as the public sector sought to extricate itself from further liabilities.

Payment for results – an outcome focus

The social enterprise, which is in simple terms a hybrid between a charity and a private business, has non-financial social goals as well as financial targets to ensure its survival. Its income comes not from charitable donations but from the delivery of key social outcomes – for example, the percentage of probationers who do not reoffend may be the target for an organisation offering prisoner rehabilitation services, with payment made for hitting key target bands.

This harsh new world of measuring social impact was a challenge for many charities, especially smaller local charities, and thus the concept of social business has grown to fill the gap, led and staffed by many who are drawn to an organisation with real purpose. It has surprised many to see the growth of the concept worldwide, and it fits into growing trends for localism as well as a social conscience and a noticeable backlash against globalisation, big business and the global elites, as can be seen from the 2016 presidential election in the US and the EU referendum in the UK.

3.2 Social value measurement

The need to measure the tangible non-financial outcomes of social services in order to secure funding has driven a growing sector of **social value** and social impact metrics, and a new vocabulary that is helping to bring the public, third and private sector closer together. In business we often hear the phrase 'if we can measure it we can manage it', and various initiatives have sprung up to measure social return on investment.

With nearly a decade of activity in this area, most of the measures and audit schemes, although well meaning and useful, cost money and time to prepare, and it is often a struggle to find a common currency to compare and contrast across social sectors and organisations. There are organisations working on this challenge with some promising results in terms of ease, cost and scalability.

In the UK, the 2012 Social Value Act requires private sector bidders for public procurement contracts to take into account the economic, social and environmental well-being of the area in their bids, possibly focused on key local issues written into the invitation to tender documentation, with a view to supporting local charities as delivery agents of the social impact. However, in order to do this, charities and businesses must improve at talking each other's language. For the private sector, the keys to good corporate citizenship lie in:

- targeted intervention addressing local need;
- strategic links to the organisation's operations;
- a focus on outcomes and impact not inputs; and
- maximum leverage in terms of savings for society.

An example is as follows:

> Banks make money from mortgages. Changing economic conditions can lead to foreclosures and homelessness. Working with homelessness charities, banks can help fund and deliver training that helps to rehabilitate homeless people, who can cost society up to £20,000pa each in the NHS and criminal justice alone. Thus a donation by a bank of £100,000 can be leveraged to a significant multiple of this figure in terms of social value, through reductions in the cost of suicides, hospitalisations, court appearances, etc., as well as long-term savings in unemployment and other welfare benefits.

Meanwhile, many organisations, including large corporations, are also rising to take on the challenge of social impact. Strategic thinking is developing to embrace this new dimension of corporate activity for a variety of reasons, including a genuine belief in the need for business to act as a good corporate citizen, or simply to anticipate further legislation and compliance in this area. It does seem clear that in future, business leaders will have to be concerned with the implicit 'licence to operate' granted by society. If only from a risk and reputation management point of view, this will be an issue that will increasingly be an agenda item in corporate governance and board meetings.

3.3 Creating shared value

That most prolific of strategy authors, Professor Michael Porter, has been addressing these issues, since 2007, when he wrote a seminal paper in the *Harvard Business Review* entitled 'Strategy and Society'. This was followed in 2011 with another *HBR* article entitled 'Creating Shared Value' (CSV), in which Porter and his co-author Kramer explored the issue of non-financial issues and externalities, as well as the traditional financial goals associated with strategic management and the search for competitive advantage.

Porter attempts to show how his core strategy models, such as the value chain, can be adapted to take into account social impacts – through the identification and treatment of negative and positive 'externalities', to use economists' language. These are the external impacts that the company has on society or society on the company. Furthermore, he put forward the idea that, in these areas and in the social services sector, there are plenty of opportunities for cost saving or revenue generation that extend beyond traditional corporate philanthropy or even the enlightened self-interest in supporting the local economy, as Nestlé does in Africa to ensure a healthy, long-living and educated work force.

Porter's objectives are noble, and the analytical tools useful. Critics of the shared value concept, such as Andrew Crane, suggest that: the thinking is not particularly new, that Porter's idealism is fine but that it was not original, that it ignores the inherent tensions between social and economic goals, that it is naive about business compliance and that it is based on a shallow conception of the corporation's role in society. Crane criticised CSV, which aims to 'reshape capitalism', and states that in reality, it is really just more of the same of all the things that have given capitalism such a bad name – a blind focus on individual corporate self-interest.

The good thing is that there is a growing debate on these issues. This emerging area is one to watch closely for anyone interested in strategy. It represents the biggest change in strategy in the past 30 years, from when Porter first hit the scene and made such an impact on strategic management. It will potentially shape the future of free market economies and capitalism, which one could say nearly collapsed in the last decade. Although Porter's shared value concept may not provide all the answers, he is at least forcing us to ask the right questions. Other management authors writing in this area include Charles Handy, and just to prove that it is not new, the late Peter Drucker in his prime. What is new is the focus on leverage and outcomes, and emerging analytical tools regarding to how to approach good 'corporate citizenship'.

This sort of enlightened approach is growing, with environmental and social reporting increasingly required by government regulation and the UK Code of Corporate Governance. The emphasis is moving from reporting on what companies have done in the past to what they are doing now and also plan to do in the future. This should stimulate continuous improvement in behaviour and impact.

The potential benefits of strategic corporate citizenship include a better society for all, as well as enhanced long-term shareholder value, through measurement of an organisation's social impact and the rebuilding of its reputational assets. Companies such as Ricoh UK are doing some ground-breaking work in this area, tracking the effect of their social initiatives and impact on employee recruitment, retention, absenteeism, performance and satisfaction.

 TEST YOUR KNOWLEDGE 8.2

a Explain the distinction between a 'social business' and a 'social enterprise'.
b What is meant by an 'outcomes' or impact rather than 'input' focus?
c What is meant by the term 'externalities' in Porter's concept of 'shared value'?

4   The role of individuals and managers

Ethics is concerned with the code of values and principles that enables a person to choose between right and wrong and therefore select among alternative courses of action. It follows that an ethical issue is one where there is a choice of alternatives and these alternatives will bring benefit or harm to others.

These exclude personal decisions that have no impact on other people and the trivial. It is only when they have consequences for other people that these choices become ethical. The law is a codification of the ethics of the society as a whole. Business and markets would be impossible without the rights and duties given to individuals and agents, the establishment of the 'rules of the game', and so on, and there is an argument that following the law is all that one has to do, and no more. Yet this may be inadequate for two reasons:

1   There are many areas of life in which the government chooses not to legislate, because of unenforceability, a desire to reduce the role of the state or because change has made previous laws out-of-date. Extreme notions of personal freedom would lead to a breakdown of many social processes.
2   Legal systems differ in different countries. In the absence of a clear legal position, the need is for some moral criteria.

Ethical issues have to be faced at the individual as well as corporate level, and can pose difficult dilemmas for individuals and managers. Such issues include:

■ the responsibility of an individual who believes that the strategy of his or her organisation is unethical (e.g. its trading practices) or is not adequately representing the legitimate interests of one or more stakeholder groups;
■ whether that person leave the company on the grounds of a mismatch of values; and
■ whether whistle-blowing is appropriate – for example, divulging information to outside bodies (such as regulatory bodies or the press).

A very recent development can be found in the concept of 'values-based' or 'values-driven' leadership, a phrase which embraces many of the elements in this chapter and embodies them in the individual leader or manager. Professor Harry M. Jansen Kraemer, Jr. of the Kellogg School of Management in Chicago wrote about rooting one's leadership style in who you are and what matters most – your values. He laid out four guiding principles of values-based leadership:

■ **self-reflection:** the ability to identify and reflect on what you stand for;
■ **balance:** the ability to see situations from multiple perspectives and differing viewpoints to gain a greater understanding;
■ **self-confidence:** accepting yourself as you are, recognising your strengths and your weaknesses, striving for continuous improvement; and
■ **humility:** never forgetting who you are or where you came from, keeping your life and career success in perspective.

Similar and overlapping themes are explored by Professor Gary Hamel in his management blog 'The MIX' (Management Information Exchange), where he talks about the concept of Management 2.0. Hamel's Pyramid in Figure 8.4 shows how enlightened management can tap into and build on the values, and thus passion, of employees to help drive innovation.

Today, in many parts of the world, confidence in leaders is low – in government as well as business. Leaders need to regain and maintain trust. Values-based leadership is an interesting approach for aligning the values of leaders with employees so as to improve the health, morale and reputation of organisations. It is a form of leadership that is based on service to others (individual), to a greater purpose (organisational and societal), and is both ethical and practical. The starting point of a good corporate citizenship/CSR and a values-driven organisation is the individual leader.

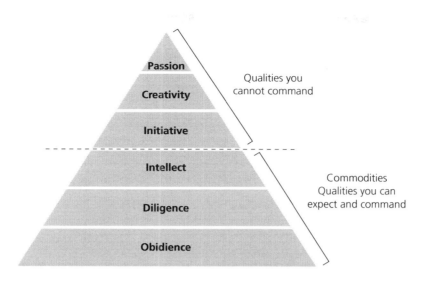

FIGURE 8.4 Hamel's Pyramid

CASE EXAMPLE 8.6

Conflicting objectives
You are a Dutch manager in charge of the mining operations of your multinational company in Namibia. You employ mainly local workers on very low wages. Your operation provides livelihood for 1,000 families and is the mainstay of the local economy. There is no other local work other than subsistence farming. You have discovered many safety problems with the mine, but the company engineer has advised that the cost of upgrading facilities would make the mine uneconomic. Closing the mine would cause a major political stir and harm the parent company's reputation, but keeping it open risks the chance of a major disaster.

Performance data
You are the recently appointed head teacher of a school that is now improving following a period of very poor performance under your predecessor. It has been made clear that one important performance indicator is pupil attendance levels, which must be brought up to the national average (95%). You have now collected all the data for your regular statistical return and notice to your disappointment that your attendance record has fallen just below your required target. On discussing this with your deputy she asks if you would like her to 're-examine and correct' the attendance data before submission.

Johnson et al. (2008, p.152)

STOP AND THINK 8.4

If you were faced with each of these dilemmas:

- What choices of action do you have?
- List the pros and cons of each choice to your organisation, the external parties and yourself.
- What you would do? Justify your actions from an ethical point of view.

Given that strategy development can be an intensely political process with implications for the personal careers of those concerned, managers can find difficulties establishing and maintaining a position of integrity. There is a potential conflict for managers between strategies that are best for their own career and those that are in the longer-term interests of their organisation and shareholders. Some organisations set down explicit guidelines that they expect their employees to follow.

CASE EXAMPLE 8.7

Texas Instruments posed these questions:

- Is the action legal? . . . If not, stop immediately.
- Does it comply with our values? . . . If it does not, stop.
- If you do it, would you feel bad? . . . Ask your own conscience if you can live with it.
- How would this look in the newspaper? . . . Ask if this goes public tomorrow, would you do it today?
- If you know it's wrong . . . don't do it.
- If you are not sure . . . ask; and keep asking until you get an answer.

TEST YOUR KNOWLEDGE 8.2

Outline the significance of the issue of individual ethics to an organisation.

CASE QUESTIONS

1 Explain how you would characterise the ethical stance of the ASO.

2 Comment on the sustainability of the ASO's previous strategy.

CHAPTER SUMMARY

- This section considered corporate social responsibility: the role that businesses and other organisations might take in society, and the ethics of the behaviour and actions of people in relation to the strategy of their organisations.
- CSR policies may be based on the principles of treating employees fairly, behaving ethically, respecting human rights, sustaining the environment for future generations and being a responsible neighbour in the communities where the company operates.
- Sustainability or sustainable development is one CSR objective. Sustainability means conducting a business in a way that sustains the environment for future environments and protects environmental resources in a way that will enable the business to continue operating into the foreseeable future. However, sustainability also recognises the need for companies to be profitable and financially secure in order to survive.
- Companies may recognise the need to be seen to adopt CSR policies in order to avoid reputational risk. Some companies use CSR initiatives for PR and marketing purposes, and there should also be commercial/financial reasons for CSR initiatives.

- There has been fast growth in the number of social businesses and enterprises, which bring private sector methods to address social problems. Metrics to measure social value are emerging, with a focus on outcomes and impact rather than inputs. This will enable to firms to leverage their resources and corporate philanthropy to maximum effect.
- Business ethics also have an impact at the individual level as ultimately it is individuals and groups in organisations who make decisions relating to strategy.
- There is an emerging concept of 'values-driven leadership' based on an alignment of individual and corporate values and service to society, customers and employees.

Implementing and evaluating strategy

■ **LIST OF CHAPTERS**

■ **OVERVIEW**

Having analysed the internal and external environment and clarified issues to do with strategic purpose, the final part of this study text looks at implementing and evaluating strategy.

We take a broad view of implementation and begin in Chapter 9 by looking at the range of choices available to organisations about the products and markets available to them, and how they position themselves against competitors choices about business level and corporate strategy as well as internationalisation.

In Chapter 10, we look at choices about how strategies are to be pursued. If an organisation's strategy calls for the enlargement of the corporate portfolios, there is a need to gain access to additional resources. It is vital that strategists and leaders choose the most appropriate strategic pathway and understand the advantages and disadvantages of the various possibilities open to them. This chapter considers three main approaches: organic development, mergers and acquisitions, and strategic alliances. The second half of the chapter discusses the success criteria by which they can be assessed and some of the techniques for evaluating strategic options.

Organisational design can be a critical issue in the success or failure of organisations. This is addressed in Chapter 11. As organisations seek to compete in ever-changing environments, they need to have appropriate organisational structures. The structural roles people play, the processes through which they interact and relationships that they build are crucial to the success of strategy. These are issues of 'organisational design'. Views about designing organisations are changing. The traditional emphasis on formal structures which suited a top-down, command-and-control view of strategy suited a more stable environment. In a world where knowledge is held by employees at all levels in the organisation, and where change is constant, relying on formal top-down structures may no longer be enough.

Chapter 12 is concerned with strategic control through the processes of performance management and Chapter 13 is about change – strategic change. To remain competitive organisations must respond to what is going on in their environment. We describe the forces that require managers to implement comprehensive change programmes and why people and organisations often resist change and how this resistance can be overcome. We also review various processes for managing organisational change and discuss contemporary change issues for managers.

■ LEARNING OUTCOMES

After reading and understanding the contents of Part Four, considering some of the Case Examples and Test Your Knowledge questions, you should be able to:

■ critically review the range of methods by which strategy might be pursued: organic development, mergers and acquisition and strategic alliances;

■ employ a range of techniques for evaluating strategic options, identify alternative directions for strategy, including market penetration or consolidation, product development, market development and diversification;

■ apply portfolio management to create value through corporate level strategy;

■ assess the extent to which strategic business units can provide sustainable competitive advantage;

■ identify sources of competitive advantage in international strategy using Porter's Diamond;

■ assess the strengths and limitations of the main structural forms;

■ recognise the role of control processes and relationships, including performance management and evaluation, technical control and administrative control;

■ distinguish the nature and significance of strategic change;

■ advise on roles in managing change including managers and change agents;

■ assess the value of change levers and tactics, including political and symbolic processes;

■ advise on managing the effects of change on people;

■ identify the issues involved in designing and managing strategic change programmes; and

■ understand why change may be resisted and how this can be overcome.

 PART 4 CASE STUDY

Strategy at London Central University (LCU)

LCU is a modern university with about 20,000 full-time students. Historically, LCU received most of its funding via government grants and awards. Recently, these grants to universities have been reduced and LCU has been forced to adopt a more business and sales-focused approach to its strategy and operations. Its academic and administrative staff are now obliged to extend their skillsets by taking on business development roles in order to identify new courses, educational partners and student segments that might develop income streams for the university.

Initially, this requirement was met by reluctance and resistance on behalf of the staff groups who seemed unwilling to enter into this new territory and who expressed nervousness and reluctance at the prospect. LCU hired a team of organisational development specialists to tackle this challenge, and they initiated the following interventions:

■ A series of cross-department working groups were established to explore and probe staff concerns, and to develop proposals to equip staff with the necessary training and support to allow them to undertake the new roles.

PART 4 CASE STUDY *continued*

- Following these meetings, the consultancy arranged a series of training programmes for the staff.
- A number of change champions were appointed (from each staff group). These individuals were selected on the basis of their ability to promote the required changes to working practices and for their enthusiasm.

The initial workshops identified that the main reason why staff were apprehensive about the new roles was a fear of failure in the new, expanded job roles. From this feedback, the consultants were able to tailor a training programme that not only helped to develop the new skills that staff required, but to promote staff confidence and morale as well. In addition, the change champions were trained to provide coaching support to staff once they finished the training, to help ensure new skills learnt and confidence gained were not simply discarded after the training programme finished. It was observable that over time – across a period of about 18 months – staff became more enthusiastic and less resistant to the changes.

The importance of the new job requirements was reinforced via incorporation of business development targets within the staff appraisal system. In a relatively short period of time, staff started to believe that their career advancement would be greatly enhanced by accepting the changes and providing evidence of achievement in the new areas required.

9 Strategic choices

■ INTRODUCTION

The first step in implementation is to choose the range of products or services the organisation is offering and how to position itself against its competitors or in relation to other providers. How and why firms outperform each other goes to the heart of strategic management. This chapter looks at the scope of strategic choice and the specific choices available to organisations: choices at the business level and the corporate strategy level, as well as the approach to internationalisation.

1 The scope of strategic choice

Strategic choices are concerned with decisions about an organisation's future and the way in which it responds to the pressures and influences that we have already discussed. There are three main sets of choices. These are shown in Figure 9.1, together with some of the possible courses of action.

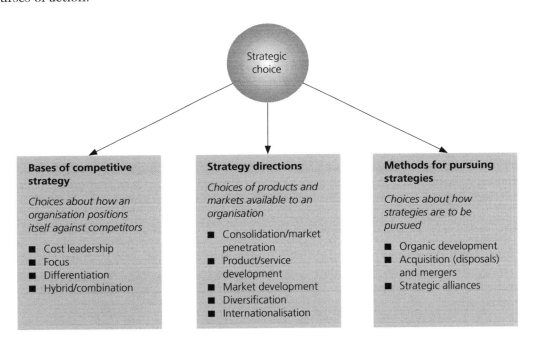

FIGURE 9.1 Strategic choices

- **Choices about how an organisation positions itself in relation to competitors**. This is a matter of deciding the overall basis of how to compete in a market. For example, if the aim is to pursue a strategy that provides competitive advantage and lasting superior financial performance, is this to be achieved on the basis of price or differentiation? These questions are addressed in the first part of this chapter.
- **Choices of the range of products and markets**. Should the organisation be very focused on just a few products and markets, or should it be much broader in scope, perhaps very diversified in terms of both products (or services) and markets? This raises questions of corporate strategy (addressed in Section 3) and international strategy (Section 4).
- **Choices about how strategies are to be pursued**. For any of these choices, should they be pursued by organic development, acquisitions or through joint ventures with other organisations? This is the theme of the first part of Chapter 10, which also looks at how these choices are to be evaluated. What are the criteria that might be used and the tools that are useful for this?

Johnson et al. (2014) point out that there is a potentially misleading distinction between undertaking the sort of strategy analysis that was explained in Part Two of the study text and considering the choices discussed in Part Three. They suggest that these are not separate and disconnected for two reasons:

1 **Key strategic issues**. Choices have to be considered in the context of the understanding of an organisation's strategic position. The key strategic issues must therefore be clear. Often the outcome of strategic analysis is a very long list of observations, but with key issues unclear. This is a matter of informed judgement and debate. The analytic tools can help inform, but are not a substitute for judgement.
2 **Strategic analysis generates strategic options**. Earlier chapters identified ways in which strategists can identify forces at work in the business environment, identify and build on strategic capabilities, meet stakeholder expectations, and be aware of the benefits and constraints of their organisation's cultural context. In understanding these forces, the strategist will have also begun to generate ideas and raise questions that generate strategic options.

STOP AND THINK 9.1

Thinking about these areas, what is the range of choices facing an organisation you know well?

TEST YOUR KNOWLEDGE 9.1

a   Identify the range of strategic choices organisations face.
b   Explain how analysis and choices may be connected in strategy.

2 Business-level strategy

2.1 Strategic business units

The starting point for business strategy is identifying the relevant business unit. A strategic business unit (SBU) supplies goods or services for a distinct domain of activity. The identification of an organisation's SBUs helps the development of business-level strategies, since these may need to vary from one SBU to another. In the sections that follow, the concepts discussed therefore relate to the SBUs that have been identified. Judgement needs to be given to the relationship of SBUs and organisational design (see Chapter 11). In the public sector, the frequent 'repackaging' of activities within ministries in central government shows how difficult these judgements can be. For example, in the UK over the last few decades 'education' has been partnered with 'science', then 'employment' and then with 'skills'.

2.2 Generic strategies

This section reviews different ways of thinking about competitive strategy, the bases on which a business unit might achieve competitive advantage in its market. Competitive advantage is about how an SBU creates value for its users that is both greater than the costs of supplying it and superior to that of rival SBUs. Competitive advantages should underpin competitive strategies. For not-for-profit organisations, the equivalent concern is the bases on which the organisation chooses to achieve superior quality of services in competition with others for funding – that is, how it provides 'best value'.

Michael Porter (1985) proposed three distinct **generic strategies** by which an organisation could achieve competitive advantage:

1 **Cost leadership**. This is based on creating a low-cost position through managing the relationships and costs throughout the value chain.
2 **Differentiation**. This is achieved by creating products or services that are unique and valued, and for which customers will pay a premium.
3 **Focus**. This involves directing attention towards narrow product lines, buyer segments or targeted geographic markets and attaining advantages through differentiation or cost leadership with a narrow target market in mind.

Figure 9.2 illustrates these three strategies on two dimensions: competitive advantage and strategic target.

Competitive advantage

FIGURE 9.2 Three generic strategies (Dess et al., 2008, p.57)

There is much debate as to exactly what each of these categories means. In particular, many confuse Porter's 'cost leadership' with 'low price'. Both casual observation and research support the notion that firms that identify with one or more of the forms of competitive advantage outperform those that do not (Ma and Karri, 2005). The lowest performers were those that did not identify with any type of advantage.

CASE EXAMPLE 9.1

Generic strategies in the British women's clothing market

Cost leadership is exemplified in the British women's clothing market by retailers such as Primark. This company seeks to use large economies of scale and tight cost discipline to serve a wide range of women with reasonably fashionable clothing at a good price. Monsoon's shops pursue a strategy of differentiation, offering arty styles ('boho chic') to women across a range of ages at significantly higher prices. Focus is exemplified by Evans, which targets only women needing larger-sized clothing, achieving a higher price for its distinctive products through a differentiation focus strategy. On the other hand, the clothing lines of the major supermarkets target shoppers who are simply looking for good-value standard clothing for their families, which is a cost focus strategy.

The rest of this section discusses these three generic strategies in more detail.

2.3 Cost leadership

Cost leadership involves becoming the lowest-cost organisation in a domain of activity. It requires a tight set of interrelated tactics that include:

- aggressive construction of efficient-scale facilities;
- vigorous pursuit of cost reductions based on experience;
- tight cost and overhead control;
- avoidance of marginal customer accounts; and
- cost minimisation in all activities in the firm's value chain, such as R&D, service, sales force and advertising.

Cost drivers include the following:

- **Input costs.** Examples include cheap raw materials or relocating call centres to low labour cost environments.
- **Economies of scale.** These are made where fixed costs are high – for example, in pharmaceutical companies in order to carry out effective research and development before launching mass-market products.
- **Economies of scope.** These may occur when an organisation is able to share resources across its operating divisions thus reducing unit costs. An example occurs in automobile manufacturing where large manufacturers, offering many brands or makes of vehicles, are able to share some of the technical resources and car-parts across all the different product ranges. VW owns Audi, Bentley, Bugatti, Lamborghini, Seat, Skoda, MAN Trucks, Scania, and Porsche and is thus able to garner economies of scale. A further example can be found in overhead delivery; large organisations might be able to centralise key overhead functions such as HRM and Finance and provide their services across all operating divisions, thus obviating the requirement to install separate overhead functions in each operating area.
- **Experience.** An important concept is the experience curve, which refers to how business 'learns' to lower costs as it gains experience with production processes. That is, with experience, unit costs of production decline as output increases in most industries. To generate above-average performance, a firm following a cost leadership position must be on a par with respect to differentiated products or elements. Put simply, there are gains in labour productivity as employees learn faster.
- **Product/process design.** Efficiency can be designed in at the outset. For example, Canon eroded Xerox's advantage (built-on service and support network) by designing a copier that needed less servicing.

 **CASE EXAMPLE** 9.2

Money is a big thing, but it is not the only thing. In the 1980s, a new car arrived from behind the Iron Curtain. It was called the Yugo and its main attraction was price. But the only way they caught on was as the butt of jokes. It offered a poor value proposition. The cars literally fell apart. The lesson was simple: price is just one component of value. No matter how good the price, the most cost-sensitive consumer won't intentionally buy a bad product.

A business that strives for a low-cost advantage must attain an absolute cost advantage relative to its rivals. This is typically accomplished by offering a no-frills product or service to a broad target market using standardisation to derive the greatest benefits from economies of scale and experience. However, such a strategy may fail if a firm is unable to attain parity on important dimensions of differentiation such as quick responses to customer requests for services or design changes.

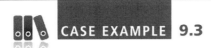

CASE EXAMPLE 9.3

Ryanair operates 1,600 flights a day in 30 countries in Europe with a fleet of 300 aircraft. It expects to carry 100 million customers in 2015–16 – the first EU airline to exceed the 100 million mark in a 12-month period. Michael O'Leary, CEO of Ryanair, makes no apologies for his penny-pinching. Want to check in luggage? You'll pay extra per bag for the privilege. Expecting free drinks and snacks? You'll be disappointed. And it is not just the passengers who are affected. Flight crews buy their own uniforms, and staff at Ryanair's spartan Dublin Airport headquarters must supply their own pens. After a customer sued Ryanair for charging for the use of a wheelchair, the company added a 'wheelchair levy' to every ticket! In 2010, after the disruption caused by volcanic ash, it initially refused to pay anything other than ticket refunds.

Yet Ryanair has been extremely successful. In 2009, its profits were €318 million and its operating margins are three times as large as BA's.

O'Leary thinks like a retailer and charges for every little thing. What Ryanair loses in seat revenue, it more than makes up by turning both planes and the Ryanair website into stores brimming with irresistible goodies, even as he charges for such 'perks' as priority boarding and assigned seating. The seats do not recline, seat-back pockets have been removed to cut cleaning time and speed turnaround of the planes, there's no entertainment, and seat-back trays will soon carry advertisements. Ryanair sells more than 98% of its tickets online.

Sounds outrageous? The strategy is clearly still working. Although there was a loss of €35 million for the last three months of 2013, there was a better-than-expected €49 million net profit for Ryanair's third quarter of 2014.

Sources: Adapted from K. Capell (2006), 'Wal-Mart with wings', *Business Week*, 27 November, pp. 44–5; N. Kumar (2006), 'Strategies to fight low-cost rivals', *Harvard Business Review*, 64(12): 104–13; BBC News, 'Ryanair Annual Reports; Ryanair raises full-year profit forecast', www.bbc.com/news/business-31088381, 2 February 2015.

Ryanair's close attention to costs helps to protect them from buyer power and intense rivalry from competitors. Thus, they are able to drive down costs and enjoy relatively high power over their customers.

STOP AND THINK 9.2

■ How easy would it be for larger airlines such as BA to imitate the strategy?
■ On what bases could other low-price airlines compete with Ryanair?

Common pitfalls of cost leadership strategies include the following:

■ **Too much focus on one or a few value-chain activities**. Organisations must pay attention to all activities in the value chain. Too often managers cut operating expenses but do not question spending on capital projects. Managers should explore all value-chain activities, including relationships among them, as candidates for cost reductions.
■ **All rivals share a common input or raw material**. Here, firms are vulnerable to price increases in the factors of production. Since they are competing on costs, they are less able to pass on price increases, because customers can take their business to rivals who have lower prices.
■ **The strategy is imitated too easily**. One of the common pitfalls of a cost-leadership strategy is that a firm's strategy may consist of value-creating activities that are easy to imitate. Such was the case with online brokers in recent years.
■ **A lack of parity on differentiation**. Above we looked at the Yugo example. Firms striving to attain cost leadership advantages must obtain a level of parity on differentiation. Often, parity can be achieved on differentiation dimensions such as reputation and quality.

■ **Erosion of cost advantages**. Erosion occurs when the pricing information available to customers increases. This is becoming a more significant challenge as the internet dramatically increases both the quantity and volume of information available to consumers about pricing and cost structures. Life insurance firms offering whole life insurance provide an interesting example. One study found that for each 10% increase in consumer use of the internet, there is a corresponding reduction in insurance prices to consumers of 3–5% (Miller and Dess, 1993).

2.4 Differentiation

As the name implies, a **differentiation** strategy consists of creating differences in the organisation's product or service offering by creating something that is perceived *industry-wide* as unique and valued by customers, so that they will pay a premium. Differentiation can take many forms:

■ prestige or brand image (e.g. BMW cars);
■ technology (e.g. Marantz stereo components);
■ innovation (e.g. Apple mobile phones and computing);
■ features (e.g. Honda Goldwing motorcycles);
■ customer service (e.g. John Lewis department stores); and
■ dealer network (e.g. Caterpillar earthmoving equipment).

Firms may differentiate themselves along several different dimensions at once. For example, BMW is known for its high prestige, superior engineering and high-quality cars. Harley-Davidson differentiates on image and dealer services.

Firms achieve and sustain differentiation advantages and attain above-average performance when their price premiums exceed the extra costs incurred in being unique. For example, both BMW and Harley-Davidson must increase consumer costs to offset added marketing expenses. Thus, a differentiator will always seek out ways of distinguishing itself from similar competitors to justify price premiums greater than the costs incurred by differentiating. Clearly, a differentiator cannot ignore costs or its premium prices would be eroded by a markedly inferior cost position. Therefore, it must attain a level of cost parity relative to competitors.

Differentiators do this by reducing costs in all areas that do not affect differentiation. Porsche, for example, invests heavily in engine design – an area in which its customers demand excellence – but it spends fewer resources in the design of the instrument panel or the arrangement of switches on the radio.

In public services, the equivalent is the achievement of a centre of excellence status, attracting higher funding from government. For example, universities try to show that they are better at research or teaching than other universities.

The success of a differentiation approach is likely to be dependent on two key factors:

1 **Identifying and understanding the strategic customer**. The concept of the strategic customer is helpful because it focuses consideration on those whom the strategy is targeting. However, this is not always straightforward, as discussed in Chapter 6. For example, for a newspaper business, is the customer the reader of the newspaper, the advertiser, or both? They are likely to have different needs and be looking for different benefits. It may be important that public sector organisations offer perceived benefits, but to whom? Is it the service user or the provider of funds?

2 **Identifying key competitors**. Who are the organisation's competitors? For example, in the brewing industry there are now just a few major global competitors, but there are also many local or regional brewers. Players in each strategic group need to decide who they regard as competitors and, given that, which bases of differentiation might be considered. Heineken appears to have decided that its 'competitor set' comprises the other global competitors – Carlsberg and Anheuser-Busch, for example.

Many companies successfully follow a differentiation strategy. These firms have taken commodity-type products and converted them to high-priced goods.

Differentiation strategy also frequently means marketing products and services on the basis on their quality in order to command and justify a price premium. According to Garvin (1987), quality may take the following eight dimensions:

- **Performance**. This refers to a product or service's operation. In the automobile industry, this might include areas such as fuel economy, acceleration, road handling, top speed and comfort.
- **Features**. These are the secondary or supplementary areas of performance. An example would be product packaging or product guides.
- **Reliability.** This reflects the probability of a product or service malfunctioning or failing to meet an expected standard. This dimension is particularly relevant in services where highly reliable service provision can be accurately measured and used as a marketing tool. An example would be a parcel delivery company quoting a high percentage of deliveries being made within a target time period.
- **Conformance**. This is the extent to which a product's or service's design and operation meets established standards. Examples include reject rates in factories and the incidence of service call outs or warranty repairs.
- **Durability**. This is the amount of usage a customer gets from a product before it deteriorates. It is not usually relevant to services.
- **Serviceability**. This refers to the speed, courtesy, competence and ease of repairs or remedial work. Specifically, it focuses on the occurrences when a product or service fails and the customer has to contact a customer care department or similar function. It can be measured by metrics such as average compliant handling times or the incidence of product breakdowns.
- **Aesthetics**. This is a subjective dimension of quality. It includes factors such as how a product or service looks, feels, sounds or tastes.
- **Perceived quality**. This is an intangible dimension and refers to factors such as: advertising, brand name and reputation. It is very important in the luxury goods industry, and can be used as an effective signal of quality and differentiation.

CASE EXAMPLE 9.4

FedEx's CEO and founder, Fred Smith, claims that the key to his firm's success is innovation. He contends his management team did not understand their real goal when they started the firm in 1971: 'We thought that we were selling the transportation of goods; in fact, we were selling peace of mind.' To that end, they were among the first in the industry to supply drivers with devices that makes it possible for customers to track their packages.

   In some markets, customers are more price-sensitive than others. So it may be that bases of differentiation are just not sufficient in the face of lower prices. Managers often complain, for example, that customers do not seem to value the superior levels of service they offer. It is easy to pile on additional costs in ways that are not valued sufficiently by customers. The historic failures under British ownership of the luxury car companies Rolls-Royce and Bentley against top-end Mercedes cars are partly attributable to the expensive crafting of wood and leather interiors, the full cost of which even wealthy customers were not prepared to pay for. Just as cost-leaders should not neglect quality, so too should differentiators attend closely to costs, especially in areas irrelevant to their sources of differentiation.

Potential pitfalls of differentiation strategy include the following:

- **Uniqueness that is not valuable**. A differentiation strategy must provide unique bundles of products and/or services that customers value highly. It is not enough just to be 'different'.

CASE EXAMPLE 9.5

Gibson came up with a unique idea: design and build an acoustic bass guitar with sufficient sound volume so that amplification was not necessary. The problem with other acoustic bass guitars was that they did not project enough volume because of the low-frequency bass notes. By adding a

CASE EXAMPLE 9.5 *continued*

resonator plate on the body of the traditional acoustic bass, Gibson increased the sound volume. Gibson believed this product would serve a particular niche market – bluegrass and folk artists who played in small groups with other acoustic musicians. Unfortunately, Gibson soon discovered that its targeted market was content with their existing options: an upright bass amplified with a microphone or an acoustic electric guitar. Thus, Gibson developed a unique product, but its potential customers did not perceive it as valuable.

- **Too much differentiation.** Firms may strive for quality or service that is higher than customers' desire. Thus, they become vulnerable to competitors who provide an appropriate level of quality at a lower price.
- **Too high a price premium.** This pitfall is quite similar to too much differentiation. Customers may desire the product, but they are repelled by the price premium.

 CASE EXAMPLE 9.6

Duracell (a division of Gillette) recently charged too much for its batteries. The firm had tried to sell consumers on the basis of its superior quality products. But the mass market was not convinced because the price differential was simply too high. At a shop just one block from Gillette's US headquarters, a pack of Energizer AA batteries was on sale at $2.99 compared with a Duracell pack at $4.59. Duracell's market share dropped 2% in a recent two-year period, and its profits declined over 30%. Clearly, the price/performance proposition Duracell offered customers was not accepted.

- **Differentiation that is easily imitated.** As was noted in Chapter 4, resources that are easily imitated cannot lead to sustainable advantages. Similarly, firms may attain a differentiation strategy that is successful for a time. However, the advantages are eroded through imitation.
- **Dilution of brand identification through product-line extensions.** Firms may erode their quality brand image by adding products or services with lower prices and less quality. Although this can increase short-term revenues, it may be detrimental in the long run.

 CASE EXAMPLE 9.7

In the 1980s, Gucci wanted to capitalise on its prestigious brand name by launching an aggressive strategy of revenue growth. It added a set of lower-priced canvas goods to its product line. It also pushed goods heavily into department stores and duty-free channels and allowed its name to appear on a host of licensed items such as watches, eyeglasses and perfumes. In the short term, this strategy worked. Sales soared. However, the strategy carried a high price. Gucci's indiscriminate approach to expanding its products and channels tarnished its reputation. Sales of its high-end goods (with higher profit margins) fell, causing profits to decline.

- **Perceptions of differentiation may vary between buyers and sellers.** The issue here is that companies must realise that although they may perceive their products and services as differentiated, their customers may view them as commodities. Indeed, in today's marketplace many products and services have been reduced to commodities. Thus, a firm could overprice its offerings and lose margins altogether if it has to lower prices to reflect market realities.

2.5 Focus

A **focus** strategy targets a narrow segment or domain of activity and tailors its products or services to the needs of that specific segment, to the exclusion of others. The essence of focus is the exploitation of a particular market niche. The focus strategy, as indicated in Figure 9.1, has two variants. In a *cost focus*, a firm strives to create a cost advantage in its target segment. In a *differentiation focus*, a firm seeks to differentiate in its target market. Both rely on providing better service than broad-based competitors who are trying to serve the focuser's target segment. Cost focus exploits differences in cost behaviour in some segments, while differentiation focus exploits the special needs of buyers in other segments. In air travel, Johnson et al. (2014) argue that Ryanair follows a cost focus strategy, targeting price-conscious holiday travellers with no need for connecting fights. In the domestic detergent market, the Belgian company Ecover follows a differentiation focus strategy, gaining a price premium over rivals on account of its ecological cleaning products.

Potential pitfalls of focus strategies include the following:

- **Erosion of cost advantages within the narrow segment**. The advantages of a cost focus strategy may be fleeting if the cost advantages are eroded over time.

 **CASE EXAMPLE** 9.8

Dell's pioneering direct selling model in the personal computer industry, was challenged and eroded by rivals as they gain experience with Dell's distribution method. Similarly, other firms have seen their profit margins drop as competitors enter their product segment.

- **Competition from new entrants and from imitation**. Some firms adopting a focus strategy may enjoy temporary advantages because they select a small niche with few rivals. However, their advantages may be short-lived.

 **CASE EXAMPLE** 9.9

There is a multitude of internet firms that specialise in very narrow segments such as ethnic foods and vintage car accessories. The entry barriers are low, there is little buyer loyalty and competition becomes intense. Imitation is easy so, over time, revenues fall, profits margins are squeezed and only the strongest survive.

- **Focusers can become too focused to satisfy buyer needs**. Some firms attempting to attain competitive advantages through a focus strategy may have too narrow a product or service. Examples include many retail firms.

2.6 Combination strategies or 'stuck in the middle'?

Porter claims that managers face a crucial choice between the generic strategies of cost leadership, differentiation and focus. Firms may end up 'stuck in the middle' if they try to attain both cost and differentiation advantages. Porter's warning about the danger of being stuck in the middle provides a useful discipline for managers. They may make incremental decisions that compromise the basic generic strategy. However, it has been suggested that the criticisms against combining generic strategies reflect a Western cultural preference for binary oppositions, as against an Eastern willingness to seek balance and synthesis. Thus Singapore Airlines has been able to combine strategies of service differentiation and low cost in a way that Western airlines have found difficult. Porter himself acknowledges that there are circumstances in which the strategies can be combined.

The major US car manufacturers are plagued by very expensive legacy costs associated with pension and healthcare obligations. They also suffer from long-term customer perceptions of mediocre quality and of being inferior to their European and Japanese rivals. Troubling quality perceptions persist despite the fact that the Big Three (Chrysler, GM and Ford) have attained approximate parity with their Japanese and European competitors in recent surveys.

The success of this strategy depends on the ability to deliver enhanced benefits to customers together with low prices whilst achieving sufficient margins for reinvestment to maintain and develop bases of differentiation. It is, in effect, the strategy Tesco has followed. It might be argued that if differentiation can be achieved, there should be no need to have a lower price, since it should be possible to obtain prices at least equal to the competition, if not higher. Indeed, there is a good deal of debate as to whether a hybrid strategy can be a successful competitive strategy rather than a suboptimal compromise between low price and differentiation. If it is the latter, very likely it will be ineffective. However, the combination strategy could be advantageous in certain situations as follows:

- **Greater volumes can be achieved than those of competitors**. Margins may therefore still be better because of a low-cost base, much as Tesco achieved in the UK.
- **Cost reductions are available outside its differentiated activities**. For example, IKEA concentrates on building differentiation on the basis of its marketing, product range, logistics and store operations, but low customer expectations on service levels allow cost reduction because customers are prepared to transport and build its products.
- **If the strategy is used as an entry strategy in a market with established competitors**. For example, in developing a global strategy a business may target a poorly run operation in a competitor's portfolio of businesses in a geographical area and enter that market with a superior product at a lower price to establish a foothold from which it can move further.

Perhaps the primary benefit to firms that integrate low cost and differentiation strategies is that it is generally harder for rivals to duplicate or imitate. This strategy enables a firm to provide two types of value to customers: differentiated attributes (e.g. high quality, brand identification, reputation) and lower prices (because of the firm's lower costs in value-creating activities). The goal becomes one of providing unique value to customers in an efficient manner.

2.7 Sustaining competitive advantage

Organisations that try to achieve competitive advantage hope to preserve it over time and much of what is written about competitive strategy takes the need for sustainability as a central expectation.

- **Sustaining cost leadership-based advantage**. An organisation pursuing competitive advantage through low costs and prices might be able to sustain this by operating with lower margins or by having a unique cost structure. Some firms may have unique access to low-cost distribution channels and be able to obtain raw materials at lower prices than competitors. An organisation may have specific capabilities so that it is able to drive down cost throughout its value chain. An example is the logistics in IKEA.
- **Sustaining differentiation-based advantage**. There is little point in striving to be different if competitors can imitate readily. For example, many firms that try to gain advantage through launching new products or services find them copied rapidly by competitors. Wine producers in France and Australia have been seeking bases of differentiation over each other for many years. So ways of attempting to sustain advantage through differentiation include creating difficulties of imitation. Imperfect mobility helps such that the capabilities that sustain differentiation cannot be traded. For example, top research scientists may be poached by competitors: they are tradable. But intangible assets, such as brand, image or reputation, are difficult to imitate or obtain. Indeed, even if the competitor acquires the company to gain these, they may not readily transfer given new ownership.
- **Strategic lock-in**. Another approach to sustainability in either case is the creation of **strategic lock-in** where an organisation achieves a proprietary position in its industry; it becomes an industry standard.

 CASE EXAMPLE   9.10

Microsoft Windows became an industry standard by working to ensure that the 'architecture' of the industry was built around it. Other businesses had to conform or relate to that standard in order to prosper.

Achieving lock-in is likely to be dependent on the size or market dominance of the organisation and is set early in the lifecycle of markets. For example, Sky, with the financial support of News Corporation, was able to undercut competitors and invest heavily in technology and fast market share growth, sustaining substantial losses over many years, in order to achieve dominance in the digital TV market. Insistence on conformity to the standard is strict so rivals will be seen off fiercely, though this can of course lead to problems, as Microsoft found when it was deemed to be operating against the interests of the market.

STOP AND THINK   9.3

Based on your knowledge of an organisation and its products or services, what is the basis of its competitive strategy and how has this been sustained?

2.8 Achieving cost leadership or differentiation

Once an organisation has decided upon its chosen generic strategy (cost leadership, differentiation or combination) then it has a number of methods that it can employ to achieve this.

A practical and efficient method entails using the value chain to conduct an audit of the various component parts in order to reduce costs (cost leadership) or add uniqueness (differentiation).

Another alternative involves using **Business process engineering** (BPR). BPR is a structured reorganisation of an organisation focused upon achieving certain efficiency goals which might include cost reduction, improving uniqueness or adding quality. According to Hammer and Champy (1993), it has the following principles:

- the merging of jobs where possible;
- empowerment of workers;
- the redesigning of processes in a more efficient order;
- maximising the sharing of process throughout the organisation;
- a reduction of checks and controls;
- elimination of duplicated tasks; and
- the use of single point of contacts for multiple functions and operations, for example, a 'one stop shop' for all customer care needs.

BPR programmes have had a controversial history since their introduction in the 1990s, with many programmes falling short of their targets owing to opposition from staff who linked BPR programmes with job losses. Hammer and Champy later concluded that it was essential not to neglect the human side of the project before embarking upon a BPR programme, and to ensure adequate levels of buy-in from the organisation's workforce.

a   Explain what is meant by a 'strategic business unit'.
b   Identify the three generic strategies.
c   Identify the potential pitfalls of a strategy based on focus.
d   How might competitive advantage be sustained?

2.9 Blue ocean strategy

Research undertaken by Kim and Mauborgne (2004, 2014) has identified a new form of strategy that has been successfully pursued by a number of organisations.

Blue ocean strategy does not set out to compete in existing industries; instead it endeavours to make competition irrelevant by creating new market space. Blue ocean industries therefore differ in a number of ways from existing and competitive red oceans, as shown in Table 9.1:

TABLE 9.1 Red oceans and blue oceans compared (based on Kim and Mauborgne, 2004)

	Red oceans	**Blue oceans**
Basis of competition	Compete in existing market space with the objective of beating competition	Create uncontested market space with the objective of eliminating competition
Customer focus	Satisfy existing demand	Create and then satisfy new demand
Generic strategy	Cost leadership or differentiation	Both cost leadership and differentiation

Blue ocean strategy therefore aims to alter the basis of competition in existing industries by either creating new ones or substantially altering existing ones. Examples of successful blue ocean strategies include Cirque du Soleil, who effectively combined elements of the theatre and the circus to create a new format of entertainment show, and Netjets, who created a system of fractional ownership for passenger jet aircraft.

Kim and Mauborgne suggest that the four actions framework (Figure 9.3) can be applied to existing industries in order to identify blue ocean opportunities that incorporate value innovation. The four actions framework requires an existing industry to be scrutinised in order to ascertain the key success factors that need to be:

- **eliminated** as they are taken for granted in the industry;
- **reduced** to below the industry standard;
- **raised** above the industry standard; or
- **created** and introduced to the industry.

However, blue ocean strategy does have a number of disadvantages:

- It may only offer temporary and transient competitive advantage, as once it is created, it is inevitable that competition will enter the industry, thus turning the colour from blue to red.
- The four actions framework can be used to identify the necessary actions required to create a blue ocean, but it cannot be assumed that the organisation has the necessary competences in this way.
- The identification of a blue ocean opportunity does not guarantee that there will be sufficient demand to make it profitable and sustainable.

Figure 9.3 demonstrates how Cirque du Soleil used the four actions framework to produce a strategy canvas that offered value innovation in an industry dominated by conventional circuses.

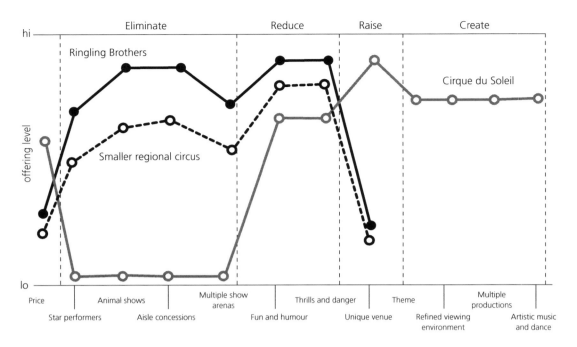

FIGURE 9.3 Four actions framework applied to Cirque du Soleil.

3   Corporate-level strategy

3.1 Scope

Section 2 was concerned with choices at the level of single business or organisational units. Many organisations do choose to grow by entering new product and market areas. For example, the Virgin Group started out in the music business, but is now highly diverse, operating in the holiday, cable, retail, air travel and rail markets. As organisations add new units, their strategies are no longer concerned just with the business-level but also with the corporate-level choices involved in having many different businesses or markets.

Even small businesses may consist of a number of business units. For example, a local builder may be undertaking contract work for local government and for local homeowners. These are different market segments with different modes of operation and capabilities needed for competitive success. The owner has to decide the appropriate investment and activity for each segment. Public sector organisations also provide different services, similar to business units in commercial organisations. Corporate-level strategy is relevant to the appropriate drawing of organisational boundaries.

Choices inform decisions about the following:

■ **Scope**. How broad to make the portfolio?
■ **Corporate parenting**. How should the 'parent' add value?
■ **Portfolio matrices**. Which SBUs should be invested in?

3.2 Strategic directions

Ansoff's (1965) product/market matrix considers the development directions available to an organisation in terms of the market coverage, products and competence base of the organisation. A useful extension by Johnson and Scholes (1998) of the traditional approach emphasises that, in the long run, development is likely to require the development of competences to cope with a changing situation. Innovation is therefore a key ingredient of strategic change.

The matrix outlines the broad types of development direction in terms of these three dimensions of markets, products and competences. These range from strategies concerned with protecting and building an organisation's position with its existing products and competences, through to major diversification requiring development and change of both products and competences to enter or create new market opportunities. Within this broad 'steer' for an organisation there are a number of specific options concerning both the direction and the method of developing the organisation's strategies (Figure 9.4).

	Existing product	New product
Existing market	**Market penetration** Increase sales (penetrate more deeply) into the existing market	**Product development** New product developed for existing markets
New market	**Market development** Existing products sold to new markets	**Diversification** New products sold in new markets

Source: Adapted from H.I. Ansoff, *Corporate Strategy*, Penguin, 1988, Chapter 6.

FIGURE 9.4 Directions for strategy development (Ansoff, 1965, adapted by Johnson et al., 2008)

An organisation typically starts in the top left-hand box, with its existing products and existing markets. According to the matrix, the organisation has a choice between penetrating still further within its existing sphere; developing new products for its existing markets; moving downwards by bringing its existing products into new markets; or taking the most radical step of full diversification, with altogether new markets and new products.

Market penetration

Market penetration, by which the organisation takes an increased share of its existing markets with its existing product range, is on the face of it the most obvious strategic direction. It builds on existing strategic capabilities and does not require the organisation to venture into uncharted territory. The organisation's scope is exactly the same. However, greater market share implies increased power over buyers and suppliers (in terms of the five forces) and greater economies of scale.

Organisations seeking greater market penetration may face two constraints:

1 **Retaliation from competitors**. In terms of the five forces, increasing market penetration is likely to exacerbate industry rivalry as competitors defend their share. Increased rivalry might involve price wars or expensive marketing battles, which may cost more than any market share gains are actually worth. In low-growth or declining markets, it can be more effective simply to acquire competitors. Some companies have grown quickly in this way.

 CASE EXAMPLE 9.11

In the steel industry, the Indian company LNM (Mittal) moved rapidly in the 2000s to become the largest steel producer in the world by acquiring struggling steel companies around the world. Acquisitions can reduce rivalry by taking out independent players and consolidating them under one umbrella.

2 **Legal constraints**. Greater market penetration can raise concerns from official competition regulators concerning excessive market power. Most countries have regulators with the powers to restrain powerful companies or prevent mergers and acquisitions that would create such excessive power. In the UK, the Competition Commission can investigate any merger or acquisition that would account for more than 25% of the national market, and either halt the deal or propose measures that would reduce market power. The European Commission has an overview of the whole European market and can similarly intervene.

Market penetration may not be an option where economic constraints are severe – for instance, during a market downturn or public-sector funding crisis. Here organisations will need to consider the strategic option of retrenchment: withdrawal from marginal activities in order to concentrate on the most valuable segments and products within their existing business.

However, where growth is still sought after, the Ansoff axes suggest further directions, as follows.

Product development

Product development is where organisations deliver modified or new products (or services) to existing markets. This is a limited extension of organisational scope.

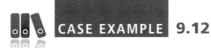 **CASE EXAMPLE** 9.12

Apple, developing its products from the original iPod through iPhone to iPad, involved little diversification. Although the technologies differed, Apple was targeting the same customers and using very similar production processes and distribution channels.

There are many reasons why companies might have a preference for product development. For example, retailers follow the changing needs of their customers by a continuing policy of introducing new product lines. A core competence for successful organisations is, therefore, the ability to analyse and understand the changing needs of a particular group of customers or clients. Strategic development can be built around such a core competence. Similarly, product development may be preferred because the company has core competences in R&D. When product life cycles are short – as with consumer electronics – product development becomes an essential requirement of an organisation's strategy, and is built around a core competence in R&D or the ability to acquire new products from elsewhere.

 STOP AND THINK 9.4

What issues arise with the introduction of new products as a development strategy?
   Why might it not be sustainable?

Product development may often raise uncomfortable dilemmas for organisations. While new products may be vital, the process of creating a broad product line is expensive, risky and potentially unprofitable, because most new products never reach the market. Of those that do, relatively few succeed. In practice, rapid rates of new product introduction can depress profitability as organisations struggle to learn new competences needed to debug production, train salespeople, etc. Johnson et al. argue that managers should ensure that the processes of innovation in the organisation are appropriate for the situation they face. There are choices about how new ideas and improvements might be fostered in the organisation and a further choice concerns the method by which innovation will be secured – whether it should be through the organisation's own internal efforts, by acquiring innovations (e.g. products, processes or whole companies) or by alliances and partnerships. The relative merits of these different methods of strategy development are discussed in Chapter 10.

In the long term, product development is unlikely to be sustainable without developing or acquiring new competences. This can occur because customers become more experienced in judging value for money. These shifts at the customer end require responses from the organisation. These may be concerned not with the basic features of the product or service, but with the need to improve other aspects of the customer experience (e.g. the quality of information provided to clients that have been regarded as peripheral).

The need to develop competences or products even to survive in existing markets is underlined by the consequences of not doing so. It is likely that the performance may become so poor in relation to that of competitors or other providers that the organisation becomes a target for acquisition, particularly by organisations that have core competences in corporate turnaround.

Market development

Most organisations have developed in ways that have resulted in limited coverage of the market by their products. If the organisation's aspirations outstrip the opportunities in existing markets and with product development, often regarded as risky and expensive, an alternative strategy is **market development**. This involves offering existing products to new markets. Again, the extension of scope is limited. Typically, of course, this may entail some product development as well, if only in terms of packaging or service.

Three common ways of doing this are:

1 **Extension**. Moving into market segments that are not currently served. This might require some modification of the product to suit it to new segments. For example, a manufacturer of branded grocery products for the premium market may enter the mainstream market through 'own-brand' sales to supermarkets. This will require the development of new competences (e.g. in key account selling).

2 **Development of new uses for existing products**. Manufacturers of stainless steel, for example, have progressively found new applications for the products that were originally used for cutlery and tableware. Innovation such as this will require competences in analysing each potential market and assessing the particular requirements of the product.

3 **Geographical spread** (nationally or internationally into new markets). Again, this may require some adjustment to product features or marketing methods. It will also require other competences (e.g. in language and cultural awareness). There are important practical implications too, including the need to reassess the way in which the organisation's structure, design and control need to change.

 CASE EXAMPLE 9.13

McDonald's expanded internationally by identifying new types of location as well as new countries. This continued growth also required competences in reducing opening costs of new outlets and being prepared to make minor adjustments to the standard offering in each country in which they operated in order to be acceptable to customers.

Diversification

Diversification is a term used in many different ways. Here, diversification involves directions of development that takes the organisation away from its present markets and its present products at the same time.

Frequently, market penetration and product development entail some diversifying adjustment of products or markets. Diversification is a matter of degree but the Ansoff matrix does make clear that the further the organisation moves from its starting point of existing products and existing markets, the more the organisation has to learn.

Diversification needs to be considered alongside its alternatives. In terms of the Ansoff matrix, it is the most radical strategic direction and might be chosen for a variety of reasons:

■ **Efficiency gains**. These can be made by applying the organisation's existing resources or capabilities to new markets and products or services: economies of scope by contrast to economies of scale. In other words, there are economies to be gained by extending the scope of the organisation's activities.

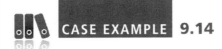

CASE EXAMPLE 9.14

Many universities have halls of residence, which they must have for their students but which are underutilised resources out of term time. These halls of residence are more efficiently used if the universities expand the scope of their activities into conferencing and tourism during vacation periods.

- **Stretching corporate parenting capabilities into new markets and products or services**. At the corporate parent level, managers may develop a competence at managing a range of different products and services which can be applied even to businesses which do not share resources at the operational unit level.

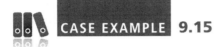

CASE EXAMPLE 9.15

The Virgin Group includes a wide range of businesses, from wine, through rail travel, to financial services, which share very few operational resources or competences. Virgin creates value for these specialised companies by adding parenting skills – for instance, the support of classic brands and the nurturing of highly creative people – that are relevant to all these individual businesses.

- **Increasing market power**. This can result from having a diverse range of businesses. With many businesses, an organisation can afford to cross-subsidise one business from the surpluses earned by another, in a way that competitors may not be able to. This can give an organisation a competitive advantage for the subsidised business, and the long-run effect may be to drive out other competitors.
- **Responding to market decline**. It is arguable that Microsoft's diversification into electronic games such as the Xbox is a necessary response to convergence in electronic and computer media.
- **Spreading risk across a range of businesses**. This is another common justification for diversification but, while managers might like the security of a diverse range of businesses, investors would prefer managers to concentrate on managing their core business. For private businesses, where the owners have a large proportion of their assets tied up in the business, it can make sense to diversify risk across a number of distinct activities.
- **Expectations of powerful stakeholders**. These can sometimes drive inappropriate diversification.

CASE EXAMPLE 9.16

Under pressure from Wall Street analysts to deliver continued revenue growth, in the late 1990s the US energy company Enron diversified beyond its original interest in energy trading into trading commodities such as petrochemicals, aluminium and even bandwidth. By satisfying the analysts in the short term, this strategy boosted the share price and allowed top management to stay in place. However, it soon transpired that very little of this diversification had been profitable, and in 2001 Enron collapsed.

Diversification can be considered under two broad headings:

1 **Related diversification**. This is development beyond the present product and market, but still within the broad confines of the 'industry' or value chain in which the company operates. For example, Unilever is a diversified corporation, but virtually all of its interests are in the fast-moving consumer goods industry. An example for a manufacturer is shown in Figure 9.5.

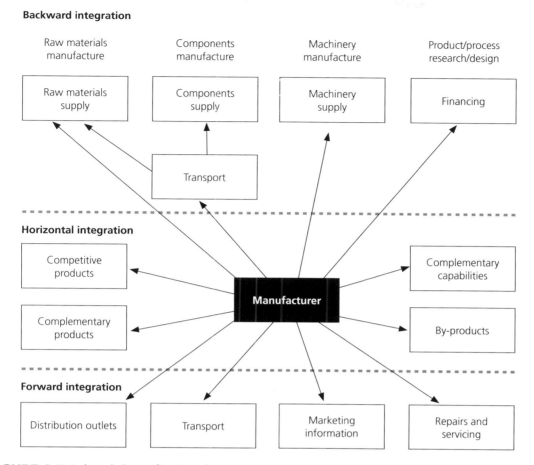

Backward integration

Raw materials manufacture · Components manufacture · Machinery manufacture · Product/process research/design

Raw materials supply · Components supply · Machinery supply · Financing

Transport

Horizontal integration

Competitive products · Complementary capabilities

Complementary products · By-products

Manufacturer

Forward integration

Distribution outlets · Transport · Marketing information · Repairs and servicing

FIGURE 9.5 Related diversification for a manufacturer

From *Exploring Strategy*, 9th edition, Johnson et al, Pearson Education Limited, © Pearson Education 2002, 2011

a) **Backward integration**. This refers to development into activities that are concerned with the inputs into the company's current business (i.e. are further back in the value chain), for example, raw materials and machinery.

 CASE EXAMPLE 9.17

In a bid to reduce premiums and improve customer service in the UK car insurance industry, Direct Line set up a limited number of wholly owned repair and development centres. These were intended to be centres of excellence, which would be supported by a larger network of recommended, but independently owned garages.

b) **Forward integration**. Refers to development into activities concerned with a company's outputs (i.e. they are *further forward* in the value chain), such as transport or distribution.

c) **Vertical integration**. Describes either backward or forward integration into adjacent activities in the value chain.

d) **Horizontal integration**. This refers to development into activities that are competitive with, or directly complementary to, a company's present activities. For example, many organisations have realised that there are opportunities in other markets for the exploitation of the organisation's core competencies.

It needs to be recognised that the 'ownership' of more value activities within the value chain does not guarantee improved performance or better value for money for the consumer or client. Indeed, there has been some degree of disillusionment with related diversification as a strategy, and more emphasis on improving performance within the value system through external linkages and the management of relationships with the various parties in the supply and distribution chains. The ability to achieve this could be a core competence. It would include the need to ensure that innovation and improvement of value for money are occurring within the other organisations (i.e. suppliers and distributors).

2 **Unrelated diversification**. This is where the organisation moves beyond the confines of its current industry. It can be divided into three categories:

   a) It may involve extension into new markets and new products by exploiting the current core competencies of the organisation.

   b) It may involve the creation of genuinely new markets. This requires very good market knowledge and the creativity to better provide for market needs.

   c) The most extreme form of unrelated diversification is where new competences are developed for new market opportunities. Not surprisingly, this extreme end of the diversification spectrum is less common.

One of the reasons why diversification strategies run into difficulties is that organisations misjudge the degree of relatedness involved. This is a clear danger in vertical integration, which moves the organisation into activities that are adjacent in the value chain (e.g. supply or distribution) but which are entirely unrelated to the organisation's current competences. Developments of this kind seek to take advantage of **synergy**, the idea that the whole can be greater than the sum of the parts. But joining individuals or work groups together does not always result in harmony! Diversified companies seek synergistic relationships as follows:

- **Market synergy**. Sales of one product reinforcing sales of another; sharing distribution channels; applying brand names across many products, and so on.
- **Operating synergy**. Filling out product ranges to occupy spare capacity; sharing infrequently used resources; recycling.
- **Technological synergy**. Sharing product or process technology among divisions; exploiting patents throughout world markets.
- **Financial synergy**. Allocating funds among units to gain the best return; using financial strength to raise new capital at low cost.
- **Management synergy**. Applying core competences learnt in one sector to another; transferring managers with special skills to areas where they are most needed.

Does diversification improve performance?

The various attempts to demonstrate the effects of diversification on performance are inconclusive. The sum total of the research is, according to Johnson et al. (2014), unclear apart from one important message: successful diversification is difficult to achieve. Since most large corporations today are diversified, scholars and policy-makers have been concerned to establish whether diversified companies really perform better than undiversified ones. After all, it would be deeply troubling if large corporations were diversifying simply to spread risk for managers, to save managerial jobs in declining businesses or to preserve the image of growth, as in the case of Enron.

Research studies of diversification have generally found some performance benefits, with related diversifiers outperforming both firms that remain specialised and those that have unrelated diversified strategies. The implication is that some diversification is good, but not too much. Diversification does not always pay. The conclusion from the performance studies is that, although on average related diversification pays better than unrelated, any diversification strategy needs rigorous questioning on its merits.

3.3 Corporate parenting

Diversification raises the related topics of the role of the corporate parent and decisions about in which business units in the portfolio to invest. The first theme is the role of the corporate-level executives who perform a corporate parent role with regard to the individual business units that make up diversified organisations' portfolios. The **corporate parent** refers to the levels of management above that of the business units, and therefore without direct interaction with buyers and competitors.

Given their detachment from the actual marketplace, how can corporate-level activities, decisions and resources add value to the actual businesses? Parents create value through management expertise. They improve plans and budgets and provide especially competent central functions such as legal, financial, human resource management, procurement, etc. Additionally, they help subsidiaries make wise choices in their own acquisitions and new internal development decisions. Such contributions often help business units to increase their revenues and profits substantially.

There is considerable scepticism about the role of corporate-level strategy. The notion of corporate strategy assumes that corporations should own and control businesses in a range of markets or products. Williamson (1998) believes that diversified corporations should only exist in the presence of 'market failures'. If markets worked well, there would be no need for business units to be coordinated through managerial structures. Business units could be independent, coordinating where necessary by simple transactions in the marketplace. The 'invisible hand' of the market could replace the 'visible hand' of managers at corporate headquarters. There would be no 'corporate strategy'.

 CASE EXAMPLE 9.18

In November 2009, after years of criticism for the failure of the corporate centre to add value to companies within the group, Cable and Wireless PLC, the UK-based telecommunications company, announced its intention to separate the Cable and Wireless Communications Group and the Cable and Wireless Worldwide Group. This reflected its belief that the businesses had reached a position where they would deliver increased value to shareholders as separately listed companies. Cable & Wireless Worldwide was subsequently acquired by Vodafone in 2012, and was fully integrated into the business the following year.

In the public sector, privatisation and outsourcing decisions can be considered as responses to the failure of public sector organisations to add sufficient value by their parenting. Units such as schools or hospitals are increasingly being given freedom from parenting authorities, because independence is seen as more effective.

Goold et al. (1994) identified five main types of activity by which a corporate parent can add value:

1 **Envisioning**. The corporate parent can provide a clear overall vision for its business units. This vision should guide and motivate the business unit managers to maximise corporation-wide performance through commitment to a common purpose. This vision can reassure shareholders about the rationale for having a diversified strategy in the first place.

2 **Facilitating synergies**. The corporate parent can facilitate cooperation and sharing across the business units, thus improving the synergies from being within the same corporate organisation. This can be achieved through incentives, rewards and remuneration schemes.

3 **Coaching**. The corporate parent can help business unit managers develop strategic capabilities, by coaching them to improve their skills and confidence. For example, corporate-wide management events bring together managers across the business to build relationships between each other and develop opportunities for cooperation.

4 **Providing central services and resources**. The centre is a provider of capital for investment and can also provide central services such as treasury, tax and human resource advice. If centralised, these services can have sufficient scale to be efficient and to build up relevant expertise.

5 **Intervening**. The corporate parent can intervene within business units in order to ensure appropriate performance. The corporate parent should be able to monitor business unit performance closely and improve performance either by replacing weak managers or by assisting them in turning around their businesses. The parent can also challenge and develop the strategic ambitions of business units, so that businesses performing satisfactorily are encouraged to perform even better.

However, there are also three broad ways in which the corporate parent can inadvertently destroy value:

1 **Adding management costs**. The staff and facilities of the corporate centre are expensive. The corporate centre typically has the best-paid managers and the most luxurious offices. It is the actual businesses that have to generate the revenues that pay for them.

2 **Adding bureaucratic complexity**. As well as these direct financial costs, there is the 'fog' created by an additional layer of management and the need to coordinate with sister businesses. These can slow managers' responses to issues and lead to compromises between the interests of individual businesses.

3 **Obscuring financial performance**. One danger in a large diversified company is that the under-performance of weak businesses can be obscured. Weak businesses might be cross-subsidised by the stronger ones. The possibility of hiding weak performance diminishes the incentives for business unit managers to strive as hard as they can. Externally, shareholders and financial analysts cannot easily judge the performance of individual units within the corporate whole.

These dangers suggest clear paths for corporate parents that wish to avoid value destruction. They should keep a close eye on centre costs, both financial and bureaucratic, ensuring that these are no more than are required by their corporate strategy. They should also do all they can to promote financial transparency, so that business units remain under pressure to perform and shareholders can be confident.

3.4 Portfolio management

A related theme is how to achieve a good mix of businesses within the corporate portfolio. Which businesses should corporate parents cultivate, and which should they divest? This section introduces an approach by which corporate parents can manage the various parts of their portfolio differently, or add and subtract business units within the portfolio. The approach focuses on the following three criteria:

1 **The balance of the portfolio**. For example, in relation to its markets and the needs of the corporation.
2 **The attractiveness of the business units**. In terms of how strong they are individually, and how profitable their markets or industries are likely to be.
3 **The fit that the business units have with each other**. In terms of potential synergies, or the extent to which the corporate parent will be good at looking after them.

Portfolio analysis examines the balance of an organisation's strategic business units. Portfolio analysis can he used to describe the current range of SBUs and to assess the strength of the mix both historically and against future scenarios. One of the most common and long-standing ways of conceiving the balance of a portfolio of businesses is the Boston Consulting Group (BCG) matrix (see Figure 9.6). Here market share and market growth are critical variables for determining attractiveness and balance. High market share and high growth are attractive, however, the BCG matrix also warns that high growth demands heavy investment (e.g. to expand capacity or develop brand). There needs to be a balance within the portfolio, so that there are some low-growth businesses that are making sufficient surplus to fund the investment needs of higher growth businesses.

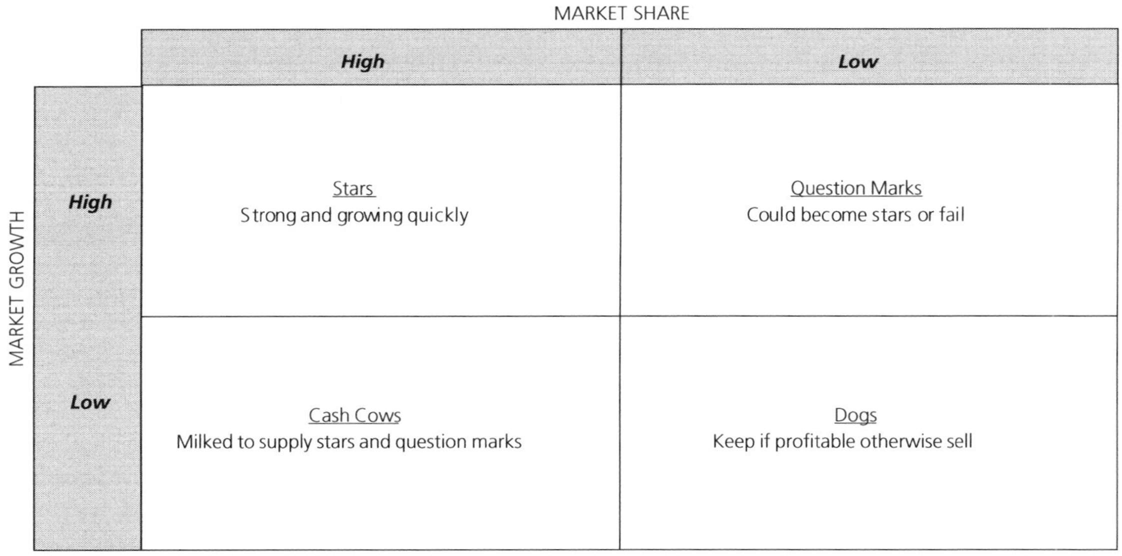

MARKET SHARE

	High	Low
High	Stars Strong and growing quickly	Question Marks Could become stars or fail
Low	Cash Cows Milked to supply stars and question marks	Dogs Keep if profitable otherwise sell

(MARKET GROWTH)

FIGURE 9.6 The Boston Consulting Group portfolio matrix

- **Star**. An SBU that has a high market share in a growing market. The SBU may be spending heavily to gain that share, but costs should be reducing over time and, it is to be hoped, at a rate faster than that of the competition.
- **Question mark (or 'problem child')**. This is also in a growing market, but does not have a high market share. It may be necessary to spend heavily to increase market share, but if so, it is unlikely that the SBU is achieving sufficient cost-reduction benefits to offset such investments.
- **Cash cow**. This has a high market share in a mature market. Because growth is low and market conditions are more stable, the need for heavy marketing investment is less. But high relative market share means that the SBU should be able to maintain unit cost levels below those of competitors. The cash cow should then be a cash provider, perhaps to finance 'question marks'.
- **Dog**. This has a low share in static or declining markets and is thus the worst of all combinations. Dogs may be a cash drain and use up a disproportionate amount of company time and resources.

Some caution is needed with portfolio analysis:

- There can be practical difficulties in deciding what exactly 'high' and 'low' mean in a particular situation.
- The analysis should be applied to strategic business units (i.e. a bundle of products or services and the associated market segments), not to whole markets.
- Corporate management must develop the ability and devote the time to reviewing the role of each strategic business unit in the overall mix of company activities. This is an important responsibility of the corporate centre. Some are sceptical of whether the corporate centre really does add value to the company through these processes of buying, selling, developing or running down individual units to keep the portfolio balanced. They suggest that the free market might allocate resources more effectively.
- The original BCG analysis concentrated on the needs of a business to plan its cash flow requirements across its portfolio. So cash cows will be used to create the funds needed for innovation and the development of question marks and stars. However, little is said about the behavioural implications of such a strategy. How does central management motivate the managers of cash cows, who see all their hard-earned surpluses being invested in other businesses?
- In many organisations the critical resource to be planned and balanced will not be cash, but innovative capacity. Question marks and stars are very demanding on these types of resource.
- The position of dogs is often misunderstood. Certainly, there may be some products that need immediate deletion but even then there may be political difficulties if they are the brainchild of people with power within the organisation. Other dogs may have a useful place in the portfolio. They may be necessary to complete the product range and provide a credible presence in the market.

 CASE EXAMPLE 9.19

Novartis uses portfolio planning approaches to help it manage its business units, which compete in a wide variety of industries, including chemicals, dyes, pharmaceuticals, crop protection and animal health. It places each business unit in a category corresponding to the BCG matrix. The business unit's goals, compensation programmes, personnel selection and resource allocation are strongly associated with the category within which the business was placed. For example, business units classified as cash cows had much higher hurdles for obtaining financial resources (from the corporate office) for expansion than question marks since the latter were businesses for which Novartis has high hopes for accelerated future growth and profitability.

a   Identify three 'grand strategies' that an organisation might pursue.
b   What is meant by 'diversification'?
c   Outline the main components of the BCG matrix.

3.5 Research and development

A necessary organisational asset that is usually required to be able to pursue generic strategies, such as diversification or product development is research and development capability (R&D).

Cooper (2001) argues that to be effective, the R&D process should be closely managed and involve a series of stages starting with idea generation and culminating with new product launches (see Figure 9.7). Each stage should also have a gate where achievements can be evaluated against pre-agreed objectives. The gatekeepers at each stage therefore have the ability and power to allow the project to proceed, suggest further refinement or recommend to top management that the project be terminated. Typically, stages become more costly as the project progresses through the different stages.

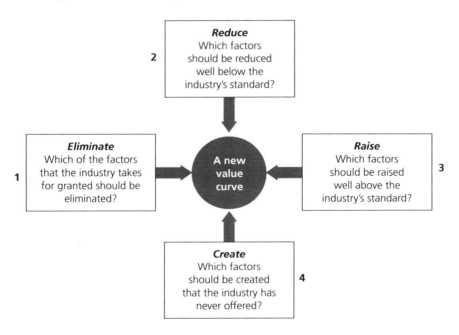

FIGURE 9.7 Example of a stage gate process

4   Internationalisation

4.1 Introduction

Section 3 introduced market development as a strategy. The focus here is on a specific but important kind of market development – operating in different geographical markets. Internationalisation raises choices about which countries to compete in, how far to modify the organisation's range of products or services and how to manage across borders. These kinds of questions are relevant to a wide range of organisations. As well as the large traditional multinationals such as Nestlé, Toyota and McDonald's, new small firms are also 'born global', building international relationships right from the start. Public sector organisations too are having to make choices about collaboration, outsourcing and even competition with overseas organisations. EU legislation requires public service organisations to accept tenders from non-national providers.

It is important to distinguish between international strategy and global strategy. International strategy refers to a range of options for operating outside an organisation's country of origin. Global strategy is only one kind of international strategy. Global strategy involves high levels of coordination of extensive activities dispersed geographically in many countries around the world.

We have had international trade for centuries, if not millennia. What is different in the past 40 years of 'globalisation' is the extent of foreign ownership of assets through the growth of FDI (foreign direct investment) and the integrated nature of supply chains, with assembly of products comprising components drawn from different parts of the world. Despite this greater intensity of foreign activity, authors such as IESE's Business School Professor Pankaj Ghemawat talk of a 'semi-globalised' or 'regionalised' world, as most foreign interaction takes place with near neighbours, often in trading blocks. Ghemawat's cultural, administrative, geographic and economic (CAGE) model explains the barriers to globalisation.

There are many general pressures increasing internationalisation. Barriers to international trade, investment and migration are all now much lower than they were. International regulation and governance have improved, so that investing and trading overseas is less risky. Improvements in communications – from cheaper air travel to the internet – make movement and the spread of ideas around the world much easier. Not least, the success of new economic powerhouses such as the so-called BRICs (Brazil, Russia, India and China) is generating new opportunities and challenges for business internationally (Friedman, 2006).

However, not all these internationalisation trends are one-way. Nor do they hold for all industries. For example, migration is now becoming more difficult between some countries. Many so-called multinationals are concentrated in quite particular markets, for example North America and Western Europe. Markets vary widely in the extent to which consumer needs are standardising – compare computer operating systems to tastes in chocolate. In short, managers need to be aware that economic integration into a single, homogenised and competitive world is wildly exaggerated and international drivers are complex.

 CASE EXAMPLE **9.20**

At the start of the 21st century, China was a magnet for Western supermarket chains. Growing at 13% a year, the Chinese market was predicted to reach $747 billion by 2010. With the local industry fragmented and focused on particular regions, large Western companies saw an advantage.

In 1995, after six years' experience in Taiwan, the French supermarket chain Carrefour was the first to enter the Chinese market in a substantial fashion. By 2006, Carrefour was the sixth largest retailer in China, though this meant only 0.6% overall market share. The world's largest retailer, the American Wal-Mart, was close behind, especially with its acquisition in 2006 of a Taiwanese chain with outlets on the mainland. These two rivals pursued very different strategies. Wal-Mart followed its standard centralised purchasing and distribution strategy, supplying as much as it could from its new distribution centre in Shenzen. Carrefour followed a decentralised strategy: except in Shanghai, where it has several stores, Carrefour allowed its local store managers, across the many different regions of China, to make their own purchasing and supply decisions.

The growth of companies such as Carrefour and Wal-Mart, as well as local chains, demonstrated that there was a substantial market for the Western supermarket experience. Carrefour, for example, was a pioneer of 'private label' goods in China, while Wal-Mart brought logistical expertise. Growing wealth and exposure to foreign ideas increased Chinese receptiveness. Nonetheless, progress was slow. Wal-Mart has yet to make a profit in China; Carrefour finally did, but its margins are significantly below those in France.

One discovery for Wal-Mart was that Chinese consumers prefer frequent shopping trips, buying small quantities each time. However, Wal-Mart had assumed that Chinese consumers would drive to out-of-town stores and fill their cars with large frozen multi-packs on a once-a-week shop, much like Americans. Now Wal-Mart supplies more of its frozen foods loose, offering customers a scoop so they can take exactly the amount they want. And in 2006, Wal-Mart allowed trade unions into its stores, in marked contrast to its policy in the rest of the world!

CASE EXAMPLE **9.20** *continued*

Another discovery for Western retailers is the amount of regional variation in a vast and multi-ethnic country. In the north of China, soya sauces are important; in central China, chilli pepper sauces are required; in the South, it is oyster sauces that matter. For fruit, northerners must have dates; southerners want lychees. In the north, the cold means more demand for red meat and, because customers are wearing several layers of clothing, wider store aisles. Northerners do not have much access to hot water, so they wash their hair less frequently, meaning that small sachets of shampoo sell better than large bottles.

Financial Times and *Wall Street Journal*, various dates

STOP AND THINK **9.5**

What might be the dangers for a large Western retailer in staying out of the Chinese market?

4.2 Drivers of internationalisation

The lesson here is that, given internationalisation's complexity, international strategy should be underpinned by a careful diagnosis of the strength and direction of trends in particular markets. Yip's 'drivers of globalisation' framework (Yip and Hult, 2012) provides a basis for such a diagnosis. The four drivers are as follows:

1 **Market drivers**. A key facilitator of internationalisation is standardisation of markets generated by similar customer needs and tastes, the presence of global customers and transferable marketing. Brands such as Coca-Cola are successfully marketed in similar ways across the world.

2 **Cost drivers**. Costs can be reduced by operating internationally. Increasing volume beyond what a national market might support can give scale economies. Companies from smaller countries such as the Netherlands become proportionately much more international than companies from the US, which have a vast market at home.

3 **Government drivers**. These can both facilitate and inhibit internationalisation. The relevant elements of policy are numerous, including tariff barriers, technical standards, subsidies to local firms, ownership restrictions, local content requirements, controls over technology transfer, intellectual property (patenting) regimes, and currency and capital flow controls. The WTO continues to push for greater openness and the EU and the North American Free Trade Agreement have made significant improvements in their specific regions.

4 **Competitive drivers**. These relate specifically to globalisation as an integrated worldwide strategy rather than simpler international strategies. Interdependence between country operations increases the pressure for global coordination and the presence of globalised competitors increases the pressure to adopt a global strategy.

The key insight from Yip's framework is that the internationalisation potential of industries is variable. There are many different factors that can support or inhibit it, and an important step in determining an internationalisation strategy is a realistic assessment of the true scope for internationalisation in the particular industry.

4.3 Porter's Diamond

As for any strategy, internationalisation needs to be based on having sustainable competitive advantage. Indeed, a foreign entrant must have significant competitive advantages to overcome the disadvantages of competing against domestic firms.

CASE EXAMPLE 9.21

Wal-Mart has been successful in many Asian markets with relatively underdeveloped retail markets, but was forced to withdraw from Germany's more mature market in 2006 after nearly a decade of failure. In Germany, unlike in most Asian markets, Wal-Mart had no significant competitive advantage over domestic retailers.

The international context raises specifically national sources of advantage that can be substantial and hard to imitate. Countries and their regions become associated with specific types of enduring competitive advantage: for example, the Swiss in private banking and the Taiwanese in computer laptops. Michael **Porter's Diamond** helps explain why some nations tend to produce firms with sustained competitive advantages in some industries more than others (see Figure 9.8). The degree of national advantage varies from industry to industry.

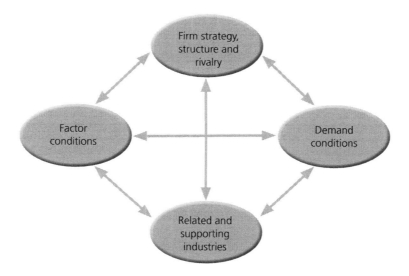

FIGURE 9.8 Porter's Diamond (Porter, 1990)

Porter's Diamond suggests that four interacting determinants of national (home base) make for advantage in particular industries. These are as follows:

1 **Factor conditions**. These refer to the 'factors of production' that go into making a product or service. For example, the linguistic ability of the Swiss has provided a significant advantage to their banking industry. Cheap energy has traditionally provided an advantage for the North American aluminium industry.

2 **Home demand conditions**. These can become a source of competitive advantage. Dealing with sophisticated and demanding customers at home helps train a company to be effective overseas. For example, sophisticated local customers in France and Italy have helped keep their local fashion industries at the leading edge for many decades.

3 **Related and supporting industries**. Local clusters of related and mutually supporting industries, often regionally based, can make personal interaction easier. Silicon Valley forms a cluster of hardware, software, research and venture capital organisations, which together create a virtuous circle of high-tech enterprise.

4 **Firm strategy, industry structure and rivalry**. German companies' strategy of investing in technical excellence gives them a characteristic advantage in engineering industries and creates large pools of expertise. A competitive local industry structure is also helpful. But if too dominant in their home territory, local organisations can become complacent and lose advantage overseas. The Swiss pharmaceuticals industry became strong in part because each company had to compete with several strong local rivals.

The argument that rivalry can be positive has led to a major government policy shift in many countries towards encouraging competition rather than protecting home-based industries. Governments can also foster local industries by raising safety or environmental standards (i.e. creating sophisticated demand conditions) or encouraging cooperation between suppliers and buyers on a domestic level (that is, building clusters of related and supporting industries in particular regions).

For individual organisations, however, the value of Porter's Diamond is to identify the extent to which they can build on home-based advantages to create competitive advantage in relation to others on a global front. For example, Dutch brewing companies, such as Heineken, have benefited from early globalisation, resulting from the nature of the Dutch home market. A key point is that before embarking on an internationalisation strategy, managers should look for sources of general national advantage to underpin their company's individual sources of advantage.

4.4 International strategies

Organisations still face difficult questions about what kinds of strategies to pursue in their markets. A key problem is the global/local dilemma: the extent to which products and services may be standardised across national boundaries or need to be adapted to meet the requirements of specific national markets. For some products and services, such as televisions, markets appear similar across the world, offering huge potential scale economies. For other products and services, such as television programming, tastes remain highly nationally specific, drawing companies to decentralise operations and control as near as possible to the local market. This dilemma leads to a range of responses, ranging from decentralisation to centralisation.

Porter (1987) identifies four kinds of international strategy, based on choices about the configuration of activities and the degree to which these activities are then coordinated internationally (see Figure 9.9). Configuration refers to the geographical dispersion or concentration of activities such as manufacturing and R&D, while coordination refers to the extent to which operations in different countries are managed in a decentralised way or a centrally coordinated way.

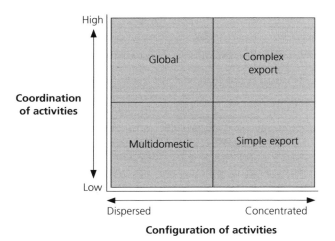

FIGURE 9.9 International strategies (Porter, 1986)

The four basic international strategies are as follows:

1 **Simple export**. This involves a concentration of activities (particularly manufacturing) in the country of origin. Marketing the exported product is very loosely coordinated overseas, perhaps by independent sales agents in different markets. Pricing, packaging, distribution and even branding policies may be determined locally.

2 **Multi-domestic**. This strategy is similarly loosely coordinated internationally, but involves a dispersion overseas of various activities, including manufacturing and sometimes product development. Instead of export, therefore, goods and services are produced locally in each national market. Each market is treated independently, with the needs of each local

domestic market given priority. This multi-domestic strategy is particularly attractive in professional services where local relationships are critical, but it carries risks for brand and reputation if national practices become too diverse.

3 **Complex export**. This still involves the location of most activities in a single country, but builds on more coordinated marketing. Economies of scale can be reaped in manufacturing and R&D, but branding and pricing opportunities are more systematically managed. Coordination demands are more complex and this is a common stage for companies from emerging economies.

4 **Global strategy**. This describes the most mature international strategy, with highly coordinated activities dispersed geographically around the world. Geographical location is chosen according to the specific locational advantage for each activity, so that product development, manufacturing, marketing and headquarters functions might all be located in different countries.

CASE EXAMPLE 9.22

US-based General Motors (GM) designed its Pontiac Le Mans at the firm's German subsidiary Opel, with its high engineering skills; developed its advertising via a British agency with the creativity strengths of London; produced many of the more complex components in Japan, exploiting its sophisticated manufacturing and technological capabilities; and assembled the car in South Korea, a location where a lower-cost, yet skilled labour force was available. All this, of course, required high investments and skill in coordination.

In practice, these four international strategies are not absolute or exclusive. Managerial coordination and geographical concentration are matters of degree rather than sharp distinctions. Companies may often oscillate within and between the four. Subsidiaries in an international firm can be managed by portfolio methods just as businesses in a diversified firm.

TEST YOUR KNOWLEDGE 9.4

a Identify three drivers of internationalisation.
b What is the purpose of Porter's Diamond?
c Identify the four main types of international strategy.

CASE QUESTIONS

1 Explain how the Garvin approach would assist with LCU's strategy setting.

2 Using examples from the case study, explain the role of the corporate parent.

CHAPTER SUMMARY

■ How and why firms outperform each other goes to the heart of strategic management.
■ Many organisations comprise a number of business units. Competitive strategy needs to be considered and defined in terms of strategic business units (SBUs). In this chapter, we identified three generic strategies for competing at business unit level: overall cost leadership, differentiation and focus. Value chain analysis can be effectively used to help support and plan cost leadership and differentiation strategies.

■ Decisions above the level of business units are the concern of corporate parents. Corporate parents can destroy value as well as create it, and should be ready to divest units for which they cannot create value.

■ Corporate strategy is concerned with development directions which can he identified by assessing the various combinations of products and markets leading to four broad categories; protect and build (current products in current markets); product development (for existing markets); market development (with existing products) and diversification (away from existing products and markets). Product diversity is often considered in terms of related and unrelated diversification. Performance tends to suffer if organisations become very diverse, or unrelated, in their business units. The BCG model helps corporate parents manage their strategic business units. Organisations need to manage their research and development process carefully in order to support new product development.

■ In recent years, a new approach to strategy, called blue ocean strategy, has emerged. At its heart, blue ocean strategy seeks not to compete with competitors, but to make them irrelevant by identifying and then occupying new market space.

■ Internationalisation potential in any particular market is determined by four drivers: market, cost, government and competitors' strategies. Sources of advantage in international strategy can be drawn from national sources of advantage, as captured in Porter's Diamond. There are four main types of international strategy, varying according to extent of coordination and geographical configuration: simple export, complex export, multi-domestic and global. Subsidiaries in an international firm can be managed by portfolio methods just as businesses in a diversified firm.

Strategy development

10

■ CONTENTS

1 Strategic pathways
2 Organic development
3 Mergers and acquisitions
4 Strategic alliances
5 Evaluating strategic options

■ INTRODUCTION

If an organisation's strategy calls for the enlargement of the corporate portfolio, then there is a need to gain access to additional resources. Given that the moves necessary to enlarge the portfolios are often of major significance to a firm, it is vital that strategists and leaders choose the most appropriate strategic pathway and understand the advantages and disadvantages of the various possibilities open to them. This chapter considers three main approaches: organic development, mergers and acquisitions, and strategic alliances. The strategist may well need to consider many possible options. The final section of this chapter therefore discusses the success criteria by which they can be assessed and some of the techniques for evaluating strategic options.

1 Strategic pathways

Once the scope of the organisation's business and competence portfolio has been decided, it will need to choose a strategic pathway to establish them. If the decision is for growth, the business will need to gain access to the required capabilities and competences. Any of the strategic directions discussed in Chapter 9 may be undertaken by a different strategic method: the means by which a strategy can be pursued. This represents another level of choice. These methods can be divided into three types: organic development, acquisition (or disposal) and alliances/joint ventures. These are summarised in Table 10.1.

TABLE 10.1 Alternative growth strategies (Thompson and Martin, 2005)

	Advantages	Possible drawbacks
Organic growth	Lower risk Allows for ongoing learning More control	Slow Lack of early knowledge – may be misjudgements
Acquisition	Fast Buys presence, market share and expertise	Premium price may have to be paid High risk if any misjudgement Preferred organisation may not be available May be difficult to sell unwanted assets
Strategic alliance	Cheaper than takeover Access to market knowledge Useful if acquisition impractical	Possible lack of control Potential managerial differences and problems

Table 10.1 continued

	Advantages	Possible drawbacks
Joint venture	As for strategic alliance plus: ■ Greater incentive and closer contract ■ Can lock out other competitors more effectively	As for strategic alliance

---

 CASE EXAMPLE **10.1**

A good example of different approaches to gaining a foothold in unfamiliar markets or technologies is the battle for dominance in the large diesel engines sector, in which Caterpillar and Cummins Engines, two big engineering companies in the US, compete.

Caterpillar is best known for its earthmoving equipment, but gains a quarter of its near sales through diesel engines. These are sold to customers in power generation, shipbuilding, trucks and industrial machinery, and are directly related to the engines Caterpillar builds for its own use.

Cummins focuses far more on engines and derives most of its annual revenues from these products, which are sold to customers similar to Caterpillar's. Both companies are about the same size in terms of revenues from diesels. Cummins is the world's biggest maker of large diesels (more than 200 hp) in units. Caterpillar is in third position.

Caterpillar and Cummins differ in their stance on moving into new markets through joining up with other businesses. In the past decade, Cummins has formulated a strategy based on joint ventures with outside groups, including customers and competitors.

For instance, Cummins built a family of engines for power generation with Wartsila of Finland and runs an engine factory in the US jointly with Case, the big US tractor and construction machine supplier. In 1996, Cummins formed a $300 million joint venture with Fiat, the Italian automotive group, to develop and make engines for tractors, buses and trucks. It also has several partnerships with Komatsu, the big Japanese company, which is second to Caterpillar in excavators and a big engine builder in its own right.

Caterpillar, by contrast, has taken a determinedly go-it-alone approach, preferring to stay in complete control of its new engine ventures. In the past, it has bought engine companies worldwide, including MaK of Germany and Perkins in the UK, makers of very large engines for electricity generation and ships, and of smaller engines suited for fitting to new families of compact construction machines, respectively.

The high cost of adapting diesel technologies for use in new types of product is driving the decisions of Caterpillar and Cummins. Both companies have spent billions of dollars since the 1930s developing their diesel know-how. Gerald Shaheeri, former head of Caterpillar's engine products division, suggests that Caterpillar has generally aimed for complete control of its new engine ventures, partly to safeguard what it regards as proprietary know-how, which feeds directly into the engines it uses internally for its construction equipment.

Cummins has taken a more flexible stance, with its smaller financial base ruling out the kinds of acquisition Caterpillar has opted for. It is also more oriented towards collaboration; virtually all its sales are built around some kind of partnership with customers, who buy engines to fit into their own products. Even so, Cummins has had to learn a new, more open way of sharing information with its worldwide collaborators.

 STOP AND THINK **10.1**

What are the strategic pathways chosen by Caterpillar and Cummins?
Why are Caterpillar and Cummins taking these different approaches to growth?

TEST YOUR KNOWLEDGE **10.1**

a   Identify the main methods of pursuing strategies.
b   Identify the main advantages of each.

2   Organic development

Organic development (also known as internal development) involves building up the organisation's own resource base and competences to develop strategy. For many organisations, organic growth or development has been the primary method of strategy development, and there are some compelling reasons for this:

- **Technical products**. It is the best way of acquiring the necessary capabilities to compete successfully where products are highly technical in terms of design or method of manufacture.
- **Knowledge and capability development can be enhanced**. For example, a business may feel that the direct involvement gained from having its own sales force rather than using agents gains greater market knowledge and therefore competitive advantage over other rivals more distant from their customers.
- **Spreading costs**. The final cost of developing new activities internally may be greater than that of acquiring other companies. However, spreading these costs over time may be a better option, particularly in small companies or public services, which may not have the resources for major, one-off investments.
- **Minimising disruption**. The slower rate of change of organic development may also minimise the disruption to other activities and avoid the problems of acquisition integration that can occur (see Section 3.3).
- **The nature of markets**. Organisations breaking new ground may not be in a position to develop by acquisition or joint development, since they are the only ones in the field. Alternatively, there may be few opportunities for acquisitions, as, for example, for foreign companies attempting to enter Japan.

The main advantages of organic development are that there is likely to be minimal change to continuing activities. There are also unlikely to be the cultural problems associated with either an acquisition or an alliance. The main disadvantage is that it is likely to be slower than if acquisition had been used, and probably slower than developing an alliance (Buzzell and Gale, 1987).

The process of internal development may occur in a variety of ways. Within certain cultures, many suggestions for offer enlargements will come from employees, the board or customers (Finlay, 2000).

CASE EXAMPLE **10.2**

3M has encouraged ideas from its employees for many years. 3M employs a loose/tight approach whereby employees are encouraged to work on research projects with their own or 'stolen' resources. This is the 'loose' part. The 'tight' part is the very strict corporate controls that are imposed when it comes to developing the initiative, since generally research is not costly: the real costs are incurred in the development phase.

In January 1999 Pearson PLC decided to establish Financial Times Management. This was a business that brought together the distance-learning management education operations of the Financial Times group with the extensive intellectual properties of Pearson Education. It aimed at providing both individual and company training. The newly appointed head reported directly to the CEO, which illustrates the Pearson approach to fledgling businesses of great potential. New businesses are left alone to get on with things, and can thus react very speedily but at the same time they have direct access to resources should they be needed.

a   Define the term 'organic development'.
b   Explain why organic development has been the principal method of strategy development.
c   Identify the main advantages of organic development.

3   Mergers and acquisitions

3.1 Introduction

An **acquisition** is where an organisation takes ownership of another organisation, whereas a **merger** implies a mutually agreed decision for joint ownership between organisations. In practice, few acquisitions are hostile and few mergers are the coming together of equals. So both acquisitions and mergers typically involve the managers of one organisation exerting strategic influence over the other. Mergers and acquisitions (M&A) frequently grab the headlines, as they involve large sums of money and sometimes public competitions for shareholder support. They can provide a speedy means of achieving major strategic objectives – but they can also go wrong. Royal Bank of Scotland's 2007 takeover of the Dutch ABN AMRO ended in commercial disaster and nationalisation by the British government.

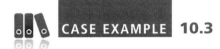

FedEx to buy rival TNT Express

US parcels delivery firm FedEx is to buy its Dutch rival TNT Express for £3.2 billion as it looks to expand its European operations. In a joint statement, the companies said both management boards had reached a 'conditional agreement'.

It comes two years after United Parcel Service (UPS) pulled out of a bid for the Dutch firm following opposition from EU competition authorities. Since then TNT has undertaken a restructuring programme, cutting costs, selling operations and investing heavily in its road network to hold on to customers in what has been a weak European market for business package deliveries.

FedEx and TNT Express expect the deal to be completed in the first half of next year and say they are confident any European competition concerns can be overcome this time. The European regional headquarters of the combined companies will remain in the Netherlands, while FedEx has promised to maintain the TNT Express brand 'for an appropriate period'. Tex Gunning, chief executive of TNT Express, said: '…while we did not solicit an acquisition, we truly believe that FedEx's proposal, both from a financial and a non-financial view, is good news for all stakeholders.' The terms of the takeover allow for a competitor to make an offer within the next eight weeks and for the current deal to be terminated if that offer exceeds the existing proposal by 8%.

Source: BBC Business, www.bbc.com/news/business-32200600, 7 April 2015.

Worldwide merger and acquisition activity takes place on a major scale, but tends to go in waves. Globally, the number of completed acquisitions tripled between 1991 and 2001. There was then a decline after 2000, but they still stood at $1.2 trillion in 2002. Since the 2007/08 recession, it has risen again and stood at almost $2.8 trillion in 2010 and $3.5 trillion in 2014. Global activity in mergers is dominated by North America and Western Europe, whereas it is traditionally less common in other economies (e.g. Japan). This reflects the influence of the differences in governance systems, although in 2014, Asia-Pacific as a whole showed a significant increase.

Who benefits from mergers and acquisitions – Customers? Shareholders? Employees? Who else benefits?

3.2 Motives for acquisitions

A compelling reason to develop by acquisition is the speed with which it allows the company to enter new product or market areas. In some cases, the product or market is changing so rapidly that this becomes the *only* way of successfully entering the market, since the process of organic development is too slow. In practice, there is a complex array of motives.

Strategic motives for M&A

Strategic motives for M&A involve improving the competitive advantage of the organisation and are often related to the reasons for diversification in general (page 200, S 3.2). Strategic motives can be categorised as follows:

- **Extension**: to extend the reach of a firm in terms of geography, products or markets. Acquisitions can be speedy ways of extending international reach. In 2010, the Chinese Geely car company bought the Swedish Volvo car company in order to build its global presence.
- **Consolidation**: to consolidate competitors in an industry. Bringing together two competitors can increase market power by reducing competition: this might enable the newly consolidated company to raise prices for customers. It can also increase efficiency through reducing surplus capacity or sharing resources – for instance, head office facilities or distribution channels. Finally, the greater scale of the combined operations may increase production efficiency or increase bargaining power with suppliers, forcing them to reduce their prices. The FedEx example in Case Example 10.3 illustrates this.
- **Capabilities**: to increase a company's capabilities. High-tech companies such as Cisco and Microsoft regard acquisitions of entrepreneurial technology companies as a part of their R&D effort. Instead of researching a new technology from scratch, they allow entrepreneurial start-ups to prove the idea, and then take over these companies in order to incorporate the technological capability within their own portfolio. Capabilities-driven acquisitions are often useful where industries are converging. For example, Google and Apple have made substantial acquisitions in order to gain a foothold in the new high-growth mobile advertising market, where there is convergence between telephony and advertising industries.

Financial motives for M&A

Financial motives concern the optimal use of financial resources, rather than directly improving the actual business. There are three main financial motives:

- **Financial efficiency**. It may, for example, be efficient to bring together a company with a strong balance sheet (i.e. it has plenty of cash) with another company that has a weak balance sheet (i.e. it has high debt). The company with a weak balance sheet can save on interest payments by using the stronger company's assets to pay off its debt, and it can also get investment funds from the stronger company that it could not have accessed otherwise. The company with the strong balance sheet may be able to drive a good bargain in acquiring the weaker company.
- **Tax efficiency**. There may be tax advantages from bringing together different companies. For example, profits or losses may be transferable within the organisation, according to legal restrictions, in order to benefit from different tax regimes between industries or countries.
- **Asset stripping or unbundling**. The underlying assets of some companies are worth more than the price of the company as a whole. This makes it possible to buy such companies and then sell (unbundle) different business units to various buyers for a total price in excess of that originally paid for the whole. Although this is often dismissed as profiteering (asset stripping), if the business units find themselves with better corporate parents through this unbundling process, there can be a real gain in economic effectiveness.

Managerial motives for M&A

Acquisitions may sometimes serve managers' interests rather than shareholders' interests. They are then self-serving and may be of two types:

- **Personal ambition**. Senior managers' personal financial incentives may be tied to short-term growth or share-price targets that are achieved more easily by large and spectacular acquisitions than gradual, organic growth. The media attention, with opportunities to boost personal reputation through interviews and appearances, may be attractive. Acquisitions may also provide chances to give friends and colleagues greater responsibility, helping to cement personal loyalty.
- **Bandwagon effects**. As suggested in section 1.1, M&A activity is highly cyclical, with booms being followed by slumps. In an upswing, there is pressure on senior managers to join the bandwagon or risk being regarded as too cautious. There may be shareholder pressure, or the business may become the target of a hostile bid itself.

 STOP AND THINK 10.3

Are mergers and acquisitions always a good thing for an organisation? What issues might arise with implementation?

In summary, there are good and bad reasons for mergers and acquisitions. The average performance of acquisitions is unimpressive, with evidence suggesting that half of acquisitions fail. The overriding problem with acquisition lies in the ability to integrate the new company into the activities of the old, which often centre on problems of cultural fit. Where acquisition is being used to acquire new competences, this 'clash of cultures' may simply arise because the organisational routines are so different in each organisation.

Reasons for mergers may be similar to those for acquisitions. However, mergers are usually the result of organisations coming together voluntarily because they are actively seeking benefits of synergy.

3.3 Advantages and disadvantages

Acquisition has some significant *advantages* over both internal development and alliances as a route towards gaining access to resources (Finlay, 2000).

- **High-speed access to resources**. The speed with which a new SBU or competence can be added to the corporate portfolio is high. An acquisition can provide a powerful brand name that could take years to establish through internal development.
- **Less likelihood of retaliation from competitors**. An acquisition only changes ownership of an SBU and thus does not alter the capacity of the competitive arena as successful internal development would. Thus less reaction from competitors might be expected.
- **They can block a competitor**. An acquisition can block off a capability or competence from a competitor. There was general agreement among commentators that one reason for the abortive bid by Kingfisher for Asda in 1999 was that it would remove a possible acquisition target from Wal-Mart.
- **They can help to restructure the operating environment**. Acquisition can be used as a means of restructuring the operating environment. Overcapacity and the need to reduce it was one of the driving forces for the worldwide wave of car mergers at the end of the 1990s.

There are also several significant *disadvantages* associated with acquisition:

- **Cultural mismatch**. There is bound to be some cultural mismatch between any two organisations. A lack of fit can be significant in knowledge-based businesses, where the value of the business resides in individuals.

 **CASE EXAMPLE 10.4**

When a large, well-established British bank bought a trading company, the cultural mismatch was palpable and this mismatch led to failure: the value of the trading company lay in its people and, dissatisfied with the merger, they simply left the organisation, thus stripping the bank of its value.

C.J. Clarke (1987), 'Acquisitions – techniques for measuring strategic fit', Long Range Planning, 20(3), 12–18

- **Mismatch in managerial salaries**. For example, the very high salaries of US senior managers compared with those of the Germans were a serious concern in the Daimler–Chrysler merger of 1998.
- **Heightened risk**. Unless very great care is taken, the acquirer will not know all there is to know about the organisation it seeks to buy. Thus there is a risk associated with the purchase. This risk will be much reduced if the organisations have been working with each other prior to the acquisition, or where the features of the competitive arena are known, such as is the case where two airlines or car companies agree to merge.
- **Disposal of assets**. Government/EU restrictions may force the buyer to dispose of assets it had prior to the acquisition. Historically, this has happened several times in brewery acquisitions in the UK, where the buyer is not allowed a monopoly of pubs in specified areas.

Acquisitions are not an easy or guaranteed route to improving financial performance (Gregory, 1997). Seventy per cent of acquisitions end up with lower returns to shareholders of both organisations. The most common mistake is in paying too much for a company. In addition, the managers of the acquiring company may be overoptimistic about the benefits of the acquisition. An acquisition will probably include poor resources and competences, as well as the better resources and competences that were the reason for the purchase. Alternatively, it may be that the capabilities of the merging organisations are not compatible.

 **CASE EXAMPLE 10.5**

In the 2004 acquisition of the UK Safeway supermarket chain by its competitor, Morrison's, among the problems encountered was the fact that Morrison's spent a year trying to integrate the IT systems of the two companies before abandoning the attempt.

For this reason, acquirers may attempt to buy products or processes rather than whole companies if possible. At the very best it may take the acquiring company considerable time to gain financial benefit from acquisitions.

3.4 Success and failure

The implementation agenda following an acquisition or merger will vary depending on its purpose. Johnson et al. (2014), summarising the evidence, suggest that there are four frequently occurring issues that account for success or failure of an acquisition/merger:

1 **Adding value**. The acquirer may find difficulty in adding value to the acquired business.
2 **Gaining the commitment of middle managers**. These managers are responsible for the operations and customer relations in the acquired business, and their commitment is important in order to avoid internal uncertainties and maintain customer confidence. Deciding which executives to retain in the acquired business needs to be done quickly.
3 **Expected synergies may not be realised**. This may be either because they do not exist to the extent expected or because it proves difficult to integrate the activities of the acquired business. For example, where the motive was the transfer of competences or knowledge it may be difficult to identify what these are.
4 **Problems of cultural fit**. This can arise because the acquiring business finds that routine, but embedded aspects of culture differ in ways that prove difficult to overcome but are not

readily identifiable before the acquisition. This can be particularly problematic with cross-country acquisitions.

3.5 Due diligence

Before embarking upon acquisition or merger preparations, both parties should ensure that they conduct the necessary research and analysis of the counterparty to confirm the soundness of the proposed transaction. Before entering into such a major commitment, it is important that the organisation adopts a holistic approach and considers all relevant factors that might impact the transaction. The due diligence process therefore involves an extensive examination of the counterparty's commercial, cultural, financial and operational positions. It is usual to adopt a risk-based approach to the examination; the due diligence findings can therefore be used to flag potential problems, risks or 'showstoppers'.

According to GE Capital, an effective due diligence process will comprise the following elements:

- **Preparation.** A comprehensive understanding of the counterparty's product lines, revenue streams and profitability and risks needs to be gathered. In this stage, a due diligence team will also need to be established with the necessary business, financial and legal skills. The team will then be required to draft out the relevant checklists and requests for information required to garner the necessary information, identify risks and advise on the soundness of the transaction. A questioning approach will, therefore, be adopted by the team, who may seek to answer questions such as the following:
  - Do the counterparty's financial statements accurately reflect its current position?
  - Would integration with the counterparty have a positive or negative impact upon profitability?
  - What is the counterparty's competitive strengths?
  - Is the counterparty exposed to any significant regulatory or liability risks?
  - Are the counterparty's supplier relationships robust?
  - What are the strengths of the counterparty's workforce?
  - Is the counterparty's corporate culture compatible?
- **Execution.** After the checklists and requests for information have been completed, the team will scrutinise and test their robustness. This may involve asking additional questions and requests for further information.
- **Closure.** In this stage the team should produce the due diligence report to senior management. The report may recommend:
  - proceeding with the transaction;
  - proceeding with the transaction but flagging possible risks that will require addressing in the integration stage;
  - stalling the transaction (should important questions remained unanswered); or
  - proceeding with the transaction but with amended terms and conditions such as a lower bid price.

TEST YOUR KNOWLEDGE 10.3

a   Distinguish between a merger and an acquisition.
b   Identify the main advantages of an acquisition as a form of strategy development.
c   Summarise the main reasons for the success or failure of a merger or acquisition.

4   Strategic alliances

4.1 Introduction

Mergers and acquisitions bring together companies through complete changes in ownership. However, companies also often work together in **strategic alliances** that involve collaboration with only partial changes in ownership, or no ownership changes at all, as the parent companies remain distinct. Thus a strategic alliance is where two or more organisations share resources and activities to pursue a common strategy. This is a popular method with companies for pursuing strategy. Accenture has estimated that the average large corporation is managing around 30 alliances at any one time (Andersen Consulting, 1999.)

Strategic alliances vary from simple, two-partner alliances co-producing a product to one with multiple partners providing complex products and solutions.

By the turn of the century the top 500 global companies had an average of 60 alliances each (Ernst and Halevy, 2002). This kind of joint development of new strategies has become increasingly popular because organisations cannot always cope with increasingly complex environments or strategies (such as globalisation) from internal resources and competences alone. They may need to obtain materials, skills, innovation, finance or access to markets, but recognise that these may be as readily available through cooperation as through ownership. However, about half of all alliances fail.

Finlay argues that an alliance must be sufficiently central to the business of at least one of the partners for it to be considered *strategically* important.

'Speculative, opportunistic and peripheral activities would generally not be considered to be strategic. The provisioning of transport or cleaning services via a joint venture would not be strategic for a bank, for example.'

 CASE EXAMPLE 10.6

Gaining competitive advantage through collaboration?

Apple has dominated the tablet market with its iPad since 2010. The lightweight touch screen and new operating system (iOS), designed from the ground up for portable performance, had won many admirers.

Market research firm iSuppli's 'teardown' analysis revealed that the $829, 4G 64GB model cost $409 to make – just 49% of its retail price. They identified Broadcom and Qualcomm as suppliers of Bluetooth and wi-fi chips, STMicroelectronics the gyroscope, Cirrus Logic the audio chip, three Taiwanese companies the touch-screen components and Sony the camera CMOS sensor. Samsung, a rival manufacturer with its own tablet, provided a significant portion of the iPad, the expensive display, battery and processor chip.

Apple was therefore at the heart of a network. However, it had always protected its intellectual property. No hardware was licensed, ensuring control of production and maintenance of its premium pricing policy. It was impossible for any independent company to manufacture cheap iPads, in the way that, for instance, Taiwanese manufacturers produced cheap IBM/Microsoft-compatible personal computers in the 1980s.

The iPad's success attracted a swarm of companies into the accessory market, supplying attractive add-ons. Apple licensed them the necessary technology for this, and benefited from attractive complementary products and royalties. However, the relationship was arm's-length, with no advanced information about new products. Controlling access to iOS, Apple opened up access for third-party apps development, stimulating the new app stores industry.

Samsung aimed to profit from business services use rather than hardware. Its Galaxy tablet's improved screen resolution and Android operating system challenged iPad's technology, and it shared many characteristics of the other ecosystem with streaming apps and a consistent user experience. Apple became embroiled in lawsuits against Samsung over its Galaxy tablet design. Samsung was counter-suing. In November 2012, Apple dropped Samsung as its provider of batteries, preferring Chinese manufacturers instead.

Sources: G. Linden, K. Kraemer and J. Dedrick (2009), 'Who captures value in a global innovation network?', *Communications of the ACM*, 52(3), pp.140–5; 'Tablet wars', the *Telegraph*, 6 November 2012; F. MacMahon, 'Tablet wars', BroadcastEngineering.com, 4 December 2012; A. Hesseldahl, 'Apple's new iPad costs at least $316 to build, IHS iSuppli Teardown Shows', 16 March 2012, allthingsd.com.

According to Johnson et al. (2014), motives for strategic alliances are of three main types:

1 **The need for critical mass**. Alliances can achieve this by forming partnerships with either competitors or providers of complementary products. This can lead to cost reduction and improved customer offering.

2 **Co-specialisation**. This allows each partner to concentrate on activities that best match its capabilities: for example, to enter new geographical markets where an organisation needs local knowledge and expertise in distribution, marketing and customer support. Similarly, alliances with organisations in other parts of the value chain (e.g. suppliers or distributors) are common.

3 **Learning**. Such learning from partners and developing competences that may be more widely exploited elsewhere. For example, first steps into e-business may be achieved with a partner that has expertise in website development. However, the longer-term intention might be to bring those activities in-house.

4.2 Types of strategic alliance

There are different types of strategic alliance. Some may be formalised inter-organisational relationships. At the other extreme, there are loose arrangements of cooperation and informal networking between organisations, with no shareholding or ownership involved.

■ **Joint ventures**. Formalised alliances where organisations remain independent but set up a newly created organisation jointly owned by the parents. Joint ventures have been a favoured means of collaborative ventures in China, for example. Local firms provide labour and entry to markets; Western companies provide technology, management expertise and finance.

■ **Consortia**. These may involve two or more organisations in a joint venture typically more focused on a particular venture or project. Examples include major aerospace undertakings, such as the European Airbus. They also exist between public sector organisations where services (such as public transport) cross administrative boundaries.

■ **Networks**. These are less formal arrangements where organisations gain mutual advantage by working in collaboration without relying on cross-ownership arrangements and formal contracts. Such networked arrangements may exist between competitors in highly competitive industries where some form of sharing is still beneficial such as Formula One racing.

The reasons why these different forms of alliance occur are concerned with the assets involved in the alliance. These assets may not just be financial or physical, but could also include access to market, skills and intellectual property. There have been four main drivers:

1 **Blurring of national boundaries**. This gives rise to greater competition. The development of the EU is an example of a political and economic factor that has reduced the economic separateness of nation-states and the protection that this affords nationally operating companies. However, Finlay (2000) argues that, as yet, this has not had much effect on the cultural separateness that divides nations and suggests that collaboration with indigenous partners is likely to be appropriate, especially with consumer offers.

 STOP AND THINK 10.4

What do you think about Finlay's argument here? What evidence can you see to the contrary?

---

2 **Political requirements**. Some countries, such as India, demand some local ownership in foreign companies entering the country. One option in satisfying this demand is for the foreign company to forge an alliance with a local company.

3 **Information technology**. This is compressing time and distance, allowing collaboration between physically separated organisations (as the collaboration between Rolls-Royce operating in the UK and General Electric (GE) operating in the US illustrates).

4 **Globalisation**. Many companies see the need to operate globally but do not have the resources to achieve the necessary presence.

4.3 Advantages and disadvantage of strategic alliances

The *advantages* of alliances over internal development and acquisition have been summarised by Finlay (op. cit.):

- **Access to complementary resources.** Offers have become increasingly complex and companies need access to a wide range of competences and capabilities that they themselves do not possess. For example, supermarkets have teamed up with banks to offer financial services. The need for extra expertise is especially required with IT.
- **Sharing of resource requirements and risk.** Some opportunities look very profitable but require significant resources to carry them out and/or are accompanied by large risks. In such cases, an alliance is an appropriate means of obtaining the resources and reducing the risks to any one member of the alliance. The Channel Tunnel development is an example of reward/ risk-sharing. In many fields, R&D is also a driver for spreading costs between partners.
- **Speeds market access.** Firms need simultaneous access to all the important markets to prevent competitors maintaining a comfortable home base and because competitive advantage is often fleeting. Without fast access, their offers will be imitated and they will not be able to appropriate the full gains.
- **Reduces political difficulties.** An alliance can provide a foreign company with the opportunity for obtaining local management, reducing risks such as expropriation and difficulties with host-country officials.
- **Enhances competences.** An alliance can help a firm remain competitive in the long run by ensuring that its competences are continuously upgraded rather than eroding over time.
- **Provides defence.** When two or more smaller firms have trouble competing with a large firm, an alliance may provide the market power to compete successfully.

The *disadvantages* of alliances are summarised as follows:

- **The costs of establishing and maintaining the alliance.** The costs associated with an alliance may be large, as senior management will be involved, together with a highly qualified team. Alliances are a tempting solution to the dilemma of a firm seeking home-based advantages of another nation without giving up its own. Although they can achieve selective benefits, they always involve significant costs in terms of coordination, reconciling goals with an independent entity, creating a competitor and giving up profits. These costs make many alliances temporary and destined to fail. Alliances may ensure mediocrity since they deter the firm's own efforts to upgrade.
- **Damage to capabilities and competences.** If a partner takes over the marketing of another firm's products, for example, then the producer may lose its feel for the marketplace and thus for what is needed to develop its offer.
- **Long development time.** The time to establish an alliance can be long, especially for it to be established well enough to achieve significant profitability.
- **Requirement to sell assets.** Government restrictions may force the buyer to sell some of its own assets.

4.4 Ingredients of successful alliances

Faulkner's (1995) study of international strategic alliances confirmed that the primary motivation to form alliances was the need for specific resources and competences to survive and succeed in globalising markets, particularly where technologies were changing too. Partners were chosen with these issues in mind. However, the success of alliances tended to be more dependent on how they were managed and the way in which the partners fostered the evolution of the partnership. For example, attitudes to commitment, trust and cultural sensitivity, clear organisational arrangements and the desire of all partners to achieve organisational learning from the alliance rather than to use partners to substitute for their lack of competences.

Johnson et al. suggest that the success of alliances depends on how they are managed and the way in which the partners foster the evolving nature of the partnership. Success factors include the following:

- **Strategic purpose.** A clear strategic purpose is helpful at the outset of an alliance. However, alliance members may have differing if compatible reasons for being part of the alliance. As an alliance develops, their expectations and perceived benefits evolve; and if they start to diverge the alliance may eventually disintegrate. If the evolving expectations remain compatible or converge, then the alliance will continue. Convergence could give rise to more formalised ownership arrangements such as a merger of the partners.

■ **Alliance expectations and benefits**. Similarly, managing partners' expectations as the alliance evolves is vital. This requires a willingness to exchange information, including performance information that would not normally be shared between organisations. Beyond this, accepting learning and experimentation as benefits is important. If one of the partners does not accept this, it may well lead to problems. There are also indications that alliances that develop knowledge-based products and services (as distinct from physical product) tend to bind alliance partners more closely together since they are likely to be mutually dependent on shared tacit knowledge in the development of such products and services.

■ **Managing alliance relationships**. Senior management support for an alliance is important. Alliances require a wider range of relationships to be built and sustained, which can create cultural and political obstacles that senior managers must help to overcome. In cross-country partnerships this includes the need to transcend national cultural differences. Consistently, research shows that trust is the most important ingredient of success and a major reason for failure if it is absent. Such trust is competence-based (each partner is confident that the other has the resources and competences to fulfil its part in the alliance) and character-based (whether partners trust each other's motives and their attitudes to integrity, openness, discretion and consistency of behaviour match). The message is that it is the quality of the relationships in an alliance are of prime importance; more so than the physical resources (Lavie, 2006).

A consistent message that recurs, is that while it may be very helpful to ensure that an alliance has clear goals, governance and organisational arrangements concerning activities that cross or connect the partners, it is also important to keep the alliance flexible so it can evolve and change.

TEST YOUR KNOWLEDGE 10.4

a   Explain what is meant by a 'strategic alliance'.
b   What types of alliance are there?
c   What influences the success of strategic alliances?

5   Evaluating strategic options

5.1 Introduction

So far in this part we have introduced an array of strategic choices. This section turns to how these might be evaluated in terms of three key success criteria that can be used to assess the viability of strategic options.

■ **Suitability**. A broad assessment of whether the strategy addresses the circumstances in which the organisation is operating – for example, the extent to which new strategies would fit with the future trends and changes in the environment.

■ **Acceptability**. Concerned with the expected performance outcomes (such as the return or risk) if the strategy were implemented and the extent to which these would be in line with the expectations of stakeholders.

■ **Feasibility**. Whether the strategy can be made to work in practice. This means an emphasis on more detailed assessment of the practicalities of resourcing and strategic capability.

Figure 10.1 shows how these various aspects of evaluation and selection can be fitted together, and builds on the issues discussed concerning strategic analysis and strategic options.

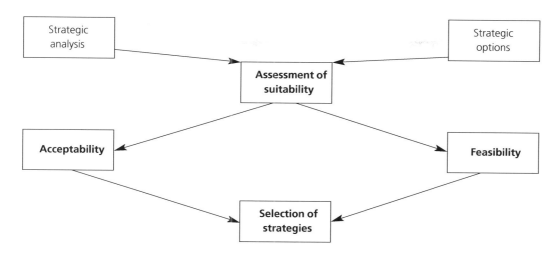

FIGURE 10.1 A framework for the evaluation and selection of strategies

5.2 Assessing suitability

Suitability is concerned with whether a strategy addresses the key issues that have been identified in understanding the strategic position of the organisation. It is therefore concerned with the overall rationale of a strategy. This means assessing how any strategic option would fit with key drivers and expected changes in the environment, exploit strategic capabilities and be appropriate in the context of stakeholder expectations and influence and cultural influences. The concepts and frameworks discussed in Part Two are especially helpful in understanding suitability and are a useful basis on which to screen options before more detailed analyses are undertaken. It is important to check that strategies are consistent with the needs of the environment, the resources and values of the organisation, and its mission.

- **Mission and objectives**. The strategy should fit the current mission and objectives of the organisation and should be acceptable to the strategic leader and other influential stakeholders. This issue is developed further in section 5.3.
- **Effect on the strategic perspective**. The strategy proposed should have the potential for improving the general competitive position of the organisation. It should seek to become, and remain, an effective competitor.
- **Current strategic position (SWOT)**. The strategy should be appropriate for the current economic and competitive environment. It should also be able to capitalise and build on current strengths, competencies and opportunities, and avoid weaknesses and potential threats. To what extent is the strategy able to take advantage of emerging trends in the environment, the market and the industry?
- **Skills, competencies and resources**. The strategies being pursued and considered must be sufficiently consistent that skills, competencies and resources are not spread or stretched disadvantageously. Check if any new proposal exploits key organisational competencies. For current businesses and strategies, the organisation should effectively add value: otherwise, a divestment strategy could be more appropriate.
- **Culture**. The strategy should fit the culture and values of the organisation. If not, there may be implications in going ahead.
- **Simplicity**. The strategy will ideally be simple, understandable and able to be communicated easily. Consider whether people are likely to be enthusiastic.

In summary, a key question is whether there is congruence between the environment, values and resources. However, as Johnson et al. make clear, the important point is that the really important issues are isolated from among all those identified in the analysis. Indeed, a major skill of a strategist is to be able to discern these key strategic issues. Evaluating the suitability of a strategy is extremely difficult unless these have been identified.

5.3 Assessing acceptability

Strategies also have to be acceptable or desirable to a variety of different stakeholders. **Acceptability** is concerned with the expected performance outcomes of a strategy, such as risk or return, if a strategy is implemented. The key issues are:

- **Strategic needs**. Timing may be important. The ability of the strategy to produce results in either the short or the longer term should be assessed in the light of the needs and priorities of the organisation.
- **The level of expected returns**. Investment decisions might concern the purchase of new technology or plant, the acquisition of another company, or financing the development and launch of a new product. The ability to raise money and the cost involved are key influences alongside two other strategic issues:
  - Does the proposed investment make sense strategically?
  - Will the investment provide an adequate financial return?
- **Synergy**. Effective synergy should lead to a better concentration of resources compared with competitors. What are the prospects for synergy in bringing an overall improvement to the organisation? Diversification into products and markets with which the organisation has no experience and which may require different skills may fit poorly alongside existing strategies and fail to provide synergy.
- **Risk**. Risk, vulnerability, opportunity and timing are linked. Where organisations, having spotted an opportunity, act quickly, there is always a danger that some important consideration(s) will be overlooked. For example, managerial competence may be stretched. Many of these issues are qualitative and require judgement. The organisation spends in considering the implications and assessing the risks, the greater the chance it has of reducing and controlling those risks. However, if managers take too long, the opportunity or the initiative may be lost to a competitor who is more willing to accept risk.
- **Stakeholder needs and preferences**. The issues here are the expectations and hopes of key stakeholders, the ability of the organisation to implement the strategy and achieve the desired results, and the willingness of stakeholders to accept the risks inherent in a particular strategy.

Strategic changes may affect existing resources and the strategies to which they are committed. Shareholders, bankers, managers, employees and customers can all be affected and their relative power and influence will prove significant. The willingness of each party to accept particular risks may also vary. The power and influence of the strategic leader will be very important in the choice of major strategic changes, and his or her ability to convince other stakeholders will be crucial.

5.4 Assessing feasibility

Feasibility is concerned with whether an organisation has the resources and competences to deliver a strategy. Important factors here include:

- **Issues of implementation and change**. The strategy should be feasible in resource terms and be possible to implement effectively. It obviously should be capable of achieving the objectives that it addresses and the organisation must be able to cope with the extent and challenge of the change implied by the option.
- **Finance and other resource availability**. A lack of any key resource can place a constraint on certain possible developments.
- **Ability to meet key success factors**. A strategic alternative is not feasible if the key success factors dictated by the industry and customer demand, such as quality, price and service level, cannot be met.
- **Competitive advantage**. The effectiveness of a strategy will be influenced by the ability of the organisation to create and sustain competitive advantage. When formulating a strategy it is important to consider the likely response of competitors in order to ensure that the necessary flexibility is incorporated into the implementation plans. A company which breaks into a currently stable industry or market may well threaten the market share and profitability of other companies and force them respond with, say, price cuts, product improvements or aggressive promotion campaigns. The new entrant should be prepared for this and be ready to counter it.

■ **Timing**. Timing is related to opportunity on the one hand, and risk and vulnerability on the other. It may be important for an organisation to act quickly and decisively once a window of opportunity is spotted. Competitors may attempt to seize the same opportunity. Timing is also an implementation issue.

STOP AND THINK 10.5

In this previous section we examined the criteria that can be employed to evaluate strategy. But are some more useful or important than others?

5.5 Real options

As part of the process of selecting strategic options, which may include mergers, acquisitions and strategic alliances, organisations need to consider the concept of real options. Real options may be considered to be options within strategic options. Real options, therefore, are embedded options that might be present within possible strategic alternatives; they exist where it is possible to alter a particular strategy in some profitable way after its commencement, but without the obligation to do so. They are therefore valuable as they serve to maintain upside risk but limit the damage from downside risk. Their value increases in times of volatility and uncertainty, and can be seen as being similar to 'hedging' in financial markets.

There are three main types of real option:

■ **The delay option.** In this real option, an organisation might be able to delay the commitment of resources for a strategy until further key information becomes available. For example, an organisation might be considering embarking upon a differentiation strategy, which might require a considerable spend on capital equipment. If it were possible to delay starting the strategy until a significant product order was received from a major customer, this would undoubtedly be valuable, as there would be a shorter wait until profitability was achieved.

■ **The abandonment option.** In this real option, an organisation tries to arrange an exit point before the strategy is completed. The exit route will be taken by the organisation if, after launch, the strategy fails to meet its targets and expectations. Exiting the strategy prematurely is therefore valuable, as it may prevent wasting further expenditure upon a doomed strategy. For example, a manufacturer might embark upon the production of a new product which will necessitate the rental of an additional factory and warehouse. If the rental contract is for five years, it would be advantageous if an exit point could be negotiated after two years so that if product sales were weak, the organisation would have the option to cease manufacturing at a reduced total cost (three years' factory rental would be saved).

■ **The platform option.** In this real option, an organisation might be able to secure the right to extend the strategy should new opportunities present themselves after its commencement. For example, an organisation might, as part of its strategy, secure a distribution contract for the sale of its manufactured tables. It might also be able to negotiate an arrangement with the distributor whereby they would start distributing the manufacturer's chairs as well as tables, should certain sales targets be achieved. The value of this option is that it allows the organisation to increase the profitability of the strategy should certain conditions be met (in this case, healthy sales of the first product).

Google has invested in a wide variety of start-ups, giving them insights into an array of new technological developments and thus real platform options to accelerate and invest more fully, should one of them hit upon the next big thing.

5.6 A word of caution

Johnson et al. (2014) suggest that there are three qualifications that need to be made to this discussion of evaluation criteria.

1 **Conflicting conclusions and management judgement**. Conflicting conclusions can arise from the application of the criteria of suitability, acceptability and feasibility. A proposed

strategy might look suitable but not be acceptable to major stakeholders, for example. It is therefore important to remember that the criteria are useful in helping think through strategic options but are not a replacement for management judgement. Managers faced with a strategy they see as suitable, but which key stake-holders object to, have to rely on their own judgement on the best course of action.

2 **There needs to be consistency between the different elements of a strategy**. Part Four has argued that there are several elements of a strategy, so an important question to ask is whether the component parts work together as a 'package'. Strategy (such as low price or differentiation), strategy direction (such as product development or diversification) and strategic method (internal, acquisition or alliances) need to be consistent. Suppose an organisation wishes to develop a strategy built on its inherent competences as a basis of differentiation that competitors will find difficult to imitate. It may believe it can do this by using those competences to develop new products or services within a market it knows well. If so, there may be dangers in looking to develop those new products through acquiring other businesses which might have very different competences and capabilities that are incompatible with the strengths of the business.

3 **Implementation**. This might suggest issues that may make organisations reconsider whether particular strategic options are, in fact, feasible or uncover factors that change views on their suitability or acceptability. This may lead to a reshaping, or even abandonment, of strategic options. This is why experimentation and low-cost probes may make sense.

5.7 Reflections – organisational fit

One of the leading and still contemporary authors on the challenges of strategic evaluation is Richard Rumelt. He defined strategy evaluation as 'the appraisal of plans and results of plans that centrally concern or affect the basic mission of the company'. This indicates the two points of evaluation – before, when choosing between alternative strategies, and then after implementing the chosen option.

We can attribute to Rumelt the need to think not only about 'where we are now' and 'where we want to get to' as part of the strategy process, but also about 'where we have come from'. He said that as an organisation has a history and culture, this cannot be ignored in shaping strategy and monitoring its success. In Rumelt's view, strategies are unique to the organisation and reflect their particular and possibly historic strengths. Take the paper mill industry. One of the leading companies may have built its competitive advantage on sourcing – being close to the forests and raw material. Another may have a relative advantage in its production being located near suitable water and hydro-electric power, skilled labour, etc. A third may be strong in distribution, being located close to a major market. We call this 'path dependency' – an organisation's current status is a result of historic decisions.

In terms of appraising strategic choices, investment analysis helps with analysis of the upfront investment, cash flow, risk and return on investment implications of alternative strategies. According to Rumelt, however, these hard, quantitative analyses are necessary but not sufficient to appraise a strategy. There is another dimension – the softer, more qualitative aspects of strategy (see the McKinsey 7S model on page 98) such as organisational fit, employee motivation, and so on. This is the corporate culture and people dimension. As Mintzberg says, success owes as much to the hundreds and thousands of activities undertaken by rank-and-file personnel as it does to the big one-off product/price/market decisions made by senior management.

Rumelt suggested four fundamental principles of strategy evaluation, which neatly summarise the earlier sections of this chapter:

■ **Consistency.** A strategy must not present mutually inconsistent goals and policies, causing 'dissonance' or conflict between divisions and staff.
■ **Consonance.** The strategy must represent a fit with the external environment and able to adapt to critical changes within it.
■ **Advantage.** The strategy must provide for the creation and/or maintenance of some sort of competitive advantage, however temporary.
■ **Feasibility.** The organisation must have the ability and motivation to carry out the strategy, and inspire the managers and staff who are responsible for implementing it.

In summary, Rumelt recommends that managers should reflect on results, looking beyond the obvious and short term to consider the origins of the results as well as the results themselves.

TEST YOUR KNOWLEDGE 10.5

a   Identify three main ways in which strategy can be evaluated.
b   Explain what is meant by acceptability in this context.
c   How might a strategy's feasibility be assessed?
d   What is 'path dependency'?

The next chapters will look at the practical issues of translating strategy into action.

 CASE QUESTIONS

1   Identify the potential disadvantages to LCU operating within a strategic partnership.

2   Discuss the advantages and disadvantages of LCU following an organic development strategy.

CHAPTER SUMMARY

- Since a strategy comprises the broad competitive strategy, the strategy direction and the method of pursuing them, these three elements need to be consistent with each other.
- This chapter identified three broad methods of strategy development:
  - Organic development has the major benefit of building on the strategic capabilities of an organisation. However, it can result in overstretched resources and is likely to require the development of those capabilities.
  - Mergers and acquisitions may have advantages of speed and the ability to acquire competences not already held 'in-house'. However, the track record of acquisitions is not good. An important part of acquisitions or mergers is an effective due diligence process to help ensure the soundness of the proposed transaction and to identify risks.
  - Forming alliances that appear to be successful where partners have a positive attitude to the evolving nature of the alliance and where there is trust between partners.
- Strategic alliances are fundamentally different from acquisitions and require a different level of understanding. While achieving full control, acquisitions bring to the acquirer all parts of the acquired entity – both strengths and weaknesses – whereas alliances match strength to strength and balance control with collaboration.
- In times of volatility, 'real options' grow in value – options embedded within strategies which will allow the firm to accelerate, delay or withdraw from certain courses of action depending on how internal and external factors evolve. Companies pay a price for this, equivalent to a hedging fee.
- The success or failure of strategies will be related to three main success criteria.
  - Suitability is concerned with whether a strategy addresses the strategic position of the organisation as discussed in Part II of this book. It is about the rationale of a strategy.
  - The acceptability of a strategy relates to three issues: the expected return from a strategy, the level of risk and the likely reaction of stakeholders.
  - Feasibility is concerned with whether an organisation has or can obtain the capabilities to deliver a strategy.
- When evaluating strategy, before or after implementation, Richard Rumelt recommends that managers consider organisational fit, including the history and culture of an organisation, and its path dependency. He offers the four key principles of consistency, consonance, advantage and feasibility, and suggests that managers look not only at results, but the origins of the results.

11 Organisational structure and design

■ CONTENTS

■ INTRODUCTION

Organisational design can be a critical issue in the success or failure of organisations. As organisations seek to compete in ever-changing environments, they need to adapt and develop to take advantage of new opportunities. To implement strategies successfully, firms must have appropriate organisational structures. The roles people play, the processes through which they interact and the relationships that they build are crucial to the success of strategy. These are issues of 'organisational design' and include the integrating mechanisms necessary to ensure that boundaries among internal activities and external parties, such as suppliers, customers and alliance partners, are flexible and permeable. Views about designing organisations are changing. The traditional emphasis on formal structures, which suited a top-down, command-and-control view of strategy, where managers at the top made the decisions and the rest of the organisation simply implemented them, suited a more stable environment. In a world where knowledge is held by employees at all levels in the organisation and where change is constant, relying on formal, top-down structures may no longer be enough. Organisational structures are changing to reflect this.

1   The nature of structure

1.1 Introduction

Organisations have a preoccupation with performance in order to achieve their stated goals and objectives. Huczynski and Buchanan (2000) describe an organisation as a 'goal-oriented system' and it is goal-seeking that creates a need for control to ensure efficiency and effectiveness. Peter Drucker (1968) describes structure as the 'means for attaining objectives and goals of the organisation', reflecting the view of structure as a means of control. Here we shall describe **organisation structure** as the formalised pattern of interactions that link an organisation's tasks, technologies and people. All organisations have to make provision for continuing activities to further their overall aims and ensure that tasks are allocated, work supervised and activities coordinated.

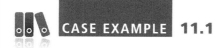 **CASE EXAMPLE 11.1**

Structural fault: Qwikster's quick demise

In 2011, Netflix, the US's largest online DVD rental and internet streaming company, faced a dilemma. Online streaming of movies was clearly a growth business; other competitors such as Amazon were beginning to enter it. On the other hand, DVD rental by mail was facing long-term decline. In September 2011, the company responded to the dilemma with a structural solution. They split the business into two separate parts: streaming would be done exclusively under the Netflix label, while DVD rental would be done exclusively in a new organisational unit called Qwikster.

In a blog post, CEO Reed Hastings explained his motivation: 'For the past five years, my greatest fear at Netflix has been that we wouldn't make the leap from success in DVDs to success in streaming…companies rarely die from moving too fast, and they frequently die from moving too slowly.' There were other reasons for the proposed split. The DVD business requires large warehouse and logistics operations, while streaming requires large internet resources. For DVDs, competitors include Blockbuster and Redbox, whereas streaming rivals include Amazon, iTunes and cable TV companies. As a standalone unit, managers in the streaming business could promote their alternative model without worrying about protecting the DVD business, still the larger part of Netflix's profits overall.

For customers, however, the split was less attractive. In future, customers would have to deal with two sites to get what they had previously got through one site. The DVD site offered many more movies, and tended to have more recent releases. Movie viewing recommendations for one site would not transfer to the other site. DVD renters would no longer receive the distinctive Netflix DVD envelopes, which had strong brand loyalty. The customer response was hostile. In the month following Qwikster's launch, Netflix lost hundreds of thousands of subscribers. The Netflix share price fell more than 60%, wiping out more than $3 billion in value.

Three weeks after the original Qwikster announcement, Hastings blogged that the new unit would not go ahead after all, and that all business would continue under the Netflix label. Despite the reversal of the structural change, repercussions were still being felt a year later: Netflix's market share of DVD rentals in 2012 had dropped from 35% to 27%, and rival Redbox had taken market leadership.

Sources: *Wall Street Journal*, 11 October 2011; Strategy+Business, 2 April 2012; *PC Magazine*, 17 September 2012.

Clearly, getting the structure wrong can be very damaging. Dess et al. (2014) go further and argue that today's managers are faced with two continuing and vital activities in structuring and designing their organisations. First, they must decide on the most appropriate organisational structure. Second, they need to decide the arrangements most helpful in enhancing the permeability of both internal and external boundaries.

Johnson et al. (2014) argue that structural issues need to be considered in the light of three key challenges for organisations in the twenty-first century:

1   The speed of change and the increased levels of uncertainty in the business environment, as discussed in Chapter 3. As a result, organisations need to have flexible designs and be skilled at reorganising.
2   The importance of knowledge-creation and sharing as a fundamental ingredient of strategic success. Organisational designs should both foster concentrations of expertise and encourage people to share their knowledge.
3   Organising for an international context has many challenges: communicating across wider geography, coordinating more diversity and building relationships across diverse cultures are some examples. Internationalisation also brings greater recognition of different kinds of organising around the world.

With this in mind, this chapter opens by looking at the influences on and elements of organisational structure. It then discusses the growth patterns of large organisations to examine further the important relationship between the strategy that an organisation follows and its corresponding structure. It then addresses the different types of traditional structure and their relative advantages and disadvantages, including a discussion of the implications of a firm's international operations for the structure of its organisation.

The chapter then discusses emerging structural forms, including the concept of the 'boundary-less' organisation. It is argued that, in rapidly changing and unpredictable environments, organisations must strive to make their internal and external boundaries both flexible and permeable. Section 4 focuses on some of the dilemmas associated with structuring and organising.

1.2 Strategy before structure?

There is a major debate regarding the relationship between the strategy and the structure of the organisation. In the past, it was considered that the strategy was decided first and the organisation structure followed – for example, PepsiCo's strategy of building on its strengths in different markets led to its decision to combine its international and beverage operations. Recent research has questioned this approach and taken the view that strategy and structure are interrelated.

Chandler (1962) studied how some leading US corporations had developed their strategies in the first half of the twentieth century. He drew the conclusion that the organisation first needed to develop its strategy and, after this, to devise the organisation structure that delivered that strategy. Consider the examples in Table 11.1.

TABLE 11.1 Structure following strategy

Strategy	Structural option
Innovation (3M)	**Organic/diverse**. A loose structure; low specialisation, low formalisation, decentralised.
Cost-minimisation (Wal-Mart)	**Mechanistic/uniform**. Tight control; extensive work specialisation; high formalisation; high centralisation.
Imitation/follower (IBM)	**Mix**. A mix of loose with tight properties; tight control over current activities and looser controls for new undertakings.

A new strategy might require extra resources, new personnel and/or equipment, any of which would alter the work of the enterprise, making a new organisational structure necessary. The task of developing the strategy took place at the centre of the organisation. The job of implementing it fell to the functional areas.

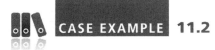 **CASE EXAMPLE** 11.2

To what extent is this approach still relevant?
Lynch (2015) argues that the environment has changed substantially, together with the workplace itself; the relationships between workers and managers, and the skills of employees, have all altered substantially. The approach advocated by Chandler is built around the notion that it is possible to choose precisely which strategies need to be introduced. Quinn (1980) has suggested that this over-simplifies the process and that strategic change may need to proceed incrementally in small stages. He called the process 'logical incrementalism', and it was discussed in Chapter 1. The implication is that it may not be possible to define the final organisation structure, which may also need to evolve as the strategy moves forward incrementally. Quinn suggests a multistage process for senior executives involved in strategy development.

   Amburgey and Dacin (1994) tested the relative impact of strategy and structure on each other by analysing the strategic and structural changes of more than 200 American corporations over 30 years. They found that moves towards decentralised structures were often followed by moves towards increasingly diversified strategies: here, structure was determining strategy. Overall, however, increased diversification was twice as likely to be followed by structural decentralisation as the other

CASE EXAMPLE 11.2 *continued*

way round. In other words, structure does follow strategy, but only most of the time. Mintzberg (1990) concludes that 'structure follows strategy as the left foot follows the right'. Strategy and structure are related reciprocally, rather than just one way. Mintzberg warns that a simple design approach to strategy and structure can be misleading. Structure is not always easy to fix after the big strategic decisions have been made. Strategists should check to see that their existing structures are not constraining the kinds of strategies that they consider. For example, PepsiCo reorganised its North American business to ensure that its strengths in the growing non-carbonated drinks market could be exploited across its full range of drinks. For an organisation to be economically effective, there needs to be a matching process between the organisation's strategy and its structure; this is the concept of strategic fit (Galbraith and Kazanjian, 1986).

In practice, the structure or form of an organisation develops over time and in response to a complex set of factors or contingencies. Handy (1993) and Robbins and Judge (2007) have identified a number of key influences that largely match those discussed when we looked at the influences on culture earlier (Chapter 5).

STOP AND THINK 11.1

Consider these influences on organisational structure. What is their impact on an organisation with which you are familiar?

1.3 Key elements of organisation structure

Handy (1993) describes structure as:

> '... the allocation of formal responsibilities, the typical organisation chart. It also covers the linking mechanisms between the roles, the co-ordinating structures of the organisation ...'

The point is that these can be arranged in various ways, and this results in varied structural forms. Robbins and Judge (2007) argue that structure is the response to six key questions:

Question	Answer
1 To what degree are tasks subdivided into separate jobs?	Work specialisation
2 On what basis will jobs be grouped together?	Departmentalisation
3 To whom do individuals and groups report?	Chain of command
4 How many individuals can a manager direct efficiently and effectively?	Span of control
5 Where does decision-making authority lie?	Centralisation
6 To what degree will there be rules and regulations to direct employees and managers?	Formalisation

Following Robbins and Judges' framework, we can distinguish six key elements of structure.

Specialisation

Specialisation describes the degree to which tasks in the organisation are subdivided into separate jobs – the division of labour. A task is divided into a series of steps or stages in which individuals specialise, completing part of an activity rather than the activity in its entirety. The early car manufacture production lines at Ford comprised small, repetitive tasks that became the job rather than the manufacture of the whole vehicle, either alone or with others. Greater specialisation assumes that:

- skills improve through repetition;
- labour costs are lowered by reducing tasks to an unskilled level;
- time is saved by reducing the need to change tasks.

The issue for organisations is that this may result in a trade-off between efficiency and job satisfaction. Individuals working on specialised tasks may find themselves working below their skill level. Specialisation was being questioned by the 1960s as manufacturers realised the serious human diseconomies from over-specialisation, in the form of boredom, fatigue and stress, which combined to offset any economic advantages. In reality work specialisation is neither obsolete nor an unending source of productivity.

Departmentalisation

Departmentalisation is the basis on which jobs are grouped together so that tasks can be coordinated. This may be done according to:

- functions such as engineering, accounting, marketing, etc. Economies of scale are achieved by placing people with common skills together;
- product/service – for example, a petroleum business may group its jobs according to fuels, waxes, lubricants. The aim is to increase accountability for individual product or service performance;
- geography, where regions are created to achieve economy from proximity;
- process; and
- customers.

 **CASE EXAMPLE 11.3**

A major UK communications business divided its organisation into strategic business units (SBUs) each aligned with the company's key customers – corporate and other major customers and small businesses and residential. These were supported by functional SBUs for the network and common services such as product development. Previously, it had a regional structure.

Chain of command

The **chain of command** is the line of authority that extends from the top of the organisation to the lowest level and clarifies who reports to whom. This can be explained by introducing two complementary concepts: authority and unity of command. **Authority** refers to the right to give instructions and expect them to be followed. The principle of **unity of command** states that an individual should have only one superior in the line to whom he or she is directly responsible. These concepts have less relevance today as developments in technology, particularly computer and communications, and trends towards empowering employees. In telecommunications companies, for example, field engineers are empowered to involve themselves in sales and have the technology to support them.

Span of control

Span of control refers to the number of reports for whom a manager is responsible and therefore determines the number of levels and managers in an organisation. As a general principle, the wider or larger the span of control, the greater the efficiency of the organisation – all other things being equal! Figure 11.1 illustrates how this might work.

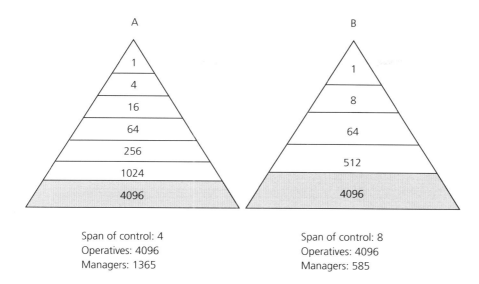

Span of control: 4
Operatives: 4096
Managers: 1365

Span of control: 8
Operatives: 4096
Managers: 585

FIGURE 11.1 Contrasting spans of control

In organisation B with double the span of control, 800 fewer managers are employed. At an average annual salary of, say, £50,000 per annum, this represents a saving of £40 million. It is therefore easy to see why wide spans of control have been part of many organisations' efforts to increase flexibility and speed decision-making, thereby reducing costs and cutting overheads. So the benefits that can arise when increasing the span of control are:

- reduced cost
- easing vertical communication
- reducing tight supervision.

 **CASE EXAMPLE** 11.4

Information technology increased the span of control at a building supply manufacturer and retailer. The company has provided its sales people with hand-held devices able to access information about products, customers and marketplace trends. The information empowers salespeople to manage their territory by making on-the-spot decisions on their own. This has increased the span of control from nine salespeople to 15.

Centralisation

The term **centralisation** refers to the degree to which decision-making is concentrated at a single point in the organisation. Typically, this means that if top management makes the organisation's key decisions with little or no input from people lower down, then it is centralised. Decentralisation occurs when decision discretion is pushed down to lower-level employees. The more decentralised an organisation, the more action can be taken quickly and the less the likelihood of alienation from the purpose of the organisation for those in the front line. For example, IBM in Europe is divided into 200 autonomous business units.

Formalisation

Formalisation is the degree to which jobs within the organisation are standardised and the degree of discretion over both what is done and when it is done within a job. Does the organisation use formal job descriptions and how restrictive are they?

CASE EXAMPLE 11.5

Jobs at McDonald's are highly formalised. To provide customers with consistent product quality and fast service, workers are expected to follow defined procedures for food preparation and service.

TEST YOUR KNOWLEDGE 11.1

a   Explain the influence of the history of an organisation on structure.
b   Outline the different ways in which an organisation departmentalises.
c   Explain what is meant by 'span of control'.

2   Traditional structural forms

2.1 Structure and growth

People often describe their organisation by drawing an organisation chart mapping out its formal structure. Structures help to ensure that resources are used effectively in accomplishing an organisation's mission. Structure identifies the executive, managerial and administrative elements of an organisation and indicates responsibilities and hierarchical relationships. It also influences the flow of information as well as the context and nature of human interactions. Formal structures reveal a great deal about the organisation, its culture and power structures. Structures may therefore be hotly debated.

Most organisations begin very small and either die or remain small. Those that survive and prosper embark on strategies designed to increase the overall scope of operations and enable them to enter new product market domains. Such growth places additional pressure on executives to control and coordinate the firm's increasing size and diversity. The most appropriate type of structure depends on the nature and magnitude of growth.

A business's strategy and structure is likely to change as it increases in size, diversifies into new product markets and expands its geographic scope. Figure 11.2 illustrates some of the common growth patterns that commercial firms may follow.

A new firm is likely to have a simple structure and may increase its sales revenue output over time. It may also integrate vertically to secure sources of supply (backward integration) as well as channels of distribution (forward integration). After a time, it may implement a functional structure to seek to increase efficiency and enhance its operations and products. This structure enables the firm to group its operations into functions, departments or geographic areas.

As its initial markets mature, a firm looks beyond its present products and markets for possible expansion. A strategy of related diversification may require reorganising around product lines or geographic markets. This leads to a divisional structure. As the business expands and domestic growth opportunities become somewhat limited, a firm may seek opportunities in international markets. At this time, a firm may structure using an international division, geographic areas, worldwide product divisions, worldwide functional and a worldwide matrix.

There are some other common growth patterns. For example, some firms may choose to move into unrelated product areas, typically by acquiring existing businesses, assets and competencies rather than developing them internally. Such a strategy requires relatively little integration across businesses and sharing of resources. Thus, a holding company structure becomes possible. There are many other growth patterns, but these are the most common. This section now looks at the most common types of organisational structure: simple, functional, divisional (SBU and holding company) and matrix, and considers their advantages and disadvantages. We close the section with a discussion of the structural implications when a firm expands its operations into international markets.

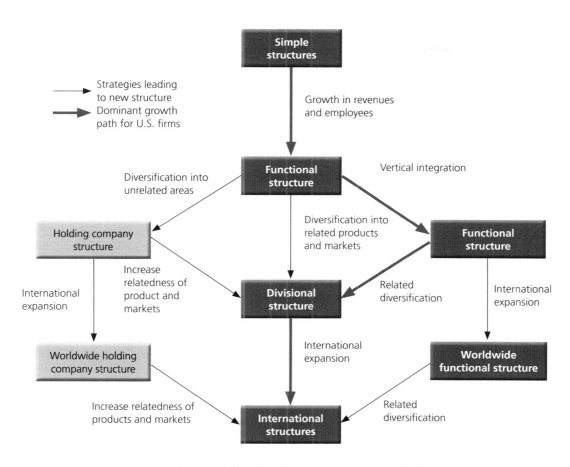

FIGURE 11.2 Structure and growth (Galbraith and Kazanjian, 1986)

2.2 Simple structure

The simple organisational structure is the oldest and most common organisational form. Most organisations are small (e.g. a small shop or firm) and have a single or very narrow product line in which the owner-manager (or top executive) makes most decisions. In effect, he or she controls all activities and the staff serve as an extension of the top executive. It is a flat organisation, with two or three levels at most. Although the owner-manager is intimately involved in almost all phases of the business, a manager is often employed to oversee day-to-day operations. This is shown in Figure 11.3.

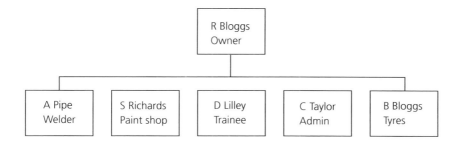

FIGURE 11.3 Simple structure

Advantages

- Highly informal and the coordination of tasks is accomplished by direct supervision.
- A low degree of departmentalism, wide spans of control, centralised authority, few rules and regulations, and an informal evaluation and reward system.

Disadvantages

- Informality may lead to problems. Employees may not clearly understand their responsibilities, which can lead to conflict and confusion.
- Employees may take advantage of the lack of regulation and act in their own self-interest. This may erode motivation and satisfaction, as well as leading to the possible misuse of organisational resources.
- Limited opportunities for upward mobility. Without the potential for future advancement, recruiting and retaining talent may become difficult.

2.3 Functional structure

When an organisation is small (15 employees or fewer), it is not necessary to have formal arrangements for groupings activities. However, as firms grow, excessive demands may be placed on the owner-manager in order to obtain and process the information necessary to run the business. The owner may not be skilled in all specialties (e.g. accounting, production, marketing) and will need to hire specialists in these functional areas. This growth in the overall scope and complexity of the business requires a functional structure in which the major functions are grouped internally. The coordination and integration of the functional areas becomes one of the most important responsibilities of the chief executive. Figure 11.4 illustrates a functional organisational structure.

FIGURE 11.4 Functional structure

Functional structures are generally found in organisations in which there is a single or closely related product or service, high production volume and some vertical integration. The functional structure provides for a high level of centralisation that helps to ensure integration and control over the related product market activities or multiple primary activities (from inbound logistics to operations to marketing, sales and service) in the value chain.

Advantages

- Bringing together specialists into functional departments enhances coordination and control within each of the functional areas.
- The structure ensures that decision-making will be centralised at the top of the organisation. This enhances the perspective of the organisational level across the various functions in the organisation.
- Provides for a more efficient use of managerial and technical talent since functional area expertise is pooled in a single department (e.g. marketing).
- Career paths and professional development in specialised areas are available.

Disadvantages

- Differences in values and orientations among functional areas lead to 'silos', which may impede communication and coordination. Departments view themselves as isolated, self-contained units with little need for interaction and coordination with other departments (see Chapter 5).

- Narrow functional orientations may lead to short-term thinking based on what is best for the functional area rather than the organisation as a whole.
- Top executives may be over-burdened as conflicts tend to be pushed to the top. No managers are responsible for the specific product lines.
- Difficult to establish uniform performance standards across the entire organisation. It may be relatively easy to evaluate production managers on the basis of production volume and cost control; establishing performance measures for, say, R&D and accounting is more problematic.

Many firms discover that as they diversify into new product-market activities, functional structures are unable to manage the increased complexity of the entire business.

2.4 Divisional structure

The divisional organisational structure is organised around products, projects or markets. Each division, in turn, includes its own functional specialists who are typically organised into departments. A divisional structure encompasses a set of relatively autonomous units governed by a central corporate office. The operating divisions are relatively independent and consist of products and services that are different from those of the other divisions. In order to attend to broader, longer-term organisational issues, top-level managers delegate decision-making to lower-level managers. Thus, divisional executives play a key role. In conjunction with corporate-level executives, they help to determine the product market and financial objectives for the division as well as their division's contribution to overall corporate performance. The rewards are based largely on measures of financial performance such as net income and revenue. Figure 11.5 illustrates a divisional structure.

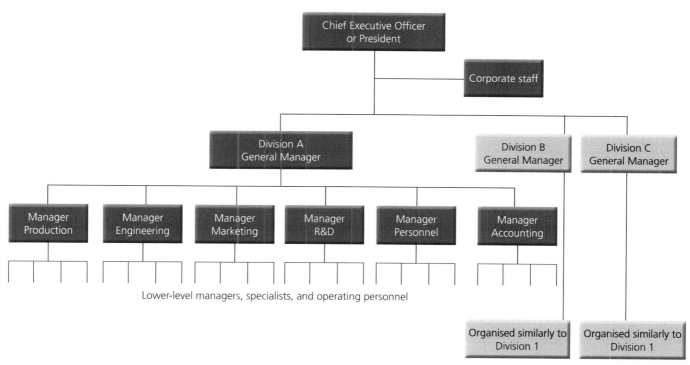

FIGURE 11.5 Divisional structure

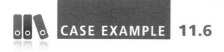

CASE EXAMPLE 11.6

General Motors (GM) was among the earliest firms to adopt the divisional organisational structure. In the 1920s the company formed five major product divisions (Cadillac, Buick, Oldsmobile, Pontiac, and Chevrolet) as well as several industrial divisions.

Advantages

- By creating separate divisions to manage individual product or service markets, there is a separation of strategic and operating control. Divisional managers can focus on improving operations in the markets for which they are responsible, and corporate managers can devote their time to overall strategic issues for the entire organisation.
- Focus on a division's markets helps the corporation respond quickly to important changes in the external environment.
- Since there are functional departments within each division of the corporation, problems associated with sharing resources across functional departments are minimised.
- As there are multiple management levels, the development of general management talent is enhanced.

Disadvantages

- A divisional structure can be expensive due to the duplication of personnel, operations and investment since each division must staff multiple functional departments.
- There can be dysfunctional competition among divisions since each tends to become concerned solely about its own operations.
- Divisional structures can discourage the sharing of ideas and resources between divisions for the common good of the whole organisation. Ghoshal and Bartlett (1995) note:

  'As their label clearly warns, divisions divide. The divisional model fragmented companies' resources; it created vertical communication channels that insulated business units and prevented them from sharing their strengths with one another. Consequently, the whole of the corporation was often less than the sum of its parts.'

- With many divisions providing different products and services, differences in image and quality may occur across divisions. For example, one division may offer 'no-frills' products or services of lower quality, which may erode the brand reputation of another division that has top quality, highly differentiated offerings.
- If each division is evaluated in terms of financial measures such as return on investment and revenue growth, there is often an urge to focus on short-term performance. Divisional managers may emphasise 'making the numbers' and minimise activities, such as advertising, maintenance and capital investments.

 **CASE EXAMPLE** **11.7**

Breaking down divisional boundaries

On the edge of Lake Michigan in Burns Harbour, Indiana, is a 50-year-old steel mill that produces steel for the car, appliance and other industries with Midwestern production plants. The steel mill struggled through the 1980s and 1990s, and went bankrupt in 2002. It was bought by ArcelorMittal Steel, the world's largest steel producer, in 2005. However, the plant faced another crisis in 2007, when it was threatened with closure unless it became more productive and efficient.

Today, this plant requires 1.32 man hours per ton of steel produced, which is 34% more efficient than the average in US steel mills. Furthermore, in 2011, the plant was 19% more efficient than it had been in 2007, and it produced twice the quantity of steel that it had in 2009. Its future as a productive steel plant is now secure.

How did ArcelorMittal achieve these gains and rejuvenate an old steel mill? By breaking down the barriers between organisation units to facilitate knowledge transfer and learning. One of the disadvantages of a divisional structure is that divisions perceive themselves as being in competition with each other and are therefore unwilling to share information to help other divisions improve. ArcelorMittal has overcome this by 'twinning' different steel mills – one efficient and one struggling – and challenging the efficient plant to help out its twin. The Burns Harbour mill was paired with a

CASE EXAMPLE **11.7** *continued*

more efficient mill in Ghent, Belgium. Engineers copied routines from that plant, implemented an advanced computer control system used in the Belgian mill, and employed automated machines similar to the ones used in Belgium.

These changes resulted in dramatic improvements in the efficiency of the Burns Harbour mill.

Sources: J. Miller, 2012, 'Indiana steel mill revived with lessons from abroad', WSJ.com, 21 May, np; www.nishp.org/bh-history.htm; and S. Markovich, 2012, 'Morning brief: Foreign investment revives Indiana steel mill', Blogs.cfr.org, 21 May, np.

The experience of ArcelorMittal demonstrates how firms can act to overcome the typical disadvantages of their divisional structure.

STOP AND THINK **11.3**

Consider the advantages and disadvantages of creating divisions along different lines, such as product, geography or technology, in a large organisation you are familiar with or a case organisation.

There are two important variations on the divisional structure.

With a strategic business unit (SBU) structure, divisions with similar products, markets and/ or technologies are grouped into homogeneous units to achieve synergies. Generally, the more related businesses are within a corporation, the fewer the SBUs required. Each of the SBUs in the corporation operates as a profit centre. The major advantage of the SBU structure is that it makes the task of planning and control by the corporate centre more manageable. At the same time, decentralisation of authority means individual businesses can react more quickly to important changes in the environment than if all divisions have to report directly to the corporate centre.

The **holding company** structure (or conglomerate) is a variation of the divisional structure. Whereas the SBU structure is used when there are similarities between individual businesses/ divisions, the holding company structure is appropriate when the businesses in a corporation's portfolio have little in common. Holding company structures are most appropriate for firms with a strategy of unrelated diversification. Companies such as Hanson Trust and ITT have used holding company structure to implement their unrelated diversification strategies. Corporate centres rely on financial controls to obtain high levels of performance from the individual businesses.

2.5 Matrix structure

One approach that tries to overcome the inadequacies inherent in the other structures is the **matrix organisational structure**. It is, in effect, a combination of the functional and divisional structures. The matrix form of organisation creates dual lines of authority and combines functional and product departmentalisation. It is often to be found in R&D organisations and consultancies. It helps coordinate the use of various specialists and focus attention on the product or service being delivered. The key issue for managers and employees alike is that it breaks the unity of command with two bosses to report to.

Most commonly, functional departments are combined with product groups on a project basis. For example, a product group may want to develop a new addition to its line; for this project, it obtains people from functional departments such as marketing, production and engineering. These people work under the manager of the product group for the duration of the project, which may vary from a few weeks to an open-ended period of time. The individuals who work in a matrix organisation become responsible to two managers: the project manager and the manager of their functional area. Figure 11.6 illustrates a matrix structure.

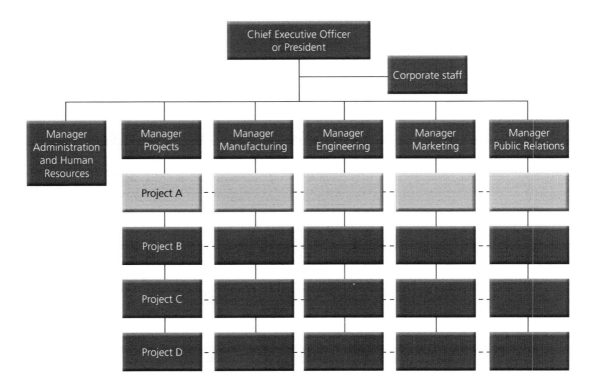

FIGURE 11.6 Matrix structure

Advantages

- Facilitates the use of specialised personnel, equipment and facilities. Instead of duplicating functions, the resources are shared.
- Individuals with high expertise can divide their time among multiple projects.
- Resource sharing and collaboration enable a firm to use resources more efficiently and to respond more quickly and effectively to changes in the environment.
- The inherent flexibility provides professionals with a broader range of responsibility. Such experience enables them to develop their skills and competencies.

Disadvantages

- The dual reporting structures can result in uncertainty and lead to power struggles and conflict over the allocation of resources.
- Working relationships become more complicated, resulting in excessive reliance on group processes and teamwork, along with a diffusion of responsibility. This may erode timely decision-making.

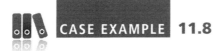 **CASE EXAMPLE 11.8**

After 50 years with a divisional structure, Procter & Gamble progressed to a matrix structure in 1987. In this structure, they had product categories (such as soaps and detergents) on one dimension, and functional managers on the other dimension. Within each product category, country managers reported to regional managers, who then reported to product managers. The structure became complex to manage, with 13 layers of management and significant power struggles as the functional managers developed their own strategic agendas that were often at odds with the product managers' agendas. After seeing their growth rate decline from 8.5% in the 1980s to 2.6% in the late 1990s, P&G scrapped the matrix structure to go to a global product structure with three major product categories, to offer unity in direction and more responsive decision-making.

Source: Based on a case in Dess et al. (2014).

2.6 International structures

To be successful in the global marketplace, managers must ensure consistency between their strategies (at the business, corporate and international levels) and the structure of their organisation. As firms expand into foreign markets, they generally follow a pattern of change in structure that parallels the changes in their strategies.

Three major contingencies that influence the chosen structure are:

- the type of strategy that is driving a firm's foreign operations;
- product diversity; and
- the extent to which a firm is dependent on foreign sales (Daniels et al., 1984).

As international operations become an important part of a firm's overall operations, managers must make changes. The primary types of structure used to manage a firm's international operations are the:

- international division;
- geographical area division;
- worldwide functional;
- worldwide product division;
- worldwide matrix.

The international division and geographical area division structures allow managers within each country to respond to local conditions. Local managers have a high level of autonomy to manage their operations within the constraints and demands of their geographic market. As a firm's foreign sales increase as a percentage of its total sales, it will likely change from an international division to a geographic-area division structure. And as a firm's product and/or market diversity becomes large, it is likely to benefit from a worldwide matrix structure.

Global strategies, on the other hand, are driven by economic pressures that require managers to view operations in different geographic areas to be managed for overall efficiency. The structures consistent with the efficiency perspective are the worldwide functional and worldwide product division structures. Here, division managers view the marketplace as homogeneous and devote relatively little attention to local market, political and economic factors.

The **transnational structure** seeks to obtain the best from the two extreme international strategies discussed above: the multi-domestic strategy and the global strategy. Looking at Figure 11.7, a global strategy would typically be supported by global divisions (e.g. a worldwide car division and a worldwide lorry division); a multi-domestic strategy would be supported by local subsidiaries with a great deal of design, manufacturing and marketing autonomy for all products (e.g. the local subsidiary responsible for both cars and lorries). International divisions refer to stand-alone divisions alongside the structures of the major home-based business, as is often the case when corporations start to internationalise (e.g. having car and lorry divisions, while overseas both businesses would be handled by the international division).

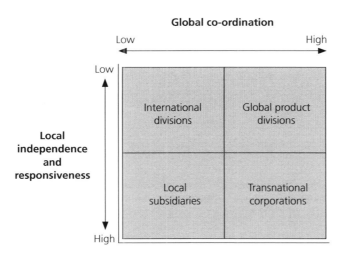

FIGURE 11.7 Global strategy (Bartlett and Ghoshal, 1998)

The transnational structure, however, attempts to achieve both high local responsiveness and high global coordination. It is like a matrix, but responds specifically to the challenge of internationalisation and tends to have more fixed responsibilities within its cross-cutting dimensions. Bartlett and Ghoshal (1990) suggest that the transnational structure has the following characteristics:

- Each national unit operates independently, but is a source of ideas and capabilities for the whole corporation. For example, in Unilever the centre for innovation in hair care products worldwide is in France.
- National units achieve greater economies of scale through specialisation on behalf of the whole corporation. Unilever in Europe has replaced its web of small national food manufacturing units with a few specialised larger factories that export its products to other European countries.
- The corporate centre manages this global network by first establishing the role of each business unit, then sustaining the systems, relationships and culture to make the network of business units operate effectively. Unilever has established a system of forums, bringing managers together to swap experience and coordinate their needs.

Deciding on the most appropriate structure when a firm has international operations depends on three primary factors:

- the extent of international expansion;
- the type of strategy (global, multi-domestic or transnational); and
- the degree of product diversity.

The success of a transnational corporation depends on the ability simultaneously to achieve global competences, local responsiveness and organisation-wide innovation and learning. This requires clarity about boundaries, relationships and the roles that the various managers need to perform. For example, functional managers such as those in finance or IT have a major responsibility for ensuring worldwide innovation and learning across the various parts of the organisation. This requires skills in recognising and spreading best practice across the organisation. These managers must be able to scan the organisation for best practice, disseminate this best practice and be the champion of innovations. Corporate (head office) managers integrate these other roles and responsibilities. Not only are they the leaders, but also they facilitate the interplay between other parts of the organisation – for example, fostering the processes of innovation and knowledge-creation and developing a strong management centre in the organisation.

International expansion occurs in most corporations after possibilities of domestic growth have been exhausted. Increasingly, we are seeing two interrelated phenomena. Dess et al. (2014) point out that many firms now expand internationally relatively early in their history, and that some firms are 'born global', being global in their activities from the beginning.

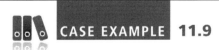 **CASE EXAMPLE 11.9**

Logitech Inc., a leading producer of personal computer accessories, was global from day one. Founded in 1982 by a Swiss national and two Italians, the company was headquartered both in California and Switzerland. R&D and manufacturing were also conducted in both locations and, subsequently, in Taiwan and Ireland.

Source: Oviatt and McDougall (2005).

The success of companies such as Logitech challenges the conventional wisdom that a company must first build up assets, internal processes and experience before venturing internationally. A global start-up has been defined as a business organisation that, from inception, seeks to derive significant competitive advantage from the use of resources and the sale of outputs in multiple countries. Right from the beginning, it uses inputs from around the world and sells its products and services to customers around the world. Geographical boundaries of nation-states are irrelevant for a global start-up. This is advantageous if the required human resources are globally dispersed, foreign financing is easier to obtain and more suitable, and target customers are located in other parts of the world. In addition, in many industries, a gradual move from domestic markets to foreign markets is no longer possible because, if a product is successful, foreign competitors may immediately imitate it.

Successful management of a global start-up presents many challenges. Communication and coordination across time zones and cultures are always problematic. Since most global start-ups have fewer resources than well-established corporations, one key for success is to internalise few activities and outsource the rest. Managers of such firms must have considerable prior international experience. Another key for success is to keep communication and coordination costs low. The boundary-less organisational designs that will be discussed in the next section are particularly suitable for global start-ups because of their flexibility and low cost.

TEST YOUR KNOWLEDGE 11.2

a Explain the link between strategy and structure.
b Contrast the functional and divisional organisational structure.
c What disadvantages arise with the matrix structure?

---

3 Emerging structural forms

3.1 Structures for innovation

Every organisation needs structures capable of producing innovation, even if these structures are only temporary. For example, a team may be formed for a particular project and disbanded once the work is completed.

From the organisational viewpoint, innovation needs integration and coordination across all the functions. Innovation is flexible, open-ended and possibly without a clearly defined or fixed objective. The process needs to be freewheeling and experimental. It is useful to distinguish between simple innovation (which might be possible in any organisation and relies on one person or a small group) and complex innovation (which may require experts drawn from a variety of business functions to form project teams). This is likely to involve larger resources and greater organisational complexity.

Mintzberg (1991) had complex innovation particularly in mind when outlining three guidelines for organising project teams:

- Flexible structures to allow experts to exercise their skills and break through conventional boundaries into new areas.
- Coordination within the team by experts with a technical background in the area, rather than a superior with authority from outside.
- Power in the team distributed among the experts, where appropriate. Much of the activity will consist of liaison and discussion among the experts as they progress their innovative ideas.

Kanter (1985) surveyed a number of US companies in the 1970s and 1980s, in an attempt to identify the organisation structures and processes that were most conducive to innovation. Among her conclusions were the following:

- **The importance of matrix structures**. These were more likely to exist in innovative companies. They tended to break down barriers and lead to the more open reporting lines that were important to the innovative process. Decision-making may have been slow and complex, but it provided the network for individuals to make the interconnections useful to innovation.
- **The need for a parallel organisation**. A separate group to run in tandem with the existing formal hierarchy was valuable. It was tasked with finding innovative solutions to problems, especially where a matrix structure was not in operation. It was able to act independently, without the day-to-day pressures and politics of the existing structure. Instead of contacts and power flowing up and down the existing structure, the parallel organisation allowed new relationships and ideas to develop.

■ **The work of a parallel organisation**. This had to be problem-solving, possibly focused on a single business problem and structured on the team. The work was integrative, flexible and with little hierarchical division. The function of such a group was often to re-examine existing routines and systems, concentrating especially on areas that were partially unknown and needed challenging.

■ **A participative/collaborative management style**. This was often employed to encourage innovation. It involved persuading rather than ordering, seeking advice and comments, and sharing the favourable results of successful initiatives.

Kanter's ideas were researched and proposed in the context of North America. Some may not work in other national cultures. But what they do illustrate is that, for strategic innovation at least, the flexible, open structure of the organisation may need to be prioritised before the innovatory strategies that subsequently emerge.

3.2 The boundary-less organisation

Former General Electric (GE) chairman Jack Welch used the term the 'boundary-less' organisation to describe his vision of what he wanted GE to become. He wanted to eliminate the effect of vertical and horizontal boundaries within GE and break down external barriers between the company and its customers and suppliers. The boundary-less organisation seeks to eliminate the chain of command, have limitless spans of control and replace departments with empowered teams. Organisations such as Hewlett Packard, AT&T and Motorola have adopted this model. What has made it possible is the ability to communicate with and through networked computers.

The term boundary-less may bring to mind a chaotic organisational reality in which 'anything goes'. This is not the case. As Welch, has suggested, boundary-less does not imply that all internal and external boundaries are completely dismantled; rather, they become more open and permeable (Afuah, 2003). It is not that boundary-less organisational designs replace the traditional forms of organisational structure; rather they should complement them.

CASE EXAMPLE   11.10

Sharp Corp. has implemented a functional structure to attain economies of scale with its applied research and manufacturing skills. However, to bring about this key objective, Sharp has relied on several integrating mechanisms and processes. To prevent functional groups from becoming vertical chimneys that obstruct product development, Sharp's product managers have responsibility – but not authority – for coordinating the entire set of value-chain activities. The company convenes enormous numbers of cross-unit and corporate committees to ensure that shared activities, including the corporate R&D unit and sales forces, are optimally configured and allocated among the different product lines. Sharp invests in this time-intensive coordination in order to minimise the inevitable conflicts that arise when units share important activities.

Source: Collis and Montgomery (1998).

There are primarily four types of boundaries that place limits on organisations. These boundaries may be:

■ **Vertical**. This is between levels in the organisation's hierarchy.
■ **Horizontal**. This is between functional areas.
■ **External**. This is between the firm and its customers, suppliers, and regulators.
■ **Geographic**. This is between locations, cultures, and markets.

Removing the *vertical* boundaries flattens the hierarchy and minimises status and rank. Methods such as 360-degree feedback and participative decision making practices are used to break down vertical boundaries. Functional departments create *horizontal* boundaries, and the way to reduce these is to replace them with cross-functional teams and organise activities around processes. Xerox, for example, now develops new products through multidisciplinary teams that work in a single process instead of around narrow functional tasks. Another way to remove horizontal barriers is to transfer or rotate people into and out of different functional areas.

The barrier-free type involves making all organisational boundaries – internal and external – more permeable. In the traditional company, boundaries are clearly delineated in the design of an organisation's structure. The roles of managers and employees are simple, clear, well-defined and long-lived. A major shortcoming is that they tend to be divisive; it leads to territorial fights. A barrier-free organisation enables a firm to bridge real differences in culture, function and goals, in order to find common ground that facilitates information sharing and other forms of cooperative behaviour. For barrier-free organisations to work effectively, the level of trust and shared interests among all parts of the organisation must be raised using teams and techniques such as brainstorming.

3.3 Flexibility, outsourcing and the modular organisation

The notion of flexibility has been addressed by both Handy's 'Shamrock' model and Atkinson's model of the 'flexible firm'.

The flexible firm concept (Atkinson, 1984) combines functional, numerical and financial flexibility by operating with workforces consisting of both core and peripheral workers, the 'core' group being permanent with a degree of functional flexibility. Peripheral workers allow numerical flexibility and can be used and discarded, as required, according to demand. Some non-core functions can be outsourced or contracted out.

The implications of the flexible firm are that organisations can minimise employment costs and become more responsive to changes in markets and technology by reorganising their employment systems in this way. But it also raises issues concerning the organisation's commitment to different types of employees (opportunities for training and development, reward, etc.) and the motivation of peripheral employees.

Charles Handy (1989) has noted:

'While it may be convenient to have everyone around all the time, having all of your workforce's time at your command is an extravagant way of marshalling the necessary resources. It is cheaper to keep them outside the organisation ... and to buy their services when you need them.'

Handy introduced the idea that an organisation could be pictured as a shamrock (Figure 11.8) representing three categories of employee, each of whom is organised, managed and rewarded differently:

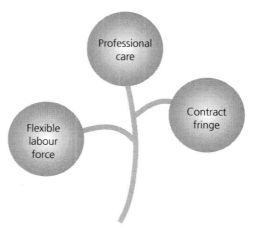

FIGURE 11.8 The shamrock organisation (Handy, 1989)

- **Professional core**. This category represents the professional worker, such as engineers, managers and specialists, who direct the organisation in its technical and professional efforts.
- **Contractual fringe**. This category comprises subcontractors of various descriptions who provide the necessary but not essential services to the host organisation. Typically, such activities are paid for by results and not time. Generally, much of the low-skill, monotonous work in organisations is contracted out at a substantial cost saving.
- **Flexible labour force**. This category represents the part-time, casual and freelance workers now common in many organisations. This category reflects the ultimate form of flexibility

in terms of number and skill in that they simply come and go as needed and are rewarded accordingly. For example, many university or college lecturers and management consultants are employed on a contract or casual basis providing only a limited range of services under a job defined by contract.

This model encourages managers to consider their organisational purpose along with the nature of the staff relationship to the organisation. As a consequence, there are implications for organisation structure that flow from the model in that the three categories of worker engage with the organisation differently and need to be managed and integrated differently from conventional employees. For example, integration between the three main categories becomes very difficult in the short term as the working patterns vary so dramatically and are not easily changed.

The implication of these flexibility models is that organisations have important relationships outside their boundaries – with customers, suppliers, subcontractors and partners.

Outsourcing is an element of strategic capability that arises from the value chain. It occurs where organisations decide to buy in services or products previously produced in-house. For example, payroll, component manufacture and IT services are common examples of outsourced activities. Two important principles are that an outside supplier can provide better value for money than in-house provision, and that core competences are not normally outsourced, since these are critical to competitive advantage.

There are important implications here. For example, outsourcing requires managers competent at maintaining performance through their management of supplier (or distributor) relationships rather than through management control systems within their own organisation. This may need considerable attention. For example, suppliers/distributors will need to be educated about the organisation's strategies, priorities and standards, and how their work impacts the final performance of the product or service. They need to be motivated to perform consistently to these required standards. Suppliers might be 'tied in' through planning systems and through cultural processes and norms. This would be important where suppliers are adding creative input to the product or service (such as designers), where the two-way interaction needs to be much more fluid. Market mechanisms could be used if a contractual approach to the relationship is not appropriate – for example, for single projects or where there is a range of potential suppliers.

The modular organisation is a way of describing an organisation that outsources non-vital functions, tapping into the knowledge and expertise of 'best in class' suppliers, but that retains strategic control. Outsiders may be used to manufacture parts, handle logistics or perform accounting activities (Jarvis, 2009). The value chain can identify the key primary and support activities, and decide which activities to keep in-house and which to outsource. The organisation becomes a central hub surrounded by networks of outside suppliers and specialists, and parts can be added or taken away. Both manufacturing and service units may be modular.

CASE EXAMPLE 11.11

Sports clothing is an industry in which the modular type has been widely adopted. Nike and Reebok, for example, concentrate on their strengths: designing and marketing high-tech, fashionable footwear. Nike has few production facilities and Reebok owns no plants. These two companies contract virtually all their footwear production to suppliers in China, Vietnam and other countries with low-cost labour. Avoiding large investments in fixed assets helps them to derive large profits on minor sales increases. Nike and Reebok can keep pace with changing tastes in the marketplace because their suppliers have become expert at rapidly retooling to produce new products.

In a modular company, outsourcing the non-core functions offers three advantages.

- A firm can decrease overall costs, stimulate new product development by hiring suppliers with superior talent to that of in-house personnel, avoid idle capacity, reduce inventories and avoid being locked into a particular technology.
- A company can focus scarce resources on the areas where it holds a competitive advantage. These benefits can translate into more funding for R&D, hiring the best engineers, and providing continuous training for sales and service staff.

- An organisation can tap into the knowledge and expertise of its specialised supply-chain partners, adding critical skills and accelerating organisational learning.

The main strategic concerns with outsourcing are:

- the loss of critical skills or developing the wrong skills, increasing dependency on suppliers;
- the loss of cross-functional skills previously acquired through the interaction of individuals in the firm; and
- the loss of control over a supplier – the outsourced products may give suppliers too much power in essence, holding the firm 'hostage'.

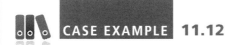 **CASE EXAMPLE** 11.12

Nike manages the potential problems of outsourcing by sending full-time 'product expatriates' to work at the plants of its suppliers. Also, Nike often brings top members of supplier management and technical teams to its headquarters. In this way, Nike keeps close tabs on the pulse of new developments, builds rapport and trust with suppliers, and develops long-term relationships with suppliers to prevent 'hostage' situations.

3.4 The virtual organisation

Outsourcing and alliances are particular cases of a general trend to rely on network relationships outside the organisation's boundaries. Taken together, they mean that more organisations have become dependent on internal and external networks to ensure success.

The logical extension of networking and outsourcing would be an organisation where in-house (owned) resources and activities are minimised, and nearly all resources and activities reside outside the organisation. These so-called **virtual organisations** are held together not through formal structure and physical proximity of people, but by partnership, collaboration and networking.

In structural terms, the virtual organisation is highly centralised, with little or no departmentalisation. Companies such as Nike, Reebok and Dell are among those that operate successful businesses without owning their own manufacturing facilities. Dell assembles its computers from outsourced parts manufacturers. These virtual organisations have created networks of relationships that allow them to contract out key functions where this can be done more efficiently and more cheaply. The major advantage this brings is flexibility – for example, allowing Dell to compete successfully against larger companies. The primary drawback is that it reduces management control over key parts of its business. A sample virtual organisation is shown in Figure 11.9.

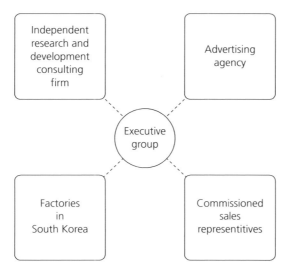

FIGURE 11.9 Virtual organisation

The important issue is that this organisation feels 'real' to clients and meets their needs at least as adequately as other organisations do. It has been argued that such extreme forms of outsourcing are likely to result in serious strategic weakness in the long run, as the organisation becomes devoid of core competences and cut off from the learning that can happen through undertaking these activities in-house. This is now an important consideration in many industries such as civil engineering, publishing and specialist travel companies, all of which are highly dependent on outsourcing aspects of their business that were once considered as core. The concern is whether short-term improvements are being achieved at the expense of securing a capacity for innovation. The danger of virtuality is that knowledge-creation and innovation only occur within the specialist 'boxes' represented by the activities of separate partners. No one has the competence or authority to integrate these pockets of knowledge.

STOP AND THINK 11.4

What are the advantages of a virtual organisation in an industry with which you are familiar? Are there any disadvantages?

TEST YOUR KNOWLEDGE 11.3

a   Distinguish transnational from multi-domestic structures.
b   How might an organisation be regarded as 'boundary-less'?
c   Explain the key components of the 'flexible firm'.

4   Determining structure

4.1 Why structures differ

Structure provides a means of balancing two conflicting forces: a need for the division of tasks into meaningful groupings and a need to integrate such groupings in order to ensure efficiency and effectiveness.

The factors in section 1.2 are the key determinants of structure, but how do particular forms emerge? Is there some kind of progression with increasing size? Handy (1993) argues that structural form is a result of the competing pressures in organisations for *uniformity* and *diversity*.

Uniformity includes:

■ cheapness of standardisation that brings economies of-scale;
■ need for interchangeability that brings common procedures – for example – on airlines;
■ need for control of process, as one unit is dependent on another;
■ need for a standard product – for example – with Tesco or McDonald's;
■ need for specialisation, which generates the division of labour; and
■ desire for central control to know what is going on.

These are the hallmarks of the 'steady state'.

Diversity includes:

■ regional, market, product and technology goals;
■ identity leading to differentiation;
■ pull for disaggregated control; and
■ need to experiment often difficult where there is systematic planning.

To an extent, large organisations prefer uniformity, predictability and efficiency. They seek to iron out diversity by smoothing the pressures for diversity by outsourcing certain functions, for example. In practice, the result is often an endless oscillation as a company seeks to adapt to the pressures of its environment! For managers and leaders, the need is to recognise and understand the tension between pressures for uniform/mechanistic structure and diverse/organic forms.

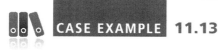 **CASE EXAMPLE 11.13**

A global communications business created a single global organisation from its separate businesses in the UK, Europe, Japan and the US. These businesses had previously been accountable for their own bottom line. This change resulted in a matrix structure and greatly reduced the role of the 'country manager', who now headed the sales operation in each major location. Common services such as marketing and product development were shared. As its markets experienced a turbulent period over the next two years, one of the responses of the chief executive was to increase local accountability. Each region was once again made accountable for its own bottom line.

4.2 Choosing structures

From the discussion in Section 2 it should be clear that functional, divisional, matrix and transnational structures each have advantages and disadvantages when it comes to dealing with the challenges posed by Johnson et al. (see Section 1). The key point is that organisational designers have to choose structures according to the particular strategic challenges (or contingencies) they face. Organisational designers face choices. If they seek control, but are less concerned with flexibility in response to change or global reach, then they might prefer a functional structure. If they want to foster knowledge and flexibility on a global scale, then they might consider a matrix or transnational structure. Structure depends on the strategic challenges the organisation faces.

In reality, few organisations adopt a structure that is just like one of the structural types discussed above. Structures often blend different types and have to be tailor-made to the particular mix of challenges face the organisation.

Goold and Campbell (2002) provide nine design tests against which to check specific tailor-made structural solutions. The first four tests stress fit with the key objectives and constraints of the organisation.

- **The Market Advantage Test**. This test of fit with market strategy is fundamental, following Chandler's classic principle that 'structure follows strategy'. For example, if coordination between two steps in a production process is important to market advantage, then they should probably be placed in the same structural unit.
- **The Parenting Advantage Test**. The structural design should fit the 'parenting' role of the corporate centre. For example, if the corporate centre aims to add value as a 'synergy manager', then it should design a structure that places integrating specialisms, such as marketing or research, at the centre.
- **The People Test**. The structural design must fit the people available. It is dangerous to switch completely from a functional structure to a multidivisional structure if, as is likely, the organisation lacks managers with competence in running decentralised business units.
- **The Feasibility Test**. This suggests that the structure must fit legal, stakeholder, trade union or similar constraints.

Goold and Campbell then propose five tests based on good general design principles.

- **The Specialised Cultures Test**. This reflects the value of bringing together specialists so they can develop their expertise in close collaboration with each other. A structure fails if it breaks up important specialist cultures.
- **The Difficult Links Test**. This test asks whether a proposed structure will set up links between parts of the organisations that are important but bound to be strained. For example, extreme decentralisation to profit-accountable business units is likely to strain relationships

with a central R&D department. Unless compensating mechanisms are put in place, this kind of structure is likely to fail.

- **The Redundant Hierarchy Test**. Any structural design should be checked in case it has too many layers of management, causing undue blockages and expense. As we have seen, delayering has been an important structural trend in recent years.
- **The Accountability Test**. This test stresses the importance of clear lines of accountability, ensuring the control and commitment of managers throughout the structure. Matrix structures are often accused of lacking clear accountability.
- **The Flexibility Test**. An important test is the extent to which a design will allow for change in the future. For instance, divisional domains should be specified broadly enough to allow divisional managers to follow new opportunities as they emerge.

STOP AND THINK **11.5**

To what extent does the structure of your organisation, or one with which you are familiar, meet these tests?

Johnson et al. identify five key dilemmas in organising:

1 Hierarchies are often necessary to ensure control and action, but they can sit uneasily with networks that foster knowledge exchange and innovation.
2 Vertical accountability promotes maximum performance by subordinates, but can lead managers to maximise their own self-interest at the expense of horizontal relationships.
3 Empowerment of employees lower down the organisation gives scope for initiative, but over the long term can lead to incoherence.
4 Centralisation might be needed for standardisation, but this can be at the cost of the initiative and flexibility fostered by devolution.
5 Having the best practice on a particular element of the organisation (e.g. financial controls) may be damaging if it does not fit with the needs of the organisation as a whole.

Managers should recognise that any organisational design is likely to face dilemmas of these kinds and is hard to optimise on all dimensions. However, they may be able to manage these dilemmas in three ways.

- By *subdividing* the organisation, so that the one part of the organisation is organised optimally according to one side of these dilemmas, while the rest responds to the other.

CASE EXAMPLE **11.14**

IBM created the PC in a specialised new venture division, kept separate from the traditional mainframe activities that were dominated by principles of hierarchy and vertical accountability highly antagonistic to radical innovation.

- By *combining* different organising principles at the same time (e.g. networks and traditional hierarchies). Organisations such as Unilever are now 'networked multi-divisionals', combining network principles emphasising horizontal integration with divisional structures ensuring vertical accountability.
- By *reorganising* frequently so that no one side of the dilemma can become too entrenched. The rate of major reorganisation for large UK companies increased from once every four years to once every three years in the last decade (Whittington and Mayer, 2002). Given this pace of reorganising, many organisations are like pendulums, constantly oscillating between centralisation and devolution, for example, without resting long on one side or another!

TEST YOUR KNOWLEDGE 11.4

a Explain what Handy means by the 'competing pressures for uniformity and diversity'.
b Identify the design tests suggested by Goold and Campbell.
c Identify five key design dilemmas.

CASE QUESTIONS

1 Review the extent to which LCU is adopting a centralised strategy.

2 Identify an optimal organisational structure for LCU.

CHAPTER SUMMARY

- Successful organisations must ensure that they have the right organisational structure. They must ensure that their firms incorporate the necessary integration and processes so that the internal and external boundaries of their firms are flexible and permeable. Such a need is increasingly important as the environments of firms become more complex, change rapidly and become unpredictable.

- The structure of an organisation is determined by factors such as environment, history, size, strategy and technology. Structural variables such as centralisation, formalisation, span of control and specialisation are the key elements of structural form.

- Most firms remain small; some continue to grow and their geographical scope may increase to include international operations. The dominant pattern of growth evolves from a simple structure to a functional structure as a firm grows in terms of size and increases its level of vertical integration. After a firm expands into related products and services, its structure changes from a functional to a divisional form of organisation. Finally, when the firm enters international markets, its structure changes again to accommodate the change in strategy.

- The main types of organisational structure are: simple, functional, divisional (including two variations – strategic business unit and holding company) and matrix, as well as their relative advantages and disadvantages. There are structural implications when a firm enters international markets.

- Emerging structural forms include the boundary-less organisation. This does not replace the traditional forms of organisational structure; rather it complements them. This is necessary to cope with the increasing complexity and change in the competitive environment.

- External relationships are also important. There are choices concerning outsourcing, virtual organisations and networks that may help or hinder success.

- Organisational structure is an outcome of competing pressures for uniformity and diversity and there are number of tests that designer can use to check the fit of structure with strategy – an important relationship.

12 Monitoring strategy

- **INTRODUCTION**

This chapter explores how the organisation ensures that its strategy is successful and *how* it measures its success. It starts by looking at the differences between efficiency and effectiveness and issues to do with the evaluation of success. It then turns to the nature of control in organisations before considering the specifics of strategic control – identifying whether an organisation should continue with its current strategy or modify it in the light of changed circumstances. The chapter closes by looking at a specific approach – the balanced scorecard.

1   Performance and effectiveness

1.1   Effectiveness and efficiency

Organisational purpose and goals, expressed through mission statements and corporate objectives, indicate the reason for an organisation's existence and the outcomes it seeks to achieve (Chapter 7). This chapter explores the other end of the equation: how the organisation ensures that its strategy is successful and how it measures the extent to which it has been successful.

Looking at the second of these first, there are two components to measurement. **Organisational effectiveness** is the degree to which an organisation realises its goals. Effectiveness is a broad concept that takes in a range of variables and evaluates the extent to which goals have been attained. Efficiency is a more limited concept that concerns the internal workings of the organisation. **Organisational efficiency** concerns the resources used to produce a unit of output. It can be measured as the ratio of inputs to outputs. If one organisation can achieve a given production level with fewer resources than another, it can be described as more efficient. Sometimes efficiency leads to effectiveness. In other organisations, efficiency and effectiveness are not related. An organisation may be highly efficient but fail to achieve its goals because it makes a product for which there is no demand. Likewise, an organisation may achieve its profitability goals but nevertheless be inefficient.

Our prime concern in this chapter is with effectiveness. How does the senior team exercise the control needed to ensure that it is meeting the goals that it has established as part of its strategy? Overall effectiveness is difficult to measure in organisations. Organisations are large, diverse and fragmented. They perform many activities simultaneously. They pursue multiple goals and they generate many outcomes, some intended and some unintended. So, managers will determine what indicators to measure to gauge the effectiveness of their organisations.

This chapter starts by looking broadly at issues to do with performance and effectiveness in organisations and then the nature of control. It then focuses on specific issues associated with strategic control and an approach to measuring effectiveness that seeks to overcome the criticisms of traditional approaches.

STOP AND THINK 12.1

How is effectiveness measured in your organisation?

1.2 Issues in evaluation

What is evaluated?

It is helpful to start by considering the issues that can determine the approach adopted towards evaluating effectiveness. Some approaches concentrate on the performance of the organisation as a whole, while others look at strategic business units, divisions, functions or the individual. What can be evaluated?

- **Profitability**. Profit has two components: cost and income. All parts of an organisation and all activities within it incur costs, and so their success needs to be measured in relation to cost. Only some parts of an organisation receive income and their success should be judged in terms of both.
- **Activity**. All parts of an organisation are engaged in activities that generate costs. Activity measures could, for example, include the number of orders received from customers as a measure of the effectiveness of marketing, the number of production runs achieved by a particular factory, etc. The concept of value is important for assessing activities: that is, to what extent do they add value to the overall output of the organisation?
- **Productivity**. This is the quantity of the product or service produced in relation to resources put in, for example so many units produced per hour, per employee or per tonne of material. It defines how efficiently resources are being used. The dividing line between productivity and activity is narrow since every activity could be said to have some 'product'.
- **Quality and service**. The quality of output can be measured by the number of production items rejected on inspection, or the number of items returned by customers as faulty. The quality of a service can be measured by the level of complaints or by favourable reaction.

A related point is whether a desire to achieve greater profitability often entails a sacrifice in some other aspect of performance. One obvious example is quality: if cheaper materials are used to make a product or less highly trained workers deliver a service, money will be saved (increasing profits), but quality will decline. It is recognised by some that economising on quality has an adverse effect in the longer term. In other cases, there may not be a clear link between an objective and the profitability objective. A company may aim to improve working conditions for its staff and measure its success in terms of the cost of improved facilities, reductions in staff turnover or absenteeism. In some cases, a company may aim to fulfil social and ethical responsibilities, for example, by incurring costs to make a manufacturing process more environmentally friendly.

Who decides what constitutes good performance?

Some approaches to evaluation are based on the viewpoint of a single interest group such as investors; others include the views of various interest groups (e.g. employees or environmental pressure groups). Within the organisation senior management oversee broad, strategic trends, but at the tactical or middle manager level exception reports can indicate deviations from standards. External stakeholders also have a role and, in the UK, regulatory bodies monitor privatised utilities, and commercial businesses are monitored by their shareholders.

Organisational purpose

An organisation may have a single, unambiguous purpose that can be translated into specific goals. Its values may be a conglomeration of the values of the different interest groups. In the former case performance evaluation can take the form of measuring progress towards targets; in the latter, the measurement needs to be far more diverse.

Types of measure

Are the measures to be used quantitative (return on investment, turnover), qualitative (employee satisfaction, aesthetics), or both? We can distinguish between *quantitative* information (capable of being measured) and *qualitative* information (can be expressed only in numerical terms with difficulty). Qualitative measures are by nature subjective and judgemental, but this does not mean they are not valuable. They are especially valuable when they are derived from different sources because they can then be expressed in a mixture of quantitative and qualitative terms, which are more meaningful overall. For example, 'seven out of ten customers consider our beds are very comfortable' is a *quantitative* measure of customer satisfaction as well as a *qualitative* measure of the perceived performance of the beds.

A general point to make here is that many managers think of measures and systems of control as built around the organisation's accounting system. True, the management of costs, cash and margins is essential in many cases; especially in businesses devoted to the pursuit of profit. Yet there are problems with the dominance of financial measures.

- The style of accounting in most organisations is narrowly focused. Driven by the need to maintain professional standards and pass formal audits, there can be too much accuracy at the expense of usefulness.
- All statements in accounts are both backward- and inward-looking. Management control should be broader than this. It should be concerned with wider aims, especially strategic ones. Examples include: enhancing product and process knowledge; broadening the customer base; developing quality; encouraging enterprise; and operating with social responsibility.

Blenkhorn and Gaber (1995) found that many managers have difficulty with the concept of evaluating effectiveness based on characteristics that are *not* subject to hard, quantitative measurements. However, top executives in some companies are finding new ways to measure effectiveness, using indicators such as customer delight and employee satisfaction. Later, we examine balanced effectiveness approaches, which integrate concern for various parts of the organisation.

1.3 General approaches to measuring effectiveness

Daft (2013) distinguishes a number of approaches to measuring effectiveness that focus on different parts of the transformation process. Organisations bring in resources from the environment and transform these into outputs that are delivered back into the environment. Figure 12.1 suggests that effectiveness might be measured at each stage.

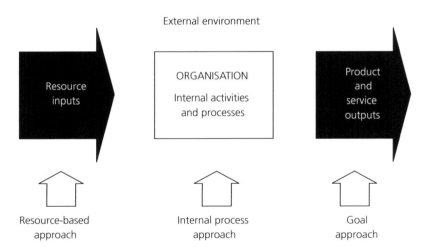

FIGURE 12.1 Approaches to the measurement of organisational effectiveness (Daft, 2001)

Goal approach

The goal approach to effectiveness consists of identifying an organisation's output goals and assessing how far the organisation has attained them. This is logical as organisations do try to attain certain levels of output, profit or client satisfaction. The goal approach measures progress towards the attainment of those goals.

CASE EXAMPLE 12.1

An important measure for any theatre or cinema is the number of tickets sold per performance. During a new theatre's first season, it might aim to sell 200–300 tickets per show. If the organisation actually averaged nearly 350 tickets per show, it indicates that it was highly effective in meeting its goal for attendances.

The goal approach is used in most business organisations because output goals can be readily measured. As we have suggested, business firms typically evaluate performance in terms of profitability, growth, market share and return on investment. However, since organisations have multiple and conflicting goals, effectiveness often cannot be assessed by a single indicator.

Daft (op. cit.) suggests that the indicators tracked with the goal approach include the following:

■ **Profitability**. The positive gain from business operations or investments after expenses are subtracted.
■ **Market share**. The proportion of the market the firm is able to capture relative to competitors.
■ **Growth**. The ability of the organisation to increase its sales, profits, or client base over time.
■ **Social responsibility**. How well the organisation serves the interests of society as well as itself.
■ **Product quality**. The ability of the organisation to achieve high quality in its products or services.

The goal approach is used in business organisations because output goals can be readily measured. As illustrated by Case Example 12.2, however, some not-for-profit organisations that aim to solve social problems also find the goal approach useful.

CASE EXAMPLE 12.2

Using a rigorous model of performance measurement based on some of the management practices at Procter & Gamble, Every Child Succeeds is a public–private partnership that aims to reduce infant mortality and improve maternal health in the area surrounding Cincinnati, Ohio, where 8.3 out of every 1,000 new-borns die before they reach their first birthday. This statistic is on a par with countries such as Lithuania and Brunei. Among the children of mothers enrolled in Every Child Succeeds, only 2.8 out of every 1,000 new-borns die before they reach their first birthday – a figure lower than that of most industrialised countries.

Unlike many social improvement programmes, Every Child Succeeds sets and measures a few narrow and specific goals organised under seven focus areas. Managers collect data that enable them to measure what is working and fix what is not. A chart hangs in the agency offices that lists 17 indicators, such as immunisation rates, rate of breast-feeding and client satisfaction, and shows how well each of the participating agencies is doing at meeting targets.

Source: Gautam Naik, 'Poverty: the new search for solutions; baby steps: Cincinnati applies a corporate model to saving infants', (Third in a Series), *The Wall Street Journal*, 20 June 2006.

In practice, any final assessment of effectiveness is likely to consider several goals simultaneously. Many organisations use a balanced approach to measuring goals and we will look at this approach below. The other issues to resolve are how to identify appropriate goals for the organisation (Chapter 7) and how to measure their attainment. For business organisations, there are usually objective indicators for some goals (e.g. profit or growth) but subjective assessment is needed for other goals (e.g. employee welfare or social responsibility). Managers rely on information from customers, competitors, suppliers and employees, as well as their own intuition, when considering these goals.

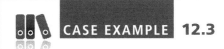

CASE EXAMPLE 12.3

Ingram Micro Inc., a Fortune 100 company bought by Chinese HNA in 2016, is the world's largest technology distributor and a leading technology sales, marketing and logistics company for the IT industry worldwide. The CEO communicates directly with hundreds of customers each week to measure the company's goal of achieving 'customer delight'. 'These direct interactions don't provide hard numbers,' he says, 'but I sure do learn a lot.'

Resource-based approach

The resource-based approach looks at the *input* side of the transformation process. It assumes that organisations must be successful in obtaining and managing valued resources in order to be effective. From a resource-based perspective, organisational effectiveness is defined as the ability of the organisation in either absolute or relative terms, to obtain scarce and valued resources and successfully integrate and manage them. Indicators of effectiveness according to the resource-based approach encompass:

- the ability of the organisation to obtain scarce and valued resources from its environment, including financial resources, raw materials, human resources, knowledge and technology;
- the ability of the organisation's decision-makers to perceive and correctly interpret the real properties of the external environment;
- the ability of managers to use tangible (e.g. supplies, people) and intangible (e.g. knowledge, corporate culture) resources in day-to-day organisational activities to achieve superior performance; and
- the ability of the organisation to respond to changes in the environment.

The resource-based approach is valuable when other indicators of performance are difficult to obtain. In many not-for-profit and social welfare organisations, for example, it is hard to measure output goals or internal efficiency. Some for-profit organisations also use a resource-based approach.

Although the resource-based approach is valuable when other measures of effectiveness are not available, it does have shortcomings. The approach only vaguely considers the organisation's link to the needs of customers in the external environment. A superior ability to acquire and use resources is important only if resources and capabilities are used to achieve something that meets a need in the environment. The resource-based approach is most valuable when measures of goal attainment cannot be readily obtained.

Internal process approach

Here effectiveness is measured as internal organisational health and efficiency. An effective organisation has a smooth internal process. Departmental activities mesh with one another to ensure high productivity. Employees are happy and satisfied. This approach does not consider the external environment. The important element in effectiveness is what the organisation does with the resources it has, as reflected in internal health and efficiency indicators. One indicator of internal process effectiveness is the organisation's economic efficiency. However, the best-known proponents of a process model are from the human relations approach to organisations. Daft (2013) cites eight indicators of an effective organisation as seen from an internal process view. These are:

1   a strong corporate culture and positive work climate;
2   team spirit, group loyalty and teamwork;
3   confidence, trust and communication between workers and management;
4   decision-making near sources of information, regardless of where those sources are on the organisational chart;
5   undistorted horizontal and vertical communication;
6   sharing of relevant facts and feelings;
7   rewards to managers for performance, growth, and development of subordinates and for creating an effective working group; and

8 interactions between the organisation and its parts, with conflict that occurs over projects resolved in the interest of the organisations.

The internal process approach is important because the efficient use of resources and harmonious internal functioning are ways to measure effectiveness. Today, many managers believe that happy, committed, actively involved employees and a positive corporate culture are important measures of effectiveness. The internal process approach also has shortcomings. Total output and the organisation's relationship with the external environment are not evaluated. Evaluations of internal health and functioning are often subjective since many aspects of inputs and internal processes are not quantifiable. This approach alone represents a limited view of organisational effectiveness.

Stakeholder approach

Each of the approaches we have looked at so far has something to offer but tells only part of the story. Other approaches try to balance a concern with various parts of the organisation rather than focusing on just one part. These acknowledge that organisations do many things, have many outcomes and combine several indicators into a single framework.

In the stakeholder approach (or constituency approach), the level of satisfaction of each stakeholder group is assessed to indicate the organisation's performance. Each will have different criteria of effectiveness reflecting their different interest in the organisation and is surveyed to learn whether the organisation performs well from their viewpoint. Daft reports a survey of seven stakeholder groups in small businesses to determine the perception of effectiveness (Table 12.1).

TABLE 12.1 Effectiveness criteria in small firms (Daft, 2013, p.146)

Stakeholder	Effectiveness criteria
1 Owners	Financial return
2 Employees	Worker satisfaction, pay, supervision
3 Customers	Quality of goods and services
4 Creditors	Creditworthiness
5 Community	Contribution to community affairs
6 Suppliers	Satisfactory transactions
7 Government	Compliance with laws, regulations

The survey revealed that a small business found it difficult to fulfil the demands of all groups simultaneously. One business may have high employee satisfaction but the satisfaction of other groups may be lower. Nevertheless, measuring all seven stakeholders provides a more accurate view of effectiveness than any single measure. Evaluating how organisations perform across each group offers an overall assessment of effectiveness.

The strength of the stakeholder approach is that it takes a broad view of effectiveness and examines factors in the environment as well as within the organisation. The approach may include the community's notion of social responsibility, which is not formally measured in the goal, resource-based and internal process approaches. It also handles several criteria simultaneously and acknowledges that there is no single measure of effectiveness. The well-being of employees may be just as important as attaining the owner's financial goals. The stakeholder approach is gaining in popularity, based on the view that effectiveness is a complex, multidimensional concept that has no single measure. Recent research has shown that the assessment of multiple stakeholder groups is an accurate reflection of effectiveness, especially with respect to organisational adaptability (Tusi, 1990). Senior managers should be careful that in satisfying some stakeholders they do not alienate others!

CASE EXAMPLE   12.4

Independent software developers are key to the success of Facebook, even though they are not necessarily customers, suppliers, or owners. CEO Mark Zuckerberg works hard to win over developers. At a developers' conference in 2010, he unveiled a new technology that lets websites install a Facebook 'Like' button for free. Users can click on it to signal their interest in a piece of content. The user's approval then shows up on his or her Facebook page, with a link back to the site. The technology will drive traffic from Facebook to other websites, and in turn drive traffic back to Facebook.

Source: Jessica E. Vascellaro, 'Facebook taps consumer card – social networking site wants to know more than just who your friends are', *The Wall Street Journal*, 22 April 2010.

TEST YOUR KNOWLEDGE   12.1

a   Differentiate between organisational effectiveness and organisational efficiency.
b   Outline the three approaches to measuring effectiveness linked to the main stages in the business process.
c   Evaluate the contribution of the stakeholder approach to measuring organisational effectiveness.

2   The nature of control

2.1 Definitions of control

While missions and goals can be set out and elaborate plans and strategies can be formulated, their implementation can easily go awry. This section focuses on the nature of organisational control. Control is the mechanism, or set of mechanisms, designed to ensure conformity with a plan and to enable corrective action (should this be necessary) and is thus one of the basic functions of management. **Control** in this sense refers to the process by which managers ensure conformity with plans and targets and has been defined as 'a process of monitoring performance and taking action to ensure intended or desired results' (Baird, Post and Mahon, 1990).

In organisational terms, control can be compared to a ship's rudder; it keeps the organisation moving in the proper direction (Barney, 1992). Without adequate controls activity can be wasteful, even though people are working very hard. For example, unhygienic conditions found in a fast-food chain could be attributed to inadequate quality controls. Similarly, in the public sector suitable controls will need to be installed and maintained if services to the public are to be equitably distributed.

However, some commentators and many managers commonly adopt a much wider definition. Tannenbaum (1962) sees control as a process in which someone determines what another person or group will do. Here, control is equated with influencing or shaping another's behaviour. A key point here is that, when viewed from a behavioural perspective, the process of management control contains many paradoxes. For example, tighter controls may result in greater resistance; and management can, under certain circumstances, most effectively 'regain control by sharing it' (Fox, 1966). In some instances, attempts to impose controls in one relatively minor area of activity can result in disastrous consequences for the whole of the enterprise. In other circumstances, as we will see, more effective controls actually appear to be associated with higher levels of satisfaction for some employees.

From a behavioural perspective the essential point is that management control is seen as a process and not merely as a set of tools and techniques. This process is social and has interactive properties. This means that the imposition of a control will trigger behavioural responses. But in other circumstances the unintended consequences of controls can be very negative. Creativity, for example, may be easily stifled under the weight of imposed formal controls.

Simply adding more control may not always be helpful – an organisation can be over-controlled. So the first challenge is to create the optimum amount of control, and the second is to use the most appropriate forms of control for the prevailing circumstances.

STOP AND THINK 12.2

Make a shortlist of the main types of control that you are aware of in your own organisation, especially those controls associated with your own current (or past) work role(s). How appropriate do you think they are?

2.2 Stages in the control process

Most descriptions of the control process depict it as comprising a number of stages. Typically, these are identified as:

- establishing standards
- measuring performance
- comparing performance against standards
- taking corrective action

As suggested above, many classic management writers and system designers have suggested that the process of management control is a reflection of this type of technical process, as shown in Figure 12.2.

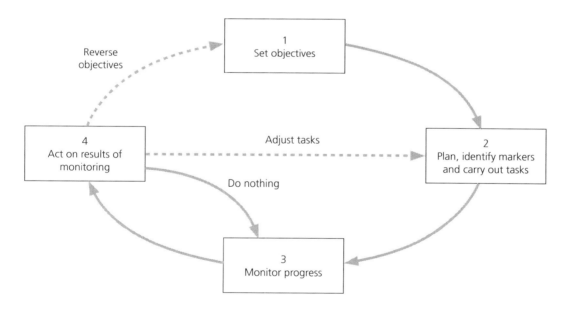

FIGURE 12.2 The control loop

STOP AND THINK 12.3

How well does this describe what occurs in your organisation?

The steps in this model are given different names by different writers, but they all represent a similar process. We will now review the steps of this process and note at each stage how the reality of management control in organisations is much more complex than this traditional model suggests.

Step 1: Establish standards of performance

These should be derived from the objectives set at the planning stage. 'Without objectives and plans, control is not possible because performance has to be measured against some established criteria' (Koontz and Weirich, 1988, p. 490). It is further recommended that the standards used should be easy to measure and definite. If objectives are vague and poorly defined, no system will be able to measure whether or not they have been attained. An example of a standard of performance, he suggests, could be 'to increase profitability by 8%'.

However, the problem is that the choice of standards can have unintended consequences.

 **CASE EXAMPLE 12.5**

During the late 1990s and into the year 2000, the UK's Department of Health highlighted the length of waiting lists for surgery as a critical performance standard. Making its reduction a priority, however, had unintended consequences: the waiting time for an initial consultation increased, and more serious but complicated cases were delayed as larger numbers of less urgent, but simpler, cases were processed.

Step 2: Measure the actual performance

Managers may develop quantitative measures of operational performance that can be reviewed daily, weekly or monthly. These may relate to quality, quantity, timeliness or customer service – or all of these as a basket of measures. As we saw above, however, there is an issue concerning the extent to which it is possible to 'manage through the numbers'. For managers of organisations there are questions about what precisely to measure and how to measure. Possible sources of information include personal observation, computer counts, written and oral reports. Each has strengths and weaknesses (Robbins, 1988). Choosing what to measure is critical: the selection of criteria can, and (if the measures are at all taken seriously) almost certainly will, influence behaviour. If disproportionate attention is given to some measures at the expense of others, the performance of the organisation can be adversely affected.

Step 3: Compare performance to standards

This step too appears deceptively straightforward when considered simply from a technical viewpoint. Managers may even be presented with computer printouts that show actual performance alongside targeted performance on a whole range of measures.

In practice, however, management control is not like a thermostat in a heating system. If actual performance measures do show a shortfall compared with targets, all manner of subjective judgements will come into play. Most managers will have some sense of priority among the measures and so will focus, quite sensibly, on the important and mission-critical measures, while paying little regard to the rest. Additionally, what is judged to be critical can change over time and is also likely to vary between different managers.

Step 4: Take corrective action

Simply comparing and noting is one thing; deciding what corrective action to take, following the interpretative phase, is quite another. Has the standard been set too high? Have circumstances changed? Are other priorities diverting attention from this particular measure? These types of issue raise all sorts of complications, including, for example, who will take 'corrective action' and what leverage they will be able to bring to bear.

 STOP AND THINK 12.4

In the light of the analysis above, return to the control model shown in Figure 12.2, identify some of the assumptions on which it is based, and make a few notes showing how these assumptions may not apply in the case of management control in an organisation.

2.3 The machine image

The previous section suggests that the technical conceptualisation of the control process is an incomplete and imperfect depiction of management control. The reality of management control is messier and more socially embedded: that is, the way in which this form of control is perceived and understood is highly conditional on social expectations, social relationships and social meanings. For example, the technical abstract model begins with the idea of setting standards. But, in an organisational setting, as we saw in Section 1, this begs a number of questions, such as: who should set the standards, with or without whose agreement, and what kind of standards should be set? Answers to each of these will vary between organisations.

Morgan (1986) considers different ways of seeing organisations as metaphors. The management control framework outlined above rests on two such metaphors: organisations as machines and organisations as information-processing systems.

Classical management theory imbues organisations with machine-like properties. Workers are seen as interchangeable and expected to have little discretion. Rather, they should carry out work precisely as instructed. Managers are responsible for devising the 'one best way' for work to be carried out. Tasks and responsibilities are precisely specified and divided into areas of specialism. The classical theorists (Taylor and others) conceived the organisation as a network of parts: functional departments, which are further specified as networks of precisely defined jobs. Job responsibilities interlock so that they complement each other as perfectly as possible (Chapter 11). The motions of the organisational structure thus produced are made to operate as precisely as possible through patterns of authority.

The machine metaphor in many organisations has been an effective foundation for management. Consider, for example, a telephone call centre, where operators respond to calls in accordance with a script that appears on a screen in front of them, and deliver scripted replies on the basis the type of customer query.

Another approach to understanding organisations rests on seeing them as information-processing systems. The central idea here is of systems that can respond to feedback from their environment so that an understanding of management control processes gives an effective foundation for performance improvement. Improving goal-setting and performance measurement, better feedback from the environment and more effective processes for adjusting behaviour in response to feedback can all be ways of improving performance. Indeed, in a failing organisation the first response is often to seek tighter management control.

The machine and information-processing metaphors of management control frameworks have a number of limitations.

■ The machine metaphor ignores the social dimension to organisations. People are not machine parts and do not generally behave as if they are.
■ Organisations often need to carry out tasks that are much less clearly specified, more complex and changeable than those that can be carried out by machines.

The machine metaphor works best for organisations carrying out straightforward tasks in a stable environment, where there is an emphasis on standard products or services and the 'machine parts' are compliant and behave as required. The information-processing metaphor is valuable in the attention it gives to the feedback process. Paradoxically, highly efficient management control processes based on feedback loops can be an impediment to improving performance, since they can strengthen a focus on a fixed set of goals that may quickly become inappropriate in a changing environment. One way of dealing with this problem is to extend the metaphor and introduce another loop. In the next section we do this with the idea of double-loop learning.

2.4 Postmodern forms of control

Some observers suggest that there is a shift in the nature of management control. Changes to the global economy have made controls characteristic of the industrial age less appropriate. In the post-industrial (or postmodern) economy, a premium is placed not on obedience and conformity but on commitment, responsiveness and flexibility. Postmodernism signals a shift from one to another set of interlocking ways of organising and controlling. The Fordist or classical model was rigid, conformist and mechanistic. New forms of competition and new market characteristics seemed to require a move towards more flexible modes of production, and even towards an 'enterprise culture', both overall and within work organisations. The characteristic modes of control of each form are summarised in Table 12.2.

TABLE 12.2 The shift to postmodern controls

Classic organisational controls	Postmodern organisational controls
Mass production of standardised products; assembly lines	Flexible production systems; multi-batch production for niche markets
Hierarchical organisation structures, bureaucratic, vertically integrated	Flat, flexible structures Decentralised
Administrative controls (rules, timetables)	Normative controls (through cultures, values, manipulation of meanings and attitudes)
Institutional controls (collective bargaining)	Identity control (e.g. through programmes such as service excellence; Total Quality Management)

The shift in organisational controls is only a small part of a radical transformation, extending across the design of organisational forms, the nature of market conditions and economic competition, technology, politics and culture which we have discussed in earlier chapters.

Individuals' responses to these kinds of question are likely to vary considerably. Critics point to the more far-reaching nature of the new controls – the way in which, for example, they make demands on the 'psyche' as well as the body. These critics suggest that such forms of control are more insidious and, by implication, more worrying. They also argue that hidden, 'manipulative' forms of control raise ethical problems. But in response it might be argued that such critics are underplaying or forgetting the defects of the Fordist model and fail to specify what changes would be necessary to render contemporary controls acceptable. Current conditions of rapid change, complexity and uncertainty may mean that traditional modes of control, such as standardisation and formalisation, are not equal to the task. Current circumstances require initiative and creativity, and rapid, informed response. These in turn suggest a need for employee empowerment; and, if empowerment were not to degenerate into anarchy, then self-control would seem necessary.

It has been suggested that self-controlling systems such as this argument implies, might be especially expected in voluntary sector organisations, where staff members may be intrinsically motivated to achieve high performance (Johnson and Gill, 1993). In so far as this may prove to be the case (and it is clearly not so for every person who happens to be employed in the voluntary sector), it shows the importance of the psychological contract in governing the way in which controls of various types are perceived and received.

 TEST YOUR KNOWLEDGE 12.2

a   Outline the management control processes in organisations.
b   Identify the limitations of the machine metaphor.
c   Explain the nature of postmodern forms of control.

3   Strategic control

3.1 The purpose and elements of strategic control

This chapter has taken a broad view of the nature of control and performance in organisations as important background, but its core is about strategic control and performance. For example, it is important to distinguish between financial monitoring (cash flow, earnings per share, etc.) and strategic controls, which may include these financial elements but also will have a broader perspective.

The purpose of **strategic control** is to identify whether an organisation should continue with its current strategy or modify it in the light of changed circumstances. Organisations must have effective strategic controls if they are to implement their strategies successfully.

Monitoring and control procedures are, therefore, an important aspect of strategic implementation because information can be used:

- to assess resource allocation choices;
- to monitor progress on implementation;
- to evaluate the performance of individual managers as they go about the achievement of their implementation tasks;
- to monitor the environment for significant changes from the planning assumptions and projections; and
- to provide a feedback mechanism and the fine-tuning essential for emerging strategy implementation, especially in fast-changing markets.

Monitoring becomes increasingly important as the concept of strategy moves from being an isolated event towards being a continuing activity. Strategy creation is seen as emerging from the way an organisation acquires, interprets and processes information about its environment. For these reasons, organisations spend significant resources on monitoring their activities. Because of the vast range of potential information, they may concentrate on the key factors for success.

Controls can take many forms: those that apply after the event and those that aim to anticipate events; those that are internal and those imposed from outside; those that rely on formal quantitative objectives and those that rely on looser mechanisms; those that are planned and those that are reactions to crises. Controls bring out the tensions in organisations: between the present and the future, coercion and motivation, efficiency and freedom, and rewards. Unless appropriately applied, controls can easily lead to counterproductive behaviour, so it is vital that strategy managers understand the advantages and disadvantages of different forms of control, and strike the appropriate balance between them.

3.2 A traditional approach to strategic control

Following the theme in the last section, the traditional approach to strategic control is usually regarded as sequential:

- Strategies are formulated and top management sets goals
- Strategies are implemented
- Performance is measured against the predetermined goal set

This is illustrated in Figure 12.3.

FIGURE 12.3 The traditional approach to strategic control

Control is based on a feedback loop from performance measurement to strategy formulation. This typically involves time lags tied to the organisation's annual planning cycle. Such traditional control systems, termed 'single-loop' learning (Argyris and Schon, 1978), simply compare actual performance to a predetermined goal. They are most appropriate when the environment is stable and relatively simple, goals and objectives can be measured with a high level of certainty, and there is little need for complex measures of performance. The appropriateness of the business strategy or standards of performance is seldom questioned.

As we have seen (Chapter 1), the idea that organisations should move forward in accordance with detailed and precise plans has come under attack from Mintzberg, Quinn and others. They argue that most strategic change proceeds incrementally. Mintzberg has called this 'crafting' strategy. His argument questions the value of rigid planning and goal-setting processes. Fixed strategic goals also become dysfunctional for firms competing in highly unpredictable competitive environments. Here, strategies need to change frequently and opportunistically. An inflexible commitment to predetermined goals and milestones can prevent the very adaptability that is required of a good strategy.

Strategic control systems monitor the main elements of the strategy and its objectives. The crucial point is to obtain information in time to be able to take action. Information for its own sake has limited value: the real test is whether it is useful and timely in revising the implementation process where required. These may include:

■ financial measures
■ customer satisfaction
■ quality measures
■ market share

It may also be necessary to assess the relative performance of the organisation under these headings against the competition.

CASE EXAMPLE   12.6

Cisco Systems' market value at one time approached $600 billion, but by 2014 it was $140 billion. Cisco has minimised the potential for such problems in the future by improving its informational control systems. Other firms such as Oracle have been more successful in anticipating change and have made appropriate corrections to their strategies.

The traditional 'feedback' approach to strategic control has limitations!

STOP AND THINK   12.5

Thinking about an organisation you know well, what are the main elements of strategic control that you can identify?

3.3 A contemporary approach to strategic control

Adapting to and anticipating both internal and external environmental change is an integral part of strategic control. The relationships between strategy formulation, implementation and control are highly interactive, as suggested by Figure 12.4, which also illustrates two different types of strategic control: informational control and behavioural control.

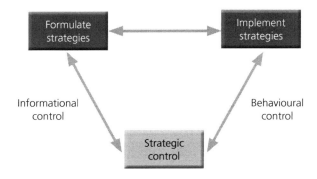

FIGURE 12.4 The contemporary approach to strategic control (Dess et al., 2014)

■ **Informational control**. This is primarily concerned with whether or not the organisation is 'doing the right things' – whether it is effective.
■ **Behavioural control**. This asks if the organisation is doing things right – whether the implementation of its strategy is efficient.

Dess et al. (2014) argue that both the informational and behavioural components of strategic control are necessary, but not sufficient, conditions for success. What good is a well-conceived strategy that cannot be implemented? What use is an energetic and committed workforce if it is focused on the wrong strategic target?

Informational control deals with the internal environment as well as the external strategic context. It addresses the assumptions and premises that provide the foundation for an organisation's strategy. The key question becomes: Do the organisation's goals and strategies still fit within the context of the current strategic environment? Depending on the type of business, such assumptions may relate to changes in technology, customer tastes, government regulation and industry competition. This involves two key issues:

1 Managers must scan and monitor the external environment, as discussed in Chapter 3.
2 Conditions can also change in the internal environment of the firm, as discussed in Chapter 4.

In the contemporary approach, information control is part of a continuous process of organisational learning that continuously updates and challenges the assumptions that underlie the organisation's strategy. In such **'double-loop' learning** the organisation's assumptions, premises, goals and strategies are continuously monitored, tested and reviewed. The benefits of continuous monitoring are that time lags are dramatically shortened, changes in the competitive environment are detected earlier and the organisation's ability to respond with speed and flexibility is enhanced.

Contemporary control systems must have four characteristics to be effective (Simmons, 1995):

1 They must focus on constantly changing information that senior managers identify as having potential strategic importance.
2 The information is important enough to demand frequent and regular attention from operating managers at all levels of the organisation.
3 The data and information generated by the control system are best interpreted and discussed in face-to-face meetings of superiors, subordinates and peers.
4 The contemporary control system is a key catalyst for continuing debate about underlying data, assumptions and action plans.

Using the control system interactively – investing time and attention on reviewing and evaluating new information – sends a clear signal to the organisation about what is important. The dialogue and debate that emerge from such an interactive process can often lead to new strategies and innovations.

 CASE EXAMPLE 12.7

Senior managers at US Today meet each Friday to discuss strategy. Each week they review information, ranging from day-to-day operations to year-to-date data. This information enables senior managers to check the pulse of the company frequently and minimises the surprises that can beset other companies that don't watch closely the available information. Senior managers frequently meet operations managers for intensive discussion to analyse the weekly information. The results of these meetings allow managers from the operating core of the newspaper to respond to industry trends and events on a real-time basis

These weekly meetings have returned significant rewards for US Today. Innovations have included a new market survey service targeted at the car industry, a potential source of high volume advertising, and adding fractional page colour advertising to increase revenue.

Behavioural control is focused on implementation – doing things right. Effectively implementing strategy requires manipulating three key control levers, such as culture and rewards. There are two compelling reasons for an increased emphasis on culture and rewards:

■ The competitive environment is increasingly complex and unpredictable, demanding both flexibility and quick response to its challenges. As firms simultaneously downsize and face the need for increased coordination across organisational boundaries, a control system based primarily on rigid strategies and rules and regulations is dysfunctional. Thus, the use of rewards and culture to align individual and organisational goals becomes increasingly important.

- The implicit long-term contract between the organisation and its key employees has been eroded. Today's younger managers have been conditioned to see themselves as free agents and view a career as a series of opportunistic challenges. The importance of culture and rewards in building organisational loyalty claims greater importance.

3.4 Control processes

As discussed in Chapter 11, structure is a key ingredient of organising for success. But within any structure, what makes organisations work are the formal and informal organisational processes. These processes control the organisation's operations and thus help or hinder the translation of strategy into action.

There are six strategic control processes considered by Johnson et al. that emphasise either input or output controls or direct or indirect controls. These are summarised in Table 12.3.

- **Input control processes**. These concern themselves with the resources consumed in the strategy, especially financial resources and human commitment.
- **Output control processes**. These focus on ensuring satisfactory results, for example the meeting of targets or achieving market competitiveness.
- **Direct controls**. These involve close supervision or monitoring.
- **Indirect controls**. These set up the conditions whereby desired behaviours are achieved semi-automatically.

TABLE 12.3 Types of control processes (Johnson et al., 2014)

	Input	Output
Direct	Direct supervision Planning processes	Performance targeting
Indirect	Cultural processes Self-control	Internal markets

Input control measures tend to require that the controllers have high levels of knowledge of what the controlled are supposed to do. In knowledge-intensive organisations, controllers may not have a good understanding of what their expert employees are doing and rely more on output controls, such as revenue or profitability targets. Direct control relies heavily on the physical presence of management or surveillance through IT systems. Organisations normally use a blend of these control processes, but some will dominate over others according to the strategic challenges. International organisations may therefore make use of indirect controls for their geographically dispersed subsidiaries. Direct control processes can be effective for small organisations on a single site.

Direct supervision is the direct control of strategic decisions by one or a few individuals, typically focused on the effort put into the business by employees. It is dominant in small organisations or larger organisations where there is little change and complexity of the business is such that a small number of managers can control strategy in detail from the centre. It is often found in family businesses and in the public sector with a history of close political involvement. Direct supervision requires a thorough understanding of the work supervised to correct errors, but not stop experimentation. It is easiest on a single site, although long-distance monitoring (e.g. of trading strategies in banking) is possible through electronic means. Direct supervision can be effective in a crisis, when autocratic control may be necessary to achieve quick results. Turnaround managers are often autocratic in style.

Planning processes

These are administrative controls, where the successful implementation of strategies is achieved through processes that plan and control the allocation of resources and monitor their utilisation (see also Chapter 11). The focus is on controlling the organisation's inputs, particularly financial. The plan shows the level of resources allocated to each area (whether that be functions, divisions or business units). For example, the marketing function may be allocated £5 million, but will need to show how this will be spent on staff, advertising, exhibitions, and so on. These costs are then monitored regularly to measure actual spend against plan. A key strength of this planned approach to strategic control is the ability to monitor the implementation of strategy.

Ways in which planning can support strategy include:

- **Standardisation of work processes** (e.g. product or service features). Sometimes these are subject to rigorous assessment and review, for example, to meet externally audited quality standards (e.g. in financial services). In many service organisations this has been achieved through IT systems. For example, the cost of transactions in internet banking is a fraction of those made through branches.
- **Enterprise resource planning (ERP) systems** (e.g. supplied by SAP or Oracle). These use sophisticated IT to achieve planning-type control. These systems aim to integrate the entire business operations, including personnel, finance, manufacturing operations, warehousing, etc. Further advantage may be gained if these systems can stretch more widely in the value system beyond the boundaries of the organisation into the supply and distribution chains, for example, in automatic ordering of supplies.
- **Centralised planning approaches**. These use a formula for controlling resource allocation. For example, in the public services, budgets might be allocated on a per capita basis (e.g. number of patients for doctors).

Planning processes work best in simple and stable conditions, where a budget or a formula can apply equally well to all the units in the organisation and where assumptions are likely to hold good for the whole of the budget or formula period. Where there is diversity in the needs of business units, standard budgets or formulas are likely to advantage some units, while handicapping others. Budgets and formulas may also be inflexible where changing circumstances contradict original assumptions.

Because of the dangers of insensitivity to diverse needs in the organisation, it is often helpful to involve those most directly involved in bottom-up planning where the corporate headquarters sets guidelines for these initial plans and subsequently reviews them. There may be several iterations of this proposal and review process and so, while it can take into account business unit needs, bottom-up planning can be very time-consuming and political.

Cultural processes

With rapid change, increasing complexity and the need to exploit knowledge, promoting self-control and personal motivation can be an effective means of control, influencing the quality of employee input without direct intervention. Many workers have a strong degree of self-control and motivation and this can help ensure appropriate kinds of performance for the (e.g. doctors have strong commitment to craft or professional standards). However, craft or professional standards can also deviate from what the organisation's strategy demands. Here managers can use cultural processes to achieve appropriate kinds of performance (Casey, 1999).

Cultural control processes are concerned with norms (as discussed in Chapter 5). Control is indirect and internalised, as employees become part of the culture. Control is exerted on the input of employees, as the culture defines norms of appropriate effort and initiative. Three processes are particularly important in shaping appropriate cultures: recruitment, socialisation (the integration of new staff through training and induction programmes, and role models); and reward. Some employees may resist these, and some cultural processes are not within formal management control, such as peer group pressure not to respond to organisational strategies. Nevertheless, cultural processes are particularly important in organisations facing complex and dynamic environments.

Performance targeting processes

An organisation's performance is judged on its ability to meet its targets. Performance targets focus on the outputs of an organisation, such as product quality, revenues or profits. These targets are often known as key performance indicators (KPIs).

Corporate centres may choose performance targets to control their business units without getting involved in the details of how they achieve them. These targets may be cascaded down the organisation as specific targets for sub-units, functions and even individuals.

In regulated markets, such as utilities in the UK, government-appointed regulators exercise control of competition through agreed performance indicators (PIs), such as service or quality levels.

In the public services, where control of inputs historically dominated, governments have moved to control processes based on outcomes, for example, patient mortality rates in healthcare.

    STOP AND THINK **12.6**

What examples are there of performance targets in an organisation with which you are familiar? Are there any types of organisations where performance targets might not be appropriate means of control?

One difficulty with targets, as we argued in Section 1, is that any particular set of indicators is liable to give only a partial view of the overall picture. In addition, some important indicators (e.g. customer satisfaction) tend to be neglected because they are hard to measure, leaving the focus on easily available data such as financial ratios. In the last decade or so, **balanced score-cards** have been increasingly used as a way of widening the scope of performance indicators. We look at these in Section 4.

Market processes

These can be brought inside organisations to control activities. This typically involves some formalised system of 'contracting' for resources or inputs from other parts of an organisation and for supplying outputs to other parts of an organisation. Control is indirect and units have simply to earn their keep in competitive internal markets.

Internal markets can be used in a variety of ways. There might be competitive bidding, or a customer-supplier relationship may be established between a central service department, such as training or IT, and the operating units. The corporate centre might set rules for service-level agreements to ensure appropriate service by an essential internal supplier.

Internal markets work well where complexity or rapid change makes impractical detailed direct or input controls. But bargaining between units consumes management time and over-zealous use of market mechanisms can lead to dysfunctional competition and legalistic contracting, thereby damaging collaborative relationships. These have all been complaints made against the internal markets in the NHS. Proponents claim that market processes free a traditionally over-centralised health service to innovate and respond to local needs, while market disciplines maintain overall control.

3.5 How can strategic controls be improved?

Bungay and Goold (1991) suggest some ways that organisations might use strategic control effectively:

- **Concentrate on the key performance indicators and factors for success**. There is a real danger that too many elements will be monitored with resulting information overload.
- **Distinguish between corporate, business and operating levels of information and only monitor where relevant**. For example, not everyone at the centre needs to know that a minor product has just achieved its sales target.
- **Avoid over-reliance on quantitative data**. Numbers are usually easier to measure but may be misleading and simplistic. Qualitative data and information that is difficult to quantify in such areas as service may be far more relevant to strategy monitoring.

- **As controls become established, consider relaxing them**. Eventually, they may interfere with the most important task of clear and insightful strategic exploration. For example, it was for this reason that Jack Welch at GE reduced them, but he did not do so until the principles had been learnt. Every organisation may need to go through this stage of learning before controls are relaxed.
- **Create realistic expectations of what the control system can do, as it is being introduced or upgraded**. Some managers may regard strategic controls as a waste of time, believing it difficult to see early results because of the long time-scales involved. Such an objection can be anticipated and it is better to acknowledge that the benefits in terms of improved strategy, resources and results will not be immediately obvious.

 TEST YOUR KNOWLEDGE 12.3

a Explain what is meant by 'strategic control'.
b Explain what is meant by the idea of 'cultural controls'.
c How can strategic control be improved?

---

4 The balanced scorecard

4.1 Introduction

One of the fundamental problems of management is how to coordinate and control the diverse people, operations and systems that make up the organisation. Without mechanisms for coordination and control there is no organisation, and hence no performance. Consequently, managers and management writers have often been preoccupied with the problem of how to link activities and behaviour in the organisation effectively with an overarching set of organisational goals.

Ask any organisation how they measure performance and the answer will usually depend on whom you ask! An operations manager may give a different answer from an accountant, who will give a different answer from someone in human resources or marketing. Of course, each perspective is related; effective performance from one perspective may depend on effective performance from another. For example, effective customer service may depend to a large extent on the effective recruitment, training and motivation of staff. There will often be trade-offs between perspectives. Improving customer service may lead to greater costs or lower operational efficiency. Improving delivery times may lead to problems with cash flow, and so on. Finally, unless measures of performance are linked to an organisation's strategic goals we are only in a position to consider economy or efficiency. To understand performance effectiveness, we need to consider how each perspective contributes to the achievement of strategic goals.

However, the accounting and finance perspective is often dominant. This section introduces a framework that brings together multiple perspectives on performance and links them to strategic objectives. Based on their research in large private sector firms in the US, Kaplan and Norton (1992) developed a framework for performance measurement, which they call the 'balanced scorecard'. Many organisations beyond the private sector have found this useful.

When Kaplan and Norton's versatile organisational performance management tool first burst on the scene, few realised quite how popular and influential it would become. The original *Harvard Business Review* article is one of the ten most read HBR articles of all time, and has become one of the classic business school models.

What exactly is a balanced scorecard? A definition often quoted is: 'A strategic planning and management system used to align business activities to the vision statement of an organisation'. The balanced scorecard attempts to relate a company's vision/mission statement into operational efficiency. Figure 12.5 shows a visual depiction of the model.

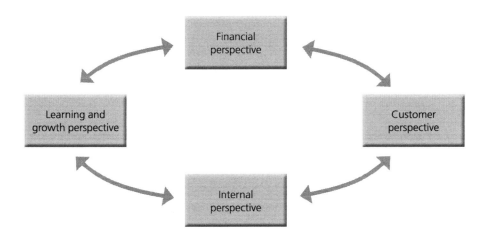

FIGURE 12.5 The balanced scorecard (Kaplan & Norton, 2007)

4.2 The scorecard approach

The balanced scorecard is a technique that has been developed to integrate the various features of corporate success; a set of performance measures that provides the framework for strategic measurement and management. The concept was developed in the belief that 'existing performance measurement approaches, primarily relying on financial accounting measures, were becoming obsolete' (Kaplan and Norton). The approach considered the intangible or 'soft' factors that had previously been considered as immeasurable, and as such, of little value. The term 'balanced scorecard' reflected the balance between short- and long-term objectives, financial and non-financial measures, lagging and leading indicators and external and internal performance perspectives. The balanced scorecard includes financial measures that records the results of actions already taken. It complements the financial measures with operational measures on customer satisfaction, internal processes and the organisation's innovation and improvement activities – operational measure that are the drivers of future financial performance.

As such, the balanced scorecard presents a more balanced view than that provided by conventional accounts. These are complemented with operational measures on customer satisfaction, internal processes and the organisation's innovation and improvement activities. These are the drivers of future financial performance. Current results are no more important than building the business for the future. Table 12.4 suggests a typical scorecard. The four sections shown correspond to four perspectives:

- **Financial**. How well are we satisfying those who put up the money?
- **Customers**. How well do we serve them?
- **Internal business**. What are we good at and how good are we?
- **Innovation and learning**. How are we improving to create better value?

Each of the four perspectives is interdependent – improvement in just one area is not necessarily a recipe for success in the other areas. Balance is needed – or in Rumelt's words, consonance, the internal consistency.

There are many variants of the basic idea of scorecards and the essence of each is practical application in each firm. The objectives and the measures of the scorecard are derived from an organisation's vision and strategy. For instance, a service business may use six areas to evaluate: competitive performance; financial performance; service quality; flexibility; use of resources; and innovation. In all cases, we see a combination of feedback and feed-forward control. Here competitive and financial performances are instances of feedback. The last four factors, on the other hand, cover 'inputs' that make the difference for the future. Thus, we best see them as examples of feed-forward control.

The successful application of the scorecard approach in a number of transformation projects identified that it could also be a medium to communicate and align a new strategic approach. It has been successful because it is able to identify linkages between the four key areas that generate and perpetuate success. The impact of scorecard measures considered in isolation would probably be minimal; success is derived from comprehensive visibility of all key influences. The added value of the scorecard is in the drawing together of all the key business areas and identifying and exploiting the linkages that deliver success. These are explained in some detail by Hoffecker and Goldenberg (1994). They emphasise that the impact of a decision in one area on the other areas can be recognised before the decision is implemented, offering more strategic management visibility than would normally be expected. This holistic approach has resulted in better performance, resulting from more informed management decision-making.

Key to the model is the determination of the key objectives in each of the four areas that will support the strategic goals. The next layer of the balanced scorecard model is the detail within each of four areas of focus, whereby management are tasked with deciding:

- key objectives;
- for each objective, the metric that can be expressed as a KPI;
- for each metric, a target number; and
- for each objective and target, the initiative or tactic that will produce the desired outcome.

Companies such as Mobil, PepsiCo and Phillips Electronics have made use of the framework.

TABLE 12.4 The balanced scorecard

Financial perspective		Customer perspective	
Goals	*Measures*	*Goals*	*Measures*
Survive	Cash flow	New products	Percentage of sales from new products
Succeed	Sales and income growth	Responsiveness	Percentage of orders supplied on time
Develop	Growth in market share and ROI	Partnership	Number of partners
Internal perspective		**Innovation and learning perspective**	
Goals	*Measures*	*Goals*	*Measures*
Technology	Quality compared with rivals	Technology	Development time Success rate
Manufacturing	Speed, cost and waste in process	Process learning	Time to learn new processes
Design	Output efficiency Measures of manufacturability	Product focus	Percentage of products as market leaders
Innovation	Meeting innovation targets	Time to reach market	Compare with benchmarks

 **CASE EXAMPLE 12.8**

Philips Electronics has over 250,000 employees in 150 countries and uses the balanced scorecard to manage its diverse product lines and divisions around the world. The company has identified four critical success factors (CSFs) for the organisation as a whole:

- competence (knowledge, technology, leadership and teamwork);
- processes (drivers for performance);
- customers (value propositions);
- financial (value, growth and productivity).

CASE EXAMPLE 12.8 *continued*

Philips uses these scorecard criteria at four levels: the strategy review; operations review; business unit; and the individual employee. Criteria at one level are cascaded down to more detailed criteria appropriate at each level. This helps employees understand how their day-to-day activities link ultimately to the corporate goals. At a business unit level, for example, the management team determine the local critical success factors and agree indicators for each. Targets are then set for each indicator based on the gap between present performance and desired performance for the current year plus two to four years into the future. These targets are derived from an analysis of the market and world-class performance.

Targets must be specific measurable, ambitious, realistic and time phased. Examples of indicators at the business unit level include:

- **Financial processes**. Economic profit; income from operations; working capital changes; operational cash flow; inventory turns.
- **Customers**. Rank in customer survey; market share; repeat order rate; complaints; brand index.
- **Processes**. Percentage reduction in process cycle time; number of engineering changes; capacity utilisation; order response time; process capability.
- **Competence**. Leadership competence; percentage of patent-protected turnover; training days per employee; quality improvement team participation.

Gumbus and B. Lyons (2002), 'The balanced scorecard at Philips Electronics', *Strategic Finance*, November, pp.45–9

Kaplan and Norton extended their scorecard idea to propose an enhanced strategic management system. Again, the central theme is to avoid over-reliance on traditional financial controls. Using a range of perspectives helps managers overcome four hurdles of strategy:

1 **Translating the vision**. Enables broad, appealing mission statements to be converted into objectives with practical meaning at all levels.
2 **Communicating and linking**. Helps managers develop a shared view through communicating the strategy throughout the organisation.
3 **Business planning**. Facilitates integration of financial and operating plans.
4 **Feedback and learning**. Ensures that feedback is used to enhance the strategy process for the future.

The power of the balanced scorecard model is how quickly it delves into operational detail. The idea of the balanced scorecard and the approaches derived from it are practical and less concerned with creating a general model of control than with correcting imbalances as they confront them. Linked to corporate strategy they apply both internal and external criteria and combine the short-term with the long-term view.

Its versatility comes from the fact that the model can be adapted to different contexts, e.g. the public sector (see Figure 12.6), and to address the non-financial goals of a variety of stakeholders. More recently, Kaplan and Norton have developed a version of the scorecard for the not-for-profit sector that charts donors, beneficiaries, processes and learning, but the model can be adapted to suit any organisation by applying the basic principles to dimensions or stakeholder groupings of interest to management.

As such, it is an important tool that balances a bias towards short-term quarterly earnings (higher profits from cutting the customer service department, for instance) and 'balances' the organisation to take into account that cutting customer service may lead to a deterioration in the customer objectives (customer satisfaction, repeat purchases, etc.). It also adapts itself to the triple bottom line, as one could add the environment, as well as community in terms of areas of focus to receive the objectives/metrics/targets/initiatives treatment. Ideally of course, these initiatives should be costed.

The balanced scorecard is versatile and can be adapted to many organisational contexts and layers of the organisation. However, critics comment on the fact that it is not an easy system to implement – it does not give the right answer, and is no substitute for deep thinking of the organisation. It overlooks the budgeting issues of the individual initiatives, or assumes that a cost-benefit analysis has already been done.

The results of using the balanced scorecard method, however, are potentially as follows:

- greater coordination across the organisation;
- improved processes and information systems;
- motivated and trained employees;
- greater customer satisfaction;
- greater financial awareness and enhanced performance;
- a more nuanced performance monitoring system; and
- an ability to address non-financial KPIs and key stakeholders beyond shareholders.

Second- and third-generation versions of the balanced scorecard are now available. Second-generation variants added strategy maps to visualise the key strategic goals. Third-generation balanced scorecards as developed by consultants such as 2GC have added a 'destination statement' – a concise agreed, quantified description of the hoped-for effect of implementing the strategy (see Figure 12.6).

FIGURE 12.6 A visual depiction of the balanced scorecard concept (source: 2GC)

In many ways, the balanced scorecard was ahead of its time when first introduced. The taking of different, balanced perspectives is fundamental to any analytical approach, but it is also highly valuable for the initiation and evolution of the strategy. Rather than being seen simply as a monitoring tool, the balanced scorecard concept can be used by company secretaries and boards as a useful tool throughout the strategy process.

4.3 Alternatives to the balanced scorecard

Although the Balanced scorecard is the most widely used performance evaluation toolkit in industry, there are two alternatives that can also be considered.

The **Results and Determinants Framework** (Fitzgerald et al., 1991) consists of six performance dimensions housed within two categories: results and determinants (see Table 12.5). The results category covers financial and competitiveness performance measures, and includes the lagging indicators. The determinants are the leading indicators.

TABLE 12.5 Results and determinants framework

Results	Financial performance
	Competiveness
Determinants	Quality
	Flexibility
	Resource utilisation
	Innovation

The **European Quality Framework Management (EFQM) Business Excellence model** links the important results to the organisation's processes and leadership (see Table 12.6). Overall firm performance is linked to:

- satisfied people (people results);
- satisfied customers (customer results); and
- a positive impact on the society (society results).

TABLE 12.6 The EQFM model

Enablers			Results	
Leadership	People	Processes	People results	Business results
	Strategy	Products	Customer results	
	Partners and resources	Services	Society results	

In order to apply the model, the organisation should develop appropriate KPIs based on the needs of the stakeholders in each of the results' categories. The organisation can then develop appropriate interventions in each of the enabling categories in order to work towards achieving these standards.

STOP AND THINK 12.7

How might the balance scorecard be applied in your own organisation? What might be measured? What possible disadvantages or dangers might the balanced scorecard technique have for organisations?

TEST YOUR KNOWLEDGE 12.4

a   Describe the purpose of the balanced scorecard as outlined by Kaplan and Norton.
b   Outline the key elements in a typical scorecard.

CASE QUESTIONS

1   Identify the implications of following a contemporary approach to strategic control for LCU.

2   Explain the advantages that there might be in using the balanced scorecard as a way of both determining strategy and measuring performance.

CHAPTER SUMMARY

■ The focus of this chapter has been on strategic control and performance. How does an organisation ensure that its strategic objectives are being met and make adjustments to ensure that these can be met or amended if they are no longer appropriate?

■ The chapter started by distinguishing effectiveness and efficiency and followed this with an examination of the most popular approaches to measuring effectiveness: goal-based, resource-based, those focused on internal processes and the stakeholder approach

■ We then looked at the nature of organisational control from the machine-based model to postmodern notions of control that take a behavioural view, and acknowledged the complexities associated with current environmental challenges. Similar patterns can be seen in notions of strategic control and we reviewed a number of ideas that can help make this process more effective.

■ Balanced scorecards combine both qualitative and quantitative measures, acknowledge the expectations of different stakeholders and relate an assessment of performance to choice of strategy. Importantly, performance is linked not only to short-term outputs but also to the way in which processes are managed – for example, the processes of innovation and learning which are crucial to long-term success.

■ Alternatives to the balanced scorecard include the Results and Determinants Framework and the European Quality Framework Management (EFQM) Business Excellence model.

13 Managing strategic change

CONTENTS

■ INTRODUCTION

This chapter is about change, strategic change, and the forces that cause organisations to make changes. It describes the forces that require managers to implement comprehensive change programmes and why people and organisations may resist change. It also reviews various processes for managing strategic change.

1   The nature of change

1.1 Elements of strategic change

We are all subject to change of one form or another; change is an inescapable part of both social and organisational life. This chapter is concerned with the management activities involved in changing strategies and in managing organisational change. Other chapters in Part Four have addressed important issues to do with the structuring of organisations and resourcing strategies, both important in effecting strategic change. However, designing a structure and putting in place appropriate resources do not of themselves ensure successful strategic implementation.

Uncertain economic conditions, global competition, the level of government regulation, and rapid developments in technology all contribute to an increasingly volatile environment. In order to help ensure its survival and future success, any organisation must be adaptable to the demands of the external environment. The organisation and its strategy must be responsive to change.

Change also originates within the organisation. Much of this change is akin to a natural process of ageing — for example, as material resources such as buildings, equipment or machinery deteriorate or lose efficiency, or as skills and abilities become outdated. Some of this change can be managed through planned, regular repairs and maintenance, such as introducing new technology or working methods. Other change can come about through effective human resource planning and training and development. But the main pressure for change is from external forces. The organisation must be properly prepared to face the demands of a changing environment. It must pay attention to its future development and success.

The effects of change can be studied over different time-scales and at different levels. Change can be studied in terms of its effects at the individual, group, organisation, society, national or international level. However, because of its pervasive nature, change at any one level is connected to changes at other levels, and it is difficult to study one area of change in isolation.

Figure 13.1 provides a structure for the chapter. It begins by explaining important issues that need to be considered in diagnosing the situation an organisation faces when embarking on strategic change, in terms of the types of change required; the variety of contextual and cultural factors that need to be taken into account; and the forces blocking or facilitating change. It then discusses the management of strategic change in terms of the styles of management and the roles played by strategic leaders and other change agents in managing strategic change. It goes on to review levers for change, including changes in structure and control, organisational routines and systems, symbols, the role of political activity and more specific tactics. Section 5 draws all this together by considering how all this might take effect and what overall lessons can be drawn about managing change programmes, and looks at the forces of change and the role played by various agents. A major problem is the tendency towards inertia and resistance to change, which is examined along with the issues associated with change programmes.

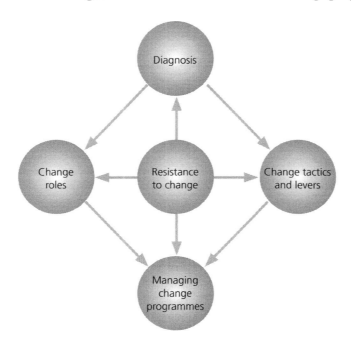

FIGURE 13.1 Elements in managing strategic change

1.2 Types of change

Martin (2001) identified four ways in which change may be experienced by an organisation, depending on the scale of change and degree of planning involved. Each cell in Figure 13.2 reflects different responses to an experienced situation and provides a basis for identifying appropriate management strategies.

- **Surprise**. Reflects situations that are unplanned and relatively minor. For example, interest rates might unexpectedly change and require finance managers to adjust loan repayment schedules.
- **Incremental**. Situations that can be anticipated and are relatively minor. For example, implementing quality circle recommendations may require small changes to the design of a component. This is likely to be only one in a series of changes to make the production process more effective.
- **Strategic**. This cell represents major planned events that attempt to position the organisation more effectively in its relationship to its environment. For example, a company making manual typewriters anticipating the growth of computer-based systems may seek to acquire a business systems or computer division.
- **Crisis**. Represents both unexpected and serious change, for example, the destruction of a factory as result of an explosion or terrorist attack. A crisis has the potential to destroy an organisation unless the response is rapid and significant.

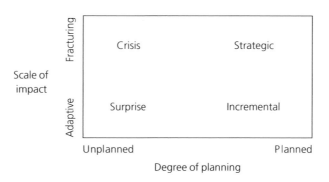

FIGURE 13.2 The change matrix (Martin, 2001)

Balogun and Hope Hailey (2004) develop this further to identify four types of strategic change (see Table 13.1) that have implications for how change might be managed.

TABLE 13.1 Types of change (Balogun and Hope Hailey, 2008)

		Extent of change	
		Realignment	*Transformation*
Nature of change	*Incremental*	Adaptation	Evolution
	Big bang	Reconstruction	Revolution

Johnson et al. (2014) argue that strategy development is typically incremental in nature. It builds on prior strategy and so is adaptive in the way it occurs, with only occasional more transformational changes. Arguably, it is beneficial for change in an organisation to be incremental since such change should build on the skills, routines and beliefs of those in the organisation. In that way, change is more likely to be understood and secure commitment. However, a 'big bang' approach might be needed on occasion, for example if an organisation faces a crisis or needs to change direction rapidly. In terms of the extent of change, the question is whether change can occur within the current culture as a realignment of strategy or whether it requires culture change. This is more akin to transformational change. Combining these two axes suggests four types of strategic change:

1   **Adaptation**. Change that can be accommodated within the current culture and occur incrementally. It is the most common form of change in organisations.
2   **Reconstruction**. Change that may be rapid and involve a good deal of upheaval, but which does not fundamentally change the culture. It could be a turnaround situation where there is need for major structural changes or a major cost-cutting programme to deal with a decline in financial performance.
3   **Revolution**. Change that requires rapid, major strategic *and* culture change. This could be in circumstances where the strategy has been so bounded by the existing culture that, even when environmental or competitive pressures might require fundamental change, the organisation has failed to respond. This might have occurred over many years and resulted in circumstances where pressures for change are extreme, for example, a takeover threatens the continued existence of a firm.
4   **Evolution**. Change in strategy that requires culture change, but over time. It may be that managers anticipate the need for transformational change. They may then be in a position of planned evolutionary change or organisational learning and development, with time in which to achieve it.

 STOP AND THINK **13.1**

Can you identify these types of change affecting an organisation or organisations known to you?

The sort of cultural analysis explained in Chapter 5 can be useful as a means of considering whether the change envisaged could be accommodated within the bounds of the existing culture, or whether it would require a really significant cultural shift. For example, a business may launch new products without requiring fundamental changes in the assumptions and beliefs of the organisation. On the other hand, some changes in strategy, even if they do not take the form of dramatic product changes, may require fundamental changes in core assumptions. For example, the shift from a production focus for a manufacturer to a customer-led, service ethos may not entail product changes, but will very likely require significant culture change.

It also helps to think of planned change in terms of order of magnitude. Robbins and Judge (2007) identify **first-order change**, which is linear and continuous. It implies no fundamental shifts in the assumptions that organisational members hold about the world or how the organisation can improve its functioning. In contrast, **second-order change** is a multidimensional, discontinuous, radical change involving the reframing of assumptions about the organisation and the world in which it operates. Others (Romanelli and Tushman, 1994) have described this as **transformational change,** which cannot be handled within the existing paradigm and organisational routines.

TEST YOUR KNOWLEDGE 13.1

a   Identify the different types of change according to Martin.
b   Distinguish revolution from evolution in the Balogun and Hope Hailey model.
c   Explain the nature of second-order change.

---

2   Understanding the context of change

2.1 Drivers of change

What are the major forces that underlie change in the external environment of organisations? Table 13.2 summarises six specific sets of forces that are acting as stimulants for change.

TABLE 13.2 Forces driving change (based on Robbins and Judge, 2014)

Force	Examples
Nature of the workforce	More cultural diversity Ageing population Increased immigration and outsourcing
Technology	Faster, cheaper, and more mobile computers and handheld devices Emergence and growth of social networking sites Deciphering of the human genetic code
Economic shocks	Rise and fall of global housing market Financial sector collapse Global recession
Competition	Global competitors Mergers and consolidations Increased government regulation of commerce
Social trends	Increased environmental awareness Liberalisation of attitudes toward gay, lesbian, and transgender employees More multitasking and connectivity
World politics	Rising health care costs Negative social attitudes toward business and executives Opening of markets in China

These are some of the key forces but there are many others that will reflect both global and local circumstances. We live in an age of discontinuity. In the 1950s and 1960s, the past was a fairly accurate guide to the future: tomorrow was essentially an extended trend line from yesterday. That is no longer true. Beginning in the early 1970s, with the overnight quadrupling of world oil prices, a series of economic shocks, developments in technology and the globalisation of world politics and economics have continued to impose changes on organisations. The global economy means that competitors are as likely to come from across the ocean as from across the city. The argument here is that successful organisations will be those that can change in response to the competition. They will be capable of developing new products rapidly and getting them to market quickly. They rely on short production-runs and product cycles, and a continuing stream of new products. In other words, they are flexible. They require an equally flexible and responsive workforce that can adapt to rapidly and even radically changing conditions. For examples of the impact of these issues on strategy, see Chapter 10.

 STOP AND THINK 13.2

How are these forces affecting your own organisation?

Organisations must therefore respond to the external environment of which they are a part.

2.2 The organisational context

Managing change in a small business, where a motivated team is driving change, would be quite different from trying to manage change in a major corporation or public sector organisation. Each may have established routines, formal structures and perhaps resistance to change, but it is unsafe to assume that approaches to change are readily transferable between contexts. For example, many government departments have sought import change management practices from consultancies or by recruiting managers from commercial firms but with varying degrees of success (Ostroff, 2006).

Understanding the challenge of managing strategic change requires an understanding of the context of change. Balogun and Hope Hailey (2004) build on this point to highlight important contextual features that need to be taken into account in designing change programmes. Figure 13.3 summarises these.

- **Time**. The time available for change could differ dramatically. A business facing immediate decline in turnover or profits from rapid changes in its markets has a quite different context for change compared with a business where the management may see the need for change coming in the future, perhaps years away, and have time to plan it carefully as a staged incremental process.
- **Scope**. The scope of change might differ in terms of either the breadth of change across an organisation or the depth of culture change required. The scope of change in a large organisation is wholly different in terms of both breadth and depth and, in consequence, likely to be a much bigger challenge than adaptive change in a successful small business.
- **Preservation**. Such preservation of some aspects of an organisation may be needed, in particular, competences on which changes need to be based. For example, a computer software business may need to preserve the expertise and motivation of its technical specialists as it grows.
- **Diversity**. A diversity of experience, views and opinions within an organisation may help the change process. Conversely, if an organisation has followed a strategy for many decades, this may have led to a very homogeneous way of seeing the world. This could hamper change. Gauging the nature and extent of diversity is important.
- **Capability**. Is there capability or experience of managing change in the organisation? There may be managers who have managed change effectively in the past, or a workforce that has been used to and has accepted past changes.
- **Capacity**. A capacity for change in terms of available resources will also be significant. Change can be costly in financial terms and in management time.

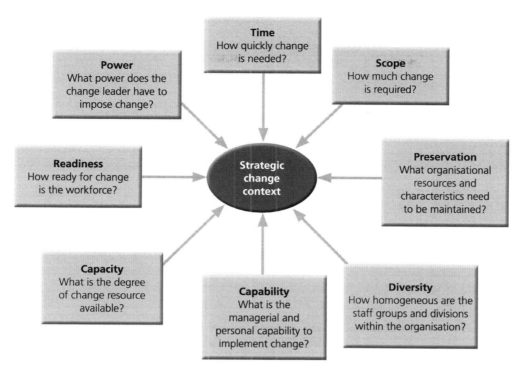

FIGURE 13.3 The context of strategic change

From *Exploring Strategic Change*, 3rd edition, Balogun and Hope Hailey, Pearson Education Limited, © Pearson Education Limited 2004, 2008

- **Readiness**. What is the readiness for change? Is there a felt need for change across the organisation or widespread or pockets of resistance?
- **Power**. Who has the power to effect change? Often it is assumed that the chief executive has the power, but with resistance from below or external stakeholders, this may not be the case. It may also be that the chief executive supposes that others in the organisation have the power to effect change when they do not.

 **CASE EXAMPLE** **13.1**

The UK Ministry of Defence (MoD) was spared the worst of government cuts imposed in 2010, but still took a 7–8% cut in budget. This was followed by a fuller strategic review in 2011 that proposed transformational change. The top eight recommendations were about structure and systems, but the underlying message was the need to address people and behavioural dimensions in the MoD.

However, the MoD had been through numerous initiatives or change but with limited success. Why?

- **Time**. Military staff move locations frequently. Someone with 35 years' service may have moved 20 times. Three years is viewed as a feasible cycle time, and those who wish to make an impact do so by initiating change, but they move on before initiatives are completed.
- **Scope**. In 2012, the MoD comprised a workforce of about 270,000 (but was reducing), which included 85,000 civilian personnel. It also relied on a further 300,000 in its supply chain. The MoD is the sum of many parts, so it is important for it to move in a coherent manner. Change in one part of the system often runs into resistance and difficulty, or has unforeseen implications for other parts of the system.
- **Preservation**. A key element to be retained is the 'can do' culture of the military. However, politicians do not recognise that, with the staff cuts of serving personnel and civil servants, they cannot expect the MoD to carry out the full spectrum of capabilities previously delivered, let alone manage major changes.

CASE EXAMPLE **13.1** *continued*

- **Diversity**. While views and expectations may differ between commanders, civil servants and outsourced operators, the different groupings are themselves highly homogeneous in their views, processes and behaviours.
- **Capability and capacity**. There is a lack of change management skills, with little investment in training in leading change. With the reduction in staff, important roles needed to deliver change were being lost. Moreover, the MoD was not clear about the skills and knowledge that it was losing as part of its downsizing.
- **Readiness**. Much past and current change fundamentally affects the roles and responsibilities of front-line command staff, and is therefore heavily resisted. Change fatigue is also rife as a result of the numerous change initiatives, few of which run long enough to take effect.
- **Power**. In typical military fashion, some senior posts have had the word 'transformation' included in their title and this is thought to get the job done. Such personnel may say the right things, but action on the ground and leading by example are in short supply.

Source: Professor Derrick Neal of the Defence Academy, Shrivenham, cited by Johnson et al. (2014), p.474.

This consideration of context needs to be borne in mind throughout the rest of this chapter. In a study of attempts to manage change in hospitals (Dennis et al., 2001) it was found that their governance and organisational structures prevented any clear authority to manage change. This, combined with resource constraints, meant that major change initiatives were unlikely to succeed. In such circumstances, it may be that the context needs to be changed before the strategic change itself can occur. For example, it could be that new managers with experience of managing change need to be introduced to enhance the capability and readiness for change and get the organisation to a point where it is ready to embark on a more significant strategic change programme. Or perhaps people with a greater diversity of experience in line with the future strategic direction need to be brought in. Or it may need to be recognised that in some contexts change has to be managed in stages. The researchers found that change tended to take place by an initiative making limited progress, then stalling, followed by a later one making further advances.

2.3 Cultural context and force-field analysis

Understanding the prevailing culture of an organisation can help decide the type of change needed, as well as an organisation's readiness for change. Chapter 5 introduced the cultural web as a means of diagnosing the culture of an organisation. Together with an understanding of the context of the organisation, this can be used to inform discussions about what changes are required. It helps identify what is problematic about the existing culture but also what might be added or introduced if change is to occur. It is useful in this respect not least because it embraces the 'softer' aspects of culture, such as organisational symbols, but also political processes and the 'harder' aspects of organisations, such as operating routines, structures and control systems. What typically emerges from such an exercise is that all these aspects of an organisation's culture can be both important blockages and facilitators to change.

STOP AND THINK **13.3**

How might the cultural web be used to help manage change?

Kurt Lewin (1951), an early writer to point out the significance of resistance to change (which we discuss further below), saw change as a matter of moving from one position of equilibrium to another. This caused him to consider what was maintaining this status quo. Through a process of **force field analysis**, he believed it possible to map the forces for change and the forces resisting change, as in Figure 13.4.

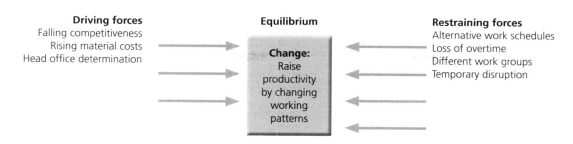

FIGURE 13.4 Lewin's force field

From *Organizational Change*, 4th edition, Senior and Swailes, Pearson Education Limited, © Barbara Senior and Stephen Swailes 2010

This is based on an understanding of the context of change, including the existing culture. It allows some key questions to be asked:

- What aspects of the current situation would block change, and how can these be overcome?
- What aspects of the current situation might aid change in the desired direction, and how might these be reinforced?
- What needs to be introduced or developed to aid change?

This can be used in a particular situation. The example in Figure 13.4 analyses the situation in an organisation seeking to achieve the strategic goal of raising productivity by changing working patterns. These issues might be attached to arrows showing the relevant forces, with their size adapted to show their relative strength.

TEST YOUR KNOWLEDGE 13.2

a Summarise the range of external trends or factors that may impact on organisational change.
b Identify the contextual factors that need to be taken into account when designing change programmes.
c Explain what is meant by 'force field analysis'.

3 Roles in the change process

3.1 The politics of change

This section is concerned with the role people play in managing strategic change and how they do it. It begins by considering the politics of change and then the roles in strategic change played by strategic leaders, middle managers, change teams and the influence of outsiders such as consultants and external stakeholders.

Change invariably affects the status quo and therefore inherently implies political activity. Many individuals high in the organisation have a lot to lose from change. They have risen to their positions of authority by developing skills and behaviours favoured by the organisation. Change may threaten those skills and patterns. What if they are no longer the ones the organisation values? This creates the potential for others in the organisation to gain power at their expense.

Politics suggests that the impetus for change is more likely to come from outside change agents, employees who are new to the organisation (and have less invested in the status quo) or from managers slightly removed from the main power structure. Some managers may be seen as major impediments to change, particularly if change is a threat to their status and position. Yet they may be expected to implement changes to demonstrate that they are not merely caretakers. By acting as agents of change they can symbolically convey to various constituencies – shareholders, suppliers, employees, customers – that they are on top of problems and adapting to a dynamic environment. When forced to introduce change, these long-time power-holders tend to implement first-order or relatively small-scale changes. Radical change is too threatening. Power struggles within the organisation will determine, to a large degree, the speed and quantity of change. Some will be sources of resistance and this is discussed in Section 5. This, incidentally, explains why boards that recognise the imperative for the rapid introduction of major change in their organisations frequently turn to outside candidates for new leadership.

Some of the mechanisms associated with managing change from a political perspective according to Johnson et al. (2014) are:

- **Controlling or acquiring resources** (or identification with important resources or expertise). The ability to withdraw or allocate resources can be a valuable tool in building readiness for change.
- **Association with powerful stakeholder groups (elites).** This can help build a power base. Similarly, association with a change agent who is respected or visibly successful can help a manager overcome resistance to change. Such resistance can vary from powerful individuals in senior positions to whole layers of resistance, perhaps in the form of senior executives in a threatened function or service.
- **Building alliances and networks.** Doing this may be important in overcoming the resistance of more powerful groups. Attempting to convert the whole organisation to accept change is difficult, but there may be parts of the organisation, or individuals within it, more sympathetic to change than others, with whom a change agent might build support. He or she may also seek to marginalise those who are resistant to change. Analysing power and interest using stakeholder mapping (Chapter 6) can, therefore, be useful to identify bases of alliance and likely resistance.
- **Symbolic change**. To build power, it may be necessary to identify initially with the very symbols that preserve and reinforce the paradigm: to work within committee structures, identify with the organisational rituals or stories that exist, and so on. On the other hand, in breaking resistance to change, removing, challenging or changing rituals and symbols may be a very powerful means of achieving the questioning of what is taken for granted.

While it is necessary to identify blockages to change and understand mechanisms of change, it is also important to consider the roles that individuals or groups play in the change process, and the sorts of skill they require.

3.2 Change agency

A **change agent** is an individual or group that effects change in an organisation. These may be at the top of the organisation, but might also come from elsewhere. The creator of a strategy may rely on others to bring the change into effect. It may also be that there is a group of change agents from within the organisation or perhaps from outside, such as consultants, who have a whole team working on a project, together with managers from within the organisation.

 STOP AND THINK 13.4

Typically, we look to senior managers as agents of change but for major change efforts, top managers may turn to temporary outside consultants with specialised knowledge in the theory and methods of change.
   What advantages and disadvantages come from using outsiders?

Personal traits of change agents are relevant. The successful change agent will need:

- to be sensitive to the external context of change – the triggers in the environment that give rise to change or the pressure from external stakeholders;
- to be sensitive to organisational context, building on or relating to the values and beliefs of those in or around the organisation who advocate or feel sympathy towards the need for change and the history of the organisation;

- to understand the overall strategy and therefore the magnitude and type of change necessary; and
- to use an appropriate style of managing change, adapting that style to the circumstances rather than imposing his or her style without regard for the specific context of change.

The literature on leadership argues that they have visionary capacity, are good at team-building and team-playing, are self-analytical, good at self-learning and have mental agility, and are also self-directed and self-confident. There is a tendency to overemphasise such personal attributes, but managing change certainly places special demands on change agents. Peters and Waterman (1982) argue that the successful manager of change in organisations masters two ends of the spectrum. By this they mean that the change agent is simultaneously able to cope with potentially conflicting ways of managing.

- They have an ability to undertake or understand detailed analysis, and, at the same time, to be visionary about the future. They need to be seen as having insight into the future, and yet action-oriented about making things happen.
- In challenging the status quo, they need the ability to maintain credibility and carry people with the change, while attacking the taken-for-granted and current ways of doing things.
- They need the ability to encapsulate often quite complex issues in straightforward ways that people can understand.

In a development programme for its senior managers, Cable and Wireless used the following competency description for a change agent:

- willingness to challenge paradigms/status quo;
- resilient in the face of resistance;
- understands and articulates the positive effects of change;
- champions change and new ideas; and
- plans for change, including management of risk, setting levels and managing relationships.

An important point is that the perspective that the change agent brings to the situation may not always be the same as the organisational context in which he or she is operating. Sensitivity to context is therefore important.

3.3 Strategic leadership

The management of change is, however, often directly linked to the role of a strategic leader. Kotter (1990) and other writers describe leadership as being about the management of change. More generally, however, leadership is seen as the process of influencing an organisation (or individuals or a group within an organisation) towards achieving an aim or goal. So a leader may not necessarily be someone at the top, but someone who is in a position to have influence in their organisation. In this sense leadership may be seen as the full-time job of a few and the part-time job of many!

Leaders are often categorised in two ways (Kets De Vries, 1994):

1 **Charismatic or transformational leaders.** These are mainly concerned with building a vision for the organisation and motivating people to achieve it. These leaders have particularly beneficial impact on performance when people see the organisation facing uncertainty (Waldman et al., 2001).

2 **Instrumental or transactional leaders.** These focus more on designing systems and controlling the organisation's operational activities.

The most successful strategic leaders are able to tailor their style to the situation (Tannenbaum and Schmidt, 1973; Goleman, 2000). Indeed, it could be a problem if they cannot as some styles might well lead to approaches to change not suited to the particular needs of the specific change context. Those at the top of an organisation will be seen by others, not least those who work for them, but also other stakeholders, as intimately associated with strategic change programmes when they occur. In this sense they are symbolically highly significant in the change process.

 **CASE EXAMPLE 13.3**

Tesco's boss, Terry Leahy

With a £250 million hole in its accounts and shareholders baying for boardroom blood, Tesco has hit a new low in 2014. By contrast, in 2004 Tesco was right at the top of its game, super-confident, relentlessly customer-focused and apparently unstoppably profitable, thanks to the leadership of its CEO.

Sir Terry Leahy, former CEO of Tesco, oversaw major transformations. Yet he is 'disarmingly ordinary … his speech is serious and straightforward. He's no showman … you are not confronted with some huge presence … he talks only about Tesco … it's like meeting a religious leader faithfully reciting a creed.' And strategically: 'He is a combination of the very smart – he's always seeing over the hill – and the very simple … you give him a problem and he'll go off and work until he's solved it. His co-workers respect him for his decision-making, but he doesn't make his moves on a whim. Everything is analysed, taken apart, discussed and put back together … he's gathered around him senior managers who've been with him and the group for years. He's in charge but he's also collegiate.' He also likes to talk and listen to people in the stores. 'What makes Leahy different is the extraordinary degree to which he chats with junior staff and absorbs their views and the attention he pays to customers.'

Since Leahy's departure in 2011, Tesco has suffered a series of setbacks including issues of undue pressure on suppliers and intense competition from the discounters Aldi and Lidl. Sir Terry's chosen successor Philip Clarke resigned in 2014 to be replaced by David Lewis, who is trying to return Tesco to its former glory. In a bold move, in January 2017 Tesco announced its £3.7bn purchase of Booker, the cash and carry giant behind the Londis and Budgens convenience chains, in a deal that will tighten its grip on the UK's £195bn food market. The deal is expected to be scrutinised by the competition authorities as Tesco is already the country's biggest retailer, with more than 3,500 stores and control of close to 30% of the grocery market. The proposed acquisition would turn Tesco into a major supplier to small retailers, serving 125,000 independent convenience stores as well as 468,000 restaurants and pubs, adding 2% to its share of UK grocery sales.

Source: Based on reports by Chris Blackhurst in *Management Today*, 2004 and 2014 and Zoe Wood and Julia Kollewe in the *Guardian* in Jan 2017

So perhaps some of the successful leadership behaviours are not all that they seem.

3.4 Middle managers and other organisational members

If we think of strategic change as a top-down process, this places middle managers as implementers of planned change. Their role is to put into effect the direction determined by top management making sure that resources are controlled appropriately, monitoring performance and, where necessary, explaining the strategy to those reporting to them. Some, however, may see managers not as facilitators of strategy, but as impediments to its success. Indeed, this is sometimes seen as one reason for reducing the numbers and layers of management to speed up communication between top management and others in the organisation. However, there is evidence that middle managers can and do provide a real benefit in both the development and the implementation of planned change. They can play three vital roles:

1   systematic implementation and control;
2   reinterpretation and adjustment of strategic responses as events unfold (e.g., relationships with customers, suppliers, and the workforce);
3   a bridge between top management and members of the organisation at lower levels.

So middle managers are likely to contribute substantially either galvanising commitment to strategy and the change process or blocking it. The critical measure of the effectiveness of a change strategy is the extent to which it affects the behaviour of those who interact with the organisation; for example, by customers buying more products, becoming more aware of a firm's benefits or making greater use of the services of a hospital or library. If this is to happen, people perhaps in very junior positions in organisations play a crucial role because they are the interface between the organisation and those affected by planned change outside the organisation. A critical question is how their commitment and understanding can best be gained. Relying on intellectual persuasion or assuming that changes in structure and control procedures are enough to effect major change may be a mistake.

CASE EXAMPLE 13.4

A senior executive in a bank, who understood the powerful blockages within the bank's culture built up over decades, had just heard the chief executive present the new strategy to 200 employees. The presentation had included a careful explanation of the strategy and the new structure demonstrated with videos, slides and glossy hand-outs. The presentation was heard in respectful silence, but as the audience left for lunch, he remarked: 'There really is no contest between a PowerPoint presentation and 100 years of culture. This is a bank; no matter how well intentioned, that talk will not change things.' The point he was making is that the day-to-day procedures and routines operating in the bank would persist.

Based on an example in Johnson and Scholes (2008)

3.5 External stakeholders and outsiders

As we saw in Chapter 6, stakeholders can be identified according to their level of interest and political influence. It is important to tailor approaches to change to these different stakeholders. For example, those with a high level of interest in the organisational change but with limited power may simply need to be kept informed of change requirements and processes, so careful thought needs to be given to means of communication. The key players are those with high power and high interest.

The use of outsiders in the change process can be productive. A new chief executive from outside the organisation may be introduced into a business to effect change. He or she brings a fresh perspective on the organisation, not bound by the constraints of the past, or the everyday routines and ways of doing things that can prevent strategic change. Consultants are often used in change processes. They may help formulate the strategy or plan and facilitate change processes. Consultants do not inherit the cultural baggage of the organisation and can therefore bring a dispassionate view to the process. They also signal symbolically the importance of the change. However, they are disadvantaged in that they often have an inadequate understanding of the organisation's history, culture, operating procedures and personnel. Outside consultants are more willing to initiate second-order change, which can be a benefit or a disadvantage, because they do not have to live with the repercussions. Other stakeholders may be key influencers of change. For example, government investors, customers, suppliers and business analysts all have the potential to act as change agents on organisations.

TEST YOUR KNOWLEDGE 13.3

a What is a 'change agent'?
b What is meant by strategic leadership?
c What contribution may external stakeholders play in strategic change?

4   Approaches to managing change

4.1 Style

Whoever the change agent is they need to consider the style of management they adopt. Different styles are likely to be more or less appropriate according to context. Kotter and Schlesinger (1979) suggest five tactics for use by organisations.

Education and communication

Any resistance can be overcome or prevented through communicating with employees to help them see the rationale for a change. This tactic assumes that people will cooperate and support change if they see the need for it. Communication can be achieved through face-to-face discussions, intranet sites, group presentations, and so on. It works, provided that management–employee relations are characterised by mutual trust and credibility. If these conditions do not exist, the change is unlikely to succeed. Assuming that reasoned argument in a top-down fashion will overcome perhaps years of embedded assumptions about what 'really matters' could be naive. Change may be more effective if those affected by it are involved in its development and planning.

CASE EXAMPLE 13.5

Michael Ying, former chairman of Esprit Asia Holdings, learned that communication could help overcome resistance to change. Ying, in trying to integrate Esprit's Asian and European operations, recognised major differences in the way they managed people and the business. The European operation was nationalistic, autocratic and had a rigid structure, whereas the Asian operation was more open-minded and willing to learn. When visiting the European managers, Ying communicated his approach to problem-solving and listened to the Europeans' concerns. This helped the Europeans to become receptive to Ying's plan of merging the two operations.

Participation

Participation in the change process is the involvement of those affected by strategic change in the change agenda; for example, in the identification of strategic issues, the strategic decision-making process, the setting of priorities, the planning of strategic change or the drawing up of action plans. It is difficult for individuals to resist a change decision in which they participated. Such involvement can foster a more positive attitude to change and people feel increased ownership of and commitment to the change process. It may therefore be a way of building readiness and capability for change. However, there is the inevitable risk that solutions will be found from within the existing culture, so anyone who takes this approach may need to retain the ability to intervene in the process.

Facilitation and support

Support may be sought for particular stages of change, such as ideas generation, data collection, detailed planning, the development of rationales for change or the identification of critical success factors, may be delegated to project teams or taskforces. The change agent retains responsibility for the change, ensures the monitoring of progress and that change is seen to occur. An advantage is that it involves members of the organisation, not only in originating ideas, but also in the partial implementation of solutions, giving rise to commitment to the change. The drawback is that it is time-consuming, expensive and offers no assurance of success.

Negotiation

One way for the organisation to deal with potential resistance is to exchange something of value for minimising the resistance. For instance, if the resistance stems from a few powerful individuals, a specific reward package can be negotiated that will meet their personal needs.

Negotiation as a tactic may be necessary when resistance comes from a powerful source. Yet one cannot ignore its potentially high costs and there is the risk that, once a company negotiates with one party to avoid resistance, it is open to the possibility that others in positions of power may want the same.

Manipulation and coercion

Coercion is an extreme form of direction. It is the imposition of change. This is the explicit use of power and may be necessary if the organisation is facing a crisis. Manipulation refers to covert attempts to twist and distort facts to make them appear more attractive, withholding undesirable information and creating false rumours to get employees to accept a change. If management threatens to close down a particular manufacturing plant if that plant's employees fail to accept a pay cut, and if the threat is untrue, management is using manipulation. Manipulation and coercion are relatively inexpensive and are easy way to use but can backfire if the targets become aware that they are being tricked or used.

Johnson et al. make some important points about the style adopted during strategic change:

- **Different styles for different stages**. Styles of managing change may need to differ according to stages in a change process. Clear direction may be vital to motivate a desire or create a readiness to change; participation can help in gaining wider commitment across the organisation and developing capabilities to identify blockages to change.
- **Time and scope**. Participative styles are most appropriate for incremental change within organisations, but where transformational change is required, more directive approaches may be more appropriate. Even where top management see themselves adopting participative styles, their subordinates may perceive this as directive and, indeed, may welcome such direction (Dunphy and Stace, 1993).
- **Power**. In organisations with hierarchical power structures a directive style may be common and difficult to break away from. In 'flatter' structures or more networked organisations, collaboration and participation will be both common and desirable.
- **Personality types**. Different styles suit different managers' personality types. However, those with the greatest capability to manage change may have the ability to adopt different styles in different circumstances.
- **Styles are not mutually exclusive**. For example, clear direction on overall vision might aid a more collaborative approach to more detailed strategy development. Education and communication may be appropriate for some stakeholders, such as financial institutions; participation may be appropriate for groups in parts of the organisation where it is necessary to build capability and readiness; whereas if there are parts of the organisation where change has to happen fast, timing may demand a more directive style.

4.2 Change tactics

So how can change be effected? The answer lies in changing established assumptions and routines and ways of doing things that are the elements of culture. But Pascale (1990) and others have argued that it is easier to change behaviours and, through this, change assumptions than it is to try to change established assumptions and thereby behaviour. This is the distinction between what is known as **programmatic change**, by which is meant the attempt to convince people by persuasion and logic of the need for change, and **task alignment**, by which is meant changes in behaviour and routines. The argument is that task alignment is a more powerful way of achieving change than the programmatic. Those who take this view argue that the style of the change agent needs to take this into account. Others argue that long-term change is best achieved by trying to create a learning organisation (see Senge, 1990), in which, in effect, all its members need to become strategic thinkers, questioning and challenging their colleagues and contributing to the development of strategy. Few organisations have succeeded in this, but some take it seriously. For example, organisations such as Motorola and Unipart have set up 'corporate universities' to develop such a capacity.

Choosing the appropriate levers or tactics, rather than following a set formula for managing strategic change, is critical. This will depend on the change context and the skills and styles of those managing change. For example, to take the extremes, if the need is to overcome resistance to achieve fast results, then the emphasis may be on achieving behavioural compliance to a change programme. On the other hand, if there is a need and the time to 'win hearts and minds' then there will need to be a focus on changing people's values and a much greater emphasis on their involvement in changing the culture of the organisation. However, most successful change initiatives rely on multiple levers for change.

Johnson et al. (2014) summarise these levers as follows.

Challenging the 'taken-for-granted'

This is the need to change often long-standing mind-sets or taken-for-granted assumptions – the paradigm. Some believe that sufficient evidence; perhaps in the form of careful strategic analysis, will itself challenge and therefore change the paradigm. However, where long-standing assumptions have persisted, they will be very resistant to change. Others argue that such assumptions can be challenged by exposing them analytically and encouraging people to question and challenge each other's assumptions so that they are more likely to be questioned. Others argue that senior managers in particular are often too far removed from the realities of their organisations and need to be brought face to face with them. They may rarely speak to customers directly or experience the services offered by their own firms.

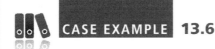 **CASE EXAMPLE 13.6**

A senior executive of a rail company explained that in the past senior executives in the organisation had always travelled first class or by chauffeur-driven car. Hardly any of them had ever travelled in a crowded railway carriage. He introduced a policy that all senior executives should travel by economy class wherever possible.

Changing operational processes and routines

The day-to-day processes and routines of the operations of the organisation that deliver strategy tend to persist over time and guide people's behaviour. Such routines can be the basis of the organisation's core competences and therefore its competitive advantage. However, they can also be serious blockages to change. Planning the implementation of an intended strategy means identifying key changes in the routines of the organisation required to deliver that strategy. In effect, strategic change needs to be considered in terms of re-engineering organisational processes (Champy and Hammer, 1993).

 **CASE EXAMPLE 13.7**

In Shell Lubricants, seven people were involved in different aspects of order-processing routines. In the search for improved efficiency and customer service, one person was given overall responsibility for an order, with the consequent reduction in order time of 75%, reduction in order processing costs of 45% and vastly improved customer satisfaction.

Changing organisational processes may also have the effect of challenging the often taken-for-granted assumptions underpinning them. As Pascale (op. cit.) argues, it is easier to change behaviour and by so doing change taken-for-granted assumptions than to try to change taken-for-granted assumptions as a way of changing behaviour. If this is so, the style of change needs to take this into account: it suggests that education and communication may be less powerful than involving people in the activities of changing.

Operational change may not simply be the outcome of planned strategic change; it could be that opportunities for operational change can stimulate innovation and new strategic thinking. Hammer gives the example of Taco Bell in the US, which saved costs and improved the quality of its offering by re-examining its operational processes in terms of best practice in manufacturing instead of fast food operations.

Even when changes in routines are not planned from the top, people do change them and this may result in wider strategic change. This may occur through the bending of routines. Managers may deliberately 'bend the rules of the game' such that new routines become acceptable. It is an incremental, experimental process that is likely to suffer setbacks and require persistence and political acumen.

The overall lesson is that changes in routines may appear to be mundane, but can have significant impact.

Symbolic processes

Change levers may also be symbolic in nature. Chapter 5 explained how the symbols of an organisation might help preserve the paradigm. Here the concern is their role in managing change. Symbols are objects, events, acts or people that convey, maintain or create meaning over and above their functional purpose. Changing symbols can help reshape beliefs and expectations because meaning becomes apparent in the day-to-day experiences people have of organisations, such as the symbols that surround them (e.g. office layout and décor), the type of language and technology used and organisational rituals.

 **CASE EXAMPLE** **13.8**

The head nurse of a recovery unit for patients who had been severely ill decided that, if nurses wore everyday clothes rather than nurses' uniforms, it would signal to patients that they were on the road to recovery and a normal life; and to nurses that they were concerned with rehabilitation. However, the decision had other implications for the nurses too. It blurred the status distinction between nurses and other non-professional members of staff. Nurses preferred to wear their uniforms. Whilst they recognised that uniforms signalled a medically fragile role of patients, they reinforced their separate and professional status as acute care workers.

Source: Michael G. Pratt and Anat Rafaeli, 'Organizational dress as a symbol of multi-layered social identities', *Academy of Management Journal*, August 1997.

This example suggests that there is an important qualification to the idea that the manipulation of symbols can be a useful lever for managing change. The significance and meaning of symbols are dependent on how they are interpreted. So a change agent's intentions in the use of symbolic levers may not be interpreted as intended.

4.3 Strategic change programmes

This section revisits the types of change identified in section 1.2 and considers which levers managers use in which contexts. It also suggests some general lessons about managing change programmes.

Reconstruction and turnaround strategy

There are circumstances where the emphasis has to be on rapid reconstruction. Without this a business could face closure, enter terminal decline or be taken over. This is commonly referred to as a **turnaround strategy**, where the emphasis is on speed of change and rapid cost reduction and/or revenue generation, and managers need to prioritise quick and significant improvements. Typically, it is a situation where a directive approach to change is required.

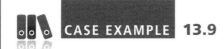

CASE EXAMPLE 13.9

The company Pace manufactures products for the digital TV markets – in particular, set-top boxes for customers such as Sky and Canal +. When Neil Gaydon took over as chief executive in 2006, the company was facing bankruptcy with a loss of £15 million on sales of £175 million and a bank facility that had just been withdrawn. By 2010, the company was reporting profits of £69.9 million on revenues of over £1 billion.

Gaydon broadened the customer base: 90% of revenue came from just two customers. By 2010, Pace had more than 100 customers worldwide. In addition, he focused on key areas of market development – in particular, on high-definition television and on pay-tv operations, which have a higher price and level, and offer better margins. He also introduced a major reorganisation of the company. He significantly pruned management and organised the company into small teams focused on particular customers. Each team was given a lot of freedom and controlled its own profit and loss account, and bonuses were linked to the teams' performance, incentivising everyone to get results. Pace, notorious for late deliveries and overruns on R&D costs, significantly improved its reliability and cost control.

Slater and Lovett (1999) describe some of the main elements of turnaround strategies as follows:

- **Crisis stabilisation**. This is required to regain control over the deteriorating position. This requires a short-term focus on cost reduction and/or revenue increase, typically involving some of the steps identified in Table 13.3. Too often turnarounds are seen as no more than cost-cutting exercises when a wider alignment between causes of decline and solutions may be important. For example, where decline is principally a result of changes in the external environment it may be folly to expect that cost cutting alone can lead to renewed growth.

TABLE 13.3 Turnaround: crisis stabilisation (Johnson et al., 2014)

Increasing revenue	Reducing costs
■ Ensure marketing mix tailored to key market segments ■ Review pricing strategy to maximise revenue ■ Focus organisational activities on needs of target market sector customers ■ Exploit additional opportunities for revenue creation related to target market ■ Invest funds from reduction of costs in new growth areas	■ Reduce labour costs and costs of senior management ■ Focus on productivity improvement ■ Reduce marketing costs not focused on target market ■ Tighten financial controls ■ Tighten control on cash expenses ■ Establish competitive bidding for suppliers; defer creditor payments; speed up debtor payment ■ Reduce inventory ■ Eliminate non-profitable products/services

- **Management changes**. These may be required, especially at the top. This usually includes the introduction of a new chairperson or chief executive, as well as changes in the board. The old management may well be the ones that were in charge when the problems developed and be seen as the cause of them by key stakeholders. It may also be necessary to bring in managers with experience of turnaround management or with different approaches to the way the organisation has operated in the past.
- **Gaining stakeholder support**. In a turnaround situation it is vital that key stakeholders such as the bank or employees are kept clearly informed of the situation and improvements as they are being made. A clear assessment of the power of different stakeholder groups is vitally important in managing turnaround.
- **Clarifying the target market(s)**. Establishing which markets are most likely to generate cash and grow profits is central to turnaround success, which involves getting closer to customers

and improving the flow of marketing information, especially to senior levels of management, so as to focus revenue-generating activities on key market segments. Indeed, a reason for the poor performance of the organisation could be because it had this wrong in the first place.

- **Refocusing.** Clarifying the target market also provides the opportunity to discontinue or outsource products and services that are not targeted on those markets, and are absorbing management time for little or no return.
- **Financial restructuring.** This typically involves changing the existing capital structure, raising additional finance or renegotiating agreements with creditors, especially banks.
- **Prioritising critical improvement areas.** i.e. the things that give quick and significant improvement.

Revolutionary strategic change

Revolutionary change is especially challenging. The need is not only for fast change, but also cultural change. At the same time, the need for change is not always as evident to people in the organisation as in a turnaround situation. This situation may have come about as a result of many years of relative decline in a market, with people wedded to products or processes no longer valued by customers or clients.

Managing such change is likely to involve the following:

- **Clear strategic direction.** In these circumstances the need to articulate a clear strategic direction and decisive action in line with that direction is critical. CEOs who are seen to provide such direction are often credited with making a major difference. They may well also become the internal and external symbol of such change.
- **Combining economic and symbolic levers.** Some of the decisions outlined for reconstruction/turnaround may be taken: for example, portfolio changes or greater market focus. However, often these are also employed to send major symbolic messages of change. In the newspaper industry, for example, Rupert Murdoch's decision in the 1970s to close his newspapers' office in Fleet Street and move to purpose-built modern premises in Wapping is still regarded as the single most significant event in modernising not only his business, but also the industry.

 STOP AND THINK **13.5**

What other symbolic levers can you think of?

- **An outside perspective.** The introduction of new managers, often at mid-level, with different perspectives is common. For example, the reform of public sector organisations has seen the introduction of managers with private sector experience. Consultants may also be used to provide a dispassionate analysis of the need for change or facilitate the change process.
- **Multiple styles of change management.** While a directive style of change management is likely to be evident, this may need to be accompanied by other styles. It may, for example, be supported by determined efforts to educate about the need for change.
- **Working with the existing culture.** It may be possible to work with elements of the existing culture rather than attempt wholesale culture change. This involves identifying those aspects of culture that can be built on and developed and those that have to be changed – in effect a force-field approach (see Section 2.3).
- **Monitoring change.** Revolutionary change is likely to require the setting and monitoring of unambiguous targets that people have to achieve. Often these will be linked to overall financial targets and in turn to improved returns to shareholders.

Evolutionary strategic change

Managing change as evolution involves transformational change, but incrementally. It can be thought of as the creation of an organisation capable of continual change. Trying to achieve this in practice is a significant challenge for management because it requires:

- **Empowering the organisation**. Rather than top-down management there is the need for a high level of participation – for people throughout the organisation to accept the responsibility for contributing strategic ideas, for innovating and for accepting change.
- **A clear strategic vision**. It is the responsibility of top management to create the context within which new ideas can emerge from below with a coherent view of long-term goals. This requires them to provide very clear guidelines (vision or mission) and to find the balance between the clarity of such a vision that allows people to see how they can contribute to future strategy whilst avoiding specifying that strategy in such detail as to constrain the enthusiasm to contribute and innovate.
- **Continual change and a commitment to experimentation**. This should occur throughout the organisation.

Sirkin et al. (2005) claim that the likelihood of success of such programmes is greatly increased if the following are in place:

- **Milestones for reviewing progress**. Change programmes should be reviewed formally by senior managers against key tasks. The criteria against which such reviews will take place also need to be explicit and widely known.
- **A high 'integrity' change team**. A team that has the skills to execute the change programme. The selection of such a team, with the required mix of skills, is a key responsibility of senior management.
- **Visible commitment to change by top management**. There should be consistency in explaining it and it needs to be accompanied by straight talking about change with those who will be affected.
- **Time and effort for managing change**. It is the responsibility of top management to make sure they have sufficient time and resource to carry out their tasks.

4.4 Kotter's change model

Kotter (1990) argues that change involves numerous phases that, together, usually take a long time and that skipping steps creates only an illusion of speed and never produces a satisfying result. Kotter's 1990 model is based on a process of change, which acknowledges that, although the journey is not a stepped one, it can still be managed. His 'Eight Steps to Transforming Your Organisation' pay particular attention to how to manage people's reaction to change. His staged approach is shown in Figure 13.5.

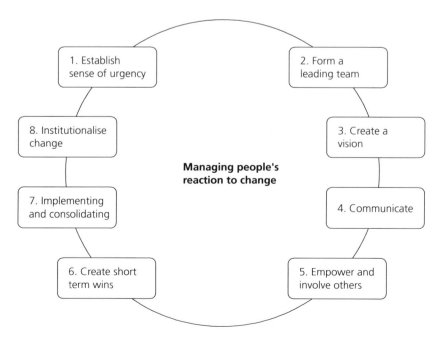

FIGURE 13.5 Kotter's change model

1 **Establish a sense of urgency**. Change proceeds in waves that begin with waking up to the need to change and unhooking from the old ways, through a period of discovery and design of a new organisation. Finally comes a period of implementing the new path with each person, which affects the very core of the organisation.

2 **Form a leading team**. A strong guiding coalition is always needed – one with the right composition, level of trust and a shared objective.

3 **Create a vision**. Vision refers to a picture of the future with some commentary on why people should strive to create that future. In a change process, a vision clarifies the general direction for change; it motivates people to take action in the right direction, even if the first steps are personally painful; it helps coordinate the actions of different people.

4 **Communicate the vision**. A great vision can serve a useful purpose even if it is understood by just a few key people. The real power of a vision is unleashed only when most of those involved have a common understanding of its goals and direction.

5 **Empower and involve others**. Employees who are affected by or involved in the change have different needs, agendas and understanding of what will happen in the change process. They often work at cross-purposes or undermine each other. Misunderstandings need to be cleared up as soon as possible. Experience of change indicates that people are more likely to resist change in which they have no input. Input or involvement engenders a sense of ownership of the situation, not to become the decision-makers, but to draw on their ideas and sustain a dialogue. With the right structure, training, systems and people to build on a well-communicated vision, companies are finding that they can tap an enormous source of power to improve organisational performance.

6 **Create short-term wins**. Major change takes time, sometimes lots of time. Zealous believers will often stay the course no matter what happens. Most of the rest expect to see convincing evidence that all the effort is paying off. Non-believers have even higher standards of proof. They want to see the clear data indicating that the changes are working and that the change process is not absorbing so many resources in the short term as to endanger the organisation.

7 **Implementing and consolidating**. Major change often takes a long time, especially in big organisations. Many forces can stall the process far short of the finish line: turnover of the key change agents, sheer exhaustion on the part of the leaders, bad luck. In these circumstances, short-term wins are essential to keep momentum going, but the celebration of those wins can be lethal if the urgency is lost. With complacency up, the forces of tradition can seep back with remarkable force and speed!

8 **Institutionalise change**. This stage is concerned with embedding and sustaining the change and focusing on looking forward. Some of the issues are establishing the new way and culture of work, and measuring and checking that you are on track; accommodating continual integration and adaptation and continuing to grow and evolve.

 TEST YOUR KNOWLEDGE 13.4

a Identify the priorities of a turnaround strategy.
b According to Kotter, what are the key stages of a strategic change approach?

4.5 Mintzberg's Change Cube

Change programmes arise for a variety of reasons, such as new product or process development, turnaround, quality management systems, etc. They may be organisation-wide or more limited in scope, but either way they are all too often carried out in a fragmented way. Mintzberg's Change Cube tries to put things into perspective.

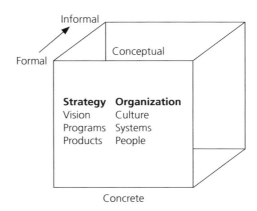

FIGURE 13.6 Mintzberg's Change Cube

From *The Strategy Process: Concepts, Contexts, Cases*, 5th edition, Mintzberg, Lampel, Quinn & Ghoshal, Pearson Education Limited, © Pearson Education Limited 2013

On the left side, change can be about strategy, on the right side about the organisation (see Figure 13.6). Both aspects have to be taken into account in a change programme. In both areas, change can be more or less strategic, esoteric or abstract, or alternatively more operational and tactical. The two sides are matched, with actions changing on one side and actors on the other. The point is that wherever you intervene in this cube, you have to change everything below and alongside.

Finally, all of this can change expressly and formally, or implicitly and informally – to use Mintzberg's own concept of deliberate or emergent. Serious change, however, includes the entire cube: strategy and organisation. This also requires leadership and management, as well as a degree of risk management that boards need to monitor in their governance systems.

5   Resistance to change

5.1 Introduction

Effective management of change requires an understanding of the resistance that frequently meets it.

Resistance can be positive. It provides a degree of stability and predictability to behaviour. If there were not some resistance, organisational behaviour would take on characteristics of chaotic randomness. Resistance to change can also be a source of functional conflict. For example, resistance to a reorganisation plan or a change in a product line can stimulate a healthy debate over the merits of the idea and result in a better decision. But there is a definite downside to resistance to change. It hinders adaptation and organisational progress.

Resistance to change does not necessarily surface in standardised ways. It can be overt, implicit, immediate or deferred.

- **Overt**. It is easiest for management to deal with resistance when it is overt and immediate. For instance, a change is proposed and employees quickly respond by voicing complaints, threatening to go on strike, etc.
- **Implicit**. Resistance efforts that are implicit are more subtle: loss of loyalty to the organisation, loss of motivation to work, more errors or mistakes, increased absenteeism due to 'sickness'. They are therefore more difficult to recognise.
- **Deferred**. Actions that are deferred cloud the link between the source of the resistance and the reaction to it. A change may produce what appears to be only a minimal reaction at the time it is initiated. Resistance surfaces weeks, months or even years later. A single change, which in and of itself might have little impact, becomes the 'straw that breaks the camel's back'. Reactions to change can build up and then explode in a response that seems out of proportion to the change action it follows. The resistance, of course, has merely been deferred. What surfaces is a response to an accumulation of previous changes.

5.2 Sources of resistance

Effective management of change requires an understanding of the resistance that frequently meets it. Fundamentally, resistance is a personal matter, although groups, organisations or whole societies can express it. The sources of resistance can therefore, for analytical purposes, be categorised by individual and organisational sources. In practice, they often overlap.

Organisational resistance

Most organisations, by their very nature, are conservative. They actively resist change. Public agencies want to continue doing what they have been doing for years, whether the need for their service changes or remains the same. Educational institutions, which exist to open minds and challenge established doctrine, are themselves extremely resistant to change. The majority of business firms, too, appear highly resistant to change.

Individual resistance

Individual sources of resistance to change reside in basic human characteristics such as perception, personalities and needs. Elisabeth Kübler-Ross developed a model of personal change after spending time analysing the emotional responses to grief by terminally ill patients. This model, commonly called the Kübler-Ross Grief Cycle, identifies the human emotional response to change over time in a cycle comprising denial, anger, bargaining, depression and acceptance. The emotional rollercoaster is shown in Figure 13.7.

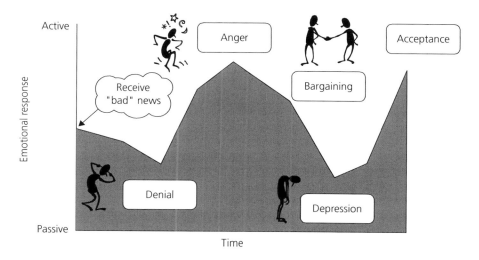

FIGURE 13.7 Stages of grief (Based on Kübler-Ross, 1969)

This emotional cycle is not exclusive to the terminally ill. It also applies to people affected by bad news. The important factor is not that the change is good or bad, but that the person or group perceives it as a significantly negative event. In organisational change these may have the impact shown in Table 13.4.

TABLE 13.4 Human reactions to change

Emotional response	Response
Denial	Suggest problem has corrected itself and it will soon be over Exhibit apathy and numbness Rationalise change away
Anger	Sabotage the change effort Play 'shoot the messenger' Withdraw from society

Emotional response	Response
Bargaining	Cut a deal to spare others harm Suggest other concerns to redirect problem solving
Depression	Express a loss of control Withdraw from society
Acceptance	Express ownership for solutions Focus on achieving benefits

Table 13.5 summarises why individuals may resist change and how managers might respond.

TABLE 13.5 Reasons for resistance (based on Kanter, 1992)

Reason for resistance	Suggested tactics
1. LOSS OF CONTROL Most people want to feel in control of what is going on around them: change is exciting when it is done by us, threatening when it is done to us. If we feel powerless or out of control, we are more likely to feel stress and behave in defensive ways.	Try to involve your team so that they feel more in control and more committed to the change. You/your team might not be involved in the design of the change but what can you control or own during the uncertainty?
2. EXCESS UNCERTAINTY People can resist when there is too much uncertainty, when they don't know where the next step takes them. It can feel safer to stay with what you know than to go forward into the uncertainty.	Try and keep your team up to date with information you can share. What can you tell them about what is happening now, what you anticipate happening next and when more information might be available? You can reduce the excess uncertainty felt by others by showing your own commitment to the change.
3. SURPRISE FACTOR People are likely to resist change when they are unprepared for decisions/outputs that are 'sprung' on them.	Where possible, choose appropriate timings for the information releases. Can you give any advanced warning, so that individuals can adjust their thinking?
4. THE DIFFERENCE EFFECT We are all supported by our own routines, habits and 'knowns'. The greater the difference, the more our own worlds are challenged and need re-establishing and the likelihood of more resistance to the change.	Review whether you need to change 'everything' around you/your team. Are there routines/ways of working that can remain the same? How much do the surroundings need to change?
5. LOSS OF FACE Changing and working in new ways often implies the old way was wrong. Some people feel threatened, that they have lost face and might defend old ways of working, rather than focusing on the new.	Try to put the old ways of working into perspective. Help your team to feel positive about the new ways of working.
6. CONCERNS ABOUT FUTURE COMPETENCE? Although often unarticulated, people are concerned about whether they have the skill set required of the future, what they will have to do and how they will do it. The result can be reasons why change should be avoided.	Identify the skills that will be needed and how can you/your team acquire them. Give messages of positive reinforcement to your team. Identify how you can help the team develop new competence.

Reason for resistance	Suggested tactics
7. RIPPLE EFFECTS Change causes ripple effects outside of the working environment, for each individual. It can affect people's plans and expectations both in and out of work, even though it can appear unrelated to the core of the change.	Find out from your individual team members what the ripple effects are. Where possible show sensitivity towards them, even though you might not be able to do anything about it.
8. MORE WORK For most people, change requires more work and more effort; there is a combination of business as usual and adjusting to the new. Those on 'change project teams' are likely to be working excessive hours.	You are able to provide support to individuals/your team. You might not have financial resources but you can recognise and acknowledge the effort and time they are putting in.
9. PAST RESENTMENTS If an individual is holding a grievance about something that happened in the past, it often surfaces when s/he is asked to do something new and hinders the change.	Such resentments are likely to only be identified by carefully listening to/observing your team. In order to move forward with your team, it might be necessary to air them and try to repair the damage.
10. SOMETIMES THE THREAT IS REAL During change, there are winners and losers. Change opens up opportunities for some and closes doors for others. All those who survive the change experience the loss of the old company/ways of working.	Avoid false promises to others. If there is bad news for someone, it is better they hear about it soon, rather than be kept in uncertainty. Give your team the opportunity to let go of, or mourn the old.

TEST YOUR KNOWLEDGE 13.5

a   What are the sources of resistance?
b   Identify the stages in the cycle of change.
c   Identify three reasons for resistance according to Rosabeth Moss Kanter.

CASE QUESTIONS

1   Use Kotter's change model to advise the CEO on the approach to take to the proposed change in LCU.

2   Advise managers on the likely impact of project change on individuals in LCU.

CHAPTER SUMMARY

- A recurrent theme in this chapter has been that approaches, styles and means of change need to be tailored to the context of that change.
- There are different types of strategic change which can be thought of in terms of the extent of culture change required and its nature – whether it can be achieved through incremental change or requires urgent action (the 'big bang' approach). Different approaches and means of managing change are likely to be required for different types of change.
- It is also important to diagnose other aspects of organisational context such as resources and skills that need to be preserved, the degree of homogeneity or diversity in the organisation, the capability, capacity and readiness for change and the power to make change happen.

- The cultural web and force-field analysis are useful as means of identifying blockages to change and potential levers for change.
- Change agents may need to adopt different styles of managing strategic change according to different contexts and in relation to the involvement and interest of different groups.
- Levers and tactics for managing strategic change need to be considered in terms of the type of change and context of change. Such levers include surfacing and challenging the taken for granted, the need to change operational processes, routines and symbols, the importance of political processes, and other change tactics.
- Frameworks such as Kotter's change model and Mintzberg's Change Cube can help develop an integrated approach to managing change.
- Resistance to change may arise for a variety of reasons and can be a key factor in throwing attempts at strategic change off course.

Afterword: Key issues in strategic management

Strategy – art, science or philosophy?

This book has introduced a lot of strategy tools, concepts and models, all offering ways to simplify the real world, and together forming the components of a 'strategy process' to help us analyse (in organisational terms) where we are now, where we need to get to and how we get there. The word 'process' itself implies a rigid, systematic and technical approach that automatically leads to the right answer. If only it were so simple. The models don't give the right answer, but they do help us to ask the right questions.

As with management, strategy is a mix of art and science. Both are under pressure, as the world reacts to a decade of credit crunch, depression and austerity as well as corporate excess and failings. Big business is under scrutiny like never before. Recent political events such as the UK's Brexit referendum vote and the election of Donald Trump as the US President in 2016 reflect a growing nationalism which seems to be a backlash against big business and globalisation, which many assumed was driving living standards up around the world through open markets and free trade.

Business at a cross roads – a crisis of leadership and governance?

Capitalism is potentially at risk. Management authors such as the UK's Tom Lloyd, in his book *Business at a Cross roads: A Crisis of Leadership*, along with people such as Gary Hamel and Michael Porter, are writing about new ways of doing business and making strategy. Strategy is not only about *what* you do but *how* you do it – how in terms of not only organising and managing people and resources, but also style, morality and ethics.

Political, banking and commercial elites are under attack, as income differentials between the boardroom and the rest of the employees grows. *The Financial Times*, one of the global newspapers of business, wrote about a 'Marie Antoinette moment' and the extremes of income inequality. Business has to react. Get it wrong and business runs the risk of losing its 'licence to operate' granted by society, with growing trade unionism, strikes and civil unrest. Get it right and we may enter a new era of long-term growth and prosperity, enjoyed by all.

The rapidly changing VUCA world that we live in presents its own challenges, of course, with technological advance driving constant disruption from start-ups in garages that, through the internet, can reach the whole world. Harnessing technology to deliver increased productivity is key to future success. The concern is that technology replaces humans, and we already see not only repetitive factory jobs but also clerical and indeed professional jobs being undertaken by machines and robots. What will replace those jobs for the people made redundant?

Purpose, values, diversity and creativity

People want purpose in their lives, and want to feel valued in a way that reflects their personal values, diversity and creativity in the workplace. Companies state that people are our greatest asset – but rarely do human resources appear as assets in the balance sheet. They are still shown as a cost in the P&L account.

The spread of Anglo-Saxon business practices, the focus on quarterly short-term earnings and the primacy of the shareholder is being challenged. The stakeholder model has been mooted as the way forward, with a focus on long-term value, where the rewards of business are shared more 'fairly' in some way. The UK's Conservative government, a right-of-centre and traditionally pro-business government, introduced new proposals about executive pay and worker representation on boards in the autumn of 2016.

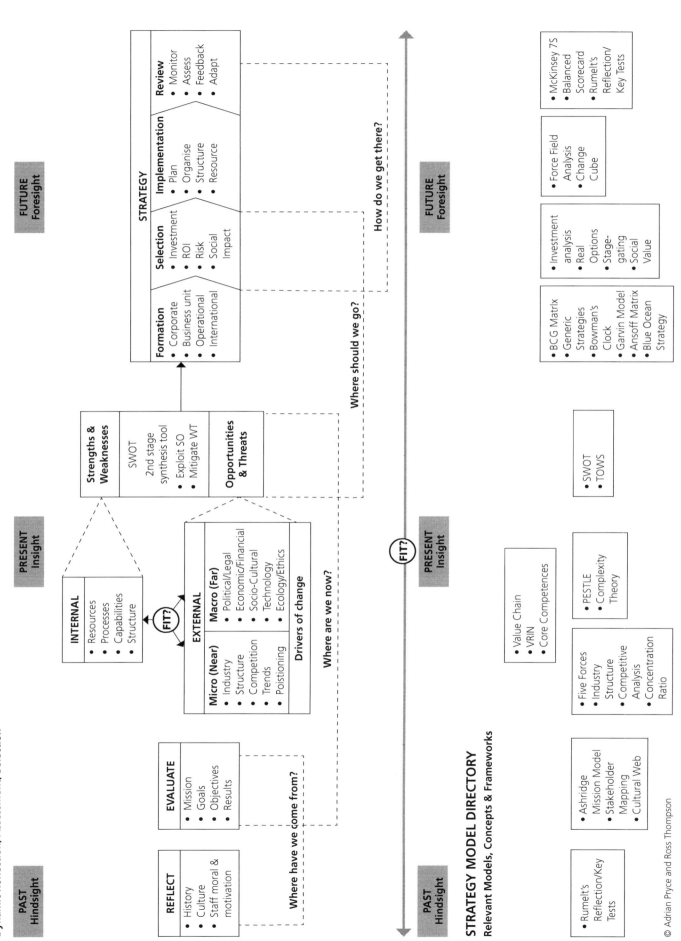

STRATEGY PROCESS MODEL
Dynamic Reflection, Assessment, Selection

STRATEGY MODEL DIRECTORY
Relevant Models, Concepts & Frameworks

© Adrian Pryce and Ross Thompson

FIGURE 1 The strategy process model framework with core models inserted

Social value and impact measurement

Boards must take note. Chartered secretaries need to be aware of the pressures building on boards. Organisations must rearticulate their purpose and mission in some way that is not solely about making money but about serving society, which, if done well and efficiently, will result in profits. At the same time, organisations need to consider non-financial objectives, heeding the call for delivering social or 'shared value' as well as financial value, the triple bottom line: social, environmental and economic. The tools and metrics for delivering social value are emerging, one of the fastest-growing and most exciting areas of strategic thinking, as it will help consolidate the thinking behind and justify good 'corporate citizenship'.

In order to have the agility to adapt quickly to the changing external environment, and the creativity and innovation to generate competitive advantage in a way that is moral and ethical, organisations will have to draw increasingly on the values and creativity of their employees, rather than rely only on the ability of the chief executive and a senior management team. This calls for a new approach not only to strategy and governance but also to management.

Strategy and Management 2.0

Mintzberg's emergent strategy seems very apt – the sum of all the hundreds of individual decisions made each day by personnel throughout the organisation, guided by some shared vision, mission and purpose. Kraemer and others propose 'values-based' leadership.

Hamel calls for Management 2.0 – management that recognises the need to manage people's values, creativity and passion: a new paradigm to manage talent and knowledge of workers. There is perhaps a parallel need for Strategy 2.0, a new framework for strategy development that addresses all the external pressures on business in a way that rebuilds trust for business in society and is more closely aligned with the values of the people working within our organisations.

We hope that this book has given the reader valuable techniques for developing strategy, but that these are applied along with some reflection, as suggested by Rumelt (see Chapter 10, page 232), on the more philosophical aspects of strategy and a real awareness of the expectations that society has of business. This will be of major concern to boards, as it is an issue of responsible governance, leadership and ultimately risk management of an organisation's very existence.

We end with a summary of the key changes in strategic thinking, as we move from hindsight through insight to strategic foresight. May your organisation enjoy enlightened leadership, good governance and successful strategy making.

Strategy as fit with resources	→	Strategy as stretch and leverage
Strategy as positioning in existing industry	→	Strategy as creating new industry space
Strategy as top management activity	→	Strategy as total organisational process belonging to all
Strategy as an analytical exercise	→	Strategy as analysis and creativity
Strategy as an annual fixed blueprint	→	Strategy as fluid and evolving
Strategy as 'hard' numbers	→	Strategy as 'soft' values and culture
Strategy as an extrapolation of the past	→	Strategy as creating the future
Strategy as science	→	Strategy as science, art and philosophy
Strategy as long-term competitive advantage	→	Strategy as a series of transient competitive advantages

FIGURE 2 Summary of key changes in strategic thinking

Source: Adapted from Prahalad (1999) and Wall et al. (2015) with authors' additions

Glossary

acceptability Concerned with the expected performance outcomes of a strategy.

acquisition An organisation taking ownership of another organisation.

authority The scope and amount of discretion given to an individual to make decisions, by virtue of the position held in the organisation.

balanced scorecard A strategic planning and management system and strategy performance management tool.

benchmarking The process of identifying, understanding and adapting exemplar practices from within the same organisation or from other organisations to help improve performance.

Blue Oceans New market spaces where competition is minimised.

business unit strategy Concerns how to compete successfully in a particular market.

centralisation The degree to which decision making is concentrated at a single point in the organisation.

chain of command The line of authority that extends from the top of the organisation to the lowest and clarifies who reports to whom.

change agent The individual or group that effects change in an organisation.

competences The skills and abilities by which resources are deployed effectively through an organisation's activities and processes.

competitive environment Factors that pertain to an industry and affect a firm's strategies.

competitive strategy Taking offensive or defensive actions to create a defendable position within an industry and a superior return on investment.

consolidation Where organisations focus defensively on their markets with current products.

control A process of monitoring performance and taking action to ensure intended or desired results.

core competences The skills and abilities by which resources are deployed through an organisation's activities and processes such as to achieve competitive advantage in ways that others cannot imitate or obtain.

core values The underlying principles that guide an organisation's strategy.

corporate citizenship The social responsibility of a business to society, including ethical, environmental and social elements.

corporate governance The relationship among various participants in determining the direction and performance of organisations.

corporate parent Levels of management above that of the business units without direct interaction with buyers and competitors.

corporate social responsibility Deals with the key issues on which an organisation exceeds its minimum required obligations to stakeholders and its relationship with its environment.

corporate strategy Concerned with the overall purpose and scope of the organisation to meet the expectations of owners or major stakeholders and add value to the different parts of the enterprise.

cost leadership A generic strategy based on appeal to the industry-wide market using a competitive advantage based on low cost.

departmentalisation The basis on which jobs are grouped together.

differentiation A strategy that seeks to provide products that are different from those of competitors and that are widely valued by buyers.

diversification A strategy that takes an organisation away from both its existing markets and its existing products.

dominant culture Expresses the core values shared by most organisational members.

'double-loop' learning Where the organisation's assumptions, premises, goals and strategies are continuously monitored, tested and reviewed.

emergent strategy Strategy that develops out of patterns of behaviour, in contrast to planned strategies that are imposed from above.

feasibility Concerned with whether an organisation has the resources and competences to deliver a strategy.

first-order change Linear and continuous change.

five forces analysis A means of identifying the forces that affect the level of competition in an industry.

focus A generic strategy based on appeal to a narrow market segment within an industry.

force field analysis Provides a view of change problems that need to be tackled by identifying forces for and against change.

formalisation The degree to which jobs within the organisation are standardised.

generic strategies Strategies by which an organisation can achieve competitive advantage: overall cost leadership, differentiation and focus.

hierarchy of purpose Organisational purpose ranging from, at the top, those that are less specific yet able to evoke powerful and compelling mental images, to, at the bottom, those that are more specific and measurable.

holding company structure An organisational form in which the divisions have a high degree of autonomy both from other divisions and from corporate headquarters.

human capital The knowledge and skills of an organisation's entire workforce. From this perspective, employees are viewed as a resource requiring continuous investment.

industry lifecycle A cycle of development stages for industries.

intangible assets Assets that are difficult to identify and account for, which are typically embedded in unique routines and practices, including human, innovation and reputation resources.

key drivers for change High-impact factors likely to affect significantly the success or failure of strategy.

market development Involves offering existing products to new markets.

market penetration Where an organisation seeks to gain market share.

market segmentation Seeks to identify similarities and differences between groups of customers or users.

matrix organisational structure An organisational form with multiple lines of authority.

merger A mutually agreed decision for joint ownership between organisations.

mission Aims to make clear to employees and stakeholders the overall purpose of the organisation.

mission statement Formal document stating the purpose of the organisation.

operational strategies Concerned with how the component parts of the organisation deliver the corporate- and business-level strategic direction.

organic development Strategies developed by building on and developing an organisation's own capabilities.

organisation structure The formalised patterns of interactions that link an organisation's tasks, technologies and people.

organisational capabilities The resources and competences that an organisation needs to survive and prosper.

organisational culture A common perception held by the organisation's members; a system of shared meaning.

organisational effectiveness The degree to which an organisation realises its goals.

organisational efficiency Concerns the number or amount of resources used to produce a unit of output.

organisational knowledge The collective experience accumulated through systems, routines and activities of sharing across the organisation.

PESTEL analysis Identification of the political, economic, social, technological, environmental and legal influences on an organisation.

planning The establishment of objectives and the formulation, evaluation and selection of the policies, strategies and tactics required to achieve these objectives.

planning horizon The time that elapses between making and executing a plan.

Porter's Diamond A framework explaining why some nations are more competitive than others, and why some industries within nations are more competitive than others.

portfolio analysis Examines the balance of an organisation's strategic business units.

power The ability of individuals or groups to persuade, induce or coerce others into following certain courses of action.

product development Where organisations deliver modified or new products to existing markets.

programmatic change The attempt to convince people by persuasion and logic of the need for change

realised strategies Those determined both by analysis and unforeseen developments in the environment, unanticipated resource constraints, and/or changes in managerial preferences.

reputation The perception that the different stakeholders have of the organisation, basing their evaluation of its performance on the available information.

resource-based view Where the competitive advantage and superior performance of an organisation is explained by the distinctiveness of its capabilities.

resources The tangible and intangible assets of an organisation.

risk The possibility that something unexpected or not planned for will happen.

risk management The process by which executive management, under board supervision, identifies the risk arising from business and establishes the priorities for control and particular objectives.

risk taking Making decisions, taking action, and committing resources without certain knowledge of probable outcomes.

rituals Repetitive sequences of activities that express and reinforce the key values of the organisation, what goals are most important, which people are important and which are expendable.

scenario planning Constructing detailed and plausible views of how the business environment of an organisation might develop in the future based on key drivers for change about which there is much uncertainty.

second-order change Multidimensional, discontinuous and radical change.

shared value A management strategy in which companies find business opportunities in social problems.

social auditing A way of ensuring that issues of CSR are systematically reviewed.

social business A business created and designed to address a social problem.

social enterprise A business set up to tackle social problems, improve communities, people's life chances, or the environment, making money from selling goods and services, reinvesting profits back into the business or the local community. In the UK, there is a separate category of incorporation at Companies House, a 'community interest company' or CIC, which must have a formal social mission and an asset lock on assets that can only

be sold or distributed for the benefit of the cause or mission.

social value Non-financial and often intangible social benefit, positive societal outcomes that are often measured as savings to the public purse as a result of corporate actions, philanthropic or otherwise.

socialisation The process that adapts employees to the organisation's culture.

span of control The number of reports for whom a manager is responsible.

specialisation The degree to which tasks in the organisation are subdivided into separate jobs.

stakeholder Any group or individual who can affect or is affected by the achievement of the firm's objectives.

stakeholder analysis A means to identify stakeholder expectations and power that helps to establish political priorities.

strategic alliance Where two or more organisations share resources and activities to pursue a strategy.

strategic business unit (SBU) structure Part of an organisation for which there is a distinct external market for goods or services that is different from another SBU.

strategic control Identifies whether an organisation should continue with its current strategy or modify it in the light of changed circumstances.

strategic drift The tendency for strategies to develop incrementally on the basis of historical and cultural influences, but fail to keep pace with a changing environment.

strategic groups Clusters of firms that share similar strategies.

strategic leadership The ability to anticipate, envisage and empower others to create strategic change.

strategic lock-in When an organisation achieves a proprietary position in its industry and it becomes an industry standard.

strategic management The analyses, decisions and actions an organisation undertakes to create and sustain competitive advantage.

strategic objectives A set of organisational goals that are used to operationalise the mission statement.

strategic planning Step-by-step procedures to develop and coordinate the organisation's strategy.

strategic planning systems Systematised, step-by-step, chronological procedures to develop strategy involving different parts of the organisation.

strategy The direction and scope of an organisation over the long term that achieves advantage for the organisation through its configuration of resources within a changing environment, to meet the needs of markets and to fulfil stakeholder expectations.

strategy canvas Compares competitors according to their performance on key success factors in order to establish the extent of differentiation.

strong culture A culture in which the organisation's core values are both intensely held and widely shared.

suitability Concerned with whether a strategy addresses the key issues that have been identified in understanding the strategic position of the organisation.

sustainable development Development that meets the needs of the present without compromising the ability of future generations to meet their own needs.

SWOT analysis Summarises the key issues from an analysis of the business environment and the strategic capability of an organisation.

synergy The idea that the whole can be greater than the sum of the parts.

task alignment Changes in behaviour and routines.

threshold capabilities Capabilities needed for an organisation to meet the necessary requirements to compete in a given market.

transformational change Where change cannot be handled within the existing paradigm and organisational routines.

transnational structure Combines the local responsiveness of the international subsidiary with the coordination advantages of global product companies.

triple bottom line The assessment of a company's performance in financial, social and environmental dimensions.

turnaround strategy Emphasises speed of change and rapid cost reduction and/or revenue generation.

unity of command An individual should have only one superior to whom he or she is directly responsible.

value chain analysis Describes the activities within and around an organisation and relates them to its competitive strength of the organisation.

value network (or system) The set of inter-organisational links and relationships necessary to create a product or service.

virtual organisations Organisations held together by partnership, collaboration and networking.

vision Concerned with what the organisation aspires to be.

VRIN criteria Capabilities for achieving and sustaining competitive advantage, characterised by value, rarity, inimitability and non-substitutability.

Bibliography

Ackerman, R.W. (1975) *The Social Challenge to Business*. Cambridge, MA: Harvard University Press.

Afuah, A. (2003) 'Redefining firm boundaries in the face of the internet: are firms really shrinking?', *Academy of Management Review*, 28(1), 34–53.

Ambrosini, V. (2003) *Tacit and Ambiguous Resources as Sources of Competitive Advantage*. Basingstoke: Palgrave Macmillan.

Amburgey, T. and Dacin, T. (1994) 'As the left foot follows the right? The dynamics of strategic and structural change', *Academy of Management Journal*, 37(6), 1427–52.

Andersen Consulting (1999) *Dispelling the Myths of Strategic Alliances*.

Andrews, K. (1987) *The Concept of Corporate Strategy*. Homewood IL: Richard D. Irwin Inc.

Ansoff, H.I. (1965) *Corporate Strategy*. New York: McGraw-Hill.

Argyris, C. and Schon, D.A. (1978) *Organisational Learning*. Reading, MA: Addison-Wesley.

Baird, I., Post, J. and Mahon, J. (1990) *Management: Functions and Responsibility*. New York: Harper & Row.

Balogun, J. and Hope-Hailey, V. (2004) *Exploring Strategic Change* (2nd edition). London: FT Prentice Hall.

Bandler, J. and Burke, D. (2012) 'How HP lost its way', *Fortune*, 21 May, pp.147–64.

Baraldi, E., Brennan R., Harrison, D., Tunisini, A. and Zolkiewski, J. (2007) 'Strategic thinking and the IMP approach: a comparative analysis', *Industrial Marketing Management*, 36, 879–94.

Barney, J. (1991) 'Firm resources and sustained competitive advantage', *Journal of Management*, 17(1), 99–120.

Barney, J.B. and Arikan, A.M. (2001) 'The resource-based view: origins and implications', in Hitt, M.A., Freeman, R.E. and Harrison, J.S. (eds), *Handbook of Strategic Management*, Oxford: Blackwell, pp.124–88.

Barney, J.B. and Hesterly, W.S. (2010) *Strategic Management and Competitive Advantage: Concepts and Cases* (international edition). Harlow: Pearson.

Bartkus, B., Glassman, M. and Mcafee, B. (2000) 'Mission statements: are they smoke and mirrors?', *Business Horizons*, 43(6), 23–8.

Bartlett, C. and Ghoshal, S. (1990) 'Matrix management: not a structure, more a frame of mind', *Harvard Business Review*, 68(4), 138–45.

Bennis, W. and Nanus, B. (1985) *Leaders: The Strategies for Taking Charge*. New York: Harper & Row.

Blenkhorn, D.L. and Gaber, B. (1995) 'The use of "warm fuzzies" to access organizational effectiveness', *Journal of General Management*, 21(2) (winter), 40–51.

Boeker, W. (1991) 'Organizational strategy: an ecological perspective', *Academy of Management Journal*, 34(3), 613–35.

Boue, C-E. (2013) *Light Footprint Management*. London: Bloomsbury.

Bower, J.L. (1972) *Managing the Resource Allocation Process* (2nd edition). Homewood, IL: Richard D. Irwin Inc.

Brodbeck, F. (2004) 'The more we blame, the less we gain', *Professional Manager*, 13(6) (November), 37.

Bungay, S. and Goold, M. (1991) 'Creating a strategic control system', *Long Range Planning*, 24(3), 32–9.

Bunting, M. (2004) *Willing Slaves*. London: HarperCollins.

Burgelman, R.A. (1983) 'A process model of internal corporate venturing in the diversified major firm', *Administrative Science Quarterly*, 28(2), 223–45.

Buzzell, R.D. and Gale, T. (1987) *The PIMS Principles: Linking Strategy to Performance*. New York: The Free Press.

Campbell, A. (1991) 'A mission to succeed', *Director*, 1 February, p.66.

Carroll, A.B. (1991) 'The pyramid of corporate social responsibility: toward the moral management of organizational stakeholders', *Business Horizons*, July–August, 39–46.

Cartwright, J. (1999) *Cultural Transformation*. London: FT Prentice Hall.

Casey, C. (1999) ' "Come, join our family": discipline and integration in corporate organizational culture', *Human Relations*, 52(1), 155–78.

Champy, J. and Hammer M. (1993) *Re-engineering the Corporation: A Manifesto for Business Revolution*. London: Nicholas Brealey.

Chandler, A. (1962) *Strategy and Structure: Chapters in the History of American Industrial Enterprise*. Cambridge, MA: MIT Press.

Chatman, J.A. and Jehn, K.A. (1994) 'Assessing the relationship between industry characteristics and organisational culture: how different can you be?', *Academy of Management Journal*, June.

Clarke, C.J. (1987) 'Acquisitions – techniques for measuring strategic fit', *Long Range Planning*, 20(3), 12–18.

Clarke, T. and Clegg, S. (2000) *Changing Paradigms: The Transformation of Management Knowledge in the 21st Century*. London: HarperCollins, Chapter 5.

Clutterbuck, D. and Snow, D. (1991) *Working with the Community – A Guide to Corporate Social Responsibility*. London: Weidenfeld and Nicolson.

Collins, J. (2001) *Good to Great*. New York: HarperCollins.

Collins, J.C. and Porras, J.I. (2000) *Built to Last: Successful Habits of Visionary Companies* (3rd edition). London: Random House Business Books.

Collis, D.J. and Montgomery, C.A. (1998) 'Creating corporate advantage', *Harvard Business Review*, 76(3), 70–83.

Coyle, B. (2010) *Corporate Governance*. London: ICSA Publishing.

Crane, A., Matten, D. and Spence, L.J. (2013) *Corporate Social Responsibility – Readings and Cases in a Global Context*. London: Routledge.

Cummings, T.G. and Worley, C.G. (2005) *Organization Development and Change* (8th edition). Mason, OH: Thompson South-Western.

Daft, R.L. (2013) *Organizational Theory and Design* (11th edition). Mason, OH: South Western College Publishing.

Daniels, J.D., Pitts, R.A. and Tretter, M.J. (1984) 'Strategy and structure of U.S. multinationals: an exploratory study', *Academy of Management Journal*, 27(2), 292–307.

Davies, S., Lukomnik, J. and Pitt-Watson, D. (2006) *The New Capitalists*. Boston, MA: Harvard Business School Press.

Deal, T.E. and Kennedy, A.A. (1982) *Corporate Cultures: The Rites and Rituals of Corporate Life*. London: Penguin.

Dennis, J-L., Lamothe, L. and Langley, A. (2001) 'The dynamics of collective change leadership and strategic change in pluralistic organizations', *Academy of Management Journal*, 44(4), 809–37.

Dess, G.G., Lumpkin, G.T. and Eisner, A.B. (2008) *Strategic Management: Text and Cases* (4th edition). New York: McGraw-Hill International.

Dess, G.G., Lumpkin, G.T. and Eisner, A.B. (2014) *Strategic Management: Creating Competitive Advantages* (7th edition). New York: McGraw-Hill International.

Drucker, P. (1968) *The Practice of Management*. London: Pan.

Drucker, P. (2001) *The Essential Drucker*. Oxford: Butterworth Heinemann.

Dunphy, D. and Stace, D.A. (1993) 'The strategic management of corporate change', *Human Relations*, 46(8), 908.

Eisenhardt, K. (1989) 'Agency theory: an assessment and review', *Academy of Management Review*, 14(1), 57–74.

Eisenhardt, K.M. (1990) 'Speed and strategic choice: how managers accelerate decision making', *California Management Review*, Spring.

Ernst, D. and Halevy, T. (2002) 'Give alliances their due', *McKinsey Quarterly*, 3, 4–5.

Faulkner, D. (1995) *International Strategic Alliances: Co-operating to Compete*. Maidenhead: McGraw-Hill.

Finlay, P. (2000) *Strategic Management: An Introduction to Business and Corporate Strategy*. London: FT Prentice Hall.

Floyd, S. and Wooldridge, B. (2000) *Building Strategy from the Middle*. Thousand Oaks, CA: Sage.

Fox, A. (1966) 'Managerial ideology and industrial relations', *British Journal of Industrial Relations*, 4.

Friedman, M. (1970) 'The social responsibility of business is to increase its profits', *New York Times Magazine*, 13 September.

Friedman, T. (2006) *The World is Flat: the Globalized World in the Twenty First Century*. London: Penguin.

Galbraith, J.R. and Kazanjian, R.K. (1986) *Strategy Implementation* (2nd edition). St Paul, MN: West Publishing.

Garratt, B. (1996) *The Fish Rots from the Head – The Crisis in our Boardrooms.* London: HarperCollins Business.

Ghoshal, S. and Bartlett, C.A. (1995) 'Changing the role of management: beyond structure to processes', *Harvard Business Review*, 73(1), 88.

Goldsmith, W. and Clutterbuck, D. (1998) *The Winning Streak Mark II.* London: Orion Business Books.

Goleman, D. (2000) 'Leadership that gets results', *Harvard Business Review*, March–April, 78–90.

Goold, M. and Campbell, A. (2002) *Designing Effective Organisations.* San Francisco, CA: Jossey-Bass.

Goold, M., Campbell, A. and Alexander, M. (1994) *Corporate Level Strategy.* New York: John Wiley.

Grant, R. (2003) 'Strategic planning in a turbulent environment: evidence from the oil majors', *Strategic Management Journal*, 24.

Grant, R. (2015) *Contemporary Strategy Analysis: Text and Cases* (9th edition). New York: Wiley.

Grinyer, P. and Spender, J-C. (1979) *Turnaround: Managerial Recipes for Strategic Success.* London: Associated Business Press.

Griseri, P. and Seppala, N. (2010) *Business Ethics and Corporate Social Responsibility.* Andover: South Western, Cengage.

Hamel, G. (2007) *The Future of Management*, HBR Press.

Hamel, G. (2012) *What Matters Now.* San Francisco, CA: Jossey-Bass.

Hamel, G. and Prahalad, C.K. (1989) 'Strategic intent', *Harvard Business Review*, 67(3), 63–76.

Hamel, G. and Prahalad, C.K. (1990) 'The core competence of the corporation', *Harvard Business Review*, 68(3), 79–91.

Hamel, G. and Prahalad, C.K. (1994) *Competing for the Future.* Boston, MA: Harvard Business School Press.

Handy, C. (1989) *The Age of Unreason.* London: Arrow.

Handy, C. (1993) *Understanding Organisations* (4th edition). London: Penguin.

Handy, C. (2015) *The Second Curve: Thoughts on Reinventing Society.* London: Random House Books.

Hatch, N.W. and Dyer, J.H. (2004) 'Human capital and learning as a source of sustainable competitive advantage', *Strategic Management Journal*, 25(12) (December), 1155–78.

Hilton, A. (2011) 'Hearts and minds', *Chartered Secretary*, April, 14. Hilton, A. (2015) 'Opening doors', *Governance and Compliance*, April, 11.

Hodgkinson, G.P., Whittington, R., Johnson, G. and Schwarz, M. (2006) 'The role of strategy workshops in strategy development processes: formality, communication, coordination and inclusion', *Long Range Planning*, 35, 479–96.

Hoffecker, J. and Goldenberg, C. (1994) 'Using the balanced scorecard to develop company-wide performance measures', *Cost Management*, Fall, 5–17.

Hofstede, G. (1980) *Culture's Consequences: International Differences in Work Related Values.* London: Sage Publications.

Huczynski, A. and Buchanan, D. (2000) *Organizational Behaviour: An Introductory Text* (4th edition). London: FT Prentice Hall.

Hudson, M. (1999) *Managing Without Profit.* Harmondsworth: Penguin International.

Hummels, H. (1998) 'Organizing ethics: a stakeholder debate', *Journal of Business Ethics*, 17(13), 1403–19.

Janis, Irving L. (1972) *Victims of Groupthink: A Psychological Study of Foreign-policy Decisions and Fiascos.* Boston, MA: Houghton Mifflin. Jarvis, J. (2009) 'How the Google model could help Detroit', *BusinessWeek*, 9 February, pp.32–6.

Johnson, G. and Scholes, K. (1998) *Exploring Corporate Strategy* (5th edition). London: Prentice Hall.

Johnson, G., Scholes, K. and Whittington, R. (2008) *Exploring Corporate Strategy* (8th edition). London: Prentice Hall.

Johnson, G., Scholes, K., Whittington, R., Angwin, D. and Regner, P. (2014) *Exploring Strategy* (10th edition). London: Prentice Hall.

Johnson, G., Yip, G.S. and Devinney, T.M. (2009) 'Measuring long term superior performance', *Long Range Planning*, 43(3), 390–413.

Johnson, P. and Gill, J. (1993) *Management Control and Organizational Behaviour.* London: Paul Chapman.

Jones, T.J., Felps, W. and Bigley, G.A. (2007) 'Ethical theory and stakeholder-related decisions: the role of stakeholder culture',

Academy of Management Review, 32(1), 137–55.

Kakabadse, A. (2015) *The Success Formula: How Smart Leaders Deliver Outstanding Value*. London: Bloomsbury.

Kanter, R.M. (1985) *The Changemasters*. London: Unwin.

Kanter, R.M. (1992) *Challenge of Organizational Change: How Companies Experience It and Leaders Guide It*. New York: The Free Press. Kaplan, R. and Norton, D. (1996) *The Balanced Scorecard*. Boston, MA: Harvard Business School Press.

Kaplan, S. and Beinhocker, E.D. (2003) 'The real value of strategic planning', *Sloan Management Review*, January.

Kellaway, L. (2000) 'Statements that sum up mission impossible', *Financial Times*, 20 March, pp.15.

Kets de Vries, M. (1994) 'The leadership mystique', *Academy of Management Executive*, 8(3), 73–92.

Kim, W.C. and Mauborgne, R. (2005) *Blue Ocean Strategy*. Boston, MA: Harvard Business School Press.

Kim, W.C. and Mauborgne, R. (2009) 'How strategy shapes structure', *Harvard Business Review*, September, 73–80.

Klepper, S. (1996) 'Industry life cycles', *Industrial and Corporate Change*, 6(1), 119–43.

Kotter, J.P. (1990) *A Force for Change: How Leadership Differs from Management*. New York: The Free Press.

Kotter, J.P. and Schlesinger, L.A. (1979) 'Choosing strategies for change', *Harvard Business Review*, 57(2), 106–14.

Lampel, J., Mintzberg, H., Quinn, J.B. and Ghoshal, S. (2014) *The Strategy Process: Concepts, Contexts, Cases*. New York: Pearson.

Laurent, A. (1983) 'The cultural diversity of western management conceptions', *International Studies of Management and Organizations*, 8, 75–96.

Lavie, D. (2006) 'The competitive advantage of interconnected firms: an extension of the resource based view', *Academy of Management Review*, 21(3), 638–58.

Lencioni, P. (2002b) 'Make your values mean something', *Harvard Business Review*, 80(7), 113–17.

Lencioni, P.M. (2002a) *The Five Dysfunctions of a Team: A Leadership Fable*. San Francisco, CA: Jossey-Bass.

Lindblom, C. (1959) 'The science of muddling through', *Public Administration Review*, 19, Spring.

Lipton, M. (1996) 'Demystifying the development of an organizational vision', *Sloan Management Review*, July.

Lloyd, T. (2010) *Business at a Crossroads – A Crisis of Corporate Leadership*. Basingstoke: Palgrave Macmillan.

Louisot, J-P. (2004) 'Risk management in practice: reputation', *Risk Management: An International Journal*, 6(3), 35–50.

Lynch, R. (2015) *Corporate Strategy* (7th edition). London: Pearson.

Ma, H. and Karri, R. (2005) 'Leaders beware: some sure ways to lose your competitive advantage', *Organizational Dynamics*, 343(1), 63–76.

Mahoney, J. (1998) ' "Editorial adieu": cultivating moral courage in business', *Business Ethics: A European Review*, 7(4), 87–192.

Mankins, P. and Steele, R. (2006) 'Stop making plans; start making decisions', *Harvard Business Review*, January.

Maritan, C.A. and Brush T.H. (2003) 'Heterogeneity and transferring practices: implementing flow practices in multiple plants', *Strategic Management Journal*, 24(10), 945–60.

Martin, J. (2001) Organizational Behaviour. London: Thomson Learning.

Mayer, C. (2013) *Firm Commitment*. Oxford: Oxford University Press.

McGahan, A. (2000) 'How industries evolve', *Business Strategy Review*, 11(3), 1–16.

McIntosh, M.,Thomas, R., Leipziger, D. and Coleman, G. (2003) *Living Corporate Citizenship: Strategic Routes to Socially Responsible Business*. London: FT Prentice Hall.

McLean, A. and Marshall, J. (1993) *Intervening in Cultures*. Working Paper, University of Bath.

Miles, L.D. (1961) *Techniques of Value Analysis and Engineering*. New York: McGraw-Hill.

Miller, A. and Dess, G.G. (1993) 'Assessing Porter's model in terms of its generalizability, accuracy, and simplicity', *Journal of Management Studies*, 30(4), 553–85.

Miller, K.D. (2002) 'Knowledge inventories and managerial myopia', *Strategic Management Journal*, 23, 689–706.

Milliken, F.J. (1987) 'Three types of perceived uncertainty about the environment', *Academy of Management Review*, 12, January.

Mintzberg, H. (1987) 'Crafting strategy', *Harvard Business Review*, July, 66–75.

Mintzberg, H. (1990) 'The Design School:

reconsidering the basic premises of strategic management', *Strategic Management Journal*, 11, 171–95.

Mintzberg, H. (1991) 'The innovative organisation', Chapter 13 in H. Mintzberg and J.B. Quinn, *The Strategy Process: Concepts, Contexts, Cases* (3rd edition), Upper Saddle River, NJ: Prentice Hall International, pp.731–46.

Mintzberg, H. (1994) *The Rise and Fall of Strategic Planning*. London: Prentice Hall.

Mintzberg, H., Ahlstrand, B. and Lampel, J. (2009) *Strategy Safari* (2nd edition). Harlow: FT Prentice Hall.

Mintzberg, H. and Waters, J.A. (1985) 'Of strategies: deliberate and emergent', *Strategic Management Journal*, 6, 257–72.

Morgan, G. (1986) *Images of Organisation*. London: Sage.

Morgan, G. (1988) *Riding the Waves of Change*. San Francisco, CA: Jossey-Bass.

Mullins, L. (2007) *Management and Organisational Behaviour*. London: FT Prentice Hall.

Murdoch, A. (1997) 'Lateral benchmarking or what Formula One taught an airline', *Management Today*, November, 64–7.

Naylor, J. (2003) *Management*. London: Financial Times/Pitman Publishing.

Nonaka, I. and Takeuchi, H. (1995) *The Knowledge Creating Company*. New York: Oxford University Press.

Ocasio, W. and Joseph, J. (2005) 'An attention based theory of strategy formulation: linking decision making and guided evolution in strategy processes', *Advances in Strategic Management*, 22, 39–61.

Ohmae, K. (1982) *The Mind of the Strategist*. Harmondsworth: Penguin.

Ostroff, F. (2006) 'Change management in government', *Harvard Business Review*, May.

Oviatt, B.M. and McDougall, P.P. (2005) 'The internationalization of entrepreneurship', *Journal of International Business Studies*, 36(1), 2–8.

Pascale, R. (1990) *Managing on the edge*. New York: Simon and Schuster.

Peters, T.J. and Waterman, R.H. (1982) *In Search of Excellence*. New York: Harper & Row.

Porter, M. (2008) 'The five competitive forces that shape strategy', *Harvard Business Review*, 86(1), 58–77.

Porter, M. and Kramer, M. (1991) 'Creating shared value', *Harvard Business Review*, 89(1/2), 62–77.

Porter, M. and Kramer, M. (2007) *Strategy and Society*. Boston, MA: Harvard Business Review.

Porter, M.E. (1980) *Competitive Strategy*. New York: The Free Press.

Porter, M.E. (1985) *Competitive Advantage: Creating and Sustaining Superior Performance*. New York: The Free Press.

Porter, M.E. (1987) 'Changing patterns of international competition', *California Management Review*, 28(2), 9–39.

Quigley, J.V. (1994) 'Vision: how leaders develop it, share it, and sustain it', *Business Horizons*, 37(5) (September–October), 37–41.

Quinn, J.B. (1980) 'Managing strategic change', *Sloan Management Review*, Summer, 59–76.

Quinn, J.B. (1995) 'Strategic change: logical incrementalism', in Quinn, J.B. and Ghoshal, S. (eds), *Strategies for Change*, London: Prentice Hall.

Robbins, S.P. (1988) *Management: Concepts and Applications*. Englewood Cliffs, NJ: Prentice Hall.

Robbins, S.P. and Judge, T.J. (2007) *Organisational Behaviour: Concepts, Controversies, Applications*. New Jersey: Prentice Hall.

Robbins, S.P. and Judge, T.J. (2015) *Organisational Behaviour, Global Edition* (16th edition). London: Pearson Education Ltd.

Roddick, A. (1992) *Body and Soul*. London: Vermillion.

Romanelli, E. and Tushman, M. (1994) 'Organizational transformation as punctuated equilibrium: an empirical test', *Academy of Management Journal*, 37(5), 1141–66.

Rutherford, D. (1995) *Routledge Dictionary of Economics* (2nd edition). London: Routledge.

Schein, E.H. (1985) *Organisational Culture and Leadership*. London: Prentice Hall.

Schwarz, M. (2004) *Knowing in Practice: How Consultants Work with Clients to Create, Share and Apply Knowledge*, Academy of Management Best Paper Proceedings.

Senge, P. (1990) *The Fifth Discipline: The Art and Practice of the Learning Organization*. New York: Doubleday.

Senior, B. and Swailes, S. (2010) *Organizational Change* (4th edition). London: Pearson.

Sexton, D.A. and Van Aukun, P.M. (1985) 'A longitudinal study of small business strategic planning', *Journal of Small Business Management*, January.

Simons, R. (1995) 'Control in an age of empowerment', *Harvard Business Review*, 73, 80–8.

Sirkin, H.R., Keenan, P. and Jackson, A. (2005) 'The hard side of change management', *Harvard Business Review*, October.

Slater, S. and Lovett, D. (1999) *Corporate Turnaround*. London: Penguin.

Slaughter, R.A. (1993) 'Looking for the real megatrends', *Futures*, October, 823–49.

Stacey, R.D. (1992) *Managing Chaos*. London: Kogan Page.

Sull, D.N. (2005) 'Strategy as active waiting', *Harvard Business Review*, 83(9), 120–30.

Tannenbaum, A.S. (1962) 'Control in organizations: individual adjustments and organizational performance', *Administrative Science Quarterly*, 2, 236–57.

Tannenbaum, R. and Schmidt, W.H. (1973) 'How to choose a leadership pattern', *Harvard Business Review*, 1 May.

Thatcher, M. (2006) 'Breathing life into business strategy', *Strategic Communication Management*, 10(2), 14–18.

Trompenaars, F. (1993) *Riding the Waves of Culture*. London: Nicholas Brealey.

Tusi, A.S. (1990) 'A multiple-constituency model of effectiveness', *Administrative Science Quarterly*, 35.

Volberda, H., Morgan, R.E., Reinmoeller, P., Hitt, M.A., Ireland, R.D. and Hoskisson, R.E. (2011) *Strategic Management*. London: Cengage Learning EMEA.

Wall, S., Minocha, S. and Rees, B. (2015)'*International Business* (4th edition). New York: Pearson.

Waterman, R.H., Peters, T.J. and Phillips, J.R. (1980) 'Structure is not organization', *Business Horizons*, 23(3), 14–26.

Wenger, E.C. and Snyder, W.M. (2000) 'Communities of practice: the organizational frontier', *Harvard Business Review*, 73(3), 201–7.

Wernerfelt, B. (1984) 'A resource-based view of the firm', *Strategic Management Journal*, 5(2), 171–80.

Williamson, O. (1991) 'Strategizing, economizing and economic organization', *Strategic Management Journal*, 12, 75–94.

Williamson, O.E. (1998) 'Strategy research: governance and competence perspectives', *Strategic Management Journal*, 20(12), 1087–1108.

Willmott, H. (1993) 'Strength is ignorance, slavery is freedom: managing culture in modern organizations', *Journal of Management Studies*, 30(5).

Worrall, L. and Cooper, C. (2007) *The Quality of Working Life 2007*. London: Chartered Management Institute.

Yip, G. and Hult, G. (2012) *Total Global Strategy*. Upper Saddle River, NJ: Pearson.

Directory

Recommended reading

Hamel, G. (2012) *What Matters Now*. San Francisco, CA: Jossey-Bass.

Johnson, G., Scholes, K., Whittington, R., Angwin, D. and Regner, P. (2014) *Exploring Strategy* (10th edition). London: Prentice Hall.

Lampel, J., Mintzberg, H., Quinn, J.B. and Ghoshal, S. (2014) *The Strategy Process: Concepts, Contexts, Cases*. New York: Pearson.

Lloyd, T. (2010) *Business at a Crossroads – A Crisis of Corporate Leadership*. Basingstoke: Palgrave Macmillan.

Lynch, R. (2015) *Corporate Strategy* (7th edition). London, Pearson.

Mayer, C. (2013) *Firm Commitment*. Oxford: Oxford University Press.

Mintzberg, H., Ahlstrand, B. and Lampel, J. (2009) *Strategy Safari* (2nd edition). Harlow: FT Prentice Hall.

Robbins, S.P. and Judge T.J. (2014) *Organisational Behaviour: Concepts, Controversies, Applications*. 16th edition, London: Prentice Hall.

Further reading

Ansoff, H.I. (1965) *Corporate Strategy*. New York: McGraw-Hill.

Dess, G.G., Lumpkin, G.T. and Eisner, A.B. (2014) *Strategic Management: Creating Competitive Advantages* (7th edition). New York: McGraw-Hill International.

Grant, R. (2013) *Contemporary Strategy Analysis: Text and Cases*. London: John Wiley & Sons.

Hamel, G. and Prahalad, C.K. (1994) *Competing for the Future*. Boston, MA: Harvard Business School Press.

Hofstede, G. (1980) *Culture's Consequences: International Differences in Work-Related Values*. London: Sage.

Kotter, J.P. (1990) *Leading Change*. Boston, MA: Harvard Business School Press.

Lampel, J., Mintzberg, H., Quinn, J.B. and Ghoshal, S. (2014) *The Strategy Process: Concepts, Contexts, Cases*. New York: Pearson.

Mintzberg, H. (1994) *The Rise and Fall of Strategic Planning*. London: Prentice Hall.

Moore, J.I. (2001) *Writers on Strategy and Strategic Management* (2nd edition). London: Penguin Business.

Porter, M.E. (1980) *Competitive Strategy*. New York: The Free Press.

Senior, B. and Swailes, S. (2010) *Organizational Change* (4th edition). London: Pearson.

Stacey, R.D. (1993) *Strategic Mangement and Organisational Dynamics*. London: FT/Pitman Publishing.

Trompenaars, F. (1993) *Riding the Waves of Culture*. London: Nicholas Brealey.

Web resources

General

Biz/ed Listing Service catalogue – bized.co.uk

Forum – www.forum.com

Institute of Healthcare Management – www.ihm.org.uk

Management Information eXchange – http://www.managementexchange.com

Oxford Economic Forecasting – www.oxfordeconomics.com

Shared Value – www.sharedvalue.org and www.fsg.org

Business news, magazines, newspapers and journals

BBC news (business) – www.bbc.co.uk/news/business

Bloomberg Business – www.bloomberg.com

CNN – www.cnn.com

Financial Times – www.ft.com

Fortune – www.fortune.com

Harvard Business Review – www.hbr.org

HR Magazine – www.shrm.org/hrmagazine

ITN – www.itn.co.uk

Learning Organization Journal – www.emeraldinsight.com/loi/tlo

Long Range Planning – www.journals.elsevier.com/long-range-planning/

Management Decision – www.emeraldinsight.com/loi/md

Management Today
  – www.managementtoday.co.uk
RSA Journal – www.thersa.org/discover
Sloan Management Review – sloanreview.
  mit.edu
Sociological Review
  – www.thesociologicalreview.com
Strategic Management Journal – smj.
  strategicmanagement.net
Strategy and Business
  – www.strategy-business.com
Sunday Times – www.sunday-times.co.uk
Workforce Online – www.workforce.com

Universities, colleges and business schools

Aston University Business School
  – www.abs.aston.ac.uk
Birmingham University Business School
  – www.birmingham.ac.uk/schools/
  business/index.aspx
Durham University Business School
  – www.dur.ac.uk/business
Edinburgh University Management School
  – www.business-school.ed.ac.uk

University of South Wales Business School
  – www.southwales.ac.uk/about/faculties-
  and schools/business-school/
Henley Business School – www.henley.ac.uk
Edinburgh Business School
  – www.ebsglobal.net
Huddersfield University Business School
  – www.hud.ac.uk/uhbs
Lancaster University Management School
  – www.lancaster.ac.uk/lums
London Business School – www.london.edu
Strathclyde University Business School
  – www.strath.ac.uk/business
UK Colleges/Universities Map – www.scit.
  wlv.ac.uk/ukinfo/index.php
The University of Manchester
  – www.manchester.ac.uk
University of Bradford Management Centre
  – www.brad.ac.uk/management
Haas Business School, University of
  California Berkeley
  – www.haas.berkeley.edu
University of Minnesota – twin-cities.umn.
  edu
Warwick University Business School
  – www.wbs.ac.uk

Index